MARKETING
for TOURISM, HOSPITALITY & EVENTS

A GLOBAL & DIGITAL APPROACH

SIMON HUDSON *and* LOUISE HUDSON

MARKETING *for* TOURISM, HOSPITALITY & EVENTS

A GLOBAL & DIGITAL APPROACH

Los Angeles | London | New Delhi
Singapore | Washington DC | Melbourne

Los Angeles | London | New Delhi
Singapore | Washington DC | Melbourne

SAGE Publications Ltd
1 Oliver's Yard
55 City Road
London EC1Y 1SP

SAGE Publications Inc.
2455 Teller Road
Thousand Oaks, California 91320

SAGE Publications India Pvt Ltd
B 1/I 1 Mohan Cooperative Industrial Area
Mathura Road
New Delhi 110 044

SAGE Publications Asia-Pacific Pte Ltd
3 Church Street
#10-04 Samsung Hub
Singapore 049483

Editor: Matthew Waters
Assistant editor: Lyndsay Aitken
Production editor: Sarah Cooke
Marketing manager: Alison Borg
Cover design: Lisa Harper-Wells
Typeset by: C&M Digitals (P) Ltd, Chennai, India
Printed in the UK by Bell and Bain Ltd, Glasgow

Library of Congress Control Number: 2016953683

British Library Cataloguing in Publication data

A catalogue record for this book is available from the British Library

ISBN 978-1-47392-663-9
ISBN 978-1-47392-664-6 (pbk)

At SAGE we take sustainability seriously. Most of our products are printed in the UK using FSC papers and boards. When we print overseas we ensure sustainable papers are used as measured by the PREPS grading system. We undertake an annual audit to monitor our sustainability.

CONTENTS

1

TODAY'S MARKETING ENVIRONMENT

2

UNDERSTANDING TODAY'S CONSUMER

3

DIGITAL MARKETING

4

THE MARKETING PLAN

5

THE TOURISM AND HOSPITALITY PRODUCT

6

PRICING

7

DISTRIBUTION

8

THE ROLE OF ADVERTISING AND SALES PROMOTIONS

9

PUBLIC RELATIONS AND PERSONAL SELLING

10

THE ROLE OF CUSTOMER SERVICE IN MARKETING

11

MARKETING RESEARCH

12

TOURISM MARKETING ETHICS

ABOUT THE AUTHORS

Dr Simon Hudson is a tourism aficionado, exploring the world, spreading his passion for travel and enlightening audiences on every kind of travel research from winter sports to film tourism. He has written eight books and over 60 research articles, many of them focused on tourism marketing. He is the Endowed Chair for the SmartState Center of Economic Excellence in Tourism and Economic Development at the University of South Carolina. An impressive title, but it basically means he researches ways to put South Carolina's tourism industry back on the map and into the black. With an eclectic background in the ski industry, retail and British and Canadian academia, Dr Hudson is a fount of international experience, amusing anecdotes and comprehensive business information. He gets his cosmopolitan and creative ideas from a background at the University of Calgary, Canada, and the University of Brighton, England, as well as visiting positions he has held in Austria, Switzerland, Spain, Fiji, New Zealand and Australia. What a great job!

A snappy and insightful travel journalist, **Louise Hudson** writes for a host of newspaper travel sections, online sites, and her own blog: www.onetwoski.blogspot.com. Published in three countries since 2005, her work has made its way into *Ski Canada*, *More Canada*, *LA Times*, *USA Today*, *Dallas Morning News*, *Boston Globe*, *Globe & Mail* and *Houston Chronicle* among many others. As well as winter sports articles, she writes tantalizing travel tales for a variety of outlets including the *Calgary Herald* in Canada, which she considers her part-time home. Meeting Simon at school in England in 1975 has led to a lifetime of adventurous travel and work abroad together, as well as a measure of audacious entrepreneurialism when they set up a very successful fashion business in the 1980s. Louise contributes cutting-edge case studies and energetic editing to this manual.

COMPANION WEBSITE

Marketing for Tourism, Hospitality & Events: A Global & Digital Approach is supported by a wealth of online resources for both students and lecturers to aid study and support teaching, which are available at: https://study.sagepub.com/hudson

For students:

- YouTube Video Links

For lecturers:

- Instructor Manual
- PowerPoint Slides
- Multiple Choice Questions Testbank

PREFACE

Festivals, events, dining out, overnight trips, vacations and adventurous travel are mainstays of everyday life. The remarkable growth of the field of tourism, hospitality and events since the 1960s has made it one of the world's largest and fastest-growing economic sectors. International tourism represents 7 per cent of total world exports and 30 per cent of services exports. Income generated by international visitors on accommodation, food and drink, entertainment, shopping and other services and goods reached an estimated $1.232 billion in 2015. But the impact of tourism goes far beyond enrichment in purely economic terms, helping to benefit environments, culture and the fight against poverty. Tourism's tentacles reach every level of society and as such it is vital for marketers to understand it in order to share the benefits.

However, the industry is subject to constant change. While established tourism destinations in Western Europe and North America are experiencing maturity, emerging destinations in Asia and Eastern Europe are competing for new generations of travellers from countries such as China and Russia. Along with these demographic shifts, technology is also having a disruptive impact on travel products and services and how they are experienced and marketed. At the same time, issues like sustainability and ethics have become forefront, while consumers are becoming increasingly demanding. Such dramatic changes require a fresh look at this exciting and dynamic industry.

This new text sets itself apart from the competition through its inclusion of the latest material on digital marketing, customer service and marketing ethics complemented by unique case studies written by a travel journalist. Students and marketing practitioners alike will be given an opportunity to gain a comprehensive understanding of marketing principles specific to the fields of tourism, hospitality and events, within a unique angle that has not yet been covered by others. The text will not only analyse these principles from a global perspective, but it will also provide real-life examples that influence the tourism and hospitality marketplace. Unique core concepts are supported by well-integrated international case studies to illuminate the practical realities of marketing within the field, focusing on the need to create a flexible, adaptive approach to marketing products and services around the globe.

Chapter 1 begins by mapping out the contemporary tourism marketing environment, looking at the key players in the tourism, hospitality and events industries. Chapter 2 is dedicated to understanding today's consumer, and then Chapter 3 focuses on digital marketing and the disruptive influence that technology has had on the industry. Chapter 4 outlines the contents of a marketing plan and, next, Chapter 5 looks at the secrets behind successful tourism products and services, describing the role of events. Chapters 6 and 7 are dedicated to pricing and distribution respectively, and Chapter 8 discusses the role of advertising and sales promotions. Chapter 9 emphasizes the importance of public relations and personal selling, and Chapter 10 illustrates the role of customer service. Chapter 11 is dedicated to understanding the role of marketing research, and finally, Chapter 12 focuses on the important topic of tourism marketing ethics.

The book also contains 36 detailed case studies that have been developed following a personal visit or in-depth interviews by the authors. These case studies follow one of three themes. Firstly, each chapter begins with '**Lessons from a Marketing Guru**', featuring the achievements of an experienced individual in the industry. In these case studies, we learn how a real guru in India has cornered the market in spiritual tourism; why ski-hill owner Charlie Locke has been honoured for his outstanding contribution to ski tourism; how an English woman is putting Kobe, Japan, on the map as a top tourism destination; why Frenchman Michel Goget is known worldwide as a hotel 'troubleshooter'; how Jo Arnett-Morrice has gone from 'dance mum' to Dance World Cup marketing expert; how a former journalist and ad agency brand strategist has created a successful magazine, guidebook and boutique travel agency; why Elena Ulko believes personalized service is the key to her success selling tours in Russia; the secrets of two Canary Island marketers – Eustasio Lopez and Marcos Van Aken; how Dionísio Pestana has developed the family business on the island of Madeira into Portugal's biggest international tourism and leisure group; how an engineer turned chartered accountant, Chitra Stern, has become the marketing maven for a chain of luxury family hotels and resorts; and why chef Magnus Berglund decided to increase accessibility at Scandic hotels, thus gaining a competitive edge.

Each chapter also contains a '**Digital Spotlight**' highlighting the cataclysmic influence that technology is having in the world of marketing communications. These Spotlights discuss the use of social media by music festivals, online marketing for the X-Games, social media listening at Marriott, the gentrification of Andermatt, Switzerland, the adoption of technology in museums, online distribution of Riads in Morocco, the sharing economy in India, Brand USA's digital marketing strategy, cooperative online marketing in Stellenbosch, South Africa, Vail Resorts and their cutting-edge app EpicMix, and how to reach technology-driven Millennials.

At the end of every chapter there is an up-to-date, relevant and detailed '**Marketing in Action**' case study, covering a variety of organizations and regions worldwide. Designed to foster critical thinking, the cases highlight actual marketing scenarios that exemplify concepts found in the chapters. In these Marketing in Action cases we learn how Myanmar is repositioning itself with a new branding campaign; why the 'bleisure' trend is forcing hotels to cater to those combining work with leisure; how Hamilton Island's innovative 'Best Job in the World' campaign resulted in over $430 million worth of PR exposure; how a game hunt in Ghana, organized by the two bands of warriors, has evolved into the popular Deer Hunt Festival; why music-themed hotels like the Beatles-themed Hard Days Night Hotel in Liverpool England, have become so popular; how low-cost carriers have expanded aggressively across the world; how the 3,000-strong National Brotherhood of Skiers' annual summit contradicts the typical skiing ethnic demographics; why marketers in Brazil decided to leverage the mega-events of the 2014 World Cup and 2016 Olympics to change a destination image; how proactive destinations like Hawaii are promoting themselves through film and television; why providing excellent customer service is critical for high-profile sporting events in Britain; why customers will receive tastier food in an open kitchen set-up; and why portraying war as a tourism attraction in Vietnam is controversial.

TODAY'S MARKETING ENVIRONMENT

1

INTRODUCTION

Chapter 1 is dedicated to the current global tourism marketing environment. The chapter starts with an introduction to the marketing of tourism, hospitality and events in general, and discusses the definition and role of marketing and its importance in international tourism. The key players in the industry are then profiled, and the remainder of the chapter examines the major environmental forces that affect an organization's ability to serve its customers.

LESSONS FROM A MARKETING GURU: THE BUSINESS OF SPIRITUAL TOURISM

'Whether you are running a business, an industry, or a nation – what is needed are insight, integrity, and inspiration' – Sadhguru Tweet

IMAGE 1.1 Sadhguru (©Sadhguru. All rights reserved. Reproduced with permission)

Located at the foot of the Velliangiri Mountains in Tamil Nadu, the Isha Yoga Center is the brainchild of Jaggi Vasudev, or Sadhguru as he is widely known. The modern-day yogi and mystic is a charismatic leader whose vision for harmony and well-being for all takes him across the world to address prestigious global forums and conferences, speaking about issues as diverse as human rights, business values and environmental responsibility. He has been invited to the United Nations' Millennium World Peace Summit, the House of Lords in the UK, Massachusetts Institute of Technology (MIT), and IMD Lausanne, Switzerland.

Surrounded by thick forests, and situated right next to the Nilgiri Biosphere reserve, the 150-acre ashram was founded by Sadhguru in 1992, and is administered by the Isha Foundation. One major attraction of the centre is the Dhyanalinga Yogic Temple, a meditative space that is said to be the first of its kind to be completed in over 2,000 years. The temple does not ascribe to any particular faith and is available to all, irrespective of religion or nationality. Open daily from 6 am to 8 pm, including national or cultural holidays, it attracts thousands of visitors from all over the world. Many of these guests take part in Nada Aradhana, an offering of sound to the Dhyanalinga that includes an ethereal blend of nonlyrical vocals, 'singing' bowls, drums and various other instruments. These twice-daily sound offerings are the only times the meditative silence of the Dhyanalinga is broken.

The ashram is also the location for major cultural events. For example, in an endeavour to preserve and promote the uniqueness and diversity of India's performing arts, the centre annually hosts Yaksha, a seven-day festival of music and dance. Various eminent artistes perform at the festival, culminating in the nightlong celebration of the Mahashivarathri Festival – one of the biggest and most significant among the sacred festival nights of India. This night is considered the darkest night of the year, and celebrates the Grace of Shiva, who is known as Aadhi (first) Guru from whom the yogic tradition originates.

The Isha Center offers all four major paths of yoga – kriya (energy), gnana (knowledge), karma (action), and bhakti (devotion), drawing advocates from all over the world. Other programmes include Inner Engineering, designed by the guru to 'establish a deep and lasting transformation'. Over two million people have completed the programme to date, all seeking advertised results such as improved mental clarity, increased energy levels, relief from chronic ailments, deepening of interpersonal relationships, and greater peace and joy in everyday life. Another programme offered by Isha Education is INSIGHT – The DNA of Success, a practitioner-oriented leadership course that draws upon the experience of several highly successful business leaders who have built and grown world-class organizations. Along with Sadhguru's guidance and involvement, other resource leaders in past programmes include Rajan Tata, Chairman Emeritus of Tata Sons Limited, and Dr Prathap C Reddy, founder of Apollo Hospitals.

Isha Sacred Walks is another branch in the guru's portfolio of product offerings, promoted not as tours, but 'a possibility for deep transformation'. The Himalayan Sacred Walks is one example, comprising two weeks of meditation, treks and camping. The guru's entrepreneurial talents have not stopped there. Sounds of Isha offers ten albums of music 'transporting you to subtler states of being, forming the basis for inner exploration'; Isha Craft produces gift items, jute pieces, paintings, metal crafts, stone artifacts and handicrafts, as well as designer clothing; Isha Life is the wellness sub-brand, a centre that provides a holistic approach to health and fitness, but also includes a fine-dining restaurant Mahamudra, an outdoor café Namma and the Shambhavi Craft Boutique; Isha Foods and Spices are a collection of snacks, drinks, tiffin mixes and pickles; Isha Arogya offers healthcare products and services and has established holistic health centres in several major cities of Tamil Nadu; and finally Isha Publications promotes Sadhguru's works and discourses in the form of books, CDs and DVDs.

The Isha Center and all of these sub-brands are promoted via a glossy magazine, a slick website, and various social media platforms including YouTube, Facebook, a blog, Pinterest and Twitter. One of his signature tweets is: 'No work is stressful. It is your inability to manage your body, mind, and emotions that makes it stressful.' Much of the income from these diverse commercial prongs is ploughed back into the foundation, an entirely volunteer-run, nonprofit organization which is 'dedicated to cultivating human potential through its vibrant spiritual movement'. The social development branch of the foundation is Isha Outreach, with a vision to empower the deprived sections of India to achieve improved health, education and environmental well-being. Another initiative established by the foundation is Project GreenHands, which aims to take corrective measures to increase the green cover of Tamil Nadu province by an additional 10 per cent, by planting trees through volunteer participation. Finally, Sadhguru's long-term vision is to raise the human spirit and rejuvenate the marginalized rural population, and so he has created Action for Rural Rejuvenation (AAR), a programme that has already reached out to 4,600 villages in over a decade of work. Not content with operating in India alone, Sadhguru is spreading his tentacles overseas, recently establishing the Isha Institute of Inner Sciences in Tennessee, US. Spread over 1,300 acres, the Institute offers a variety of programmes 'that provide methods for anyone to attain physical, mental and spiritual well-being'. Two powerful meditation spaces are the main features of the Isha Institute. Mahima, which means grace, is a 39,000 sq ft domed meditation hall and home to many of the programmes offered at the Institute: basic programmes that do not require any prior knowledge of yoga or meditation, as well as advanced programmes for those who wish to take a step further in their spiritual growth. The second space is the Adi Yogi: Abode of Yoga, a meditative space established as a tribute to the Adi Yogi, who offered the yogic sciences to the world over 15,000 years ago.

Sources: Personal visit by authors: February 2016; www.ishafoundation.org; http://isha.sadhguru.org/blog/lifestyle/everything-you-need-to-know-about-the-isha-yoga-center-and-more/

THE TOURISM MARKETING ENVIRONMENT

The opening case study depicts a successful entrepreneur in India who has responded to the growing demand for spiritual and wellness tourism. By understanding and adapting to a changing environment, Jaggi Vasudev's vision for harmony and well-being for all has made him an extremely influential figure in India. What the case also shows is that tourism can be a powerful economic force providing employment, foreign exchange, income, and tax revenue for countries all over the world. The tourism market reflects the demands of consumers for a very wide range of travel and hospitality products, and it is widely claimed that this total market is now being serviced by the world's largest industry. Players in this industry are operating in a global environment where people, places and countries are increasingly interdependent. Countries once considered inaccessible to Western tourists, because of geographical, cultural and political barriers, are now becoming accessible and their very remoteness makes them an attractive choice for travel today. An example is Myanmar, one of the most impoverished parts of the world and, until recently, a country in isolation, unwelcoming to visitors. But social and economic reforms in the 2010s, and a new branding campaign, have resulted in a surge of international visitors (see Marketing in Action at the end of this chapter).

The globalization of tourism has cultural, political and economic dimensions. Cultural globalization is characterized by cultural homogenization as Western consumption and lifestyle patterns spread throughout the world, a process facilitated by the flow of travellers from the West to the Third World. Travel also enhances friendships between peoples and facilitates cultural exchange. Political globalization involves the undermining of the roles and importance of nation states as borders are opened up to free trade and investment. Economic globalization has both positive and negative effects. On the one hand, it could be argued that a key aspect of economic globalization has been the trend towards increasing power in the hands of a small number of travel organizations, leading to oligopolistic control in the industry. On the other hand, tourism brings with it economic rewards and opportunities for host communities, in particular, to benefit from foreign exchange and enhance their livelihood options.

There are many examples in tourism and hospitality industries of companies operating in a global environment. The Hard Rock brand, a favourite on tourists' T-shirts the world over, is a good example. The chain was founded by music lovers Isaac Tigrett and Peter Morton with one London restaurant in 1971, and by 2015 the chain included nearly 200 cafes in more than 60 countries. Hard Rock International, now owned by the Seminole Tribe of Florida, is also known for its collectible fashion and music-related merchandise, Hard Rock Live performance venues, and an award-winning website that in 2015 was featuring this brand video: https://www.youtube.com/watch?v=L9Wf8PYsLO0.

The increased globalization of tourism is reflected in the statistics related to the industry. The number of international arrivals rose from 25 million in 1950 to 1.18 billion in 2015 (see Figure 1.1). In the same year, income generated by international visitors on accommodation, food and drink, entertainment, shopping and other services and goods reached an estimated $1.232 billion.

Despite occasional shocks, tourism has experienced continued expansion and diversification to become one of the world's largest and fastest-growing economic sectors

FIGURE 1.1 International tourism arrivals and receipts for 2015 (Source: World Tourism Organization, 2016a: ©UNWTO 92844/20/16)

in the world. International tourism represents 7 per cent of total world exports and 30 per cent of services exports (see Figure 1.2). As a world export category, tourism ranks third after fuels and chemicals, and ahead of food and automotive products, and in many developing countries, tourism ranks as the first export sector. In 2015, the total export value from international tourism amounted to $1.4 trillion, with the sector being responsible for 10 per cent of the world's GDP, and accounting for one in 11 jobs.

Figures 1.3 and 1.4 come from HowMuch.net, a cost information site, and show inbound and outbound tourism expenditures around the world. For inbound tourism expenditures, the US is far ahead of all the others, bringing in about $220 billion each year from tourists, followed by France ($66.8b), Spain ($65.1b), the UK ($62.8b) and China ($56.9b). Western and Asian countries enjoy the highest levels of inbound tourism expenditures by far; out of the top 20 countries, every single one of them is either in the West or in Asia. Chinese people spend more on tourism to other countries than any other group with $164.9 billion in outbound expenditures, followed by the US ($145.7b), Germany ($106.6b), the UK ($79.9b) and France ($59.4b).

The United Nations World Tourism Organization (UNWTO, 2015) forecasts that international arrivals worldwide will increase by 3.3 per cent per year between 2010 and 2030 to reach 1.8 billion by 2030. Figure 1.5 depicts how money travels in the tourism economy and shows that, in short, travel pays. But the impact of tourism goes far beyond enrichment in purely economic terms, helping to benefit the environment and culture and the fight to reduce poverty. Over the past decade, the annual growth rate of tourists visiting developing countries has been higher than the world average. In fact, the market share of emerging economies increased from 30 per cent in 1980 to 45 per cent in 2014 and is expected to reach 57 per cent by 2030, equivalent to

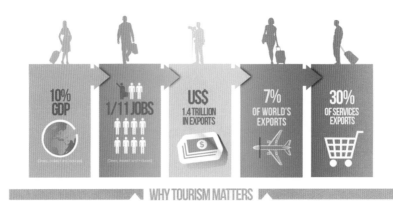

FIGURE 1.2 Significance of tourism in the world's economy (Source: World Tourism Organization, 2016b: ©UNWTO 92844/20/16)

over 1 billion international tourist arrivals. Tourism can serve as a foothold for the development of a market economy where small and medium-sized enterprises can expand and flourish. And in poor rural areas it often constitutes the only alternative to declining farming opportunities. In Ghana, Africa, for example, tourism has become the country's third source of foreign income after gold and cocoa exports, taking in over $853 million in 2013 and directly supporting 124,000 jobs (see Marketing in Action in Chapter 4 for more on Ghana).

Big emerging markets (BEMs), like Brazil, India, Turkey and Vietnam, also see the potential of tourism as a powerful economic force. The Vietnam National Administration of Tourism (VNAT), for example, has been actively encouraging war tourism as part of its marketing plan (see Marketing in Action in Chapter 12). VNAT

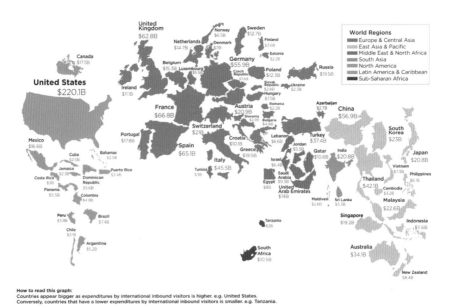

FIGURE 1.3 Inbound tourism expenditures (Source: cost information website. Courtesy of How Much.net. Reproduced with permission)

FIGURE 1.4 Outbound tourism expenditures (Source: cost information website. Courtesy of HowMuch.net. Reproduced with permission)

is focusing on increasing state management of tourism, strategic planning and forecasting, human resource training, and the easing of formalities within the industry. The intention is to attract overseas investment and develop tourism as a dominant foreign exchange earner for Vietnam.

Research has shown that destinations that promote themselves to potential tourists experience significantly greater employment and economic growth beyond the visitor economy. Through a statistical analysis of more than 200 cities over more than 20 years, case studies, interviews and a literature review, Oxford Economics (2014) revealed the broad economic benefits reaped by US destinations which spent an estimated $2 billion on promotion and marketing to encourage leisure and convention travel. The visitor economy was found to drive broader economic growth through four primary channels (see Figure 1.6).

1. Destination promotion supports development of transportation infrastructure, providing greater accessibility and supply logistics that are important in attracting investment to other sectors.

2. Destination promotion builds awareness, familiarity, and relationships in commercial networks that are critical in attracting investment. Similarly, destination promotion raises the destination profile among potential new residents, supporting skilled workforce growth that is critical to economic development.

3. By securing meetings, conventions and trade shows for local facilities, destination marketing organizations (DMOs) create valuable exposure among business decision-makers and opportunities to deepen connections with attendees.

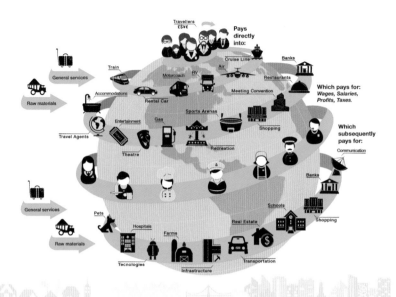

FIGURE 1.5 Travel pays (©World Travel and Tourism Council. All rights reserved. Reproduced with permission)

FIGURE 1.6 The catalytic impacts of destination promotion (©Tourism Economics. All rights reserved. Reproduced with permission)

4. Destination promotion supports amenities and a quality of life that are integral to attracting investment in other sectors in the form of human capital, corporate relocations and expansion.

THE INFLUENCE OF MARKETING ON TOURISM

Marketing has been defined as 'the process of planning and executing the conception, pricing, promotion, and distribution of ideas, goods, and services to create exchanges that satisfy individual (customer) and organizational objectives' (Kotler, 1984). The marketing concept is a business philosophy that defines marketing as a process intended to find, satisfy and retain customers while the business makes a profit. Central to all definitions of marketing is the role of the customer and the customer's relationship to the product, whether that product is a good, a service or an idea. The tourism, hospitality and events sector, like other service sectors, involves a combination of tangible and intangible products. A hotel is a mixture of goods (beds, food, telephone and communication systems) that are linked with a range of services (front desk, housekeeping, room service, finance and accounting). A tourist attraction, such as a national park, is a combination of facilities (hotels, shops, visitor centres) situated within a physical attraction (the mountains, forests, beach or rivers, for example), offering a range of services (guided tours, interpretation, education and so on). This whole package of tangible and intangible products is perceived by the tourist as an experience, and represents the core of the tourism product.

With international tourism being the largest service export for many countries (including the USA), it is important to understand the nuances of international marketing. International marketing is defined as the business activities designed to plan, price, promote and direct the flow of a company's goods and services to consumers or users in more than one country for profit (Cateora, Gilly and Graham, 2013). The important difference between this definition and the one given above for marketing in general is that international marketing activities take place in more than one country. The uniqueness of foreign marketing comes from the range of unfamiliar problems and the variety of strategies necessary to cope with different levels of uncertainty encountered in foreign markets. A number of cases in this book highlight some of the challenges organizations encounter when they expand abroad, and the marketing strategies they have employed to overcome these challenges.

Figure 1.7 illustrates the environment of an international marketer. The inner circle depicts the domestic controllable elements that constitute a marketer's decision area, such as product, price, promotion, distribution and research decisions. The second circle encompasses those environmental elements at home that have some effect on foreign-operation decisions, and the outer circles represent the elements of the foreign environment for each of the foreign markets in which the marketer operates. As the outer circles illustrate, every foreign market in which the company operates can present separate problems involving certain uncontrollable elements. Examples of uncontrollables include political instability, economic climate, cultural problems and the level of technology. To adjust and adapt a marketing programme to foreign markets, marketers must be able to interpret effectively the influence and impact of each of the uncontrollable elements on the marketing plan for each foreign market in which they hope to do business. When Disney opened theme parks in France and Hong Kong, management was insensitive to cultural differences, and the parks experienced consequent teething problems (Hudson, 2008). More market research and better environmental scanning would have helped make some of the hiccups at least foreseeable, if not entirely controllable.

Key obstacles facing international marketers are not limited to environmental issues. Just as important are difficulties associated with the marketer's own self-reference criteria (SRC) and ethnocentrism. SRC is an unconscious reference to one's own cultural values, experiences, and knowledge as a basis for decisions. Closely connected is ethnocentrism, which is the notion that one's own culture or company knows best how to do things. Both limit the international marketer's ability to understand and adapt to differences prevalent in foreign markets. A global awareness and sensitivity are the solutions to these problems. In the 2000s, Americans were accused of ethnocentrism, and this led to the country developing a poor image overseas. This in turn adversely affected tourism visits to the country. Destination marketers in the US have since engaged in a series of strategies to overcome this problem (see Digital Spotlight in Chapter 3).

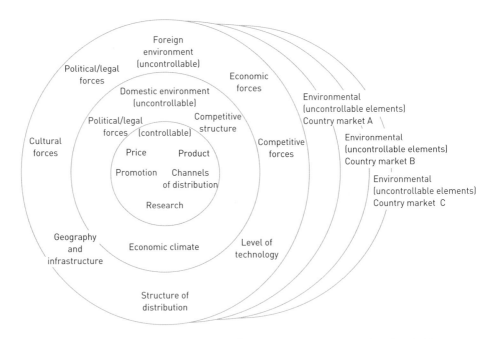

FIGURE 1.7 The international marketing task (©McGraw-Hill Education. Reprinted with permission)

TOURISM AND HOSPITALITY MARKETING

Marketing is a subject of vital concern in tourism because it is the principal management influence that can be brought to bear on the size and behaviour of this major global market. Tourism marketing has been recently defined as 'customer focus that permeates organizational functions and processes geared towards: 1) making promises relating to products and services required when travelling to stay in places outside one's usual environment for leisure, business and other purposes for less than one year; 2) enabling the fulfilment of individual expectations created by such promises; and 3) fulfilling such expectations through support to customers' value-generating processes' (Dolnicar and Ring, 2014: 44). Figure 1.8 shows the vital linkages between demand and supply in tourism, which are fundamental to an understanding of the role of marketing. The figure shows the relationship between market demand, generated in areas of origin, and product supply, mainly at visitor destinations. In particular, the model shows how the main sectors of the tourism industry – travel organizers, destination organizations, transportation, various product suppliers – combine to manage visitors' demand through a range of marketing influences.

The marketing mix is in the centre of the diagram, and it is discussed in detail in this book. However, it is important to note that the influence of this marketing activity is likely to vary according to visitors' interests and circumstances. For example, domestic visitors travelling by car to stay with friends or relatives may not be influenced by destination marketing in any way, whereas first-time buyers

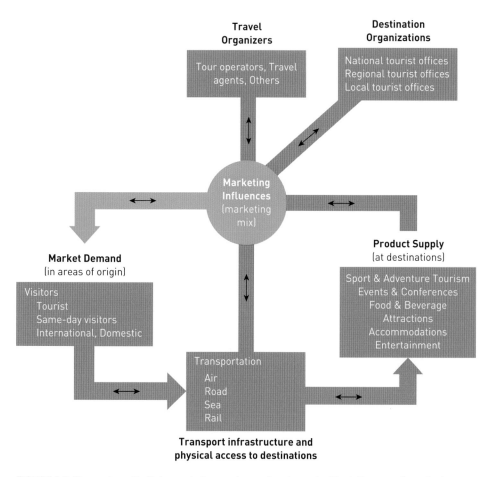

FIGURE 1.8 The systematic linkages between demand and supply: The influence of marketing (Source: Middleton and Clarke, 2012)

of package tours to exotic destinations may find that almost every aspect of their trip is influenced by the marketing decisions of the tour operator they choose. In between these two examples, a business traveller will select his or her own destination according to business requirements, but may be influenced as to which airline or hotel he or she selects.

Knowledge of the customer, and all that it implies for management decisions, is generally referred to as consumer or marketing orientation. A detailed understanding of consumer characteristics and buying behaviour is central to the activities of marketing managers and therefore consumer behaviour is the topic of Chapter 2.

DIGITAL SPOTLIGHT: APP-DAPTING FOR MUSIC FESTIVALS

Music tourism is big business worldwide. In the UK, for example, it generates approximately $3.1 billion in spending and provides the equivalent of 38,238 full-time jobs. A key component of music tourism is the music festival phenomenon which has been gaining ground in recent years. In the US, consulting firm Beacon Economics gauged the economic activity of music festivals run by dance-music promoter Insomniac to be around $3.2 billion over 48 events between 2010–14. The 2015 report listed direct spending at around $327 million, with festival attendees spending another $866 million on transportation and hotels, and the remainder comprising spin-off income and local business benefits. All this activity created the equivalent of 25,000 full-time jobs and contributed about $180 million in state and local taxes.

IMAGE 1.2 Bonnaroo 2016 (Courtesy of Bonnaroo/Andrew Jorgensen)

One of the secrets to the success of music festivals is expert and, increasingly, innovative use of social media marketing aimed at selling their brands and encouraging customer loyalty. The Bonnaroo Music and Arts Festival, held annually in Manchester, Tennessee, relies heavily on aggressive digital marketing campaigns both to generate publicity and attract visitors. Tactics include establishing relationships with bloggers to stimulate excitement for the concerts, leveraging social media sites such as Facebook and Twitter to achieve maximum exposure, and exploring mobile technology.

Set on a 700-acre farm, Bonnaroo typically attracts 85,000 attendees annually to its four-day camping festival each June. Ranked as one of the '50 Moments that Changed Rock & Roll' by *Rolling Stone* magazine, it was developed by Superfly Presents and AC Entertainment in 2002 and they continue to produce it annually, utilizing social media to sustain the momentum. Superfly's website says that it 'transformed bonnaroo.com from a website with information about the festival to a content-rich and socially-driven destination for "good stuff"'.

At Bonnaroo 2011, an air-conditioned barn in the middle of the festival ground, sponsored by Fuse TV, offered a private concert with an up-and-coming artist for those who checked into the barn via Foursquare. Once a visitor had checked in, their followers would be able to see that they were at the Fuse TV barn and then choose to go there themselves. Organizers provided the fans with a free buffet, ice-cold water, and a chance to see an intimate live show with just 40 other people. In return for their simple check-in on Foursquare, fans were rewarded with an experience not found anywhere else in the festival.

This music and camping festival, with added attractions such as an on-site salon sponsored by Garnier and a Red Bull music academy courtesy of Red Bull, notched up over $50 million in economic impact in 2012 according to a study by Greyhill Advisors. Also in 2012, instead of following the regular method and announcing the musical lineup on the official website, Bonnaroo announced its lineup on the music-streaming social media programme Spotify. The initiative was a big success attracting over 25,000 subscribers who were able to listen to songs from all the attending bands and discover new, exciting acts playing at the festival.

But perhaps the organizers' greatest success with social media in 2012 was the use of radio frequency identification (RFID) technology to foster engagement. Each attendee was given a wristband which served as the only form of ticket to the festival. The wristbands had built-in RFID technology and could be swiped by attendees at one of 20 check-in portals around the venue. Scanning their wristbands at the towers would check visitors in on Facebook, enabling their friends to see exactly where they were and what band they were seeing. This could be used not only to share experiences, but also to provide a location so that friends at the festival could find them. At the end of the day, the system made a second post to each guest's Facebook: a recap of all of the acts the person had seen that day with a link to Spotify which provided each act's Bonnaroo set list and a playlist of studio tracks of those songs.

Now featuring 150 acts over 12 stages, Bonnaroo recently branched out into 'glamping', offering prepitched specialty tents, state-of-the-art cabanas and RVs. All of its annual innovations are broadcast through its multiprong social media presence via Tumblr, Twitter, Facebook, Spotify, YouTube and Instagram. Marketing initiatives, such as merchandise design contests, #Bonna-YOU story-sharing, a volunteer programme, Ticketmaster's #FESTGOALS Sweepstakes to win free tickets, custom Bonnaroo shoes and 'Respect The Farm' environmental efforts, are all communicated through these outlets.

Since Woodstock in 1969 – probably the most famous music event of all time – the music festival sector has grown to be a sizeable industry, comparatively resilient to the 2008–13 global economic downturn. Worldwide, there are more than 800 music festivals of various types in 57 countries. The industry is generally made up of independent operators and entrepreneurs, but bigger umbrella groups such as Live Nation, Music Festivals and Festival Republic are emerging. Few researchers have examined the promotion or marketing of music events, although Rivero found that organizers of music festivals in Spain do not aggressively promote their festivals from a touristic

(Continued)

(Continued)

point of view – relying instead on positive word of mouth to build a loyal following. But we do know that social networks are key delivery channels for festivals and organizers owing to the large amount of information that can be provided through them, such as artist information and schedules, and general festival information, much of which is delivered for many months leading up to the event.

Sources: Hudson and Hudson (2013); Hudson et al. (2015); Shah (2015); Rau (2014).

CASE STUDY QUESTIONS

1   Account for the growth of music festivals around the world.

2   How are music festivals adapting to the changing marketing environment?

3   What more could music festivals do to engage with consumers via social media?

KEY PLAYERS IN THE GLOBAL TOURISM INDUSTRY

The key players in the tourism industry are outlined in Figure 1.9. They include private and nonprofit sector services, public sector services, suppliers (transportation, accommodations, food and beverage services, attractions, and events and conferences), intermediaries, and the customers (tourists/travellers) themselves. Each will be discussed in turn below.

1 PRIVATE AND NONPROFIT SECTOR SERVICES

The private and nonprofit sector includes tourism industry associations such as travel agency or tour operator associations, financial and banking services, educational institutions, the media and insurance services. A key player in this sector is the destination marketing organization (DMO), an organization responsible for the marketing of an identifiable tourism destination with an explicit geopolitical boundary (Pike and Page, 2014). Although DMOs date back to the twentieth century, it was after the Second World War that the number of DMOs grew considerably, with many establishing their core marketing role in the 1960s and 1970s alongside the rise of the package holiday, introduction of jet aircraft and the rise of the holiday brochure. The 1980s and 1990s saw the creation of many new DMOs as additional places recognized the value of a coordinated approach to destination promotion. It is estimated that there are now well in excess of 10,000 DMOs around the world (Pike and Page, 2014).

2 PUBLIC SECTOR SERVICES

Public sector involvement often comes in the form of national, regional or destination management or marketing organizations. Under the umbrella of each provincial tourism organization, there are a number of public, quasi-public and independent organizations, which work independently and in cooperation with others to create more attractive tourism products. The United Nations World Tourism Organization (UNWTO) is a well-known public sector agency tasked with the promotion of responsible, sustainable and universally accessible tourism. As the leading international

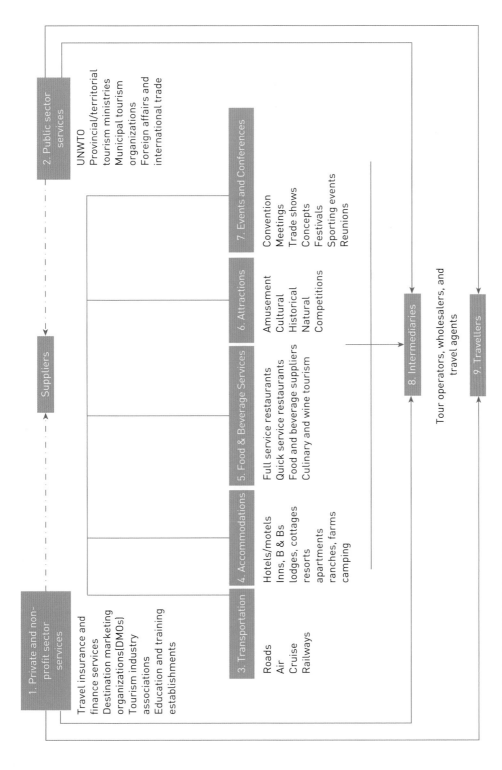

FIGURE 1.9 Key players in the tourism industry

organization in the field of tourism, UNWTO promotes tourism as a driver of economic growth, inclusive development and environmental sustainability and offers leadership and support to the sector in advancing knowledge and tourism policies worldwide. UNWTO's membership includes 156 countries, six Associate Members and over 450 Affiliate Members representing the private sector, educational institutions, tourism associations and local tourism authorities.

3 TRANSPORTATION

(A) ROADS

A good transportation infrastructure is crucial for the tourism industry to thrive in any country. Developing countries, in particular, are investing millions to improve their transportation systems. In India, for example, tourism growth has been hampered for many years due to its poor infrastructure. However, in 2000 India began the Golden Quadrilateral Project. This endeavour connects the top four metros of India by a four-lane highway, connecting Srinagar to Kanyakumari and Silcher to Saurashtra. The project has had a very positive impact on tourism, particularly domestic tourism. A strong transportation system is important for the growing RV tourism sector, the growth driven by the development of RV parks and campgrounds and the rise in the number of aging Baby Boomers with a taste for RV retirement lifestyle. Global shipment of RV vehicles is expected to reach seven million units by 2020. Prideaux and Carson (2012) have edited an excellent book about the drive tourism market around the world. Thirty-three authors contribute to 26 chapters and the focus is on drive tourism to and from a destination and on travel between destinations. The last chapter of the book is written by the editors and provides a good conclusion, recommending themes for future research in drive tourism. The authors suggest that our understanding of drive tourists as consumers of information requires further investigation, particularly as social networking and mobile technologies continue to expand and evolve. They also propose that the economics of drive tourism have not been well conceptualized and that, beyond expenditure, the economic implications of drive tourism development for destinations are not well understood. The chapter also points to a future characterized by a continued rapid rise in the volume of drive tourism across the globe – even in the face of rising fuel costs and increasing environmental concerns.

(B) THE AIRLINE INDUSTRY

The airline sector is a highly competitive one as barriers to entry are low due to liberalization of market access, a result of globalization. According to the IATA (International Air Transport Association), about 1,300 new airlines were established in the last 40 years (Cederholm, 2014). Recently, there has been a wave of industry consolidation resulting from mergers and acquisitions, which has reduced competition in a few regions. Mergers of major US airlines, for example, have resulted in a reduction in the number of key players from 11 in 2005 to just six in 2015. The six major airlines in the US – including Delta Air Lines, Inc., United Continental Holdings Inc., Alaska Air Group, Inc., JetBlue Airways Corporation, Southwest Airlines Co., and American Airlines – account for 94 per cent of market share by capacity. However, airlines based in the Persian Gulf are shaking up the North American market by offering high-quality service at lower prices. In 2014, Emirates, Qatar Airways and Etihad Airways boosted their number of US flights by 47 per cent and now serve 11 cities (McCartney, 2014).

Despite this competition, and the impacts of high-profile terrorism acts and natural disasters over the last decade, the world's airlines are experiencing increasing demand. Rising economic growth is spurring travel demand in Asia and Europe, and airline deregulation around the world has led to the development of no-frills, low-cost air-lines, operating mainly out of secondary airports. Airports themselves are spending millions in adapting their facilities to handle the new style outsize jets. Heathrow, for example, is investing more than $5 billion over the next decade to upgrade its facilities. Airports play a vital role in keeping the tourism sector growing in many countries, and competition among airlines is increasingly waged on the ground, especially in the Persian Gulf where fast-growing airlines having been driving construction of air-ports that are creating new expectations for travellers. They are following a strategy pioneered in Singapore and other Asian hubs, where the airport becomes part of the fun of the trip, rather than just an entry and exit.

(C) THE CRUISE INDUSTRY

The cruise sector is increasingly recognized as a successful and dynamic subsector of the global tourism industry (Weedon, Lester and Thyne, 2011). The global cruise industry generated revenues of $37.1 billion in 2014, making a significant recovery after revenues fell below $25 billion during the 2009 global recession. The number of passengers carried by the cruise industry has grown year-on-year and is expected to exceed 24 million in 2018. In 2013, the average cruise passenger brought in revenue of $1,728, but with expenses per passenger also high, the average profit was only $185 in 2013. Traditionally cruises were the preserve of the rich and famous who travelled in luxury with no financial or time restraints on such vessels as the *Lusitania* and the *Queen Elizabeth II*. Nowadays, the trend is towards bigger ships that carry over 3,000 passengers in an attempt to improve economies of scale in purchasing and operating expenses. These mega-ships can offer all-inclusive fares for about $100 per person per day, less than half the cost on most small ships, and comparable to resorts on shore. In 2016, Royal Caribbean launched the world's largest cruise ship, *Harmony of the Seas*. The vessel is 361m (1,187ft) long and can carry 6,780 passengers. It features 20 restaurants, 23 swimming pools and took more than two-and-a-half years to construct.

(D) RAILWAYS

Some countries around the world have turned to the railways to solve their transporta-tion problems. In mainland Western Europe and Japan, for example, governments have invested massive sums in dedicated high-speed lines and trains offering city-to-city services at speed in excess of 200 kmph. The British Conservative Party recently put forward high-speed trains as a solution to current environmental concerns and as a means of boosting the country's economy. Major new projects are also planned in many other countries. In China, the railway connecting China to Tibet has had a huge impact on tourism in Tibet. Until the first train made its way over the mountains in July 2006, a passage to Tibet involved a back-breaking bus journey or an expensive flight beyond the reach of many Chinese tourists. In 2014, 7.5 million passengers rode the railway from Golmud to Lhasa – more than double the population of Tibet itself. China now plans to build a 540-kilometre strategic high-speed rail link between Tibet and Nepal, passing through a tunnel under Mt Everest. Luxury train travel is another important component of the transportation sector. According to the world's travel agents, the Maharajas' Express in India is the number one luxury train, winning the

'World's Leading Luxury Train' award at the World Travel Awards for three consecutive years in 2012, 2013 and 2014. Owned and operated by Indian Railway Catering and Tourism Corporation, the Maharajas' Express is the most expensive train in the world. It runs on five circuits covering more than 12 destinations across Northwest and Central India, mainly centred on Rajasthan, between the months of October to April.

4 ACCOMMODATIONS

The accommodation sector consists of a great variety of types of accommodation facilities to meet the consumers' needs. These include youth hostels, bed and breakfasts, tourist residences, holiday dwellings, timeshare apartments and campsites. But the subsector of hotels is perhaps the most important, and hotel chains are particularly significant in large cities. In London and Paris, for example, their share of the bed capacity amounts to 50 per cent. An example of the global nature of the hotel sector is the Hilton group. Hilton has nearly 4,200 hotels in 93 countries and is busy spreading its traditional US brands such as Conrad, Doubletree, Embassy Suites, Hampton Inn and Hilton Garden to other parts of the world. Hilton is currently focusing its main international expansion on China, India and Eastern Europe for the high-demand mid-price market. Hilton will tailor the brand for different parts of the world, for example increasing the food and beverage offering in India to attract Western travellers. The recent purchase of Starwood Hotels by Marriott International is certain to shake up Hilton and other key players in the hotel sector. The deal created the world's largest hotel company, with more than 5,000 owned or franchised hotels with 1.1 million rooms around the world (Picker, 2015).

5 FOOD AND BEVERAGE SERVICES

The food and beverage sector involves companies that process, package and distribute fresh and prepared foods, as well as prepackaged foods, and both alcoholic and nonalcoholic beverages. Essentially, this sector encompasses any product consumed by humans, excluding pharmaceuticals. The countries driving most of the growth of the food and beverage sector are the primary emerging market economies of China and India, along with Brazil, Mexico, and a number of countries in Southeast Asia, such as Singapore and Malaysia. Food consumption and food production in China and India are, and have been for several years now, increasing at significantly faster rates than those in developing countries. China's total grocery food sales, as of 2015, exceeded those of the US. Its annual wheat production has increased substantially since the turn of the century, while US wheat production has only been steady to slightly down. There have been significant increases in sales of both alcoholic beverages and soft beverages in emerging market nations as well. Major beverage companies such as Coca-Cola and Pepsi have made significant investments in marketing their own brands and in creating partnerships with local firms for marketing new products.

6 ATTRACTIONS

As with other sectors of the tourism industry, attractions are increasingly polarized between a few large attractions and thousands of small and micro-sized enterprises. Within the range of visitor management techniques available to attractions, marketing is increasingly seen as fundamental to success. It is recognized as the best way of generating revenue to contribute to the cost of operation and maintenance of the resource base, to develop and sustain satisfying products, to create value for money, and to influence the volume and seasonality patterns of site visits. Tourist attractions can be classified as natural or human-made and, increasingly, consumers are drawn to attractions that provide entertainment. For example, throughout the world, 223.5 million people visited the top 25 theme parks in 2014. Disney Parks are well represented on this list of most visited theme parks, with nine parks landing in the top ten. Walt Disney World's four theme parks (water parks excluded) are included in those nine. With 19,332,000 guests, Magic Kingdom was once again the most visited theme park in the world, seeing a 4 per cent increase from 2013. However, the growth in the industry is expected to come outside of the US, particularly in China and India, where the middle classes are growing rapidly and are undersupplied with entertainment opportunities.

7 EVENTS AND CONFERENCES

Events and conferences often play a key role in bringing business and leisure travellers to destinations. These events can vary from conventions and exhibitions for the business market to huge sporting events like the Olympics or the Soccer World Cup, which attract millions of sport tourists. Events play a significant role in today's society and for tourism destinations they are important due to their tourist, social and cultural functions (Getz, 2007), as well as their role in local and regional development (Wood, 2005). First, and foremostly, events are a great anchor for attracting tourism, providing tourists with a prime opportunity to get to know the local culture and experience the essence of the place. During an event, visitors have a unique chance to interact with the local community, gaining a deeper experience of the ambience, customs and local culture. Events can also help in improving a place's image, creating a window for positive media coverage. Finally, for the residents themselves, events are a unique occasion to celebrate the local culture and interact within the community. For Edinburgh in Scotland, festivals make a huge contribution to the quality of life, international reputation and economic vitality of Edinburgh and Scotland. A recent study found that the city's festivals attract audiences of more than 4.5 million generating an impact of over $350m. The same report found that 94 per cent of attendees stated that festivals are part of what makes Edinburgh special as a city, and 68 per cent of local festival goers agreed that festivals increased their pride in Edinburgh as a city (BOP Consulting, 2016).

There are certainly a number of components to event marketing, and Figure 1.10 lists those activities and their purpose.

Conference travel is another important sector of the travel industry. In the last 20 years, the meeting and convention industry has gone from being an ancillary service provider to the Fortune 500 to a major industry that contributes more to the GDP than the air transportation, motion picture, sound recording, performing arts, and spectator sport industries. In the US alone, meetings bring $114 billion to the economy, 12 per cent of all travel, and 940,000 jobs. Of the 1.8 million meetings per year, 1.3 million are classified as corporate or business meetings, 270,000 are conventions, conferences or congresses, 11,000 are trade shows, and 66,000 are incentive meetings (Sadmin, 2016).

8 INTERMEDIARIES

The key intermediary players in the tourism industry are tour operators and wholesalers, travel agents, travel specialists, and Web-based intermediaries (a detailed analysis

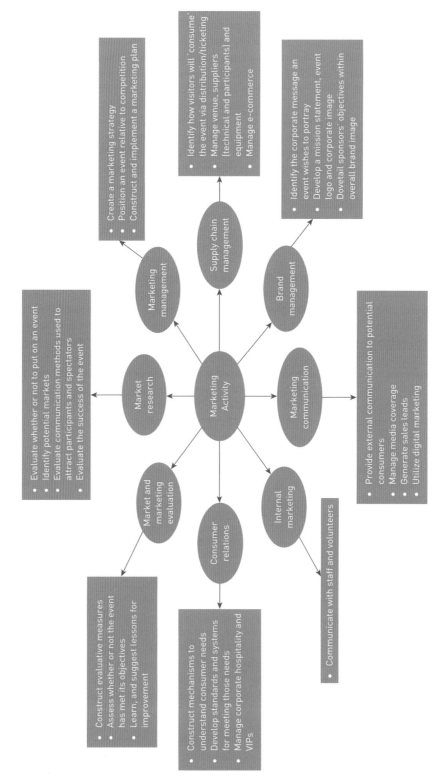

FIGURE 1.10 The components of event marketing practice (Source: Adapted from Jackson, 2013)

of intermediaries can be found in Chapter 7). Both tour operators and wholesalers are organizations that offer packaged vacation tours to the general public. These packages can include everything from transportation, accommodation and activities, to entertainment, meals, and drinks. Travel agents are the most widely used marketing intermediaries in the tourism industry and, with the advent of the Internet, online travel agents play an increasingly important role. This is explored more in depth in Chapter 3.

9 THE TOURISTS

The final key player in the tourism industry is the tourist. As mentioned above, international tourist arrivals reached an all-time record of 1.18 billion in 2015. Chapter 2 will focus on the tourist in more detail.

INFLUENCES ON THE TOURISM MARKETING ENVIRONMENT

MICROENVIRONMENT

The marketing environment is made up of a microenvironment and a macroenvironment. The microenvironment consists of forces close to the organization that can affect its ability to serve its customers: the organization itself, marketing channel firms, customer markets and a broad range of stakeholders or publics (see Figure 1.11). For a tourism marketer, these factors will affect the degree of success in attracting target markets, so it is important to understand their importance. This book discusses most of these components in detail: customers in Chapter 2, competitors in Chapter 4, intermediaries in Chapter 7, and the various publics in Chapter 9. However, it is important to acknowledge the influence that the company and its suppliers will have on achieving marketing objectives.

Marketing managers need to work closely with other departments in the company, as all of these departments will have some impact on the success of marketing plans. Every tourism organization will differ as to how many departments it has and what they are called. However, finance is normally responsible for finding and using the funds required to carry out marketing plans, accounting has to measure revenues and costs in order to evaluate marketing objectives, and human resources will be crucial in supporting a service marketing culture (see Chapter 10). Suppliers also have an important role to play in supporting marketing objectives. Suppliers are firms and individuals that provide the resources needed by the company to produce its goods and services.

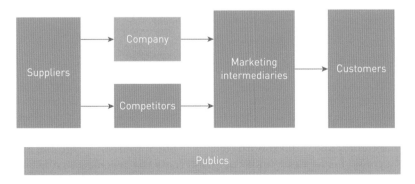

FIGURE 1.11 Major components in a company's microenvironment

Marketing management must pay close attention to trends and developments affecting suppliers, and to changes in supply availability and supply costs. At a micro level, hotels and exhibition centres contract with restaurant companies to supply food and beverage services. In turn, these restaurants will have their own favoured suppliers of produce. On a macro basis, tourist destinations will need suppliers in the form of airlines, hotels, restaurants, ground operations, meeting facilities, and entertainment.

MACROENVIRONMENT

The macroenvironment comprises the larger societal forces that affect the entire microenvironment, and this will shape opportunities and pose threats. The macroenvironment consists of the eight major forces shown in Figure 1.12, and tourism businesses need to take into consideration the fact that they operate in a competitive national and international environment. Although an organization cannot control many of these external factors, they should never be allowed to come as a total surprise. A planned response to potential environmental issues allows for a balanced, thoughtful reaction – a process often referred to as 'environmental scanning'.

FIGURE 1.12 Major forces in a company's macroenvironment

1 COMPETITIVE FORCES

Being aware of who the competition is, knowing what their strengths and weaknesses are, and anticipating what they may do are important aspects for understanding the macroenvironment. Competition tends to centre on the destination. Countries, states, regions, and cities now take their role as tourist destinations very seriously, committing considerable effort and funds towards enhancing their touristic image and attractiveness. As a consequence, destination competitiveness has become a significant part of tourism literature, and evaluation of the competitiveness of tourism destinations is increasingly being recognized as an important tool in the strategic positioning and marketing analysis of destinations (Hudson, Ritchie and Timur, 2004). Today, competition is intensifying to grab a larger share of the expected growth in outbound travel from China. The World Tourism Organization expects that by the year 2020, China will become one of the world's major outbound tourism markets, generating globally 100 million tourists, or 6.2 per cent of the world total. Competitive product, price, and quality, as well as access to and delivery of tourism goods and services, will be the major success factors in attracting new Chinese outbound tourists and encouraging repeat travellers in the next decade and beyond.

2 DEMOGRAPHIC FORCES

Demographics are statistics that describe the observable characteristics of individuals, including our physical traits, such as gender, race, age and height; our economic traits, such as income, savings and net worth; our occupation-related traits, including education; our location-related traits; and our family-related traits, such as marital status and number and age of children. According to David Foot, author of *Boom, Bust and Echo*, demographics explain about two-thirds of everything (Foot, 2000). For example, the dramatic increase in popularity of golf between 1990 and 2010 can be explained by golf's popularity among aging Baby Boomers who were entering a stage of life that enabled them to spend more time on the golf course. In fact, the single most notable demographic trend in many countries is the aging population. The over-50 segment is nearly 30 per cent of the population, and this market has a keen interest in travel and leisure services. Other demographic trends affecting the marketing of tourism worldwide include the relatively slow population growth, the continued increase in education and service sector employment, increasing ethnic diversity, the demise of the traditional family, and the geographic mobility of the population. In addition to understanding general demographic trends, marketers must also recognize demographic groupings that may turn out to be market segments because of their enormous size, similar socioeconomic characteristics, or shared values. Such segments are discussed in Chapters 3 and 4.

3 ECONOMIC FORCES

Economic forces in the environment are those that affect consumer purchasing power and spending patterns. Total purchasing power depends on current income, prices, savings and credit, so marketers must be aware of major economic trends in income and of changing consumer-spending patterns. The global recession that began in 2008 had long-lasting impacts for many countries, although some did benefit from an increase in domestic tourism (Papatheodorou, Rosselló and Xiao, 2010). Price changes can also have a significant impact on tourism. In the airline sector, airlines based in the Persian Gulf have been shaking up the North American market by offering high-quality service at lower prices. In 2014, Emirates, Qatar Airways and Etihad Airways boosted their number of US flights by 47 per cent and now serve 11 cities (McCartney, 2014). Finally, exchange rates can impact travel, and research has shown the importance of maintaining a relatively stable exchange rate to attract tourist arrivals (De Vita, 2014). Agiomirgianakis, Serenis and Tsounis (2014), for example, found that there is a negative relationship between exchange rate volatility and tourist inflows into Turkey. In the summer of 2016, Britain's intended exit from the European Union impacted travel between the UK and America. The hit delivered to the British pound by Brexit made travel to the US more expensive for holders of UK currency, and for US travellers heading to England, a stronger US dollar gave them more buying power abroad and a greater bang for each buck (Burris, 2016).

4 ENVIRONMENTAL AND NATURAL FORCES

The last four decades have witnessed a dramatic increase in environmental consciousness worldwide. Media attention given to the greenhouse effect, acid rain, oil spills, ocean pollution, tropical deforestation, and other topics has raised public awareness about environmental issues. This environmental awareness has had an impact on the tourism industry. International leisure travellers are increasingly motivated by the quality of destination landscapes in terms of environmental health and the diversity and integrity of natural and cultural resources. Studies of German and US travel markets indicate that environmental considerations are now a significant element of travellers' destination-choosing process, down to – in the case of the Germans – the environmental programmes operated by individual hotels. The growing concern among consumers for the protection of the environment has clearly attracted the attention of companies seeking to profit from environmentally sound marketing practices. Surveys have shown that consumers are more likely to choose one brand over another if they believe the brand will help the environment, and environmental quality is a prevailing issue in making travel-related decisions. This has led to the 'greening' of attractions, hotels, and even resorts, and to an increase in the number of environmentally friendly tourism products. An increasing emphasis is also being placed upon evaluating the likely environmental impacts of any tourism development, with environmental audits, environmental impact analysis, and carrying capacity issues being taken more seriously.

Finally, uncontrollable natural forces can have a negative impact on the tourism industry. For example, the South Asian tsunami of 2004, due to the number of victims among foreign visitors and among workers of the tourism sector, constitutes the greatest catastrophe ever recorded in the history of tourism. Before the tsunami, tourism was at an all time high in many of the affected countries. A two-year ceasefire between the Sri Lankan government and the Tamil Tigers had helped produce an 11 per cent increase in the number of tourists there. Thailand was continuing its strong growth with a 20 per cent rise from the previous year. The tsunami devastated tourism in many countries. Due to its magnitude and repercussions, the disaster took on a global scale, reflecting the world-wide reach tourism has today. Another uncontrollable health scare that impacted tourism more recently – particularly in Brazil – was the Zika virus. Early in 2016 the World Health Organization declared the virus a global public-health emergency, leading to fears that travellers would cancel their plans to attend that summer's Olympic Games (Kiernan and Jelmayer, 2016).

5 TECHNOLOGICAL FORCES

The most dramatic force shaping the future of tourism and hospitality is technology, discussed in more detail in Chapter 3. The accelerated rate of technological advancement has forced tourism organizations to adapt their products accordingly, particularly in terms of how they develop, price, distribute, and promote their products. Technology facilitates the continual development of new systems and features that improve the tourism product. Technology has allowed for extra security in hotels and resorts, thanks to security systems and safety designs. It has also created new entertainment options for travellers, such as in-room movies and video games. The majority of hotels, and even airplanes, now offer Internet services to cater to the technological needs of today's consumer.

The Internet fits the theoretical marketing principle in the travel industry because it allows suppliers to set up direct links of communication with their customers. Technology is also beginning to have an impact on consumer research, as tourism organizations realize the potential of database management and the value of relationship marketing. Databases of customer profiles and customer behaviour are the basis for effective direct marketing. In tourism, the collection and analysis of data streams that now flow continuously through distribution channels and booking systems provide the modern information base for strategic and operational decisions of large organizations. The rate of technological change as databases connect and interact indicates that the speed and quality of information flows will be further enhanced in the coming decade.

6 POLITICAL FORCES

Marketing decisions are strongly affected by developments in the political environment. This environment is made up of government agencies and pressure groups that influence and limit the activities of various organizations and individuals in society. Government policies can have far-reaching implications for the tourism industry. The political turmoil in Greece in 2015, for example, had a negative impact on tourism. Tourism is a vital industry in Greece, representing about 17 per cent of the country's gross domestic product and supporting an estimated 70,000 jobs. Political actions can also have a positive impact on tourism. In some parts of the world, the relaxing of political barriers is making areas more accessible to tourists. An example is Cuba, where economic and political reform has led to a steady growth in international tourists (Hingtgen et al., 2015).

Terrorism can also have a devastating impact on tourism around the world. Since 11 September 2001, there have been thousands of major terrorism attacks worldwide, most of which have impacted the tourism industry. After the terrorism attack in Tunisia in June 2015, the tourism minister predicted that the industry would lose $500 million that year due to the attack. Media attention to these attacks is usually enough to sway many international travellers towards reconsidering their vacation plans, and negative media and foreign office warnings are usually enough to deter tourists. The terrorists themselves target tourism destinations in order to force governments to rethink and abandon specific policies, or to deny governments the commercial and economic benefits of tourism.

At the time of writing, more than one-quarter of the world's countries was deemed to be either entirely or partly off limits by the British Foreign Office (FO). The FO was advising against journeys to all, or parts, of more than 60 countries. The majority of these were in Africa or the Middle East, with many of them – Afghanistan, Iran, Iraq, Libya, Sierra Leone, Somalia, South Sudan, Syria and Yemen among them – considered unfeasible destinations by all but the most intrepid travellers (Leadbeater, 2015).

7 CULTURAL AND SOCIAL FORCES

Marketing's consumer focus relies on an understanding of who the markets are, what motivates them, and how to appeal to them. Understanding the cultural environment is thus crucial for marketing decision-making. This cultural environment includes institutions and other forces that affect society's basic values, perceptions, preferences, and behaviours. Cultural values influence consumer behaviour, and marketers tend to concentrate on dominant cultural values or core values.

A grouping technique that is used to track trends in cultural values is psychographics, which determines how people spend their time and resources (activities), what they consider important (interests and values), and what they think of themselves and the world around them (opinions). Psychographics is discussed more fully in Chapter 2. Core values are slow and difficult to change, but secondary values are less permanent values that can sometimes be influenced by marketers. Many major cultural trends affect the tourism industry, and the final section of Chapter 2 focuses on ten key trends or demands in consumer behaviour that are influencing tourism and hospitality marketing today.

8 LEGAL FORCES

The tourism industry has witnessed an increase in legislation and regulation that affects business, normally enacted to protect companies and consumers from unfair business practices. An example comes from Mille Lacs Lake in Minnesota in 2015, when a ban on fishing from the state's Department of Natural Resources, devastated the local economy which is dependent on anglers who rent charter boats, stay in nearby motels, and eat in bars and restaurants (Bosman, 2015). Government regulation also aims to protect society's interests against unrestricted business behaviour, as profitable business activity does not always improve the quality of life within a society. Hence the regulations in many parts of the world that restrict smoking in restaurants and hotels. In fact, government agencies have become involved in the regulation of everything from food-handling practices in restaurants to fire codes for hotels. Travellers are seen as good sources of revenue by politicians, as witnessed by the increasing number of cities, states or provinces that are implementing hotel taxes. Travel is one of the most heavily taxed activities in the US, and the Global Business Travel Association, a trade and lobbying group for travel managers, says that travellers pay taxes that total, on average, 57 per cent more than if they just paid the normal general sales tax (McCartney, 2012). Laws regarding landing taxes for aircraft, health regulations, gaming licences and entry permits all affect the tourism industry in one way or another. Song et al. (2012) have documented how visa restrictions in China have resulted in a major loss in tourism arrivals over the years.

CHAPTER SUMMARY

Tourism is a powerful economic force, providing employment, foreign exchange, income and tax revenue for countries all over the world. The key players in the industry are private and nonprofit sector services, public sector services, suppliers (transportation, accommodations, food and beverage services, attractions, and events and conferences), intermediaries and the customers (tourists/travellers) themselves. The marketing environment is made up of a microenvironment and a macroenvironment. The microenvironment consists of forces close to the organization that can affect its ability to serve its customers: the organization itself, marketing channel firms, customer markets and a broad range of stakeholders or publics. The macroenvironment forces are competitive, demographic, economic, environmental and natural, technological, political, cultural and social, and legal. Marketing is a subject of vital concern in tourism because it is the principal management influence that can be brought to bear on the size and behaviour of this major global market.

REFLECTIVE QUESTIONS

1 What are the key challenges facing the global tourism and hospitality industry today? Which of these are controllable and which are uncontrollable?

2 Which of the key players in the tourism industry outlined in Figure 1.9 are more vulnerable to external influences such as terrorist attacks and tsunamis?

3 Choose one of the transport sectors discussed in the chapter and update the material presented in the text. How is this sector performing in today's environment?

MARKETING IN ACTION: LET THE JOURNEY BEGIN (AGAIN)

In 2012–13 Myanmar, a country labelled by the US government ten years before as 'an outpost of tyranny', launched a nationally coordinated tourism branding campaign for the first time in decades. The purpose: to change forever a negative destination image.

IMAGE 1.3 Ngapali Beach, Myanmar - opening frame for 'Let the Journey Begin' television commercial (Image Diplomacy. Used with permission)

Historically, the country has faced many challenges to tourism growth, including a lack of trained human resources and insufficient public services and infrastructure. Attempts to launch mass tourism have failed before, blockaded in particular by politics. New laws, including the 1990 Tourism Law – which ended state monopolies on hotels, transportation and tour guiding – began the process of opening up Myanmar's tourism offerings. But the resulting reports of mass upheaval, human rights' violations, conscripted labour and population displacement while developing facilities led many groups to oppose tourism. As well as groups outside Myanmar, the naysayers included Aung San Suu Kyi, leader of the Democratic Party, and winner of the Nobel Peace Prize in 1991. At one point, she and her party urged travellers to refrain from visiting Myanmar until there was a political transition to democracy. Her anti-tourism campaign proved to be successful, with travellers and their dollars staying away. While tourism expanded rapidly in neighbouring Asian countries, Myanmar received relatively few tourists over the last few decades. Nearby Thailand annually attracts more than ten million visitors but it took until 2012 for Myanmar to top one million.

(Continued)

(Continued)

In 2011, however, everything changed. The Government of the Republic of the Union of Myanmar (GOM) began to transform its political and socioeconomic system to enhance inclusive economic growth, accelerate poverty reduction and increase living standards for Myanmar's multiethnic population. Led by President Thein Sein, the new regime completely revamped the investment law, covering more than 20 sectors, opening up the 'Golden Land' for new investment opportunities. Aung San Suu Kyi became a member of parliament, sitting alongside members of the party that once imprisoned her. The reform process opened significant opportunities for business, investment and human capital. The World Bank, which was investing $2 billion to bring health and energy to the poor, estimated Myanmar's economic growth rate at 8.4 per cent for 2014 and 2015, a figure higher than any other nation it surveyed, including China.

In 2012, a professional international marketing firm, ImageDiplomacy (iD) was contracted to create and deliver Myanmar's new branding campaign. Headed up by Brit, Sorcha Hellyer and Italian partner, Gabriele Villa, the creative company launched their tantalizing tagline 'Let the Journey Begin' at the World Economic Forum on East Asia in 2013. The multilayered campaign included a television commercial (shown on BBC World and Channel News Asia among other places) and a branding booklet. As Hellyer said: 'Aligning custom publishing initiatives with other branding endeavours ensures greater longevity of brand exposure.' Besides the audiovisual elements of the campaign at the WEF (including the TV commercial, the show reel and tourism showcase), iD put together a coffee-table book full of photos of Myanmar that was given to all the high-level delegates in a branded gift bag, along with a folder of information about the campaign and a USB key with the films on.

Despite this promising progression, the country is still facing hurdles. As one commentator recently put it: 'For all the encouraging change from 2010 to 2014, Burma is still a place of two parallel universes in a race for time. One is of prosperity and progress, iPhones and donut shops. The other is of grinding poverty, greed, and medieval religious understanding.' Reforms in Myanmar resulted, however, in an initial surge of curious international travellers. Between 2011 and 2012 visitor arrivals increased by 29.7 per cent, and, for the first time in its history, Myanmar received over one million visitors. In 2012, the Ministry of Hotels and Tourism (MOHT) – the agency mandated by GOM to oversee the systematic development of tourism – prepared the Myanmar Tourism Master Plan. It set out strategic programmes, priority projects and activities in a long-term implementation framework covering 2013–20 and a short-term action plan for 2013–15. The Master Plan set a high target of 3.01 million international visitors in 2015 and 7.48 million in 2020. Based on this high-growth scenario, tourism receipts were projected to increase from a baseline of $534 million in 2012 to $10.18 billion in 2020, with the number of tourism-related jobs rising from 293,700 to 1.49 million. The Plan identified a number of strengths and opportunities for Myanmar's tourism industry to build on, constraints to overcome and risks to manage.

Htay Aung, Minister for Ministry of Hotels and Tourism said that they timed the launch to coincide with, and capitalize on, the platform of the World Economic Forum: 'Not least because of the relevant themes of the East Asia summit – those of courage, transformation, inclusion and integration.' Aung also said that the various elements of the campaign 'all aimed to portray the inherent cultural values of the old Myanmar and the optimism of the new Myanmar'. Deputy Minister for National Planning and

Economic Development, U Set Aung said he hoped the campaign would show that Myanmar is now a 'responsible member of the community'.

The new brand was also rolled out at the World Travel Market, one of the leading global events for the travel industry, held annually in London. Exhibiting at the event were several Myanmar-based companies and individuals who as a group promoted Myanmar as a desirable destination. Such activities are coordinated by the Myanmar Marketing Committee (MMC), the marketing arm of Myanmar Tourism Federation (MTF). MMC selects target markets and promotes the destination by participating in travel shows, organizing road shows, organizing familiarization trips and media trips.

ImageDiplomacy said it wanted the nation-branding campaign to appeal to both visitors and investors, and to focus on Myanmar's rich cultural heritage: 'People are not aware of what Myanmar has to offer, so we wanted to create an alluring campaign that would inspire travellers and investors alike,' said Vila. As for the tagline, the team was determined to steer clear of adjectives. 'There are destinations using words like "amazing" or "incredible" or "sparkling" – some of which have been effective but others fail to fully capture the essence of the national identity,' Villa explained. iD considered over 70 taglines before deciding on 'Let the Journey Begin': 'We feel that it expresses Myanmar's current situation as well as the desire to welcome people to explore and better understand the country after a long period of isolation.'

Myanmar has played host to other major international events since the reforms, including the Southeast Asia Games in 2013, the Association of South East Asian Nations (ASEAN) in 2014, and the ASEAN Tourism Fair in 2015. The 2013 Southeast Asia Games, which took place in Naypyidaw, the new capital, as well as in the main cities of Yangon, Mandalay and Ngwesaung Beach, marked the nation's biggest sporting event hosted since 1969. Myanmar has continued to host events that highlight the changes taking place – for example, the inaugural 'Myanmar Summit' in 2015 which examined the 'state of play' for its economic and political systems and the implications for business and investors. Tourism arrivals continue to climb with the country attracting over three million foreign visitors in 2014 to surpass the government's expectations.

Sources: Hudson (2007); Hudson (2016); Personal visit by authors Feb 2016.

CASE STUDY QUESTIONS

1   Do some research and find out what the political situation in Myanmar is today.

2   Give examples from other countries around the world where politics is having a negative impact on tourism.

3   Apart from political factors, what other environmental factors are influencing tourism in Myanmar?

REFERENCES

Agiomirgianakis, G., Serenis, D. and Tsounis, N. (2014). 'Exchange rate volatility and tourist flows into Turkey', *Journal of Economic Integration*, 29(4): 700–25.

BOP Consulting (2016) *Edinburgh Festivals 2015 Impact Study*, July. www. edinburghfestivalcity.com/assets/000/001/964/Edinburgh_Festivals_-_2015_Impact_ Study_Final_Report_original.pdf?1469537463 (accessed 5 December 2016).

Bosman, J. (2015) 'A fishing ban helps walleye but hurts tourism', *New York Times*, 13 August, A11.

Burris, R. (2016) 'How Brexit could impact South Carolina', *The State*, 24 June. www.thestate.com/news/business/article85892047.html (accessed 5 December 2016).

Cateora, P. R, Gilly, M. C. and Graham, J.L. (2013) *International Marketing*. New York: McGraw-Hill/Irwin (16th edn).

Cederholm, T. (2014) 'Low-entry barriers intensify competition in airline industry', *Market Realist*, 29 December. http://marketrealist.com/2014/12/low-entry-barriers-intensify-competition-airline-industry (accessed 5 December 2016).

De Vita, G. (2014) 'The long-run impact of exchange rate regimes on international tourism flows', *Tourism Management*, 45: 226–33.

Dolnicar, S. and Ring, A. (2014) 'Tourism marketing research: Past, present and future', *Annals of Tourism Research*, 47: 31–47.

Foot, D. (2000) *Boom, Bust and Echo: Profiting from the Demographic Shift in the 21st Century*. Toronto: MacFarlane Walter & Ross.

Getz, D. (2007) *Event Studies. Theory, Research and Policy for Planned Events*. Oxford: Butterworth-Heinemann.

Hingtgen, N., Kline, C. M, Fernandes, L. and McGehee, N. G. (2015) 'Cuba in transition: Tourism industry perceptions of entrepreneurial change', *Tourism Management*, 50: 184–93.

Hudson, S. (2007) 'To go or not to go? Ethical perspectives on tourism in an "outpost of tyranny"', *Journal of Business Ethics*, 76(4): 385–96.

Hudson, S. (2008) *Tourism and Hospitality Marketing: A Global Perspective*. London: Sage.

Hudson, S. (2016) 'Let the journey begin (again). The branding of Myanmar', *Journal of Destination Marketing and Management*. Online first at: www.sciencedirect.com/science/article/pii/S2212571X16300907?_rdoc=1&_fmt=high&_origin=gateway&_docanchor=&md5=b8429449ccfc9c30159a5f9aeaa92ffb (accessed 5 December 2016).

Hudson, S. and Hudson, R. (2013) 'Engaging with consumers using social media: A case study of music festivals', *International Journal of Events and Festivals Management*, 4(3): 206–23.

Hudson, S., Ritchie, J. R. B. and Timur, S. (2004) 'Measuring destination competitiveness: An empirical study of Canadian ski resorts', *Journal of Tourism and Hospitality Planning and Development*, 1(1): 79–94.

Hudson, S., Roth, M. S., Madden, T. J. and Hudson, R. A. (2015) 'The effects of social media on emotions, brand relationship quality, and word of mouth: An empirical study of music festival attendees', *Tourism Management*, 47: 68–76.

Kiernan, P. and Jelmayer, R. (2016) 'Zika virus saps Brazil's tourism hopes', *Wall Street Journal*, 4 February: A5.

Kotler, P. (1984) *Marketing Management: Analysis, Planning, Implementation and Control*. Upper Saddle River, NJ: Prentice Hall (8th edn).

Leadbeater, C. (2015) 'Is the world getting riskier for tourists?' *Daily Telegraph*, 4 July, T6.

McCartney, S. (2012) 'The best and worst US cities for travel taxes', *Wall Street Journal*, 18 October, D3.

McCartney, S. (2014) 'Now landing: Tough challengers', *Wall Street Journal*, D1, 4.

Middleton, V. T. C. and Clarke, J. R. (2012) *Marketing in Travel and Tourism* (3rd edn). Oxford: Butterworth-Heinemann.

Oxford Economics (2014) *Destination Promotion: An Engine of Economic Development*. Oxford Economics, November.

Papatheodorou, J., Rosselló, A. and Xiao, H. (2010) 'Global economic crisis and tourism: Consequences and perspectives', *Journal of Travel Research*, 49(1): 39–45.

Picker, L. (2015) 'Marriott to buy Starwood Hotels, creating world's largest hotel company', *New York Times*, 16 November, www.nytimes.com/2015/11/17/business/marriott-to-buy-starwood-hotels.html?_r=0 (accessed 5 December 2016).

Pike, S. and Page, S.J. (2014) 'Destination marketing organizations and destination marketing. A narrative analysis of the literature', *Tourism Management*, 41: 202–27.

Prideaux, B. and Carson, D. (eds) (2012) *Drive Tourism. Trends and Emerging Markets*. London: Routledge.

Rau, N. (2014) 'Bonnaroo brings in big acts, bigger bucks', *The Tennessean*, 11 June. www.tennessean.com/story/money/industries/music/2014/06/11/bonnaroo-brings-big-acts-bigger-bucks/10347135 (accessed 5 December 2016).

Sadmin, P.M. (2016) 'Economic impact of the meeting industry', *Premier Meeting Services*, 24 May. www.premiermeetingservices.com/economic-impact-meeting-industry (accessed 5 December 2016).

Shah, N. (2015) 'How music festivals pump billions into the US economy', *Speakeasy, Wall Street Journal*, 31 July. http://blogs.wsj.com/speakeasy/2015/07/31/how-music-festivals-pump-billions-into-the-u-s-economy/#:erMaZUzLloG8xA (accessed 5 December 2016).

Song, H., Gartner, W. C. and Tasci, A. D. A. (2012) 'Visa restrictions and their adverse economic and marketing implications – evidence from China', *Tourism Management*, 33: 397–412.

UNWTO (2015) *UNWTO Tourism Highlights. 2015 Edition*. The United National World Tourism Organization. www.e-unwto.org/doi/pdf/10.18111/9789284416899 (accessed 5 December 2016).

ValueWalk (2016) 'How much money do tourists spend in each country?' *ValueWalk*, 10 August. www.valuewalk.com/2016/08/how-much-money-do-tourists-spend-in-each-country (accessed 5 December 2016).

Weedon, C, Lester, J-A. and Thyne, M. (2011) 'Cruise tourism: Emerging issues and implications for a maturing industry', *Journal of Hospitality and Tourism Management*, 18: 26–9.

Wood, E. (2005) 'Measuring the economic and social impact of local authority events', *The International Journal of Public Sector Management*, 18(1): 37–53.

World Tourism Organization. (2016a) 'International Tourism,' *Infographic*, UNWTO, Madrid. http://media.unwto.org/content/infographics (accessed 5 December 2016).

World Tourism Organization. (2016b) 'Why Tourism Matters,' *Infographic*, UNWTO, Madrid. http://media.unwto.org/content/infographics (accessed 5 December 2016).

UNDERSTANDING TODAY'S CONSUMER

2

INTRODUCTION

This chapter looks at behavioural trends in tourism, and begins by reviewing the factors that influence consumer behaviour. The second part of the chapter focuses on typologies of tourists, and the third section looks at the stages of the buying process. This is followed by a section devoted to organizational buying behaviour, as tourism marketers need to understand both the decision-making criteria used and the process of decision-making that groups and organizations go through in buying tourism services. The final section looks in-depth at some of the trends in consumer behaviour affecting tourism marketers today. Case studies in this chapter discuss a leading ski hill operator, the marketing of the X Games, and the 'bleisure' trend.

LESSONS FROM A MARKETING GURU: CHARLIE LOCKE KEEPING ONE STEP AHEAD

In 2015 Lake Louise was named Canada's Best Ski Resort at The World Ski Awards in Kitzbühel, Austria for the third year running. At the same time, owner Charlie Locke was honoured with the trophy for Outstanding Contribution to Ski Tourism for the Americas, the winter sports' Oscar. 'This is the high point of my career,' said Locke at the time. These kinds of awards are extremely competitive and don't come to resorts by chance. It has been Locke's intuition and careful research into consumer needs over decades that have led to such universal appreciation of both his resort and his own endeavours.

IMAGE 2.1 Charlie Locke (Courtesy of Charlie Locke)

Over more than 37 years, Locke has seen dramatic changes in the winter sports' world. 'These range from IT, to grooming, to snowmaking, to lifts, to food service, to difficulties with the environmental lobby, to the way we do our marketing, to the way we distribute our food, rent skis, and teach lessons,' he says. Lake Louise has led the way in Canada in many of these respects, anticipating and responding to trends. One particular innovation was the provision of a volunteer ski guiding team available to orientate customers around the slopes and at the resort base all season. 'We initiated the "ski friend" idea, and copyrighted the name,' Locke explains. Another front-running initiative was the provision of discount cards for lift tickets. 'Originally, at Lake Louise we called these "Blue Cards" as a brewery provided us with a sizable contribution to our marketing costs in exchange for naming it after one of their brews. The card later became the Louise Card which I believe is one of the most successful skier incentive cards in North America,' Locke says.

He ranks marketing and social media among the most dynamic challenges for the ski industry in recent years, with many more mediums to juggle and real time response the fundamental key to success. But, while grassroots and guerilla marketing-type endeavours still resonate, traditional PR and media relations remain important, he believes. Vital aspects of the techie trend evidenced at Lake Louise include direct-to-lift cards, debit-loadable passes, efficient IT systems for purchasing and rentals, as well as wi-fi, recharging stations for phones, and computer terminals.

Lake Louise was an early adopter of social media and in the 2014/15 season one of the first resorts on Snapchat. Locke employs a dedicated social media guru to keep up with the latest trends and platforms online. The resort is also exploring sophisticated methods of tracking progress and benchmarking the online platforms where skiers and snowboarders are interacting and making purchase decisions. In the main lodge there are cellphone-recharging stations, computer terminals, ATMs and wi-fi. Lake Louise also has its own blog and is active on Facebook, Twitter, Pinterest, YouTube, Google+ and Instagram.

Good customer service goes beyond social media management, he maintains, requiring hands-on contact with every detail. With snow being crucial to the success of a ski resort, Locke's typical day starts with a review of the snow report, the grooming report and the run-open report. 'It ends with reviewing the skier count for the day and comparing it, and the year to date numbers, with budgets,' Locke adds. He also takes time to compare the Lake Louise reports with those disseminated by umbrella area marketer, Ski Banff Lake Louise, and occasionally suggest amendments: 'For example, this morning I noted that the report said 20 cm of snow in the last 48 hours, when in reality, there was 20 cm in the last 36 hours. This minor change could make the difference of 100 skiers or so and all of the incremental revenue flows to the bottom line.' Other daily preoccupations include skier demographics, particularly important in today's changing landscape where both the industry and the skier are maturing. In response to this Lake Louise introduced a super senior pass for just $20 and also promotes ski nostalgia with interpretive heritage photos around lodges, retro events, a growing seniors' club, and Throwback Thursdays, a retrospective of photos and videos posted on social media.

In order to mitigate the aging skier trend, most ski resort operators are diversifying, offering myriad activities – rather than depending on just ski tickets – to ensure a sustainable year-round business model. Thus Lake Louise is responding with a fuller activity menu including a new dedicated service entitled 'Experience Lake Louise', a booking and information facility for snowmobile tours, heli-hiking, heli-snowshoeing, heli-skiing, cat-skiing, dog-sledding, tubing, guided snowshoe tours and sleigh rides, complete with customization options. A new ski and yoga retreat is also in the offing with discussions ongoing regarding yoga/health and wellness retreats at Skoki Lodge. The resort is also continually upgrading mountain food service to include the latest trends in healthy, vegan and gluten-free eating.

In terms of ethical consumption and sustainability, Lake Louise has always been in a unique position, subject to the more stringent practices required from operating within Banff National Park UNESCO World Heritage Site. The first ski area in the Canadian Rockies to introduce an Environmental Management Department to oversee 'green' operations and projects, Lake Louise features cutting-edge water conservation, waste management and energy-saving endeavours, delivery of interpretive programmes and the supporting of staff in graduate level research. Other initiatives include green groomers, eco-upgrades to snowmaking, water and energy conservation in lodges, efficient lighting and heating, recycling, community clean-ups and an established Corporate Social Responsibility programme.

(Continued)

(Continued)

Committed to education and enrichment, Lake Louise creates educational pro-grammes and installations to deliver key conservation and heritage tourism messages to visitors to Banff National Park. As well as supporting an international exchange programme focusing on culture, nature and conservation, there are Avalanche Awareness, Outdoor Education and Backcountry Skiing courses. In winter, Lake Louise offers Ski Friends Winter Heritage tours (free of charge) and snowshoe tours which combine activity with tidbits on the area, animals, geography and history. And in summer there are interpretive hikes, a Junior Ranger programme and an Interpretive Centre.

As Locke says, looking after Lake Louise is a legacy for the future: 'We don't just own the resort but are active in the day-to-day operations, keeping in touch with our customers and what makes them happy. Having multiple generations involved gives us a variety of perspectives and insights into what people want now, and will as we develop our resort over the next 20 years. Our involvement also allows us to make decisions more effectively and to respond to changes and trends of our customers as they happen. Whether it's learning from our social media community, building new products for the next generation or following trends in tourism, it's ultimately important that we never forget who we are as a brand and the type of experience we want to offer.'

Sources: Personal visit and interviews with Charlie Locke (2015 and 2016).

FACTORS INFLUENCING CONSUMER BEHAVIOUR

The cornerstone of marketing theory is the satisfaction of the consumer. Therefore, the marketer needs to understand three related aspects of consumer behaviour analysis: consumer motivations, consumer typologies and the consumer purchasing process. Most tourism and hospitality organizations have an imperfect picture of their customer, and many of them do not monitor patterns of consumer behaviour at a level of detail necessary to remain competitive (Hudson and Hudson, 2015). Many organizations consider that they are sufficiently close to their visitors and therefore do not commit resources to more formal consumer studies. Others are constrained by limited marketing budgets and by the fact that researching consumer motivation and the buying process can be a time-consuming and difficult procedure. In fact, most organizations rely almost entirely on the scanning of secondary consumer data, combined with management observation and judgment. However, in a rapidly chang-ing environment, conclusions drawn from secondary data can be out of date in no time. Consumer patterns recorded in 2017, for example, will most likely have changed by the year 2020, but many companies might still be using this type of information as a benchmark.

Figure 2.1 shows the seven key factors that influence a consumer's behaviour. Motivation is often seen as a major determinant of consumer behaviour, but cul-tural, personal and social influences will also have an important effect on consumer purchases. Each of the influences in Figure 2.1 will be discussed in turn.

FIGURE 2.1 Factors influencing behaviour

1. MOTIVATIONS

Motivations are inner drives that cause people to take action to satisfy their needs, and monitoring consumer motivation is one of the most effective ways of gaining competitive differential advantage. Understanding the key triggers that lead to the purchase of a tourism or hospitality product, such as a visit to an attraction or making a hotel booking, is recognized as one of the main factors in the success of competitive organizations. Central to most content theories of motivation is the concept of need. Needs are seen as the force that arouses motivated behaviour, and it is assumed that, to understand human motivation, it is necessary to discover what needs people have and how they can be fulfilled. Maslow, in 1943, was the first to attempt to do this with his needs' hierarchy theory, now the best known of all motivation theories (see Figure 2.2).

One of the main reasons for the popularity of Maslow's hierarchy of needs is probably its simplicity. Maslow suggested that human needs are arranged in a hierarchy, from the most pressing to the least pressing. These needs, in order of importance, are physiological needs, safety needs, social needs, esteem needs and self-actualization needs. A person tries to satisfy the most important need first. When that need is satisfied, it will stop being a motivator, and the person will then try to satisfy the next most important need. It could be argued that traveller philanthropy is an outcome of the modern consumer seeking to satisfy self-actualization needs, since all the other needs in Maslow's hierarchy have been met. Certainly, most experts would agree that consumer demand for self-actualization is set to grow across socioeconomic levels, geographic borders and cultural boundaries (Pedraza, 2013).

Attempts to explain tourist motivation have aligned with Maslow's hierarchy. Mills and Morrison, for example, see travel as a need or want satisfier, and show how Maslow's

FIGURE 2.2 Maslow's hierarchy of needs (Source: Based on Maslow, 1943)

hierarchy ties in with travel motivations and the travel literature (Mills and Morrison, 1985). Similarly, Dann's tourism motivators can be linked to Maslow's list of needs. He argues that there are basically two factors in a decision to travel: the push factors and the pull factors (Dann, 1977). The push factors are those that make you want to travel, and the pull factors are those that affect where you travel. Krippendorf, in an enlightening book on tourism, sees a thread running through all these theories of tourism motivation. Firstly, travel is motivated by 'going away from' rather than 'going towards' something; second, travellers' motives and behaviour are markedly self-oriented. The author classifies these theories into eight explanations of travel: recuperation and regeneration, compensation and social integration, escape, communication, freedom and self-determination, self-realization, happiness, and broadening the mind (Krippendorf, 1987).

Other factors influencing motivation and purchase include: learning, beliefs and attitudes, and perception. Learning refers to the way in which visitors receive and interpret a variety of stimuli. People gain experience through taking holidays, by listening to others and through a variety of other sources. From these experiences a consumer will develop a mental inventory of expectations about places – a catalogue of good and bad holiday experiences. These form the basis of learned criteria that will be recalled when selecting future holidays and destinations. Beliefs refer to the thoughts that people have about most aspects of their life. As far as tourism is concerned, consumers will have beliefs about companies, products and services, including tourism offerings and destinations. Such thoughts can be positive, such as trust or confidence in a certain hotel or tour guide, or negative, such as a feeling about lack of security on airlines, or fear of injury on the ski slopes. Attitudes are more difficult to change, as they are ingrained feelings about various factors of an experience. Finally, perception is an overall mind-picture of the world, shaped by information that people filter and then retrieve. Thus, perception is inextricably bound to the concepts of bias and distortion. People choose to interpret different stimuli in different ways, ignoring some factors while enhancing others. This is known as selective perception.

2. CULTURE

The second key factor from Figure 2.1 that influences a consumer's behaviour is culture. Culture can be defined as the norms, beliefs and rituals that are unique to each person. These different factors influence how we live, communicate and think about certain things. Culture can also dictate how a person will act in a certain situation. In terms of self-image and the satisfaction of underlying tensions, most people seek to satisfy their desires in a way that fits into societal norms. For example, it is acceptable to be a green consumer in tourism, but sex tourism is viewed disparagingly. The last few decades have witnessed an increased interest in cross-cultural studies, driven by forces such as the globalization of the market and an increase in cross-cultural encounters in daily life (Marsella, 1998). To understand the source of cross-cultural differences, psychologists have identified meaningful dimensions of cultural variability that can describe the subjective elements of culture. Hofstede (1980), for example, developed a well-known set of four dimensions: Individualism Versus Collectivism, Power Distance, Uncertainty Avoidance and Masculinity.

More recently, Hofstede (2001) incorporated a fifth dimension called Long- Versus Short-Term Orientation. Of Hofstede's five dimensions, individualism-collectivism has become the most widely studied and has been conceptually linked to many psychological differences across cultures. Triandis (1994, 1995, 2001), in particular, has championed this dimension and used it to explain many cross-cultural similarities and differences in relationships. Another landmark study by Markus and Kitayama (1991) linked individualism-collectivism on the cultural level with the concept of self on the individual level. They posited that individualistic cultures foster the development of independent self-construals, which in turn have consequences for mental processes and behaviours. Likewise, they suggested that collectivistic cultures foster the development of interdependent self-construals, which have different consequences.

In the last few decades, players in the tourism and hospitality industry have witnessed a form of cultural globalization as Western consumption and lifestyle patterns have spread throughout the world, a process facilitated by the flow of travellers from the West to the Third World. However, it is still critical for tourism and hospitality marketers to have an understanding of different cultures in markets in which they operate. For example, Koreans are one of the most homogenous people in the world with few cultural or racial variations and virtually no ethnic minorities among them. In Myanmar, on the other hand, there are an estimated 135 ethnic minority groups with over 100 languages and dialects spoken in the country. In China, foreign multinationals are having to adjust their business models and align them with the latest trends and fashions in the world's second-largest economy. In 2015, for example, the Chinese suddenly developed a taste for English bitter, after Chinese President Xi Jinping dropped in for a pint at an English country pub with Britain's Prime Minister, David Cameron. Within a few weeks, monthly sales in China of the beer they drunk, Greene King IPA, soared from 6,000 bottles a month to 80,000 bottles a month. Such volatile and unpredictable consumer behaviour is becoming increasingly common in a country where brands are emerging from nowhere to be worth a billion dollars in 12 to 18 months (Chen, 2016).

IMAGE 2.2 Greene King IPA (Courtesy of Greene King)

3. AGE AND GENDER

A traditional way of segmenting markets has been by age. For example, many travel suppliers are today targeting the growing senior market. This market is both lucrative and unique because it is less tied to seasonal travel, involves longer trips, and is not wedded to midweek or weekend travel, so it can boost occupancy rates for business and leisure travel opportunities. Others are focusing their attention on Millennials, those born between 1980 and 1999. There are currently around 79 million Millennials in North America – that is three million more than Baby Boomers who are predicted to dwindle to just 58 million by 2030. Children of the Digital Age, Millennials are profiled in detail in Chapter 4.

In some societies gender can influence consumer behaviour in terms of societal expectations of the roles men and women should play. Gender segmentation has long been used in marketing clothing, hairdressing, cosmetics and magazines. But more recently it has been applied to tourism and hospitality products and services. For example, the number of women travelling for work purposes has been growing steadily for two decades, and vocal women travellers have influenced the introduction of better-lit parking garages, higher-quality soaps and lotions in hotel bathrooms, and improved room-service fare. Travel industry experts say that women travellers are more demanding and discerning than their male counterparts. Their main concerns are safety and security, followed by comfort and convenience.

4. SOCIAL CLASS

Social class is an important external factor influencing consumer behaviour. Social class is the position one occupies within society, and it is determined by such factors as income, wealth, education, occupation, family prestige, value of home and neighbourhood. Social class is closely linked to the existence of social institutions. The role and status positions found within a society are influenced by the dictates of social institutions. The caste system in India is one such institution. The election of a low-caste person – formally called an 'Untouchable' – as President made international news because it was such a departure from traditional Indian culture. Decades ago, touching or even glancing at an Untouchable, was considered enough to defile a Hindu of high status. Even though the caste system has been outlawed, it remains a visible part of the culture in India, and it is difficult for people to move out of the class into which they were born.

In the West, it is easier for people to move into social classes that differ from their families', although the class system is becoming increasingly difficult to categorize. In the UK, for example, classes have traditionally been labelled as upper, middle and lower classes, and, just ten years ago nearly half the population could be placed in the 'middle' bracket (Brean, 2006). However, a recent study from the London School of Economics identified a new model of class with seven classes ranging from the Elite at the top, to a 'Precariat' at the bottom (Savage et al., 2013). The researchers devised a new way of measuring class by the combination of three different economic, cultural and social resources (called in the study 'capitals') that people possess. Table 2.1 lists and describes those seven classes. The UK (and North America) is also witnessing an increasingly polarized society with the gap between rich and poor continuing to widen. In London, for example, the last 30 years have seen a 60 per cent increase in poor households and a 33 per cent increase in wealthy households (Boffey, 2015).

TABLE 2.1 A new model of social class (based on Savage et al., 2013)

Class	Description
Elite	This is the most privileged class in Great Britain, people who have high levels of all three capitals. Their high amount of economic capital sets them apart from everyone else
Established middle class	Members of this class have high levels of all three capitals although not as high as the Elite. They are a gregarious and culturally engaged class
Technical middle class	This is a new, small class with high economic capital but seem less culturally engaged. They have relatively few social contacts and so are less socially engaged
New affluent workers	This class has medium levels of economic capital and higher levels of cultural and social capital. They are a young and active group
Emergent service workers	This new class has low economic capital but has high levels of 'emerging' cultural capital and high social capital. This group is young and often found in urban areas
Traditional working class	This class scores low on all forms of the three capitals although they are not the poorest group. The average age of this class is older than the others
Precariat	This is the most deprived class of all with low levels of economic, cultural and social capital. The everyday lives of members of this class are precarious.

5. LIFESTYLE

Marketers are increasingly segmenting their markets by consumer lifestyles. Lifestyle analysis examines the way people allocate time, energy, and money. Lifestyle analysis tends to exclude demographic traits, so researchers in marketing have combined demographic and psychological variables into a concept called 'psychographics.' Psychographic analysis attempts to measure people's activities, interests, and opinions. By profiling the way groups of people live, it is possible to predict their travel motivations and purchases (Hudson, 2007). One of the best-known categorizations in this area is the VALS™ (Values and Lifestyles) framework that divides the US population into different lifestyle groups, defined according to psychological factors that correlate with purchase behaviour. VALS distinguishes between eight psychographic groups: innovators, thinkers, achievers, experiencers, believers, strivers, makers and survivors. Members of each group have different psychological profiles and maintain different lifestyles. The position of a person in the VALS framework depends on the person's primary motivations (ideas, achievement or self-expression) and resources, including income, education, self-confidence, health, eagerness to buy and energy level. The VALS tool can be used to help businesses develop and execute more effective strategies. For example, a cruise company in the US used VALS to identify and understand consumers most interested in its specialized tours. By designing direct mail creative to appeal to targeted consumers and mailing to key ZIP codes, the cruise line increased reservations by 400 per cent.

6. LIFE CYCLE

The concept of the family life cycle – the stages through which families might pass as they mature – is based on the premise that when people live together, their way of life changes. Single people are likely to behave differently than couples, and if couples subsequently have children, their lifestyle changes more radically, as does their level of financial and other commitments. Many authors have applied the life-cycle model to tourism, suggesting that travel patterns and destinations vary as people move through their life cycle (Pearce, 1993). The model works well when investigating the traditional nuclear family composed of two parents and one or more children. It does not, however, purport to represent the increasing proportion of households that do not fall into this pattern, such as single-parent families, extended family networks, and those who remain single throughout their life. Tourists may also change their behaviour patterns over time, so if the life-cycle model is used to predict behaviour, then trends in consumer behaviour need to be monitored. For example, research has shown that backpackers are no longer just young people aged between 18 and 25. They have been joined by an older, and wealthier, segment of backpackers who are changing the structure of the backpacker market (Hudson, 2008).

7. REFERENCE GROUPS

Learning also takes place through sharing values and expectations with others in a variety of social reference groups, including the family, college, workplace or church. This brings exposure to a normative set of values, those that set a tone as to how we should behave morally in society. For example, experienced travellers, who have been exposed to other cultures and to people who are less fortunate than they, are influencing the new trend of volunteer tourism. The UNWTO, and other tourism organizations that monitor trends in the travel industry, say it is precisely the growing number of well-heeled, well-educated older travellers – people who are indeed concerned with 'doing something good for society' – that has been driving the demand for such developing niche markets as educational tourism, eco-tours, agri-tourism, and cultural tourism. Travellers can take a 'volunteer vacation' and give their time and expertise to help in projects in developing countries. These trips aren't free, but they're often cheaper than conventional tours.

DIGITAL SPOTLIGHT: MARKETING EXTREME SPORTS EVENTS – THE X GAMES

IMAGE 2.3 Slopestyle Elimination at the X Games in Tignes, France, 2013 (©Red Bull Media House)

Launched in 1995 in Newport, Rhode Island, the X Games is an extreme sports competition encompassing skateboarding and motocross and, since 1997, winter sports including snowboarding, skiing and snowmobiling. It acts as an incubator for the latest hip sports both for summer and winter. Targeting Generations X, Y and Millennials, the annual X Games competitions are put on by American sports broadcaster ESPN and also shown on ABC Sports. Since 2002, the winter event has been held at Aspen's Buttermilk ski hill. The Summer X Games moved from Los Angeles to Austin, Texas in 2014.

(Continued)

(Continued)

Chris Schuster, President and Founder of the Association of Freesking Professionals (AFP), provides the management team for X Games under his company Event Production Specialists (EPS Events). AFP is the global organizing and sanctioning body for competitive freeskiing – halfpipe, slopestyle and big air – via a variety of events on the AFP World Tour. The X Games is a platinum-level event within this tour.

Based in North Lake Tahoe, Andrew Gauthier is AFP's World Tour Manager. 'As a member of the EPS team, we manage all sports and competition at X Games. We are responsible for coordinating between ESPN Live TV, the athletes, the judges, hospitality, medical, and the course builders,' says Gauthier. 'As a crucial pivot point for these events to occur, we ensure that the timing, the safety, the competition process are all aligned. Furthermore, we also are responsible for coordinating athlete practices for each discipline.'

Marketing and sales are Gauthier's chief areas, with a wide involvement in sponsorships and partnerships, social media strategy, event promotion, athlete membership drives, and also basic video editing for exclusive AFP content. The AFP World Tour is another of his responsibilities. 'I accept and review all event sanctioning applications, update athlete rankings with new event results and manage the AFP judging programme,' he explains. This includes procurement, education and scheduling for all AFP Certified Judges.

Alongside Jeff Schmuck (Editor of Forecast Ski Magazine – @ForecastSki – and Communications Director for the AFP) and Connor Clayton (the World Tour Coordinator of AFP), he also manages all event media and content on afpworldtour.com and is responsible for athlete communications. Gauthier creates and distributes all formal AFP documentation, manages the inventory logistics including banners, signage, cameras, equipment, etc. And he distributes analyses and post-season surveys to both athletes and event organizers.

When it comes to marketing plans, AFP and the X Games are heavily weighted towards social media and online advertising. 'In the past, many marketing campaigns have focused on product. Today we see many brands moving away from product-focused content and more towards entertainment and building a personality of their brand,' Gauthier explains. 'See Salomon's *Freeski TV*, The North Face's *The Rise* and Atomic's recent video series, all live on YouTube. In addition, you find many brands have a dedicated online theatre, if you will, to present this content. What's particularly interesting here is that this is the most difficult type of campaign to track back to the bottom line, yet companies continue to invest.'

Gauthier's boss, Eric Zerrenner (Executive Director of AFP) says content is king these days: 'Brands – both hard goods and soft goods – are looking to create their own, unique content. Typically this has resulted in brands looking to their sponsored athletes to provide them with this content – whether it's action footage at a comp, lifestyle footage from the offseason, training, or travels or general freeskiing content. Because of social media, and the scope and immediate reach via those channels, brands are able to tap into an athlete's audience to help them get their brand/marketing message out to a relevant and receptive audience.'

Media, both traditional and especially social media are paramount, says Zerrenner: 'As the main source for competitive freeskiing, we want to be as informative as possible about the competitions, courses, athletes and results. If we're not able to be at an event – or even at every competition at an event – social media provides instant access. We rely on this information to keeps us informed and current on what's happening within our sport and culture.' Responsible for the successful leadership and management of the AFP according to the strategic direction set by the Board, Zerrenner ensures programme excellence, rigorous evaluation, and consistent quality of finance, administration, fundraising, communications and rankings. As well as developing an operational plan for the organization, he oversees both operations and strategic direction to improve deliverables to members, events and sponsors: 'Through the organization and management of a 16 country, 65-event World Tour, we bring structure and governance to the sport – which ultimately led to freeskiing's inclusion in the 2014 Winter Olympics.'

Sources: Personal interview with Andrew Gauthier, Nov. 2014; personal interview with Eric Zerrenner, Dec. 2014; personal interview with Jeff Schmuck, May 2016.

CASE STUDY QUESTIONS

1. Briefly sum up the X Game's digital marketing strategy.

2. Why do marketers of extreme sports place such a heavy emphasis on digital marketing?

3. Go to www.redbull.com/us/en/events and then write a short typology of consumers interested in these events.

TYPOLOGIES OF TOURISTS

The discussion so far has been about the variables that influence tourist behaviour. But many tourism researchers have tried to explain tourist behaviour by developing typologies of tourists who carry out various tourism roles. The tourist motivation model proposed by Stanley Plog is one of the most widely cited typologies of tourists (Plog, 1974). According to Plog, travellers may be classified as allocentrics or psychocentrics. Travellers who are more allocentric are thought to prefer exotic destinations, unstructured vacations rather than packaged tours, and more involvement with local cultures. Psychocentrics, on the other hand, are thought to prefer familiar destinations, packaged tours and 'touristy' areas. Later, Plog changed these labels to more 'reader-friendly' terms: specifically, psychocentrics became dependables and allocentrics changed to venturers (Plog, 2002). Figure 2.3 presents a visual picture of the old and new concepts as applied to a normal population curve. Plog found that the majority of the population was neither allocentric nor psychocentric but midcentric – somewhere in the middle. It has been argued, however, that Plog's theory is difficult to apply, as tourists will travel with different motivations on different occasions. There are many holidaymakers who will take a winter skiing break in an allocentric destination, but will then take their main holiday in a psychocentric destination.

In addition to Plog, other tourism researchers have tried to explain tourist recreational behaviour by developing typologies of tourist roles. Most are based on empirical data obtained from questionnaires and/or personal interviews. Cohen's typology – one of the first – proposed four classifications of tourists: (1) the organized mass tourist,

highly dependent on the 'environmental bubble', purchasing all-inclusive tours or package holidays; (2) the individual mass tourist, who is more autonomous and free than those in the previous group; (3) the explorer, who seeks new areas but would sometimes opt for home comforts; and (4) the drifter, who avoids any kind of 'tourist establishment' (Cohen, 1972).

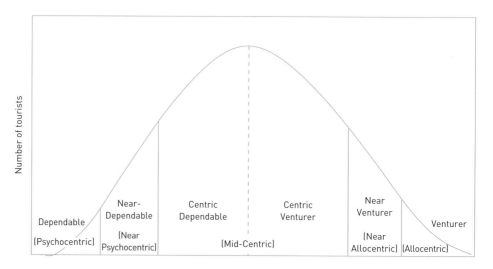

FIGURE 2.3 Plog's psychographic personality types: current versus (previous)

(*Source:* Adapted from Plog, 1974 and 2002).

Plog and others have developed travel personality quizzes, so that travel professionals can understand the unique needs of different travellers (see http://besttripchoices.com/travel-personalities/quiz/). The Canadian Tourism Commission (CTC) has also developed a tool – the Explorer Quotient – to help attract international visitors to Canada. Launched in spring 2006, this online self-examination tool allows each potential traveller an opportunity to discover his or her individual explorer 'type'. Once the consumer's type is determined, a host of experiences are presented to encourage travel to Canada. 'The EQ tool provides an understanding of which explorer types will resonate best in which markets', said Michele McKenzie, President and CEO of the CTC. 'This way we can give clear advice about how to package existing products to better appeal to those customers' (Hudson and Ritchie, 2009). Travel professionals in Canada are still using the EQ tool, and many national parks and national historic sites have introduced experience opportunities based on the Explorer Quotient.

Some believe there are scientific explanations for different traveller types. In 1999, four scientists from UC Irvine published a paper titled 'Population migration and the variation of dopamine D4 receptor (DRD4) allele frequencies around the globe' that explored the migration patterns and gene pool distribution of prehistoric human beings. They were originally researching for links between dopamine receptor D4 (DRD4) and Attention Deficit Disorder. While conducting the study, they discovered another correlation: people with the DRD4 genes tend to be thrill seeking and migratory. And almost all study participants with this gene had a long history of travelling. So according to some, there are genetic reasons why some people are more prone to travel than others (Xu, 2015).

THE BUYING PROCESS

Before discussing the buying process, it is important to recognize that various buying situations will have an influence on this process. First of all, consumers are likely to display various levels of commitment, depending on the nature of the purchase. It has been suggested that there are three such levels (Howard and Sheth, 1969):

1. **Extended problem-solving.** In this situation, such as the decision to take a long-haul holiday, the consumer is likely to have a deep level of commitment, to make a detailed search for information, and to make an extensive comparison of the alternatives.

2. **Limited problem-solving.** In this situation, the consumer will have some degree of knowledge or experience already, but many factors will be taken for granted and the information search will be far more limited. A second holiday at a favourite skiing destination may be purchased in this way.

3. **Habitual problem-solving.** This is a repeat purchase of a tried and tested short break or day excursion, which requires little or no evaluation. The purchase is made primarily on the basis of a previous satisfactory experience and a good understanding of the destination or brand name of the tourism or hospitality offering.

Role adoption will also influence the buying process, and it is proposed that there are five roles (Engel et al., 1990):

1. **Initiator:** the person who starts the purchasing process and who gathers information.

2. **Influencer:** a person or persons who express preferences in choice or selection of information – this can be a group of friends, relatives, or a partner.

3. **Decider:** the person who has the financial control and possibly the authority within a group of people to make the purchase.

4. **Buyer:** the person who actually makes the purchase, visits the travel agent, and obtains the tickets, etc.

5. **User:** the person or persons who consume the purchase and actually go on the trip.

A recent study suggests that children have significant decision-making power when it comes to making travel plans (PRWeb, 2015). The study found that the vast majority of parents (85% US, 76 % UK, 86% France, 95% Germany, 94% Spain) give their children some say in deciding where they want to go on vacation. Millennial parents are most likely to give kids full control of where they want to go on vacation (19% versus 2% of parents over the age of 55).

ORGANIZATIONAL BUYER BEHAVIOUR

DECISION-MAKING FOR ORGANIZATIONS

Tourism marketers need to understand both the decision criteria used and the decision-making process undergone by groups and organizations in buying tourism services. The process is likely to be quite different for group buyers, and there can be many individuals or groups involved in making decisions for the conference market. These include the users, influencers, deciders and buyers. It has been argued that in order to close a sale within a business-to-business market, the supplier has to identify and satisfy all stakeholders in the decision-making unit and treat each accordingly.

A marketer will also need to understand the buying phases for organizations. The conference market, for example, follows a pattern of group decision-making, and the 'buy phase' has been described as follows: problem recognition, general need description, product specification, supplier search, proposal solution, supplier selection, order routine specification and performance review (Radburn, 1997). These buy phases sometimes take a long period of time, depending on the size of the conference or the complexity of arrangements, with lead times of two or three years in some instances and longer ones for mega events such as the World Cup soccer tournament.

The process is also affected by the nature of the purchase, as it can be a new purchase, a modified rebuy, or a straight rebuy. A new purchase involves a high degree of risk, as the client is buying a facility or service for the first time. A modified rebuy is less risky, as the client has bought a service offering before, perhaps at another hotel or conference centre within the group, but now seeks to modify the purchase. This might mean a new venue or new specifications for service levels. The straight rebuy is the least risky purchase situation, as it involves, for example, reordering a service at the same venue.

Having identified the key decision-makers and phases in the purchase process, the marketer must then establish which criteria the decision-makers use to differentiate between suppliers. Webster and Wind suggest that four main factors influence the decision-making criteria of organizational buyers: environmental, organizational, interpersonal and individual (Webster and Wind, 1972). These factors are constantly changing, so it is essential to reevaluate market trends frequently.

THE BEHAVIOUR OF BUSINESS TRAVELLERS

The behaviour of business travellers is significantly different from that of leisure travellers. In fact, according to experts, executives do not see travel as a perk but rather as another source of stress (Cohen, 2000). Executives feel that they have no proper balance between home life and work life, and that it causes problems in their relationships with partners and children. And it is not just the business traveller who suffers. One study found that people whose spouses travel frequently on business suffer more mental health problems than those whose partners remain at home (Tong, 2002). Short, frequent trips away from home have a worse effect on people than longer, less frequent trips. The study recommended that workers travel no more than 90 days a year and that companies allow employees to decline making too many trips; it also suggested video-conferencing and flexible work arrangements as substitutes for travel. Unfortunately, few businesses pay attention to the damaging effect travel can have on their employees. The paradox is that travel costs the company money, and much business travel has been made redundant by modern communication technologies such as telephone-conferencing and video-conferencing. One current travel trend is the 'blurring' of business and leisure travel (Pullman, 2013), and this is discussed later in the chapter.

Airlines spend a lot of time and money trying to understand the needs of their business travellers. As the demographic gets wider for this group (as it has been doing for the last decade), zeroing in on which services and programmes would most appeal to this group is becoming more difficult. The group is not necessarily unified in terms of age, dress or tastes, or in terms of what its members want to do or have in business class. Whether a flight is inbound for business or outbound for home makes a difference in what a customer expects from an airline, and the key for airlines is to offer their customers the ability to work or play. Work-related technology – laptop power plugs in-air phones and wi-fi – are now obligatory for any airline interested in attracting the business traveller. For passengers' downtime, not much has changed: movies, food, and drink remain required staples.

GLOBAL TRENDS IN CONSUMER BEHAVIOUR

In a rapidly changing environment, it is critical that tourism and hospitality marketers stay on top of consumer trends. The following section, therefore, presents ten consumer trends that are shaping the world of tourism.

1. LEARNING AND ENRICHMENT

One of the major trends in tourism today is the desire of the tourist to have a learning experience as a part of the vacation. One survey of North American travellers found that half of them want to visit art, architectural or historic sites on vacations, while one-third would like to learn a new skill or activity. Today's travellers are seeking experiences that provide them with a greater insight, increased understanding, and a personal connection to the people and places they visit. Learning and enrichment travel refers to vacations that provide opportunities for authentic, hands-on or interactive learning experiences, featuring themes such as adventure, agriculture, anthropology, archaeology, arts, culture, cuisine, education, forestry, gardening, language, maritime culture, mining, nature, science, spirituality, sports, wine and wildlife – to name only a few!

Travel and learning is a neglected area of tourism research (Falk et al., 2012), but historical events such as the Grand Tour are often used as examples of the importance of travel and learning. In fact, the growing subsectors of academic and educational tourism have their roots in these early efforts to 'broaden the mind' through travel and experiential learning (Brodsky-Porges, 1981). These days educational travel is packaged to all market segments and is becoming increasingly creative. An example is Curiosity Retreats, a 'thought leadership getaway' hosted by Colorado luxury resort, Gateway Canyons. The five-night retreats offer small groups of guests the chance to learn about technology, science, the human spirit and civilization through lectures while mixing with global thought leaders like Deepak Chopra, Vint Cerf and violinist Charles Yang. Guests can also take part in sunrise yoga, horseback rides, guided photography, nature hikes and stargazing sessions (Atkinson, 2014). Another example of educational travel catering to a younger audience come from Hong Kong, where the theme park Ocean Park has an educational arm called Ocean Park Academy, that provides over 30 different courses to secondary school, primary school and kindergarten students and their teachers. In addition, the academy will tailor educational programmes for university students (see Image 2.4 below).

IMAGE 2.4 Author Simon Hudson with his Semester at Sea students on an educational field trip at Ocean Park, Hong Kong

2. ETHICAL CONSUMPTION

In the last few decades, responsible tourism has emerged as a significant trend in the Western world, as wider consumer market trends towards lifestyle marketing and ethical consumption have spread to tourism. Tourism organizations are beginning to realize that promoting their ethical stance can be good business as it potentially enhances a company's profits, management effectiveness, public image and employee relations. Consumers are demanding openness from companies – more information, responsibility and accountability (Mintel, 2014).

International leisure travellers are increasingly motivated to select a destination for the quality of its environmental health and the diversity and integrity of its natural and cultural resources. Studies indicate that environmental considerations are now a significant aspect of travellers' destination-choosing process. According to a travel study in 2012, the 'green' travel trend is gaining momentum, as 71 per cent of travellers surveyed said they planned to make more eco-friendly choices in the ensuing 12 months compared to 65 per cent the previous year (TripAdvisor, 2012). Traveller philanthropy is also gathering momentum, whereby civic-minded travellers and travel businesses are giving time, talent and financial resources to further the well being of the places that they visit. The phenomenon is expected to grow exponentially, benefiting from trends in giving, travel and globalization. An example is WHOA Travel (Women High on Adventure), where founders Allison Fleece and Danielle Thornton lead women from around the world on life-altering adventures, such as climbing

Mount Kilimanjaro, while connecting with the local women in the countries they visit. Travellers are also seeking foods that adhere to animal welfare, organic and other standards, so restaurant chains like Chipotle are catering to these changing consumer tastes (more about Chipotle in Chapter 12).

3. WELLNESS

Wellness travel is a $439 billion market, fuelled by an increasingly health-conscious consumer. In the US, the market segment that is focused on health and fitness has been labelled the LOHAS segment.

LOHAS is an acronym for Lifestyles of Health and Sustainability, and describes an estimated $290 billion marketplace for goods and services focused on health, the environment, social justice, personal development and sustainable living (French and Rogers, 2010). Research shows that one in four adult Americans is part of this group – nearly 41 million people. A more health-conscious society is often attributed to the influence of the baby boomer. Baby Boomers are generally healthier, financially better off, better educated and more interested in novelty, escape, and authentic experiences than were previous cohorts of older people. But younger generations, too, are health and wellness focused. Millennials, for example, are dieting less frequently than other generations, but consuming fewer calories daily. They spend money on gym memberships, running gear and energy bars and seek out specific health foods like whole grain breads, nuts and seeds, and quinoa (Forbes Consulting Group, 2012). This generation is also driving the demand for self-tracking, wearable technologies (Ericksson, 2013). Sales of wearable technology trebled in 2014 from a year before – and the market could increase more than fivefold to more than 100 million units by 2018 (Hamlin, 2015).

The tourism sector is responding to this wellness trend with health and wellness centres springing up in many destinations. Mountain resorts are combining alternative health and wellness services with winter sport tourism. The Montage Deer Valley, Utah, for example has a signature spa treatment called SURRENDER that creates a customized regimen for each guest which is transferable to other Montage properties. The Montage is also responding to the demand for healthier foods. Culinary teams collect copious notes on dietary restrictions of customers so that associates can address the guests in advance of their orders when they come to the tables, helping reassure guests that they are recognized and that their dietary needs are being taken to heart in preparing their meals.

4. CUSTOMIZATION, CONVENIENCE AND SPEED

Consumers are increasingly looking for customized solutions that fit their specific needs, becoming more engaged with product creation, a process that has been facilitated by advances in technology (BDC, 2013). In the restaurant sector, computer software and Internet reservations systems like OpenTable and Rezbook have pushed service to another level, allowing restaurant owners to amass a trove of data with ease. Because of advances in technology, many restaurants are tracking their customers' individual tastes, tics, habits and even foibles (Craig, 2012).

Requests for customized and personalized vacations are also rising sharply, and both agents and traditional tour operators are changing their businesses to meet that demand.

In addition to booking air and hotel reservations, travel providers are arranging customized wine tastings, visits to artisan workshops, and private after-hours tours of attractions such as the British crown jewels and the Vatican. Destinations targeting winter sport tourists are also responding to this trend. At the Grand America in Salt Lake City, for example, Director of Guest Experience, Annie Fitzgerald says: 'We ensure all employees are empowered to make each guest's stay exceptional and a personalized experience. If our employees learn something about our guests that will enhance their stay, we will recognize and deliver. For example, if we learn upon arrival that a couple is celebrating an anniversary, we will deliver a cake and card wishing them a Happy Anniversary, likewise with honeymoon couples who receive chocolate-covered strawberries and a card. We recognize birthdays and we love taking care of guests who bring their children. We often provide balloons or small welcome toys for the little ones.'

The increasing desire for convenience and speed is also having a great impact on various sectors of the tourism industry. In the restaurant sector, drive-through sales are on the rise; in transportation, self-check-in terminals are increasingly popular; and in accommodation, business travellers are seeking convenient rooms for shorter stays. There is also the suggestion that travel in the future will be geo-local, meaning that people will travel much closer to their home – more within their homeland and continent, and less outside it. A survey by the European Commission in 2013 found that EU residents generally stay in their home country during their time off – 57 per cent of people in the EU take a trip within their own country (Karaian and Yanofsky, 2014).

5. POP-CULTURE TOURISM

Pop-culture tourism refers to the rising number of people looking to journey to locations featured in popular literature, film, music, or any other form of media (Larson, Lundberg and Lexhagen, 2013). As 'fandom' becomes more ingrained in our culture, pop-culture tourism is likely to become even more prevalent (Rellihan, 2015). Increasingly, movies and television shows are becoming a source of inspiration for travel. The phenomenon of Harry Potter – or 'Pottermania' – had huge domestic and international repercussions for tourism in the UK. Pottermania was thoroughly and successfully exploited by VisitBritain to rescue the country's ailing tourism industry hit by the 9/11 terrorism in 2001 and then the foot-and-mouth crisis (Hudson, 2008). In an integrated marketing strategy, VisitBritain utilized the books and the films for their promotional potential, increasing tourist visits throughout Britain and, in particular, to destinations featured in the books and movies.

Pop-culture tourism is not just confined to tourism inspired by movies or TV shows. Music-based tourism is also big business; in the US alone, music-based tourism constitutes approximately 17 per cent of the tourism industry (Connell and Gibson, 2003). Music festivals, in particular, are more popular than ever, attracting millions of fans. Worldwide, there are more than 800 music festivals of various types in 57 countries (Schwartz, 2013). But tourists are also attracted to music-inspired attractions and accommodations. Music-themed hotels have become increasingly prevalent, particularly in big cities. Examples include the Beatles-themed Hard Days Night Hotel in Liverpool, to the rock-themed Backstage Hotel in central Amsterdam, to Hotel BPM, a music-themed hotel in New York City, to the nhow Berlin, a new lifestyle hotel focused on music and fashion, to Porto's Hotel da Música that takes a classical angle on its theme. Marketing in Action in Chapter 5 provides more on music-themed hotels.

6. THE SHARING ECONOMY

The sharing economy is having a disruptive influence on the travel industry, with the basic idea being to use resources more efficiently, whether this is accommodation, transportation or other services. As the Internet enables us to share information with unprecedented ease, the idea of a sharing economy is potentially huge. Pooling resources in various ways is becoming integral to urban life and is likely to impact the future of cities (Euromonitor, 2015). Ericksson (2015) found in recent research that more than half of smartphone owners are already open to renting other people's leisure equipment rooms and household appliances.

Travel-oriented peer-to-peer (P2P) websites are rapidly expanding, allowing travellers to rent lodging, cars, sports equipment and more from individuals. Such sites link visitors with tours from locals, meals and other services. The collaborative-travel trend has been enabled by technology, but has also been inspired by the troubled economy (Clark, 2014), and increasingly expectant consumers (ITB, 2014). In the accommodation sector, Airbnb has over 1,500,000 listings in 34,000 cities and 190 countries, making it one of the ten largest hospitality brands in the world. Fast-expanding Uber has taken a dramatic amount of business from taxi companies in cities where it operates. For consumers, these companies are attractive because they offer lower prices, better accessibility, great flexibility, ease of use and 'a user focused mission' including transparency and interactive communication (ITB, 2014). The sharing economy is discussed in more detail in Chapter 7.

7. SERVICE EXCELLENCE

Service quality has been increasingly identified as a key factor in differentiating service products and building a competitive advantage in tourism. The process by which customers evaluate a purchase, thereby determining satisfaction and likelihood of repurchase, is important to all marketers, but especially to services' marketers because, unlike their manufacturing counterparts, they have fewer objective measures of quality by which to judge their production. Satisfying customers has always been a key component of the tourism industry, but never before has it been so critical. With increased competition, and with more discerning, experienced consumers, knowing how to win and keep customers is the single-most important business skill that anyone can learn. Becoming customer-centred and exceeding customer expectations are therefore requirements for business success (Hudson and Hudson, 2013).

Consumers worldwide are willing to spend more on service excellence. One study found that seven in ten Americans are willing to spend an average of 13 per cent more with companies they believe provide excellent customer service (AMEX, 2011). The same study found a similar willingness in other countries (Australia and Canada, 12%; Mexico, 11%; UK, 10%; France, 9%; Italy, 9%; Germany, 8%; and Netherlands, 7%). In India, consumers would spend 22 per cent more for excellent customer service. Another recent study found that the value of great customer service in the US economy is a staggering $267.8 billion per year (STELLA Service, 2010). This figure was calculated based on the average spend per person per year with each type of company. Value is the extra percentage that people are willing to spend if they know they will receive great service. If the consumers surveyed received great customer service, 70 per cent would use the same company again, and 50 per cent would make recommendations to family and friends. In the hospitality sector, the study found that consumers are willing to spend 11 per cent more for great service, higher than most other sectors.

8. ENGAGEMENT AND CONNECTIVITY

We are witnessing a new mobile lifestyle (Roberti, 2011) that is revolutionizing where, when and how we communicate personally and with businesses. Mobile devices are having a profound effect on the traditionally defined silos between managed and unmanaged travel. A recent study found that 43 per cent of international travellers always take their mobile professional devices with them on holiday or on weekend trips (Ali et al., 2013). Always-connected consumers expect to receive real-time services from travel companies (Euromonitor, 2015). Championed by Google and cemented by Apple Pay, mobile transactions will become the new normal, as consumers will be able to buy products simply by placing their phones in front of a sensor at check-out. Taking a page from Uber, an increasing number of apps, such as Airbnb and OpenTable, now offer digital transactions that link to credit cards. Such connectivity has also upended how consumers engage with tourism destinations. After visiting, they often enter into an open-ended relationship with the destination, sharing their experiences online through social media (Edelman, 2010). Virtual reality technology is a further way consumers can engage with travel providers. Giving a new meaning to armchair travel, virtual reality is the development of computer-generated simulation of an environment that can be interacted with, in a seemingly real or physical way, by a person using special electronic equipment, such as a helmet with a screen inside or gloves fitted with sensors. Chapter 3 provides more details about virtual reality.

9. BLEISURE

'Bleisure' or Blurring', whichever term you prefer, is the gradual intermingling of professional and personal activities, and is a global trend that is transforming the organization of private and work lives. Frequent travellers are connected and can be reached at all times. As a result, they are blurring the frontiers between work and personal life. A recent survey of international travellers has found an increased blurring of their private and professional lives, partly due to the fact that mobile professional devices (PCs, smartphones and tablets) are increasingly commonplace in this target group (Pullman, 2013). BridgeStreet Global Hospitality (2014), in a similar study of this blurring phenomenon, found that 60 per cent of international travellers have combined business with leisure travel in the past, with most respondents adding two vacation days to business trips. Conference and meeting planners have to be cognisant of these changes, ensuring that they incorporate an element of leisure when they plan their meetings. An example is a conference, organized by research specialists, Qualtrics, that the author attended in Salt Lake City in February 2015 which included a day's skiing in Park City as part of the conference. The case study at the end of this chapter shows how hotels are responding to this 'bleisure' trend.

10. AUTHENTICITY

There is a trend towards inconspicuous consumption in the developed world with a desire by people to express their identity in more subtle ways than in the past. Visible expressions of status are becoming less important and instead a more fluid and less elitist concept of luxury is emerging that is driven by consumer concerns about authenticity, experience and individualism. Increasingly, luxury is about the pursuit of authentic and exotic experiences and services, rather than scarcely available, high-value goods. Intangibles such as time and experience will therefore define the luxury holiday of the future, creating challenges for companies who presently offer more traditional luxury holidays that focus on exclusivity and price. Demand is growing for authentic travel that engages the senses, stimulates the mind, includes unique activities, and connects in personal ways with travellers in an emotional, physical, spiritual or intellectual level. A related trend is 'experience caching' whereby consumers continually collect, store and display their experiences for private use, or for friends, family, even the entire world to peruse (Hudson and Hudson, 2015).

The travel industry is responding to these demands, as it is naturally keen to meet the needs of niche and mainstream markets interested in authentic, experiential travel. These companies are experience providers who sequence and stage carefully choreographed activities, personal encounters, and authentic experiences, designed to create long lasting memories, engaging travel, and increased customer loyalty. A new wave of travel services is connecting consumers to local people, social networks and influencers at destinations. My Plus One in Berlin is an example, offering guests the chance to connect with local experts to discover bars and stores and get the insider's perspective. In London, The Ace Hotel in Shoreditch, has monthly cycling tours led by artists and influencers, to enhance the local flavour. Hallo Hallo, a pop-up restaurant in Copenhagen Airport, offered diners the chance to meet other socially minded travellers over dinner, and Six Degrees, a social networking platform launched by Marriott, includes mobile apps that connect like-minded guests (JWT Intelligence, 2015).

CHAPTER SUMMARY

Factors that influence consumer behaviour include motivation, culture, age and gender, social class, lifestyle, life cycle and reference groups. Many tourism researchers have tried to explain tourist behaviour by developing typologies of tourists. According to Plog for example, travellers may be classified as allocentrics or psychocentrics. It has been suggested that there are three levels of buying commitment: extended problem-solving, limited problem-solving and habitual problem-solving. It is also proposed that there are five buying roles: initiator, influencer, decider, buyer and user. Trends in consumer behaviour affecting tourism marketers today are learning and enrichment, ethical consumption, wellness, customization, pop-culture tourism, sharing economy, service excellence, engagement and connectivity, bleisure and authenticity.

REFLECTIVE QUESTIONS

1. Using the Digital Spotlight on the X Games, and all the material on consumer behaviour in this chapter, create a profile of a typical attendee at extreme sporting events.

(Continued)

(Continued)

2. Thinking back to any family holidays you have been on, discuss the roles that each member of the family plays in the decision-making process when choosing a holiday. Is there any evidence that children have an influential role?

3. Consider the trends in consumer behaviour discussed at the end of the chapter. How would you rank them in order of importance? Can you think of any other trends that have emerged since this book was published?

MARKETING IN ACTION: HOTELS RESPONDING TO 'BLEISURE' TREND

IMAGE 2.5 Pullman's global nomad (©Accor Hotels. Reproduced with permission)

As mentioned above, the lines between business and leisure travel are becoming increasingly blurred. Fuelled by the proliferation of mobile devices and the ability to stay connected, over half of business travellers now extend their business trips into leisure trips – recently dubbed 'bleisure'. Blurring, or the gradual intermingling of professional and personal activities, is a global trend that is transforming the organization of both private and work lives. Frequent travellers are connected and can be reached at all times. As a result, they are merging their work and personal life.

Recent research supports this trend. Pullman, AccorHotel's upscale hotel brand, and research institute IPSOS, surveyed over 2,200 seasoned international travellers and found an increased blurring of their private and professional lives, partly due to the fact that mobile professional devices (PCs, smartphones and tablets) are increasingly commonplace in this target group. The survey's key findings reveal that 'blurring' increases freedom and efficiency for travellers, with 82 per cent of the survey panel believing that having a mobile professional device allows them to work more freely. The same study found that 43 per cent of international travellers always take their mobile professional devices with them on holiday or on weekend trips. Around 33 per cent of them spend at least 30 minutes a day browsing the Internet for personal reasons (reading the news, booking holidays, consulting bank accounts, and checking their Facebook page).

BridgeStreet Global Hospitality, in a similar study, found that 60 per cent of international travellers have combined business with leisure travel in the past, with 30 per cent of those respondents adding two vacation days to business trips. A hefty 78 per cent of respondents agreed that adding leisure days to business travel adds value to work assignments. More than half of these travellers take their families with them. BridgeStreet found that younger travellers are significantly more likely to combine business and leisure travel. Finally, a study by corporate travel company, Expedia confirmed that younger travellers are fuelling this blurring trend. In its survey of business travellers, it found that 56 per cent of Millennials (19–30 year olds) extend their business trips into leisure trips. They, more than other groups, are demanding new tools and apps inspired by the leisure travel and retail industries. With a majority working for companies that don't have managed travel programmes, they are seeking to take advantage of deals on everything from Airbnb to HotelTonight, as well as low-cost carriers.

So, how are hotels responding to this trend? For Bill Lacey, General Manager at The Sanctuary, Kiawah Island Golf Resort, in South Carolina, golfers are his key market segment seeking to combine business with pleasure. 'In the resort sector, so much business happens on the golf course – the two have always married themselves together, so that people will come to us with that specific goal in mind.' With five golf courses, Lacey says that often companies will buy out a whole golf course for corporate events: 'The company employees will then bring their families with them, so wives and children will be out enjoying our other leisure facilities, while the husbands are at the corporate event. Everybody wins.' Lacey says that sometimes companies will even take over the 250-room Sanctuary Hotel: 'We have a big car manufacturer coming in this month for three days – and they are taking over the whole hotel.' Lacey says for these guests the technology has to be top-notch. 'We have found ourselves continuously having to upgrade our broadband width in the building. I always go back to the mindset that what the guests experience at home – whether it be their bed, food and beverage, their wi-fi and so on – if these things are not better when they come to a five-star hotel, then why would they go? We aim to always try and exceed those types of benchmarks that people have.'

Combining business and leisure travel is certainly a trend observed by Westin Hotels & Resorts, and according to Brian Povinelli, SVP, Global Brand Leader at Westin & Le Meridien, this trend can be attributed to several factors. 'Travellers have greater flexibility in their schedules as a result of mobile devices that enable working remotely, opening the possibility to remain in a destination for a longer period of time, even past when business has wrapped,' he says. 'Millennials, who are entering their peak spending years, typically take the greatest advantage of business trips by extending them a day or two to experience a new city or destination.' The various Westin offerings and programmes make it possible for guests to get the most out of their stay, including a dedicated Westin Weekend programme that has a late 3 pm Sunday check-out and

(Continued)

(Continued)

extended breakfast hours all weekend long. 'The Westin Weekend late check-out lets our guests, especially those interested in "bleisure" travel, make the most out of their getaway,' says Povinelli. 'Our RunWESTIN programme is also a fantastic way for our guests to explore their destination between meetings or after a business trip has wrapped. It features three- and five-mile running maps, and New Balance® shoes and clothing for guests to use during their stay for only $5 USD or local equivalent.' Westin has also introduced Tangent™, an innovative workspace concept that meets the changing needs of today's mobile business traveller. 'This new flexible workspace reinvents the small meetings' model and has proven highly successful – receiving rave reviews and high usage from both guests and neighbouring businesses,' says Povinelli.

Hotels are beginning to promote both leisure and business services in targeted marketing communications. Pullman Hotels & Resorts, AccorHotels, for example, has introduced a 'Time for Pleasure by Pullman' promotion, designed to convert business travellers into leisure travellers. The package, which requires a minimum three-night stay, includes 'unlimited Internet access', 'Lounge Connectivity by Pullman' services, breakfast buffet, and a discount on hotel services such as the bar, restaurant and video-on-demand. Xavier Louyot, Senior Vice-President, Brand Content AccorHotels LUXE, Global Brand Marketing, says 'Our hotel offer has evolved to meet the expectations of this new generation of curious, cosmopolitan, hyper-connected travellers who travel both for business and leisure. The results of our survey confirm our vision of upscale international hospitality which is based on "work-hard, play-hard" and reflects our customers' lifestyle.' In May 2015, Pullman unveiled its new television ad, targeting this new consumer, depicting the hero, Pullman's 'global nomad', moving through life in a series of swift encounters, both personal and professional, and ensconced in the pursuit of a work–life blend.

Sources: Pullman (2013); BridgeStreet Global Hospitality (2014)

CASE STUDY QUESTIONS

1. Explain why the lines between business and leisure travel have become increasingly blurred.
2. What is the hotel sector doing to cater to this trend?
3. Think of other ways that the hospitality sector can respond to the bleisure trend.

REFERENCES

Ali, R., Clampet, J., Schaal, D. and Shankman, S. (2013) '14 global trends that will define travel in 2014'. www.fairtrade.travel/source/websites/fairtrade/documents/Skift_Trends_2014.pdf (accessed 12 December 2016).

AMEX (2011) 'AMEX Global Service Barometer 2011 Press Release'. www.thetrainingbank.com (accessed 6 December 2016).

Atkinson, K. (2014) 'Chopra meets cosmology at Colorado's Curiosity Retreats', *Forbes*, 2 April. www.forbes.com/sites/forbestravelguide/2014/04/02/chopra-meets-cosmology-at-colorados-curiosity-retreats (accessed 6 December 2016).

BDC (2013) 'Mapping your future. Five game-changing consumer trends', Business Development Bank of Canada, October. www.bdc.ca/Resources%20Manager/study_2013/consumer_trends_BDC_report.pdf (accessed 6 December 2016).

Boffey, D. (2015) 'How 30 years of a polarized economy have squeezed out the middle class', *Guardian*, 7 March. www.theguardian.com/society/2015/mar/07/vanishing-middle-class-london-economy-divide-rich-poor-england (accessed 6 December 2016).

Brean, J. (2006) 'Where suburbia was born', *National Post*, 21 October: A14.

BridgeStreet Global Hospitality (2014) *The Bleisure Report 2014*. http://skift.com/wp-content/uploads/2014/10/BGH-Bleisure-Report-2014.pdf (accessed 6 December 2016).

Brodsky-Porges, E. (1981) 'The Grand Tour: Travel as an educational device 1600–1800,' *Annals of Tourism Research*, 8(2): 171–86.

Chen, S. (2016) 'Riding on emotions,' *China Daily*, 26 April: P1.

Clark, J. (2014) 'Making connections via peer-to-peer travel', *USA Today*, 31 January: 8B.

Cohen, A. (2000) 'Business takes all the fun out of travel', *National Post*, 31 January: C17.

Cohen, E. (1972) 'Toward a sociology of international tourism', *Social Research,* 39(1): 164–82.

Connell, J. and Gibson, C. (2003) *Sound Tracks: Popular Music, Identity and Place.* London: Routledge.

Craig, S. (2012) 'Getting to know you', *New York Times*, 5 September: D1, D5.

Dann, G. (1977) 'Anomie, ego-enhancement and tourism', *Annals of Tourism Research,* 4: 184–94.

Edelman, D. (2010) 'Branding in the digital age', *Harvard Business Review*, 88(12): 62–9.

Engel, J. F., Blackwell, R. D. and Miniard, P. W. (1990) *Consumer Behavior.* Orlando, FL: Dryden.

Ericksson (2013) '10 Hot Consumer trends 2014'. www.ericsson.com/res/docs/2013/consumerlab/10-hot-consumer-trends-report-2014.pdf (accessed 6 December 2016).

Ericksson (2015) '10 Hot Consumer trends 2015'. www.ericsson.com/res/docs/2014/consumerlab/ericsson-consumerlab-10-hot-consumer-trends-2015.pdf (accessed 6 December 2016).

Euromonitor (2015) *Top 10 Global Consumer Trends for 2015*. London: Euromonitor International. www.siicex.gob.pe/siicex/documentosportal/alertas/documento/doc/810395732radDD19D.pdf (accessed 6 December 2016).

Falk, J. H., Ballantyne, R., Parker, J. and Benckendorff, P. (2012) 'Travel and learning: A neglected tourism research area', *Annals of Tourism Research ,* 39(2): 908–27.

Forbes Consulting Group (2012) 'Millennials', *Insight Series.* www.forbesconsulting.com (accessed 6 December 2016).

French, S. and Rogers, G. (2010) *Understanding the LOHAS consumer: The rise of ethical consumerism. A strategic market research update from the Natural Marketing Institute (NMI).* http://www.lohas.com/Lohas-Consumer.

Hamlin, K. (2015) 'Wear it well', *Breaking Views*, 31 December. www.breakingviews.com/wearable-tech-will-go-from-novelty-to-necessity/21179435.article (accessed 6 December 2016).

Hofstede, G. (1980) 'Motivation, leadership, and organization: Do American theories apply abroad?' *Organizational Dynamics*, 9: 42–63.

Hofstede, G. H. (2001) *Culture's Consequences: International Differences in Work-Related Values* (2nd edn). Beverly Hills, CA: Sage Publications.

Howard, J. A. and Sheth, J. N. (1969) *The Theory of Buying Behavior.* New York: Wiley.

Hudson, S. (2007) 'It's all about psychographics: Ten consumer trends impacting the hospitality industry today', *Alberta Hospitality,* Winter.

Hudson, S. (2008) *Tourism and Hospitality Marketing: A Global Perspective.* London: Sage.

Hudson, S. and Hudson, L. J. (2013) *Customer Service for Hospitality & Tourism.* Oxford: Goodfellow Publishers Ltd.

Hudson, S. and Hudson, L. J. (2015) *Winter Sport Tourism: Working in Winter Wonderlands.* Oxford: Goodfellow Publishers Ltd.

Hudson, S. and Ritchie, J. R. B. (2009) 'Branding a memorable destination experience. The case of Brand Canada', *International Journal of Tourism Research*, 11(2): 217–28.

ITB (2014) *ITB World Travel Trends Report 2014/15*, IPK International, Germany. www.itb-berlin.de/media/itbk/itbk_dl_en/WTTR_Report_A4_4_Web.pdf (accessed 12 December 2016).

JWT Intelligence (2015) 'JWT Tomorrowscope: Travel'. http://jwttomorrowscope.com/future-100/view/travel (accessed 6 December 2016).

Karaian, J. and Yanofsky, D. (2014) 'Where Europeans go on vacation, once they leave their country', *Quartz.com,* 14 February. http://qz.com/177366/where-europeans-go-on-vacation-not-so-far-from-home (accessed 6 December 2016).

Krippendorf, J. (1987) *The Holidaymakers.* London: Heinemann.

Larson, M., Lundberg, C. and Lexhagen, C. (2013) 'Thirsting for vampire tourism: Developing pop culture destinations', *Journal of Destination Marketing and Management*, 2(2): 74–84.

Markus, M. and Kitayama, S. (1991) 'Culture and the self: Implications for cognition, emotion, and motivation', *Psychological Review,* 98(2): 224–53.

Marsella, A. J. (1998) 'Toward a "global community" psychology', *American Psychologist*, 53: 1282–91.

Maslow, A.H. (1943) 'A theory of human motivation', *Psychological Review,* 50: 370–96.

Mills, A. S. and Morrison, A. M. (1985) *The Tourism System: An Introductory Text.* Englewood Cliffs, NJ: Prentice-Hall.

Mintel (2014) *Consumer Trends 2015.* London: Mintel Group Ltd.

Pearce, P.L. (1993) 'Fundamentals of tourist motivation', in D. Pearce and W. Butler (eds), *Tourism and Research: Critiques and Challenges*, pp. 113–34. London: Routledge.

Pedraza, F. (2013) 'Why self-actualization is the next big market', *Huffington Post*, 10 May. www.huffingtonpost.com/francis-pedraza/why-selfactualization-is-_b_3247465.html (accessed 6 December 2016).

Plog, S. C. (1974) 'Why destination areas rise and fall in popularity', *Cornell Hotel and Restaurant Administration Quarterly,* 14(4): 55–8.

Plog, S. C. (2002) 'The power of psychographics and the concept of venturesomeness', *Journal of Travel Research*, 40: 244–51.

PRWeb (2015) 'New HomeAway survey reveals the strong influence of kids on family travel plans'. www.prweb.com/pdfdownload/12725790.pdf (accessed 6 December 2016).

Pullman (2013) '"Blurring" A growing trend amongst international travelers', Accor Hotels, 30 September. www.accorhotels-group.com/fileadmin/user_upload/Contenus_Accor/Presse/Pressreleases/2013/UK/20130930_pr_pullman_survey_ipsos.pdf (accessed 6 December 2016).

Radburn, D. (1997) 'Organizational buyer behavior', in L. Lumsdon (ed.), *Tourism Marketing*, pp. 52–63. London: Thomson Business Press.

Rellihan, K. (2015) 'Travel trends for 2015'. www.travelchannel.com/interests/hot-topics/articles/travel-trends-for-2015?refcd=n-def&nl=TCN_123114_featlink1&c32=c7e67d6b7c89533e9015acf696e3693075004d36 (accessed 6 December 2016).

Roberti, J. (2011) 'Q&A', *Marketing Week*, 2 June, 29.

Savage, M., Devine, F., Cunningham, N., Taylor, M., Li, Y., Hjellbrekke, J., Le Roux, B., Friedman, S. and Miles, A. (2013) 'A new model of social class? Findings from the BBC's Great British Class Survey experiment', *Sociology*, 47(2): 219–50.

Schwartz, K. (2013) 'Music festivals drive U.S. tourism in warm weather months', *Destinations*. http://skift.com/2013/04/17/music-festivals-drive-u-s-tourism-in-warm-weather-months (accessed 6 December 2016).

STELLA Service (2010) 'The value of great customer service: The economic impact for online retail and other consumer categories'. http://media.stellaservice.com/public/pdf/Value_of_Great_Customer_Service.pdf (accessed 6 December 2016).

Strategic Business Insights (2015) 'US framework and VALS types'. www.strategicbusinessinsights.com/vals/ustypes.shtml (accessed 6 December 2016).

Tong, T. (2002) 'Business travelers' spouses pay psychological price', *National Post*, 8 March: A1.

Triandis, H. (1994) *Culture and Social Behavior*, New York: McGraw-Hill.

Triandis, H. (1995) *Individualism and Collectivism*, Boulder, CO: Westview Press.

Triandis, H. (2001)'Individualism and collectivism: Past, present and future', in D. Matsumoto (ed.), *Handbook of Culture and Psychology*, pp. 35–50. New York: Oxford University Press.

Thiyagaraj, V. (2015) 'Lohas: The rise of ethical consumerism'. *International Journal of Scientific Research*, 4(7): 702–3.

TripAdvisor (2012) 'TripAdvisor survey reveals travelers growing greener'. www.tripadvisor.com/PressCenter-i5154-c1-Press_Releases.html (accessed 6 December 2016).

Webster, F. and Wind, Y. (1972) *Organizational Buying Behavior*. Englewood Cliffs, NJ: Prentice Hall.

Xu, X. (2015) 'The genetic reason why some people are born to travel all over the world', *bit.of.news*, 24 April. http://news.bitofnews.com/the-wanderlust-gene-why-some-people-are-born-to-travel-all-over-the-world (accessed 6 December 2016).

DIGITAL MARKETING 3

INTRODUCTION

Chapter 3 begins by looking at the disruptive impact of technology on marketing communications, and this is followed by describing the four stages of the new consumer decision journey. This journey is heavily influenced today by social media (see later in this chapter, pp. **77–83**). The final part of Chapter 3 focuses on the challenges of digital marketing such as the loss of control for marketers over the evaluation process, and the difficulty of measuring return on investment for online campaigns. Case studies describe the digital marketing efforts of a public relations expert in Japan, how Marriott has taken social media listening to a new level, and Hamilton Island's 'Best Job in the World' campaign.

LESSONS FROM A MARKETING GURU: KOBE'S LOUISE DENDY

I first met PR expert, Louise Dendy, via Twitter – @Kobe_PRS. I was looking for a tourism organization for the city of Kobe, Japan and her Twitter contact was the first recognizable entry to come up. I had actually tried to find a similar contact in Tokyo first but to no avail.

IMAGE 3.1 Louise Dendy (Courtesy of Louise Dendy)

From that simple Google search emanated a chauffeur-driven FAM trip around many of Kobe's top attractions, guided by Dendy and her colleague, Mr Azuma. Culinary highlights over the two days included eating Kobe's world famous beef at Kobe Plaisir, sampling a selection of sakes at Fujuku Sake, trying Kobe's succulent sweets at Takasugi Tea Room, feasting on fish fresh from the harbour at traditional ryokan-style Kurakura Restaurant in Tarumi Ward, and decadent dining in Kobe's Chinatown. Dendy incorporated a stroll and ride to the top of the Akashi Kaikyo Bridge, the world's longest suspension bridge, to give us a 360-degree panoramic perspective of the city, the harbour islands and the mountains. Other attractions included visiting the 100-year-old Weathercock House in the quaint Kitano European Settlement, checking out cutting-edge anti-earthquake construction techniques at the Takenaka Carpentry Tools Museum and appreciating Kobe's foremost industrial and nautical achievements at the Kawasaki World and Maritime Museum. A shopping spree around Harborland topped off the innovative itinerary.

Born in Northampton, UK, Dendy had been in Kobe for five years by 2016. She initially visited Japan as part of a university study abroad programme, spending five months in Tokyo with a short visit to Kobe. 'I came to Kobe to study at Kobe University on a summer course for two weeks, which made me want to come to Kobe again – my top preference was Kobe,' she says. So, after graduation in 2011, she chose Kobe's calm and cosmopolitan charm over the more frenetic Tokyo to return to teach English as part of the JET programme. 'With both traditional appeal and Western charm, I consider Kobe to be a microcosm not just of Japan but of the entire world,' she explains.

Dendy quickly moved up to a position as translator and interpreter in the City Hall International Department in 2013 before being offered her current job as PR specialist for Kobe City Government in April 2015. Due to her proficiency in Japanese, as well as Spanish, French, Italian and German and her native English, she still interprets for the Mayor of Kobe at many important events and missions both in Japan and abroad, including a visit to San Francisco and Silicon Valley. 'Knowing a variety of languages is a great advantage in PR and marketing, as it allows you to reach a much wider audience than only speaking one,' she acknowledges. 'Being able to speak someone's native language enables you to connect with them and understand them on a deeper level. Multilingualism, and having experience living and working in other countries and cultures, also offers you a broader perspective on your work from day to day, even if it does not directly involve speaking other languages.'

With its prime position between the sea and mountains, Dendy loves Kobe for its relaxed atmosphere, beautiful natural attributes and, of course, her pivotal job. This entails promoting the city to non-Japanese visitors, dealing with foreign media and providing information to non-Japanese citizens. She also plays an integral part in strengthening Kobe's image as a cosmopolitan, international city within Japan. 'I run the city's official English Facebook account, Instagram account (in English and Japanese) and my own Twitter account, which I use to provide news, information and beautiful pictures, as well as sharing what I love about the city and what I'm up to,' she says. She posts weekly news, gourmet suggestions and travel tips along with her photos.

As well as encouraging and entertaining foreign media, she fine-tunes the city's English homepage and disseminates her love of the area via her own hands-on articles to various newspapers. 'Every two months I have a page in the Kobe paper, where I visit an area in the city and spotlight its hidden attractions. I write the original printed version in Japanese but I also translate it into English and upload it to my page on the Kobe website,' she says.

In 2016 Dendy spearheaded an innovative initiative to harness the social networks of local key influencers to help promote the city. 'As well as running the City's social media and homepage, I have just recently launched the PR Ambassador scheme. Under the scheme, 19 non-Japanese people who live, work or study in Kobe are using their social media to promote the city,' she explains. Dendy specifically targeted Kobe's sizeable JET community because of their international reach: 'These participants are broadly involved in a profusion of activities throughout the city. Being a JET participant means becoming a lifelong member of a vast, ready-made network extending around the world. There are a multitude of former participants who are using their JET connections to do valuable work at various organizations in Japan and abroad.'

These Ambassadors, profiled on the Kobe City website (www.city.kobe.lg.jp/foreign/english/media/kobepra/index.html) are volunteers for a year. 'During this time they will deepen their knowledge and experience of Kobe through tours, events and newsletters, meet likeminded PR Ambassadors, and share their own Kobe with the world,' says Dendy. 'Posts will be shared on the Kobe PR Ambassadors official Facebook and Twitter accounts, hubs for all PR Ambassador activity.' By May 2016, the dedicated Facebook page (www.facebook.com/KobePRA) had already featured photos and videos from an assortment of contributors.

The Ambassadors' year was launched with an appointment ceremony, a chance to learn more about the scheme and get to know all the participants. Events and tours were scheduled for June, August, October and January with an opinion exchange meeting set up midway and a closing ceremony at the end. As a guide, a monthly Kobe PR Ambassador newsletter complements the regular meetings. The Ambassadors now circulate their opinions in English about Kobe's daily life on all their social media outlets, pinpointing highlights such as the cherry blossom, the sake, sweets and cuisine as well as an array of activities. As well as participating in various bigger events and familiarization tours, they are also encouraged to seek out the hidden charms of Kobe.

Sources: *Personal visit by the authors to Kobe with Louise Dendy in January 2016 and interview in May 2016.*

THE IMPACT OF TECHNOLOGY ON MARKETING COMMUNICATIONS

We are witnessing a rapidly changing communications environment dominated by digital technology. To illustrate how quickly technology is advancing, take the example of Steven Spielberg's sci-fi thriller *Minority Report*. In 1999, the director convened a three-day think tank to gather insights from 23 top futurists for the making of the movie, which depicted the world of 2054. The goal was to create a realistic view of a plausible future 50 years ahead. Projecting out from the present day's marketing and media technologies, Spielberg depicted an advertising-saturated society where billboards call out to passers-by on a first-name basis, cereal boxes broadcast animated commercials, newspapers deliver news instantly over a broadband wireless network, holographic hosts greet customers by name at retail stores, and where biometric retina scans deduct the cost of goods instantly from bank accounts (Mathieson, 2002). The technologies portrayed in the film were far from science fiction, and today many are in use or are in development – an indication of the rapid pace of technological development.

Technology and the Internet have fundamentally altered the way the world interacts and communicates. Traditional approaches to branding that put emphasis on mass media techniques are less and less effective in a marketplace where customers have access to massive amounts of information about brands, product and companies and in which social networks have, in some cases, supplanted brand networks (Keller, 2009). In the new media environment, consumers are increasingly in control. Not only do they have more choices of media to use, they also have a choice about whether and how they want to receive commercial content. In response, marketers are employing more varied marketing communications techniques than ever before. Table 3.1 summarizes some of the interactive marketing communication options that are now available.

One relatively new method of communication on this list is virtual reality, computer-generated simulation of an environment that can be interacted with in a seemingly real or physical way by a person using special electronic equipment, such as a helmet with a screen inside or gloves fitted with sensors. Destination marketing using virtual reality is gathering momentum. British Columbia in Canada was one of the first destinations to use virtual reality for tourism marketing, providing trade, media partners and end consumers with a new and unique way to experience the province from their desk chairs. 'As the headsets become more widely available to consumers, virtual reality gives them a 360-degree experience – immersing them in the extraordinary travel opportunities that British Columbia offers, from raw wilderness to refined cities,' said Marsha Walden, CEO of Destination British Columbia (Rellihan, 2015). While the Destination BC virtual-reality experience was developed for the Oculus Rift headset, it can be transferred to other technologies as they become available. Samsung's virtual-reality headset, Gear VR, is the first virtual reality headset available to consumers; it costs $200.

Marriott Hotels have also been testing virtual reality with their 'teleporter', a telephone booth-like structure equipped with a headset, wireless headphone and 4-D sensory elements to provide a virtual travel experience. Marriott partnered with creative studio Framestore to develop the teleporter. Framestore used a new technique to capture 3-D, 360-degree live-action video, then mixed it with computer-generated imagery

TABLE 3.1 Digital marketing communications options (Source: Adapted from Keller, 2009)

• **Website**	Companies must design websites that express their purpose, vision, products and history. A key challenge is to design a site that is attractive enough on first viewing and which continues to raise people's interest to allow repeated visits. Dedicated websites for mobile devices are on the increase
• **Mobile marketing**	Mobile marketing will become increasingly important. Particularly, smartphone use is growing among travellers
• **Social media**	Companies are embracing social media because of its potential for collaboration and engagement with consumers. Social media advertising will yield relatively stronger results due to its ability to tightly target audiences based on social media activity
• **Display ads**	Display ads are small, rectangular boxes with text and perhaps a picture that companies pay to place on certain websites. The larger the reader, the more the placement costs
• **Internet-specific ads and videos**	With user-generated content sites (i.e. YouTube, Google Video, MySpace Video), consumers and marketers can upload ads and videos to be shared virally by millions of people
• **Email**	Email uses only a fraction of the cost of a 'd-mail', or direct mail campaign. Three times more effective in prompting purchases than social media
• **Blogs**	Blogs are commonly maintained by an individual with regular entries of commentary, description of events, or other material such as graphics or video. Most blogs with high quality are interactive, which allows visitors to leave comments and even message each other
• **Microsites**	A microsite is a limited area on the web managed and paid for by an external advertiser. A microsite is an Internet web design term referring to an individual web page or a small cluster (around 1–7) of pages which are meant to function as a discrete entity within an existing website or to complement an offline activity
• **Search ads**	Paid-search or pay-per-click ads, represent 40% of all online ads. 35% of all searches are reportedly for products or services. The search terms serve as a proxy for the consumer's consumption interests and trigger relevant links to product or service offerings alongside search results from Google, MSN and Yahoo! Advertisers pay only if people click on the links
• **Virtual reality**	Destination marketing using virtual reality is gathering momentum
• **Online brand communities**	Many firms sponsor online communities whose members communicate via postings, chat discussions and instant messaging about special interest related to the firm's products and brands

and 4-D elements such as wind, heat and mist. At a preview of the technology at the New York Marriott Marquis, reporters and Marriott employees donned goggles and headphones for a few minutes. Firstly, they saw the lobby of a Marriott Hotel. Then they saw 360-degree images of Hawaii's Wai'anapanapa Black Sand Beach in Maui and heard waves crashing with a mist spraying on them. Next, they were transported to London and lifted slightly off the ground to see the skyline from the viewpoint of the Tower 42 skyscraper. 'We wanted to show London and Hawaii because these are aspirational destinations,' said Michael Dail, vice president of Marriott Hotels Brand Marketing (Trejos, 2014).

In a less sophisticated 2013/14 campaign, Monarch Airlines in the UK created a 360-degree virtual reality guide to ski resorts served by the airline. As part of a direct marketing campaign by marketing agency WDMP, consumers were 'transported' to a virtual ski slope, with high-quality graphics and a 360-degree 'Photosphere' view complete with realistic falling snow and sound. Navigation around the mountain was possible by moving and tilting a smartphone or tablet to travel around and access new areas. By touching icons, consumers could visit each of the ski resorts accessible via Monarch's routes. Users could also watch ski tip videos from the Ski Club of Great Britain, access the latest snow reports, and enter a 'Postcard' competition to win free flights. This encouraged sharing of the campaign by 'posting' a virtual, personalized postcard to friends via social media.

Certainly, to communicate effectively and efficiently, tourism marketers have to go where the consumers are – and this is increasingly online (Phocuswright, 2013). The Internet is moving marketers much closer to one-to-one marketing. The Web not only offers merchants the ability to communicate instantly with each customer, but it also allows the customer to talk back, and that makes it possible for companies to customize offers and services. The Internet also allows organizations to provide seven-day, 24-hour service response. In fact, the main reason consumers have adopted the Internet is that it enables them to shop 24/7 in the comfort of their home with no time zone worries. Ease of navigation is then the primary reason for variations in purchase decisions between different online products.

The latest evolution on the consumer technology front is the widespread use of smartphones. The pervasiveness of mobile technology is creating what MTN, the South African-based telecommunications and mobile finance brand, calls a whole mobile lifestyle (Roberti, 2011). Providing accessibility to banking and credit facilities, travel itineraries, insurance, utilities services, as well as voice and Internet connectivity, is revolutionizing where, when, and how we communicate personally and with businesses. With total activity on smartphones and tablets accounting for 60 per cent of digital media time spent in the US, there's no denying that reaching users while on mobile devices is the next big wave in advertising. Mobile advertising comprised nearly 70 per cent of Facebook's revenue and about 85 per cent of Twitter's in 2014, and two-thirds of social media advertising spend is forecasted to go towards mobile ads in 2018, creating a $9.1 billion market on mobile (Ganguly, 2015). This, coupled with the fact that over half of mobile phone users globally will have smartphones in 2018, means that social media advertising on mobile is a huge growth market in the next few years.

Smartphone use is growing among travellers; nearly two-thirds of US travellers who plan their travel online now own a smartphone, and just under a third own a tablet. Hotels are capitalizing on this in order to speed up or personalize more services for guests. The Park Hyatt Tokyo and Park Hyatt Seoul, for example, give guests free access to over 2,300 international newspapers on their smartphones or tablets using the hotel's wi-fi network and an app called Press-Reader. A growing number of hotels are also allowing guests to unlock their guest rooms with their phones. Starwood began offering smartphone apps in its Aloft, Element and W hotel brands in 2014, and Hyatt Hotels and Resorts, Hilton Worldwide, Marriott and others have followed suit since then. 'We believe this will become the new standard for how people will want to enter a hotel,' said Frits van Paasschen, Starwood's CEO. 'It may be a novelty at first, but we think it will become table stakes for managing a hotel' (Karmin, 2014). Some technology offerings extend beyond the hotel's walls. The Park Hyatt Tokyo rent guests a pocketsize mobile wi-fi connector to use with an iPhone, iPad, Blackberry or laptop to make international calls and get Internet access wherever they go during their stay (Weed, 2013).

Smartphone technology is continually evolving, presenting tremendous opportunities to tourism marketers. The Digital Spotlight in Chapter 5 describes how a 2011 campaign in Poland brought art to a whole new generation thanks to smartphones and QR codes. People visiting the Sukiennice National Museum in Krakow, could use their phones to scan the paintings and, when they did so, it used augmented reality to act out scenes from the paintings and bring the whole museum to life. The application for use on an iPhone provides eight 2D video films depicting the most interesting painting masterpieces which are presented at the exhibition. It can often be hard to relate to artwork that is hundreds of years old but the stories told through video brought a whole new understanding of the artwork, enhancing appreciation and recall. The campaign itself was a huge success with the tour booked months in advance, and the initiative picked up mainstream attention on television, media, blogs and online in general.

IMAGE 3.2 The National Museum in Krakow (Courtesy of Polska Organizacja Turystyczna)

The use of augmented reality has spread to other sectors of travel and tourism. In 2012, destination marketers in Hawaii and Mexico experimented with Aurasma to lead the future of tourism marketing with their cross-media creative campaigns. Aurasma is a visual browser – a new platform technology that merges the physical world with the virtual. Available as a free app for iPhone 4, iPad 2 and high-powered Android devices or as a free kernel for developers, Aurasma uses advanced image and pattern recognition to recognize and understand real-world images and objects in much the same way that the human brain does. It then seamlessly blends the real world with rich interactive content such as videos and animations called 'Auras'. Auras can be created for printed images, product packaging, clothing and physical places and users can even use the app to create and share their own.

To capture the public's attention and further entice travel to Hawaii and Mexico, these destinations used Aurasma's ability to transport visually their vacation hotspots to potential travellers. In Chicago and San Francisco, pedestrians could position their mobile devices over outdoor print ads of Hawaii and use Aurasma to see the printed ads dissolve into videos of Hawaii. Those interested in getting more information could then tap on their mobile touch screen to be automatically directed to gohawaii.com. Mexico used Aurasma to offer exclusive content to media and key influencers in North America via postcards. When the Aurasma viewer saw the front of the postcard, the image triggered a series of video testimonials from recent trips to Mexico. To incentivize recipients to unlock the digital content and watch the video, marketers also included a nice prize. One lucky viewer could win an iPad 2.

Some have suggested that the popularity of Nintendo's Pokémon Go augmented reality game could be the harbinger of a revolution in travel (tnooz, 2016). What makes Pokemon Go different from its predecessors like Second Life is that it has created a virtual world overlaid atop the real world. The game has proven itself capable of affecting real-world places by creating in-game reasons for being at a certain geographical location. People who own stores or sites in the real world can, for example, pay Nintendo approximately $1.19 per hour for 'lures', which encourage the spawning of valuable in-game creatures in a real world location. These lures create foot traffic and potential purchases in the real world. L'inizio's Pizza Bar in New York was one of the earliest businesses to tap deliberately into the real-world windfall from the game. Manager Sean Benedetti spent about $10 on 'Lure Modules' and saw food and drink sales spike by about 30 per cent. 'People are coming out of the woodwork because of this game,' he said (Mosendz and Kawa, 2016).

Finally, a relatively new technological innovation influencing travel, referred to in Chapter 2, is the use of wearable technologies for monitoring and tracking health and performance. For example, a new technology called Trace from the makers of AlpineReplay, provides winter sport tourists with real time data. The Trace sport tracker weighs just 40 gm and clips easily on to skis and snowboards to measure speed, distance, turns, vertical, airtime, airs, calories burned, and more. The data accumulated allows athletes to track their progress and learn what areas of riding need to be improved on. Also included is Trace Cam, which syncs with all Bluetooth-enabled video devices, including GoPro, iPhone and Android and allows users to relive their experience instantaneously on the slopes through professional-quality highlight videos. Amadeus (2015) recently published a travel infographic that shows the array of technology available and under development to create a truly personalized experience for travellers from smart clothes to wearable technologies. The infographic is available at: http://www.amadeus.com/documents/shaping-the-future-of-travel/Amadeus-Infographic-Wearable-Technology.jpg

Many of the new technologies discussed above are having an impact on events and festivals. The 'M Live' case in this chapter notes how Marriott is creating social media content about special events to engage guests and business partners, and the Digital Spotlight in Chapter 1 described the influence of social media on music festivals. Music events are also experimenting with virtual reality. In 2016, the Coachella festival offered music fans outside of Coachella's Indio, California location the opportunity to experience the weekend in virtual reality. Using a dedicated app, those equipped with a VR headset could go on tours of the festival's site thanks to a team up with Vantage.tv. The VR experience also included exclusive interviews with performing acts which included The Kills, The Last Shadow Puppets and Ellie Goulding.

IMAGE 3.3 Attendees at GeekWire sporting their LiGo badges (Courtesy of Limefy)

New apps are also revolutionizing the experience for attendees at business events. The organizers of the 2016 Seattle GeekWire Startup Day, for example, wanted to increase attendee engagement and have a way to measure the event effectiveness – a desire shared by many other event producers. They also wanted to overcome the difficulties of networking and help engage attendees with each other in a more meaningful way, making each individual a participant rather than an observer. LiGo smart badges were therefore given out after registration and attendees used a LiGo mobile app to program the device. Attendees were able to select a profile, who they were attending the event as, and who they wanted to meet and talk to. As the attendees walked around, LiGo badges lit up in the same colour alerting the two people that they were looking for each other and should start up a conversation. The mobile app also helped pinpoint who the match was with by providing a picture of the person and more information about the 'match' such as their LinkedIn profile. LiGo helped create a total of 9,459 matches at the Seattle GeekWire Startup Days event and helped bridge the gap between all sorts of people looking to engage in productive conversations and generate new business opportunities. Founders were able to identify and talk to investors quickly about their ideas, business service providers were able to locate the startup founders that needed their help, and recruiters were able to find engineers and technologists that matched their needs (Korovkin, 2016).

THE NEW CONSUMER DECISION JOURNEY

According to McKinsey & Co, the Internet has upended how consumers engage with brands to the extent that consumers are promiscuous in their brand relationships (Edelman, 2010). They connect with myriad brands through new media channels often beyond the marketer's familiarity or control. In the past, marketing strategies emphasized brand awareness and ultimate purchase. However, after purchase, consumers now remain aggressively engaged, actively promoting or assailing the products they have bought, and collaborating in the brand's development. The touch points when consumers are most open to influence have changed, requiring a major adjustment to realign marketers' strategy and budgets with where consumers are actually spending their time. McKinsey have developed a model of consumer decision-making that depicts this new journey (see Figure 3.1).

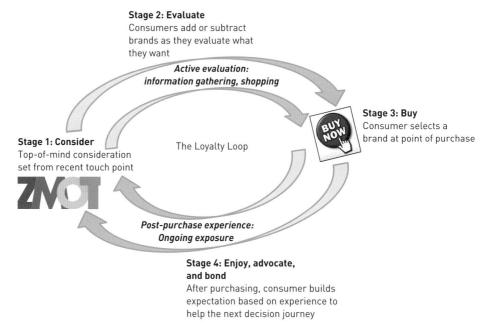

FIGURE 3.1 The new consumer decision journey (©2016 Mckinsey & Company. All rights reserved. Reprinted by permission)

They developed their model from a study of the purchase decisions of nearly 20,000 consumers across five industries and three continents. Their research revealed that rather than systematically narrowing their choices until they had decided what to buy, consumers add and subtract brands from a group under consideration during an extended evaluation stage. After purchase, they often enter into an open-ended relationship with the brand, sharing their experience with it online through social media. McKinsey & Co suggests that top-performing brands are actively shaping these decision journeys, for example by capturing insights about customers and feeding them back into their marketing programmes to improve performance (Edelman and Singer, 2015).

The four stages of the consumer decision journey are: (a) consider; (b) evaluate; (c) buy; and (d) enjoy, advocate and bond. New media make the 'evaluate' and 'advocate' stages increasingly relevant. Consumers' outreach to marketers and other sources of information is much more likely to shape their ensuing choices than marketers' efforts to persuade them. An addition to the original model is the 'Zero Moment of Truth' (ZMOT). Online marketers have coined this term to describe the new reality where marketers have to compete for shoppers' attention online long before a purchase decision is made (Lecinski, 2011).

Travellers rely on a range of information sources when comparing and choosing travel products for their trips, but online information sources – including websites and apps – dominate the travel shopping process (Phocuswright, 2013). Websites via computer are by far the leading source of information for shopping; seven in ten trips are planned using this channel. Companies must design websites that express their purpose, vision, products and history. A key challenge is to design a site that is attractive enough on first viewing and continues to raise people's interest to repeat visit. Companies will often work with web design specialists to create or improve their websites. Celebrity Cruises, for example, recently partnered with SDL and digital consultancy Building Blocks to improve the mobile journey for its website. 'At Celebrity Cruises, it's important that our customers have a consistent and local web experience on the device of their choosing. SDL and Building Blocks helped us to achieve this, rolling out a successful mobile-first strategy that we continue to develop to meet the needs of our growing customer base,' said Toby Shaw, Director of Marketing & PR, Celebrity Cruises (SDL, 2015). 'We couldn't be more delighted with the seamlessness and success of this project. Their combined digital vision and innovative solutions has produced the superior mobile experience that reflects the modern luxury experience our customers have come to expect.' The site's improved itinerary content, powerful imagery and simplified booking process has improved conversion rates for Celebrity Cruises.

Despite the increasing importance of social media, it is important to recognize that at the early stages of the consumer decision journey, email remains a significantly more effective way to acquire customers than social media – nearly 40 times that of Facebook and Twitter combined (see Figure 3.2). According to McKinsey & Co, this is because 91 per cent of all US consumers still use email daily, and the rate at which emails prompt purchases is not only estimated to be at least three times that of social media, but the average order value is also 17 per cent higher (Aufreiter,

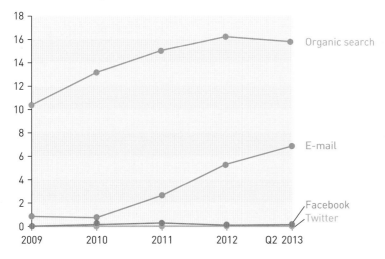

FIGURE 3.2 US customer acquisition growth by channel: percentage of customers acquired (Exhibit from "Why marketers should keep sending you e-mails", January 2014, McKinsey & Company, www.mckinsey.com. Copyright ©2016 McKinsey & Company. All rights reserved. Reprinted by permission)

Boudet and Weng, 2014). This does not mean marketers should bombard customers with mindless spam. McKinsey's iConsumer survey reported a 20 per cent decline in email usage between 2008 and 2012 as a share of time spent on communications, with the medium surrendering ground to social networks, instant messaging, and mobile-messaging apps. However, McKinsey suggest that marketers should not be too hasty in shifting budgets away from email – they just need to recognize that: (a) email is merely the first click (literally) in a consumer's decision journey; (b) every email is an opportunity to learn more about their consumer; and (c) emails should be personal and customized (Aufreiter, Boudet and Weng, 2014).

After purchase, a deeper connection begins as the consumer interacts with the product and with new online touch points. Vail Resorts has taken advantage of this 'enjoy, advocate and bond' stage with its EpicMix campaign (described in the Digital Spotlight in Chapter 10). Of course, a key part of leveraging the online consumer journey is social media listening – tuning into the conversations that are organically driven by the customer (Eduljee, 2010), a process that leads to new insights and discoveries (see Figure 3.3). Chapter 11 on marketing research goes into more detail about this, giving examples from various sectors of the tourism and hospitality industry on how listening to social media has benefited individual companies. The case study below shows how Marriott has created M Live in order to gain rich, unmediated consumer insights faster than ever before.

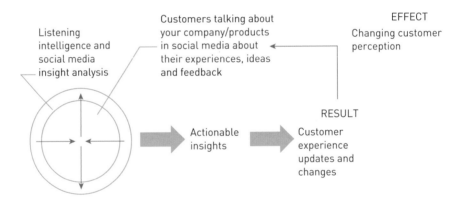

FIGURE 3.3 Social media listening (©Mark Eduljee. Used with permission)

DIGITAL SPOTLIGHT: MARRIOTT TAKES SOCIAL MEDIA LISTENING TO A NEW LEVEL

'If it's not on social media, it didn't happen,' says Vanessa Saw, Digital Executive for Marriott's Creative & Content Marketing department. Stationed at Marriott's Hong Kong regional office, Saw's job is to oversee 'M Live APAC', the company's new Asia Pacific state-of-the-art marketing and brand newsroom Command Center, which has become Marriott's epicentre of real-time marketing to customers in the region.

Marriott first unveiled the Marriott ('M') Live concept at its US headquarters in Bethesda, Maryland early in 2015. The concept brings together all marketing disciplines

IMAGE 3.4 M Live APAC Command Center in Hong Kong (©Marriott International, Inc. All rights reserved. Reproduced by permission)

to track conversations, trends, global performance, marketing campaign performance and brand reputation on social media, while also proactively creating original content based on what is trending, or anticipated to trend, on social media. With full-time staff able to monitor data displayed on multiple split screens within the M Live APAC Command Center, Marriott authentically engages customers as relevant social conversations trend. 'The region-specific goals at M Live APAC are to help identify online trending stories that our brands can leverage as marketing opportunities, identify breaking news – i.e. local news and if our properties are affected by it – and customer stories – i.e. influencers and brand mentions our properties can amplify – since real customer experiences are the new word of mouth on social,' says Saw.

In addition to responding to social conversations, M Live APAC has created a calendar of topics expected to trend, such as Chinese New Year, the Seoul Marathon, the Rugby Sevens in Hong Kong, and the India Premier Cricket League. By anticipating what will trend, M Live is able to plan its creative and content strategy in concert with the other marketing and brand disciplines within Marriott International. 'The changing consumer is at the centre of everything we do at Marriott,' says Anka Twum-Baah, Vice President, Customer Loyalty & Content, Asia Pacific at Marriott International. 'M Live is another example of how we are putting our marketing in the context of next generation travellers' lives that is immediate, relevant and authentic. With the opening of the Hong Kong M Live studio and the building out of a network, M Live will help make our new approach to marketing become truly global.'

(Continued)

(Continued)

M Live allows Marriott not only to seize more chances to engage with consumers quickly, but also to identify opportunities by brand, by discipline, by market and by channel to create memorable and shareable experiences. Tony Chow, Director of Creative & Content Marketing for Asia Pacific, is heading up the M Live initiative in Hong Kong. 'We are the first brand in Asia Pacific to have a real time listening platform for social media. In today's very fast evolving marketplace you can't talk so much but you have to listen more. That is the philosophy behind M Live. Sysomos built the system for us called "heartbeat", to pull data and information across social channels using key words. Marriott-related keywords have been built into heartbeat to allow us to monitor across social media – Twitter, Instagram, YouTube and Facebook. Such social media platforms are expanding rapidly across Asia. Indonesians, for example, are heavy users of Twitter, sending out a minimum of five million tweets a day.'

Chow acknowledges that they can't utilize WeChat in China as access to personal information is not allowed, but they will soon be monitoring Weibo, the 'Facebook of China'. By analysing the four real-time screens at the Hong Kong command centre, Chow's team can react to social media conversations immediately. For example, the team will track key influencers – those with more than a half million followers – and if they talk about their experiences with Marriott (good or bad) they will act. 'We contact the hotel,' says Chow, 'to make sure that their experience can be amplified. We give the General Manager a call and ask if they have seen what has been posted and we see how we can engage with the influencer – not in a bribery way – but answer back to their very positive comments. We know the faster we react to something, the better you keep your customers.' The team will also track celebrity conversations: 'In India, a lot of the Bollywood actors stay in JW Marriott properties, so we track them.'

The team will look for comments like 'I love that', or 'I will think of staying there next time.' 'We then leap on it and try to nurture that sale,' Chow explains. 'Building trust and creating a relationship.' Chow believes traditional advertising has lost its impact. 'The first call of a lot of conversation is online. We call it word of mouth advertising. That is the kind of reality and we want to be there.' One of the screens at the command centre is dedicated to pop-culture in Asia Pacific – food, fashion, clubs, etc. 'People take pictures or videos of the food they are eating all the time,' says Chow. 'It's catching on so quickly in Asia – in the Philippines nobody touches their food until they have posted their photo on Facebook. And in Japan and Korea people will watch live videos of our customers eating. If you watch them eating, you experience it with them.'

The team will also work with individual properties to create videos to post on social media. In a recent initiative, drones were used in the Mekong Delta to fly over and film the new rooftop Liquid Sky Bar at the Renaissance Riverside Hotel in Vietnam. The promotional video will be uploaded to YouTube, and M Live will monitor the reaction. 'Social media is now the hot ticket item for us,' says Blair Fowler, General Manager at the Ho Chi Minh City property. 'Many of our hotels are moving away from printed collateral towards digital. We are trying to get as much exposure as we can for the new bar through digital, and this video will help to do that. Making content of special events that engage our guests and business partners not only provides an event review, it also acts as a great branding tool, too... and with a new outlet, such as the Liquid Sky Bar, we need to create as much awareness and engagement in the market as we can.'

To date, M Live in Asia has created a number of successful real-time marketing efforts. One recent piece of news, published in the *South China Morning Post* but trending across Asia on Instagram and Facebook, focused on the most expensive apartment sold in Hong Kong – about US$65 million. 'When we saw that trending topic we thought there was something we could do,' says Chow. 'I thought that the view from that apartment was similar to something we had from one of our properties – so we found a picture of a room in our Renaissance Harbor View hotel with a view, and put it side by side with the most expensive property sold.' The pictures were posted and linked to the *South China Morning Post*, suggesting that you could live like a millionaire by staying in this Marriott property. 'Exposure amplified immediately, and within an hour we had around 700 likes and many positive comments. Everyone started asking for that room with the view, showing that you can actually drive transactions by leveraging social media,' says Chow. As well as linking M Live's initiatives directly to bookings, the team is able to measure its success in terms of brand awareness through amplified social media presence. Analysing the statistics from this presence, they are then able to engage with followers, turn trust into transaction, and eventually convert conversations to sales.

The M Live Asia Pacific is the first to come on board outside the US, but M Live Europe, Middle East & Africa, and Caribbean and Latin America all had planned launches in 2016. Marriott chose Asia Pacific as the second location because Asia, with 4.4 billion people and approximately 500 million in the emerging middle classes, will provide substantial opportunities for tourism growth. And the region's next-generation travellers are among the fastest growing customer segment within the hospitality industry.

Sources: Personal visit to M Live Hong Kong and Renaissance Riverside Hotel in Vietnam by authors in January 2016.

CASE STUDY QUESTIONS

1. Apparently although over 80 per cent of hotels have a social media strategy, only 20 per cent actually monitor and listen to social media conversations. Why do you think that is?
2. Why should hotels be monitoring social media conversations?
3. If you were working in the M Live lab and saw via Twitter that a popular celebrity was staying in a Marriott hotel, what would you do?

THE INFLUENCE OF SOCIAL MEDIA

Social media platforms are emerging as a dominant digital communications channel with social media advertising coming a long way in a relatively short period of time. When Facebook launched its first advertising option in May 2005, no one could have predicted that social media advertising revenue would have reached around $8.4 billion in 2015, just ten years later. Social media spending is currently 13 per cent of marketing budgets, and in five years marketers expect to spend more than 21 per cent of their budgets on social media (Duke's Fuqua School of Business, 2014).

A recent study by McKinsey & Co found that the impact of social media on buying decisions is greater than previously estimated and growing fast, with 50 to 60 per cent of customers looking to social media recommendations for products like travel. They also found that online articles written by journalists prompt consumers to seek out social media to inform purchase further (and that PR spending to generate such articles is therefore a worthwhile investment). Furthermore, consumers who use search engines to gain initial knowledge of a product are more likely to tune in to social media before a purchase. Therefore companies that spend effectively on search-engine optimization (to move their product mentions to the top of search results) can expect to benefit from a great social media impact. As consumers spend more time on social networks, decisions about what to purchase often reflect interactions with friends and other influencers.

A large percentage of consumers read reviews of hotels, attractions and restaurants prior to vacation, and while on vacation over 70 per cent post vacation photos on a social network or update their Facebook status (Lab42, 2012). It is therefore important that marketers in the travel industry provide the opportunity for visitors to use social media (for example by providing free wi-fi), and encourage them to do so. Figure 3.4 is an example of a destination – Fernie Alpine Resort in British Columbia, Canada – reminding visitors to share their experiences via social media.

FIGURE 3.4 Poster at Fernie Alpine Resort encouraging visitors to 'get social' (Courtesy of Resorts of the Canadian Rockies)

Marketers have embraced social media because of its potential for engagement and collaboration with these networked consumers. Figure 3.5 shows just some of the ways social media is being used by marketers in the tourism and hospitality sector to engage customers and gain loyalty over the long-term.

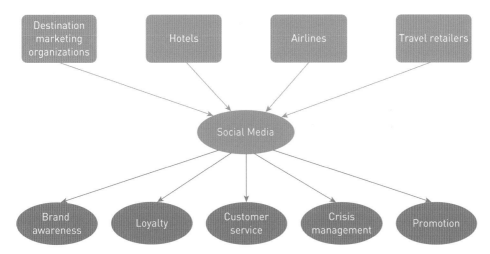

FIGURE 3.5 Engaging customers through social media (©Euromonitor International. Reprinted by permission)

While many marketers are gaining considerable consumer insights, faster than ever before, through social media, others see the value of social media in its networking. According to Facebook, the average user has 350 friends on the social network, and when people hear about a product or service from a friend, they become a customer at a 15 per cent higher rate than when they find out about it through other means. The growth of social networking is mainly driven by Facebook, which reaches 90 per cent of US social media users and 85 per cent of European users, and is the most popular social networking site (see Table 3.2).

TABLE 3.2 Ten most popular social networking sites (Source: Adapted from eBiz, 2014. ©eBizMBA. com. Reproduced with permission)

Social networking site	Estimated unique monthly visitors (1,000s)
1. Facebook	1,100,000
2. YouTube	1,000,000
3. Twitter	310,000
4. LinkedIn	255,000
5. Pinterest	250,000
6. Google Plus +	120,000
7. Tumblr	110,000
8. Instagram	100,000
9. Reddit	85,000
10. VK	80,000

Companies are also using social media to promote their brands. Virgin Atlantic Airways (VAA), for example, leverages the power of social media to reinforce its brand (Barwise and Meehan, 2010). The VAA customer promise is innovation, fun, informality, honesty, value, and a caring attitude. VAA uses social media to support these brand values. For example, the most-read section of its Facebook page includes travel tips from crew members – communication that comes across as honest, informal and caring. VAA builds trust by delivering on that promise. Trust is mainly about service delivery, but when things go wrong, keeping customers informed can prevent that trust from eroding. During the volcanic-ash crisis in Europe in 2010, VAA's website couldn't keep pace with the rapidly changing situation, so it used Facebook and Twitter to communicate with customers.

Twitter is increasingly being used as a standalone marketing tool to generate awareness for a tourism product or service. A few years ago, the Virginia Tourism Corporation (VTC) won a marketing award for a wine tourism promotion called 'Vintage Tweets' – a cutting-edge public relations effort that utilized social media to promote wine tourism in Virginia. VTC organized Vintage Tweets to kick off their annual October Virginia Wine Month. The state tourism agency used Twitter to target media, bloggers and consumers who were passionate about wine travel, who lived in and around Washington, DC, and had a significant number of Twitter followers. VTC used Twitter to invite 40 of those consumers to a wine reception, featuring six different wineries from across the state. The guests tweeted about their wine tastings and also took part in Virginia Wine Travel Twitter trivia. In total, Vintage Tweets was able to reach over 43,000 consumers in just 24 hours, providing key facts and travel ideas to potential visitors from across the country.

One social media platform that is helping tourism and hospitality businesses is the emergence of geolocation sites such as Foursquare, Gowilla and Loopt. Foursquare encourages consumers to broadcast their whereabouts (or 'check-in') in exchange for discounts or coupons, for instance. People use the Foursquare app on their smartphones to check in to places like restaurants, pubs and hotels, and just about any other type of physical and even nonphysical location. Once they check in, users often share that information with friends, families and followers on Facebook and Twitter. Foursquare users compete for badges, points, and 'mayorships,' awarded to those who check in to a place most frequently. Business owners claim their venue on Foursquare (for free) and reward people simply for checking in, for checking in a certain number of times, for checking in with friends, or reward the person who checks in the most (the 'mayor'). For example, Chili's Grill & Bar, a national restaurant chain in the US, rewards its customers with free chips and salsa every time they check in. Chili's makes money on the deal because customers don't walk into Chili's just for free chips and salsa and leave. They order appetizers, entrées and drinks.

Dutch Airline KLM used Foursquare as part of an innovative social media campaign that focused on random acts of kindness. An effective way to connect emotionally with consumers is through random acts of kindness designed to produce customer gratitude. Gratitude is a powerful and potentially quite profitable emotion to inspire (Palmatier et al., 2009). The airline's 'How Happiness Spreads' campaign of 2010 employed a 'Surprise Team' to give passengers tailored, unexpected gifts at the airport (Trendwatching, 2011). When passengers checked in at KLM's Foursquare locations, the KLM Surprise Team used social networks such as LinkedIn, Twitter and Facebook to find out more background information. The KLM Surprise Team then used this information to come up with a personalized gift to surprise the passenger. The team followed up after giving the passenger the gift by monitoring the conversation generated on social networks by that person and their friends. They also took photos of the people they had surprised and posted them to the KLM Facebook page. KLM has previously proven its social media savvy with a popular Facebook application allowing users to create luggage tags using their Facebook photos. In 2006 the company had another success with an award-winning viral video for its Fly for Fortune game.

User-generated video contests have become an increasingly popular communication tool for many destinations which use them to engage consumers and prompt them to become digital ambassadors for their brands. Users are encouraged to submit a personal video to the competition's website, from which they can be selected to win a free dream holiday in a reality TV-like process. In return, the lucky winners are expected to share their impressions on Facebook, Twitter, YouTube, Flicker and blogs, serving as the place's ambassadors. Perhaps one of the most successful campaigns of this type was the 'Best Job in the World' Queensland campaign profiled in the case study below.

Tourism and hospitality brands are teaming up more and more with social media influencers to create videos that will drive engagement, reach and awareness. Marriott, for example, recently rolled out its own global content studio, partnering with five top social media influencers to create a dedicated series on a daily interactive channel (What's Trending) that allowed the viewer to follow the featured influencers as they travelled and documented their unique adventures. Influencers chosen were YouTubers Jeana Smith from PrankVsPrank, Louis Cole from FunForLouis, Tom from TheSyndicateProject, Steve Zaragoza from Sourcefed, and Meghan Camarena from Strawburry17. By using this YouTuber marketing strategy, Marriott garnered close to four million views in four months. Marriott also partnered with top YouTuber Casey Neistat to drive a campaign where he travelled to various locales, sharing his entire experience with Marriott. David Beebe, the VP of Global Creative & Content Marketing for Marriott International, advises that 'rather than dictating the topic and type of content you want from the influencers, let them come back to you with a concept that plays to their strengths and social credibility' (Mediakix, 2015).

Another type of social media leverage by travel marketers is the online brand community (Kunz and Seshadri, 2015). Brand communities are defined as 'specialized, nongeographically bound communities, based on a structured set of social relationships among admirers of a brand' (Bagozzi and Dholakia, 2006: 45). The emergence of brand communities has coincided with the growth in consumer empowerment. They are venues where intense brand loyalty is expressed and fostered, and emotional connection with the brand is forged in customers. Research on such communities has found that commitment to a brand can be influenced (positively) by encouraging interactions with groups of like-minded customers and identification with the group in social context offered (and sponsored) by the firm and the brand, but controlled and managed primarily by the consumers themselves.

As use of the Internet becomes more pervasive, so too have online brand communities become effective tools for influencing sales. One study of online brand communities (Adjei, Noble and Noble, 2010) found that the quality of the communication exchanged between customers reduces the level of uncertainty about the company and its products, which relates to increased profits for the company in terms of immediate purchase intentions, and the number of products purchased. It also found that the impact of negative information is not as strong as the benefits of positive information. So maintaining a brand community that allows customers to know the company more intimately through peer-to-peer conversations will work in the company's favour, even if negative information is shared.

A challenge in building and managing online brand communities is that consumers can easily associate marketers' efforts with extrinsic motives of profit exploitation and thus become less likely to engage with, and contribute to, such a community (Algesheimer, Dholakia and Herrmann, 2005; Lee, Kim and Kim, 2011). Finding the right tone for effective communication in online communities is therefore critical (Kunz and Seshadri, 2015). One possible solution is to develop a platform of online brand communities encouraging consumers to share and exchange their ideas voluntarily rather than imposing the organization's own ideas, such as sales coupons or sweepstakes. This implies that marketers should employ a passive role when facilitating brand communities.

A good example of this passive engagement in a brand community is the Walt Disney World Moms' Panel. This is a forum where online 'Moms' answer questions and offer advice about family vacations to Disney. The Moms are selected to be panellists because they have demonstrated an excellent knowledge of Disney products. Being familiar with the Parks, Resort hotels, dining and entertainment, shopping, and recreational activities, they can offer the help and tips consumers need when planning their vacations. As Leanne Jakubowski, who oversees the programme, says: 'It is important that the Moms' Panel is made up of real guests and represents a diverse spectrum of thoughts and perspectives so we can offer honest, heartfelt and useful information' (Walt Disney World, 2011). Panellists receive a trip to the Walt Disney World Resort for their participation and in 2012 the Panel boasted 43 panellists whose expertise spanned Walt Disney World Resort, Disney Cruise Line, Disney Vacation Club, Adventures by Disney and Disneyland Resort offerings. The Moms' Panel offers guests vacation insights on a variety of platforms including exclusive 'How-To' videos from panellists and celebrities, dedicated Facebook content, personal Disney Parks Blog posts and in-Park meet-ups.

Because brand community members have a strong interest in the product and in the brand, they can also be a valuable source of innovation. In a study of brand community members, research found that the stronger the identification with the brand, and the higher the brand trust, the more likely a consumer was willing to contribute to open innovation projects initiated by a brand. This activity has been called 'crowdsourcing', a term coined in 2006 by *Wired* magazine Contributing Editor, Jeff Howe (Sullivan, 2010). Crowdsourcing-led innovation means opening the door to allow customers, employees, or the general public at large into the innovation process to help improve products, services or marketing efforts. Consumers get a direct line to the company and the opportunity to steer offerings to reflect their needs better, while companies benefit from getting more insights, opinions and wisdom that can be translated into actionable innovation ideas for less money than a typical R&D initiative.

For Virgin Atlantic Airways, the greatest social media opportunity lies in gathering insights to drive continual incremental improvements (Barwise and Meehan, 2010). For example, in response to online-community suggestions, it launched a system to arrange taxi sharing on arrival with passengers from the same flight. Fresh insights from social media also reinforce the innovation aspect of the brand. Facebook interactions helped the company appreciate the extensive planning that goes into a big trip, so they launched Vtravelled, a site dedicated to inspirational journeys. Customers moderate the conversation and exchange information, stories, and advice. The site leads to some sales, but its main benefit to VAA comes from brand reinforcement and new customer insights.

Club Med used crowdsourcing in 2014 to engage consumers in the development of a ski resort in the French Alps town of Val Thorens. The all-inclusive brand rolled out a seven-phase marketing campaign via Facebook which encouraged fans to contribute to the development process for the Club Med resort. The Facebook campaign had three tracks, one to Discover the Resort, another to Join the Vote and one that outlined available Prizes for participation. Beyond simply marketing the upcoming launch of the resort to the community, the voting functionality allowed fans to select a series of components of the new experience. For example, voters chose 'Val Thorens Sensations' over 'Val Thorens Titanium' for the new brand name, and decided on a climbing wall versus a modern atrium as part of the design.

Club Med offered a seven-day stay at the new resort to participating fans, and the winners were the first two guests to experience the resort fully. In the release supporting the rollout, VP of Marketing for Club Med North America, Jerome Hiquet said: 'Club Med welcomed almost 200,000 guests at its Alpine ski resorts last year and has launched this innovative platform in order to engage with discerning travellers and empower them to create their ideal ski resort. We greatly value our guests and want to ensure they are able to take part in this new generation of resorts. With the resort opening in December of this year, it's vital for the brand to get out in front of the opening to ensure a place in consumers' travel budgets and to get those rooms booked. Delivering a drip marketing campaign will contribute to significant buzz amongst Club Med evangelists, while also offering up a multimonth marketing campaign to fill up the social media pipeline with compelling, engaging and ultimately shareable content' (tnooz, 2014).

CHALLENGES OF DIGITAL MARKETING

One downside to the proliferation of online social networking for tourism marketers is the loss of control over the consumer evaluation process (Kim and Hardin, 2010). While reasonable criticisms taken from social networking sites could lead to further improvements in services, consumers can easily distribute damaging information using social media, without the opportunity for companies to resolve consumer complaints. However, it is important that marketers embrace social review sites – even to the extent of publishing negative reviews – as they are a major influence in the decision process for visitors. A recent study by Medallia found that hotel properties that actively engage with social media reviews grow occupancy at double the rate of properties that don't (Hertzfeld, 2015). Hotel companies like Marriott, IHG, Starwood, Wyndham and Accor have started to post guest reviews on their websites, even if it means allowing less-than-glowing opinions. Clay Cowan, Starwood's vice president for global digital said reviews were 'uniquely important in travel, compared to other things that are sold online. There are no trials, no exchanges, no previews,' he said. 'You rely on others who have been there to tell you about it' (Levere, 2014).

Another challenge with social media marketing is measuring the return on investment and its impact on the bottom line. Brands that conduct social media interactions with consumers in a meaningful way are beginning to see a positive return (Cruz and Mendelsohn, 2010; Hudson et al., 2016), but there are too few research studies that can support this claim. One study by Dholakia and Durham (2010) did show a clear relationship between social media engagement and the bottom line. The experiment set up a company's Facebook page and measured the effect on customer behaviour. The partner in this experiment was Dessert Gallery (DG), a popular Houston-based bakery and café chain. The researchers launched a Facebook page and invited everyone on a DG customer mailing list to become a fan. DG updated its page several times a week with pictures of goodies, news about contests and promotions, links to favourable reviews, and introductions to DG employees. Three months later, they resurveyed customers, this time receiving 1,067 responses from DG's Facebook fans, Facebook users who did not become fans, and customers not on Facebook. They analysed the data sets separately and then compared participants in the first survey with those in the second who had become DG fans.

Facebook changed customer behaviour for the better. People who had replied to both surveys and had become fans ended up being DG's best customers. Though they spent about the same amount of money per visit, they increased their store visits per month after becoming Facebook fans and generated more positive word of mouth than non-fans. They went to DG 20 per cent more often than non-fans and gave the store the highest share of their overall dining-out dollars. They were the most likely to recommend DG to friends and had the highest average Net Promoter Score – 75, compared with 53 for Facebook users who were not fans and 66 for customers not on Facebook. DG fans also reported significantly greater emotional attachment to DG – 3.4 on a four-point scale, compared with 3.0 for other customers. Additionally, fans were the most likely to say they chose DG over other establishments whenever possible.

Mulhern (2009) suggests that the digital revolution poses a serious challenge for media companies, agencies, and brand marketers who have constructed a sophisticated infrastructure to send messages to target audiences through media channels, but do not have the mindset or the technical expertise to master the data analysis and modelling of the digital media world. The data analysis (or data mining) is both a challenge and an opportunity for tourism marketers in the digital era. Travel companies have access to mind-boggling data: everything from basic personal information to preferred airline seats, in-flight entertainment preferences, favoured television channels in hotels, meals in restaurants, and credit card usage. They have the means to paint detailed pictures of consumers that will drive marketing initiatives to engage them deeply. Yet few of them truly maximize the potential of the data at their disposal (Carey, Kang and Zea, 2012). Those in the travel sector could follow the example of Amazon, which became the thorn in the side of every bookseller by mining data to craft individualized customer experiences full of conversion-ready streams of recommendations.

Finally, the ability to choose the most effective mix of online and offline marketing channels has become a critical issue for marketers in recent years (see Marketing in Action below). The integration of online marketing within overall marketing strategy is complicated by diversity in current and emerging online applications, and measurement issues. Marketers are aware that traditional communications channels have retained their historically favoured attributes, especially trust and reliability of information (Danaher and Rossiter, 2011). But they are unsure if existing marketing communications models such as advertising persuasion, consumer behaviour, and 'reach, frequency, and impact' apply in online media (Valos, Ewing and Powell, 2010). To accommodate a digital world, scholarly research must adopt new approaches to theory and method. Most of the research about digital media deals with small behavioural questions about online behaviour, and even then the work it often outdated before it is published (Mulhern, 2009). So researchers are beginning to conduct deeper exploration of consumer emotional responses to digital media (see Hudson et al., 2015 for example).

CHAPTER SUMMARY

Technology is having a disruptive impact on marketing communications, and a new consumer decision journey has emerged that has changed how consumers engage with tourism and hospitality providers. This new decision journey is heavily influenced by social media, and as consumers spend more time on social networks, decisions about what to purchase often reflect interactions with friends and other influencers. Some of the challenges of digital marketing include the loss of control for marketers over the evaluation process, and the difficulty of measuring return on investment for social media campaigns.

REFLECTIVE QUESTIONS

1. Take a look at the new consumer decision journey in Figure 3.2. Find an example that is not in the book of a tourism or hospitality provider (or an event) engaging with consumers in the last stage of the journey (enjoy, advocate and bond).

2. The text suggests that one downside to the proliferation of online social networking for tourism marketers is the loss of control over the consumer evaluation process. How can this lack of control be managed?

3. The chapter mentioned that some destination marketers are using virtual reality to communicate with potential tourists. What are the advantages and disadvantages of this from the destination point of view? What about for the consumer?

MARKETING IN ACTION – HAMILTON ISLAND BEST JOB IN THE WORLD CAMPAIGN

Arguably one of the most successful digital/traditional marketing initiatives ever was the 'Best Job in the World' Queensland campaign. In January 2009, Tourism Queensland embarked on a global search to find an Island Caretaker to explore Australia's Great Barrier Reef and report back to the world about the experience.

(Continued)

(Continued)

IMAGE 3.5 Ben Southall (©Tourism and Events Queensland and Ben Southall. Reproduced by permission)

Director of Experience Engagement and Digital Channels for Tourism and Events Queensland, Chris Chambers says it was a marketing campaign that had a strong digital marketing and PR element: 'But there was a great variety of elements that contributed to its success, including trade engagement and newspaper and traditional advertising.'

The job was touted through recruitment adverts placed in 15 countries on 12 January 2009. On offer was a salary of AUD $150,000 for a six month position with live-in luxury accommodation on Hamilton Island and the opportunity to explore all that the region had to offer. Over 34,000 would-be caretakers from all over the world uploaded a 60-second video to demonstrate their creativity, skills and aptitude for the plum job.

From celebrities, writers, tour guides, environmentalists, students, to mums, dads and retirees, everyone was vying for the Best Job in the World, so much so that the submission website was overloaded with visits and video uploads, crashing two days after the launch of the campaign. This was caused, says Chambers, by the tremendous amount of attention the campaign garnered in the Northern Hemisphere. 'The site was launched with three servers hosting, one database server and two servers load balanced to manage the traffic,' he explains. 'Over the first week of the campaign we extended the hosting to eleven servers. Even with this increased hosting in place, there were times the site struggled with the visitation.'

A shortlist of 50 applicants from 22 countries was narrowed down to a final 16 – 15 of these were chosen by Tourism Queensland and the 16th, a 'wild card' applicant Claire Wang from Taiwan, was chosen by popular vote. The job went to ostrich-riding, bungee-jumping charity worker, Ben Southall from Hampshire, England, who was still there in 2011, reporting via blogs on his adventures. 'Being involved in the Best Job in the World campaign was an incredibly exciting, groundbreaking experience from start to finish,' says Southall. 'There had never before been a marketing campaign that had gripped the globe like this. From the unique YouTube application process that received nearly 35,000 entries, through the intense media coverage that followed, to the three-day final on Hamilton Island on the Great Barrier Reef... it was an honour and a total surprise to be there at the last and named the Caretaker of the Islands of the Great Barrier Reef.'

Worldwide media attention included the Oprah Winfrey Show which hosted Southall for a ten-minute slot on the highly popular daytime TV programme, which was broadcast in 140 countries. As well as appearing on the BBC, ABC and CNN and in *Time Magazine* and *Private Eye*, he also made a six-part show for National Geographic, retracing Captain Cook's route from 240 years before and took part in the Australian children's TV show, *Totally Wild*. Via YouTube clips, Facebook, Twitter, online discussion groups, bulletin boards, blogs and websites, social media was heavily utilized to spread the word about the job applications and subsequently Southall's adventures – all of which helped emphasize the allure of Queensland and the Great Barrier Reef as a tourism and lifestyle destination. Three years later British television and newspapers were still covering the story, focusing on the outcomes of the job for Southall in 'where is he now' style articles.

Tourism Queensland claims that the inaugural Best Job in the World campaign generated more than $80m of equivalent media advertising space – for an investment of just $1m (Sweney, 2009). The campaign, developed by the Brisbane-based agency, Nitro, won three top prizes at the Cannes Lions International Advertising Festival in 2009, including the awards for PR, direct marketing and best website and interactive campaign sectors in the Cyber Lions category. It went on to win more awards than any other campaign in 50 years.

Tourism Queensland used much footage from Southall's stint on its blog, *Hello Sunshine*, including Southall's tips on nailing the Hamilton Island video job interview. More jobs on similar lines were developed over the following few years under the tagline 'The Best Jobs in the World', encompassing diverse job titles such as Wildlife Caretaker, Chief Funster, Park Ranger, Taste Master, Outback Adventurer and Lifestyle Photographer.

Capitalizing on his own elevated media profile, Southall subsequently wrote a book, *The Best Job in the World: How to Make a Living from Following Your Dreams* (2014), publicized via his blog and website: www.bensouthall.com/best-job-in-the-world-2009/ and bensouthall.com. 'Since winning the Best Job the consequent doors that have opened to me have allowed me to continue to travel, embark on my own expeditions and pursue a career in adventure television production on both sides of the camera,' says Southall. Now an adventure advocate, digital journalist and presenter, he is also a motivational speaker, presenting around the world at conferences, conventions, university events, charity balls, trade shows and government functions. His Facebook page is consequently entitled 'Best Life in the World': https://www.facebook.com/Bestlifeintheworld. While contributing to this article he was filming a television series in Nepal at Everest Base Camp!

(Continued)

(Continued)

An article in UTalkMarketing.com set the initial Tourism Queensland campaign reach via islandreefjob.com in 2009 at three billion people. Other results included 34,684 video applications from 197 countries; more than 475,000 votes for the Wild Card entrant; in excess of 8,465,280 website visits; 55,002,415 page views; and average time spent on site 8.22 minutes. Social media impact included 378,735 Facebook referrals to islandreefjob.com; 24,782 Twitter referrals and 610 hours of user generated content on islandreefjob.com/YouTube following the application process. All this campaign reach and consumer engagement inevitably led to bookings: over 9,000 visitors from the UK, Ireland and Nordic regions booked Queensland trips in the period following campaign activity. And the total PR value of the initiative was valued at $430 million.

Sources: Email interview with Ben Southall, May 2016 – bensouthall.com and bestlifeintheworld. com; Email interview with Chris Chambers, May 2016; Sweney (2009); Enoch (2012), UTalkMarketing. com (2010).

CASE STUDY QUESTIONS

1. The first line of the case suggests this was 'one of the most successful digital/traditional marketing initiatives ever'. Do you agree? Why or why not?

2. How did Tourism Queensland measure the success of this campaign? Do you see any problems with any of the metrics used?

3. Take a look at what Ben Southall is up to these days. After evaluating his social media activities, what do you think are his goals?

REFERENCES

Adjei, M., Noble, S. and Noble, C. (2010) 'The influence of C2C communications in online brand communities on customer purchase behavior', *Journal of the Academy of Marketing Science*, 38(5): 634–53.

Algesheimer, R., Dholakia, U. M. and Herrmann, A. (2005) 'The social influence of brand community', *Journal of Marketing*, 69: 19–34.

Amadeus (2015) 'Travel infographic – wearable technology and the opportunities for the travel industry', *Amadeus*. http://www.amadeus.com/documents/shaping-the-future-of-travel/Amadeus-Infographic-Wearable-Technology.jpg

Aufreiter, N., Boudet, J. and Weng, V. (2014) 'Why marketers should keep sending you e-mails', *Insights & Publications*, McKinsey & Company, January. www.mckinsey.com/business-functions/marketing-and-sales/our-insights/why-marketers-should-keep-sending-you-emails (accessed 12 December 2016).

Bagozzi, R. and Dholakia, U. (2006) 'Antecedents and purchase consequences of customer participation in small group brand communities', *International Journal of Research in Marketing*, 23(1): 45–61.

Barwise, P. and Meehan, S. (2010) 'The one thing you must get right when building a brand', *Harvard Business Review*, 88(12): 80–4.

Carey, R., Kang, D. and Zea, M. (2012) 'The trouble with travel distribution', *McKinsey Quarterly*, February.

Court D., Elzinga, D. Mulder, S. and Vetvik, O. J. (2009) 'The Consumer Journey', *McKinsey Quarterly*, June. www.mckinsey.com/business-functions/marketing-and-sales/our-insights/the-consumer-decision-journey (accessed 12 December 2016).

Cruz, B. and Mendelsohn, J. (2010) 'Why social media matters to your business', Chadwick Martin Bailey. www.cmbinfo.com/cmb-cms/wp-content/uploads/2010/04/Why_Social_Media_Matters_2010.pdf (accessed 6 December 2016).

Danaher, P. J. and Rossiter, J. R. (2011) 'Comparing perceptions of marketing communication channels', *European Journal of Marketing*, 45(1/2): 6–42.

Dholakia, U. M. and Durham, E. (2010) 'One café chain's Facebook experiment', *Harvard Business Review*, 88(3): 26.

Duke's Fuqua School of Business (2014) 'The CMO survey: Social media spending high, but impact difficult to prove', 3 September. www.fuqua.duke.edu/newscontent/news_releases/cmo-survey-moorman-social-media#.VjoKsRNVikr (accessed 6 December 2016).

eBiz (2014) 'Top 15 most popular social networking sites', *eBiz*, December. www.ebizmba.com/articles/social-networking-websites (accessed 6 December 2016).

Edelman, D. (2010) 'Branding in the digital age', *Harvard Business Review*, 88(12): 62–9.

Edelman, D. and Singer, M. (2015) 'The new consumer decision journey', *McKinsey & Co.*, October. www.mckinsey.com/insights/marketing_sales/the_new_consumer_decision_journey (accessed 6 December 2016).

Eduljee, M. (2010) 'The difference between monitoring and listening to social media', *The Quantum Mousetrap*, 27 November. www.markeduljee.com/the-difference-between-monitoring-and-listening-to-social-media (accessed 6 December 2016).

Enoch, N. (2012) 'Whatever happened to the man who got the best job in the world on a desert island paradise? He worked too hard, lost his girlfriend and got stung by poisonous jellyfish', *Daily Mail Online*, 24 April. www.dailymail.co.uk/news/article-2134388/Ben-Southall-What-happened-man-got-best-job-caretaker-Hamilton-Island.html (accessed 6 December 2016).

Euromonitor (2014) *Trends Shaping Online Travel*. London: Euromonitor International. www.tti.org/assets/files/presentations/2014/Spring2014/Caroline_Bremner_Euromonitor.pdf (accessed 6 December 2016).

Ganguly, S. (2015) 'Why social media advertising is set to explode in the next 3 years', *Marketing Land*, 17 March. http://marketingland.com/social-media-advertising-set-explode-next-3-years-12169 (accessed 6 December 2016).

Hertzfeld, E. (2015) 'Social media boosts hotel occupancy', *Hotel Management*, 24 March. www.hotelmanagement.net/technology/social-media-boosts-hotel-occupancy-30683 (accessed 6 December 2016).

Hudson, S., Huang, L., Roth, M. S. and Madden, T. J. (2016) 'The influence of social media interactions on consumer-brand relationships. A three-country study of brand perceptions and marketing behaviors', *International Journal of Research in Marketing*, 33(1): 27–41.

Hudson, S., Roth, M. S., Madden, T. J. and Hudson, R. A. (2015) 'The effects of social media on emotions, brand relationship quality, and word of mouth: An empirical study of music festival attendees', *Tourism Management*, 47: 68–76.

Karmin, C. (2014) 'The new hotel-room key: Your smartphone,' *Wall Street Journal*, 27 January: B1.

Keller, K. (2009) 'Building strong brands in a modern marketing communications environment', *Journal of Marketing Communications*, 15(2/3): 139–55.

Kim, J. and Hardin, A. (2010) 'The impact of virtual worlds on word-of-mouth: improving social networking and servicescape in the hospitality industry', *Journal of Hospitality Marketing and Management*, 19(7): 735–53.

Korovkin, C. (2016) 'Why event badges will never be the same again. Case study,' *EventMB*, 9 June. www.eventmanagerblog.com/smart-badges-and-networking-results (accessed 6 December 2016).

Kunz, W. and Seshadri, S. (2015) 'From virtual travelers to real friends: Relationship-building insights from an online travel community', *Journal of Business Research*, 68(9): 1822–8.

Lab42 (2012) 'Techie traveler. The behavior of today's tech-based travel aficionado', April. http://blog.lab42.com/techie-traveler (accessed 6 December 2016).

Lecinski, L. (2011) 'Winning the zero moment of truth', *Knowledge@Wharton*, 11 May. https://www.thinkwithgoogle.com/research-studies/2011-winning-zmot-ebook.html (accessed 12 December 2016).

Lee, D., Kim, H. and Kim, J. (2011) 'The impact of online brand community type on consumer's community engagement behaviors: consumer-created vs. marketer-created online brand community in online social-networking web sites', *CyberPsychology, Behavior & Social Networking*, 14(1/2): 59–63.

Levere, J.L. (2014) 'How was your stay? Post it,' *New York Times*, 14 January: B6.

Mathieson, R. (2002) 'The future according to Spielberg: *Minority Report* and the world of ubiquitous computing', *Mpulse Magazine*, August. www.rickmathieson.com/articles/0802-minorityreport.html (accessed 6 December 2016).

Mediakix (2015) 'Social media influencers help travel and hospitality brands reach untapped audiences', *Mediakix*, 5 August. http://mediakix.com/2015/08/travel-hospitality-brands-marketing-with-social-media-influencers/#gs.null (accessed 12 December 2016).

Mosendz, P. and Kawa, L. (2016) 'Pokemon Go brings real money to random bars and pizzerias', *Bloomberg*, 11 July. https://www.bloomberg.com/news/articles/2016-07-11/pok-mon-go-brings-real-money-to-random-bars-and-pizzerias (accessed 12 December 2016).

Mulhern, F. (2009) 'Integrated marketing communications: From media channels to digital connectivity', *Journal of Marketing Communications*, 15(2–3): 85–101.

Palmatier, R. W., Burke, C. B., Bechkoff, J. R. and Kardes, F. R. (2009) 'The role of gratitude in relationship marketing', *Journal of Marketing*, 73: 1547–7185.

Phocuswright (2013) *Ski Traveler Snapshot. US Skier and Ski Traveler Report*, New York: Phocuswright Inc.

Rellihan, K. (2015) 'Travel trends for 2015', travelchannel.com. www.travelchannel.com/interests/hot-topics/articles/travel-trends-for-2015?refcd=n-def&nl=TCN_123114_featlink1&c32=c7e67d6b7c89533e9015acf696e3693075004d36 (accessed 6 December 2016).

Roberti, J. (2011) 'Q&A', *Marketing Week*, 2 June, 29.

SDL (2015) 'Celebrity Cruises, Guinness World Records and Adama Agricultural Solutions improve customer experience with SDL and Building Blocks', 22 July. www.sdl.com/about/news-media/press/2015/sdl-building-blocks-improve-customer-experience.html (accessed 6 December 2016).

Sullivan, E. (2010) 'A group effort', *Marketing News*, 28 February: 22–8.

Sweney, M. (2009) '"Best job in the world" campaign storms Cannes Lions advertising awards', *Guardian*, 23 June. www.guardian.co.uk/media/2009/jun/23/best-job-advertising-awards (accessed 6 December 2016).

tnooz (2014) 'Club Med crowdsources elements of latest ski resort in the French Alps', 18 February. www.tnooz.com/article/Club-Med-crowdsources-latest-ski-resort-in-French-Alps/#sthash.rWKo7nbd.dpuf (accessed 6 December 2016).

tnooz (2016) 'What does Pokemon Go mean for the travel industry?' tnooz, 13 July. https://www.tnooz.com/article/articlewhat-does-pokemon-go-mean-for-the-travel-industry (accessed 6 December 2016).

Trendwatching (2011) *11 Crucial Trends for 2011*. www.trendwatching.com/trends/11trends2011 (accessed 6 December 2016).

Trejos, N. (2014) 'Marriott "teleports" guests to Hawaii, London', *USA Today*, 22 September. www.usatoday.com/story/dispatches/2014/09/22/marriott-hotels-virtual-travel-transporter/15904019 (accessed 6 December 2016).

UTalkMarketing.com (2010) 'Tourism Queensland "Best Job In The World" social media campaign', *UTalkMarketing*, 12 April. www.utalkmarketing.com/pages/article.aspx?articleid=17349&title=tourism_queensland_best_job_in_the_world_social_media_campaign (accessed 12 December 2016).

Valos, M.J., Ewing, M.T. and Powell, I.H. (2010) 'Practitioner prognostications on the future of online marketing', *Journal of Marketing Management*, 26(3–4): 361–76.

Walt Disney World (2011) 'It all started with an "M" and it wasn't "Mouse" but "Moms!" – Disney Parks announces fifth annual Walt Disney World Moms Panel Search'. *PRNewswire*, 13 September.

Weed, J. (2013) 'The "smart" trend in hotels', *New York Times*, 23 April: B5.

THE MARKETING PLAN | 4

INTRODUCTION

The marketing plan serves a number of purposes within any tourism organization: it provides a roadmap for all marketing activities of the firm for the future; it ensures that marketing activities are in agreement with the corporate strategic plan; it forces marketing managers to review and think objectively through all steps in the marketing process; it assists in the budgeting process to match resources with marketing objectives; and it creates a process to monitor actual against expected results. There are eight logical steps in a systematic marketing planning process and this chapter describes each in turn. Case studies in the chapter focus on hotel troubleshooter Michel Goget, the Gentrification of Andermatt, Switzerland, and the Deer Hunt Festival in Winneba, Ghana.

LESSONS FROM A MARKETING GURU: MICHEL GOGET, GLOBETROTTING HOTEL TROUBLESHOOTER

Globetrotter, Michel Goget has had a multifaceted career in hospitality over the past 40 years from chef, to sales and marketing, to general manager. After starting out with

Loews Hotels in Monte Carlo, Monaco in the 1970s, he has worked for Marriott International, Euro Disney Paris, as VP Europe for Dolce International in France, GM for Ritz Carlton International LLC, GM for Ritz Carlton Sanya, Senior Vice President Operations for The World, SVP North America & China for EDL Hospitality, and now back to Ritz Carlton where he is GM at their Chicago property.

Graduating from Florida International University in Miami with a Bachelor of Science degree in International Hotel Management, Goget speaks fluent English, French and has a basic knowledge of Spanish. During his seven-year stint from 2007 to 2014 on China's Hainan Island, Goget was charged with keeping the Ritz Carlton Sanya at the number one position in Hainan Island. He was named 'Outstanding Entrepreneur' by the Sanya City Government and Tourism Bureau and, under his leadership, the hotel earned

IMAGE 4.1 Michel Goget (Courtesy of Michel Goget)

more than 100 awards including the 2012 Ritz Carlton Hotels' Best Hotel Award and Best GM of the Year.

As Senior Vice President, Operations for The World – the largest privately owned residential ship on earth – he was responsible for developing and directing strategic business plans and initiatives for Hotel Operations – including Food & Beverage, Housekeeping, Spa & Wellness Centre, Enrichment, Front Office and Administration – both on board the ship and in the company's corporate office in Fort Lauderdale, Florida.

Semi-retired, he was called back to Ritz Carlton in 2015 to spearhead a marketing plan for their Chicago hotel. 'It is an interesting story. Through August 1 last year, it was a Ritz Carlton but was not affiliated with Ritz Carlton as a company,' says Goget. It was being run by Four Seasons, using their channels of distribution and marketing strategy but still had the Ritz-Carlton name: 'It was a kind of loose situation, the name Ritz Carlton, but run by Four Seasons, confusing for the consumer and an odd situation.'

Extremely successful all the way through the 1990s, it was the first multi-unit complex of its kind in the world, with the luxury hotel, a big shopping centre and 250 units of apartments located right in the heart of Chicago. The first task in rebranding was to instigate a $45 million overhaul in order to bring it up to today's high standards. 'One of the requirements with Ritz Carlton LLC, which operates 92 hotels in the world, is that Ritz Carlton has to appoint the GM,' Goget explains. 'And since I was kind of retired

I was readily available and they needed someone with a lot of experience to transition that property to a Ritz Carlton-branded hotel.' With the first phase of renovation completed in 2016, the second phase was planned for the first part of 2017 – 'by June of next year it will have been given back a bit of that luster of yesteryear and will be in the upper luxury area,' Goget says.

With rivals like the Peninsular and Park Hyatt literally across the street and Trump and the Waldorf Astoria nearby, it is a very competitive market. That's where Goget's expertise and vast experience comes to the fore: 'From a marketing sales point what I'm doing now (and did very successfully in China) is to really position the hotel properly in the market. It's a question of really understanding the market and the way you're being perceived. And I'm going to do that through a very formal exercise in positioning which will take place probably in December and then by early next year we will have the plan.' He intends this clear and thoroughly researched vision to coincide with completion of the hotel's renovations.

Reinforced by Team 1 from Saatchi and Saatchi, the research will involve a $30,000 analysis and in-depth appraisal of the marketplace, bearing in mind the sentiments of customers towards the hotel. Realistically, Goget admits that the hotel had suffered from a lack of focus in more recent years. 'Everyone sees us as a Ritz Carlton and for the average customer it was a Ritz Carlton. A number of loyal, regular customers know it was run by Four Seasons, however. For the majority of our customers we need to prove that we are better than Four Seasons and this will be an interesting process,' he says.

Fundamental to the success of his marketing plan will be a full understanding of the hotel's culture, character and market position, which can then be translated to all stakeholders. Once that is ascertained, Goget will be looking for ways to differentiate it from, and outperform, other rival brands and also communicate this to the world. 'Firstly, find the vision, and then stick to it,' he says. 'It takes two months to lose rate and two years to gain rate.'

Sources: Michel Goget (2012) and (2016).

STEPS IN THE MARKETING PLAN

The opening case study highlights the importance of successful positioning and planning in today's marketing environment. As Michel Goget recognizes, positioning is critical in the hotel sector, as it is in other sectors of tourism and hospitality. In its principles, marketing planning is no more than a logical thought process in which all businesses should engage. It is an application of common sense, as relevant to a small bed-and-breakfast as it is to Ritz Carlton. The term marketing plan is widely used to mean a short-term plan for two years or less. This chapter is devoted to the development of such plans. A strategic marketing plan, on the other hand, is different, as it covers three or more years. A systematic marketing planning process consists of eight logical steps, as outlined in Figure 4.1. For the strategic marketing plan, the first four stages may be more detailed, but any short-term marketing plan should also include an assessment of these steps. Each step feeds into the next one. A marketing plan is not a standalone tool, so the first stage is examining the goals and objectives of the organization as a whole and then developing a marketing plan that will support the company's mission statement, corporate philosophy, and corporate goals. Once the corporate connection has been clarified, the next two stages involve defining the current situation, reviewing the effectiveness of current activities, and identifying opportunities. These are the analysis and forecasting stages. The fourth stage is concerned with defining marketing goals and objectives derived logically from the previous stages of the planning process.

Next, target markets should be selected from the previously developed list of available segments, and once the market has been segmented and a target market identified, the subsequent step in the marketing plan is positioning. Market positioning is ultimately how the consumer perceives the good or service in a given market, and

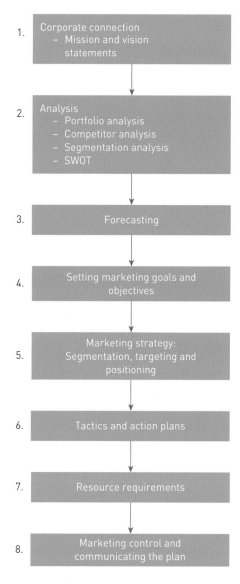

FIGURE 4.1 Marketing planning: an eight-step process

is used to achieve a sustainable competitive advantage over competitors. The sixth stage of the marketing plan involves selecting and developing a series of tactics and action plans that effectively bring about the required results. This part of the plan shows how the organization intends to use the 7 Ps. The marketing plan needs to address the resources required to support the strategies and meet the objectives, and resource requirements are the focus of the plan's seventh stage. The eighth stage of the marketing plan is concerned with marketing control and how objectives will be achieved in the required time, using the funds and resources requested. This final stage of the marketing plan also involves communication, both internally and externally, to achieve maximum impact.

The role played by each section of the marketing plan will now be discussed in more detail.

1. THE CORPORATE CONNECTION

A good marketing plan begins with the fact that the only purpose of marketing is to support the enterprise. Marketing planning should therefore reflect the goals and objectives of the organization as a whole. The mission or vision statement reflects the organization's philosophy, and the goals and objectives as set out in the business plan become the basis of planning for all departments. Marketing's responsibilities in relation to the corporate vision are usually outlined in one or more separate marketing-specific documents. Goals can be defined in terms such as sales growth, increased profitability, and market leadership, whereas objectives are the activities that will accomplish the goals. A vision statement usually answers the question 'What do we want to be?' while the mission statement will answer the question 'What business are we in?' Whereas the vision describes where the organization wants to be in some future time, the mission is a broader statement about an organization's business and scope, goods or services, markets served and overall philosophy.

Vision and mission statements can vary. The mission for adventure travel operator G Adventures, for example, is to empower its customers to help do good in the world by travelling with purpose and leaving a positive impact on the places in which the company operates. Many of its trips offer a unique opportunity to help the underserved communities travellers visit, often through its Planeterra Foundation, an organization founded in 2003 with a focus on social enterprise support and development. By 2015, 25 social enterprise projects were incorporated in the supply chain of G Adventure itineraries with the goal of helping communities more directly and enable them to benefit consistently from tourism. And Founder/Owner Bruce Poon Tip plans to increase that number. 'We're going all in with our social enterprise business model,' said Poon Tip in reference to G Adventure's '50 in 5' campaign. This will see the introduction of 50 new social enterprises into its tours by the end of 2020, ensuring more than 90 per cent of travellers will visit at least one. 'We're celebrating what we've done but also doubling down on our original mission, which is to have positive impact in the places we travel,' he said (Birnbaum, 2015). Poon Tip's goals to reduce poverty through tourism, empower women and help preserve traditional cultures are being helped by the increasing number of travellers who are searching for tour operators that espouse social and environmental priorities.

Another company with a strong mission is Four Seasons Hotels and Resorts, which has been driven by four key pillars put in place decades ago by founder Isadore

IMAGE 4.2 G Adventures CEO, Peru Lares Trek Mountain View (©G Adventures, Inc. Reproduced by permission)

Sharp. The company's first pillar is based on the early decision to manage only mid-sized luxury hotels: 'We will only operate medium-sized hotels of exceptional quality with an objective to be the best,' Sharp emphasizes. He has kept true to his word and, having no other business diversification, has ensured a sturdy brand. The second Four Seasons' core value is about service – 'True luxury will be defined not by architecture or décor, but by service. So we must make the quality of our service our distinguishing feature and a competitive advantage.' Sharp has made a science out of anticipating peoples' needs. Third comes the company's world-renowned culture, based on the simple premise of the 'Golden Rule', which guides employees' actions towards its guests, business partners and with each other. The fourth is brand, reflecting a decision to manage rather than own its hotels: 'We will grow as a management company and build a brand name synonymous with quality.' This credo has always been accompanied by external quality control audits resulting in nearly 300 operating standards which are under regular assessment (Hudson and Hudson, 2013).

2. ANALYSIS

The next stage of the marketing plan is defining the current situation. It is essential that each component of the business be reviewed in order to ensure that resources can be allocated efficiently. Several models exist for reviewing effectiveness and identifying opportunities, but those proven by time and practical application across a range of industries include portfolio analysis, competitor analysis, segmentation analysis, SWOT (strengths, weaknesses, opportunities, and threats) analysis and forecasting.

PORTFOLIO ANALYSIS

Portfolio analysis first became popular in the 1960s, when many organizations sought to improve their profitability by diversifying their activities so as not to keep all their eggs in one basket. The Boston Consulting Group (BCG) model was one of the most popular approaches to evaluating a very diverse group of goods and services, based on long-term planning and economic forecasts. The model adopts the view that every product of an organization can be plotted on a two-by-two matrix to identify those offering high potential and those that are drains on the organization's resources.

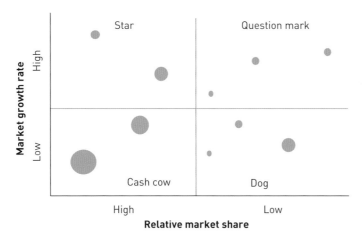

FIGURE 4.2 The Boston Consulting Group (BCG) model

In Figure 4.2, the horizontal axis represents market share, and the vertical axis represents anticipated market growth. High market share means that a business is a leader in that good or service; low market share indicates that either the market-place is heavily competitive or a good or service has not had widespread market acceptance. A good or service can then take up one of four theoretical positions on the model. A cash cow is a product that generates cash and turnover, but the long-term prospects are limited. The company in Figure 4.2 operates two cash-cow businesses. A dog provides neither cash flow nor long-term opportunities and does not hold great promise for improved performance. In the illustration, the company has three dogs.

Stars are products that have a dominant share of a fast-growing market. Although they may not generate a large amount of cash at present, they have potential for high returns in the future. Question marks are fairly speculative products that have high-risk potential. They may be profitable, but because they hold a small market share, they may be vulnerable to competition. Goods or services go through the product life cycle, which can affect where they are positioned on the BCG model. A new product may be in the 'question mark' cell; as it becomes successful it moves into the 'star' category, and then moves on to become a 'cash cow' before it starts to decline and becomes a 'dog'.

A good example of a tourism product that has taken up all four positions in the BCG model is the British Airways Concorde jet airplane. Beginning as a question mark, the delta-winged marvel, a product of 1960s technology and optimism, quickly became a star as business executives and famous celebrities asserted their status by happily spending thousands of dollars to save a few hours of travelling time. The product soon became a cash cow, and more than 2.5 million passengers flew on Concorde airplanes after they entered service in 1976. However, filling the 100 seats on a Concorde became increasingly difficult, and between 2000 and 2003, Concorde could be classified as a dog. In April 2003 it was announced that the supersonic airline run by British Airways and Air France would be retired that year because of slumping ticket sales. But it may not be the end of the story for this product. According to recent reports, a group of Concorde fans ('Club Concorde') has raised $186 million in the hopes of getting a Concorde to fly again by 2019. The group plans to buy two Concorde planes and restore one for flying use and turn the other into a tourist attraction that will reside near the London Eye (Hoeller, 2015).

COMPETITOR ANALYSIS

Information on the number and type of competitors, their relative market shares, the things they do well, and things they do badly will assist in the planning process. Competitor analysis will also highlight market trends and the level of loyalty of consumers. Competitors can be divided into four broad categories: direct competitors offer similar goods and services to the same consumer at a similar price; product category competitors make the same product or class of products; general competitors provide the same service; and budget competitors compete for the same consumer dollars. In addition to the existing competition, there is also the threat of potential competition in the form of new entrants (Porter, 1980).

If one looks at the competitiveness of the ski resorts sector in the US as an example, resorts can be broken into three categories (Hudson and Hudson, 2015). Firstly, there are national resorts that attract people generally from within a state, province, or region within a country. Secondly, there are regional resorts, those that skiers will travel several hundreds of miles to reach. Lastly, there are top-class international destination resorts (three to four hundred in total) that attract skiers from all over the world. In the US the largest ski resort operator, with over a third of the market share, is Vail Resorts Inc. which operates resorts in the US, Canada and beyond. Vail has a real estate and a lodging segment in addition to the mountain segment which includes the six ski resorts of Vail, Beaver Creek, Breckenridge, Keystone, Northstar at Tahoe and Heavenly. In 2014, Vail added Park City Mountain Resort in Utah to its portfolio, and then in 2015 expanded outside of North America by acquiring Perisher in Australia. In 2016 Vail Resorts purchased Whistler Blackcomb in Canada, and then in 2017 added Stowe, Vermont to its portfolio. Other major players in the US include Intrawest Corporation which operates Snowshoe, Steamboat, Stratton and Winter Park Resorts, and Boyne Resorts, a Michigan-based company that operates ten ski resorts in North America. POWDR Corporation is based in Park City, Utah and owns nine resorts in the US including Copper Mountain and Killington in Colorado. Figure 4.3 shows the major players in the US ski industry in 2015 along with their market shares.

To understand relative competitiveness, organizations may often undertake a feature analysis to see if their products and services are better (or worse) than those offered by competitors. For example, when they were developing a new city walks app, New York-based UX Design conducted a feature analysis with four of the top competitors in the travel and event spaces (see Table 4.1). Through this process they were able to identify best practices and areas of opportunity for the new application. For example, finding activities near the user's current location was a feature that most of UX Design's competitors lacked. So UX included this feature within their app to give users the ability to find a walk close to them and quickly.

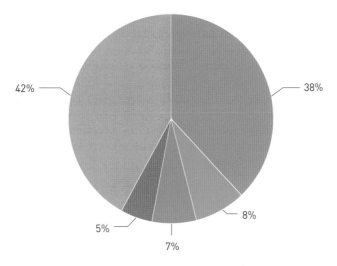

42% — 38%

8%

5% — 7%

FIGURE 4.3 Major players in the US ski industry sector tourism (Source: IBISWorld.com, 2016)

TABLE 4.1 Feature analysis for the walk the walk app (Source: www.xiaohandesign.com/walk-the-walk. ©Xiao Han. All rights reserved. Used with permission)

	YPlan	Guide Pal	TimeOut New York	TimeOut Walks
Categorize by active type	√	√	√	×
Bookmark events for the future	√	×	×	×
Sort by price	√	×	×	×
Sort by topic	√	√	√	×
Editor's pick	√	√	√	×
Tells you how many people are going	√	√	√	×
Can book in app	√	√	×	√
Maps	√	√	√	×
How long to destination/directions	×	√	×	×
Activities near your current location	√	×	×	×
Activities for today and this weekend	√	×	√	×
Curated guides	×	√	√	√
Users can add guides	×	√	×	×
Uber link	×	√	×	×
Rating	√	√	√	×
Comments	√	√	√	×
Expert reviews	×	√	√	×
Invite friends	√	×	×	×
Video for event	√	×	×	×
Guided tours	√	√	√	√
Audio tour	×	×	×	√
Walking tours	√	√	√	√

Key: Yes √ No ×

Michael Porter suggests that there are only three generic strategies for dealing with competition: low-cost leadership, differentiation and focus (Porter, 1980). Low-cost leadership is the simplest and most effective strategy, but it requires large resources and strong management to sustain. A low-cost leadership strategy is used when a firm sets out to become the low-cost producer in its industry. Low-cost producers typically sell a standard, or no-frills, product and place considerable emphasis on reaping scale or absolute cost advantages from all sources. It may be short-lived, as it is easy for competitors to match a low price in an attempt to drive off the challenge. The low-cost airlines that have sprung up all over the world are examples of companies following such a strategy.

Differentiation is a strategy that consists of an innovative technological breakthrough, which can take competitors a long time to imitate. A competitive advantage can be gained by a product that is newer, better and/or faster. The improvement can be in performance, durability, reliability, or service features. Airbus's new 560-ton jet, the A380, carries up to 800 passengers and has differentiated itself from competitors by becoming the world's biggest commercial airliner. A focus strategy concentrates on designing a good or service to meet the needs of one segment of the market better than the competition does. Bruce Poon Tip from G Adventures, mentioned above, follows such a strategy in the adventure tourism business. All three of these generic strategies are based on the organization's creation of a unique position for itself, which distinguishes its offerings from those of its competitors by price, product features, or the way in which it serves the needs of a particular segment. This process, known as 'positioning', is discussed later in this chapter.

SEGMENTATION ANALYSIS

Segmentation analysis refers to the way in which organizations identify and categorize customers into groups defined by similar characteristics and similar needs or desires. The concept of segmentation is widely adopted in tourism marketing, as few companies in the industry attempt to appeal to an entire market. The principles of segmentation are based on the premise that a market can be readily divided into segments for the commercial purpose of targeting offerings. The core advantage of segmentation is that customers will be more satisfied with the product because it has been designed with their needs in mind. Their social needs are also satisfied because they will be mixing with people like themselves and avoiding incompatible types. If an organization knows exactly which segments it wishes to reach, it can select the media most likely to be read, heard, or seen by those consumers, and so spend less on general mass-market advertising. If it knows the lifestyles and attitudes of that segment and the benefits they are seeking from the product, the advertising message can be made more persuasive.

The criteria used most often by tourism and hospitality suppliers to segment the market are as follows.

(a) Demographic segmentation uses the primary variables of age, gender, family life cycle, and ethnicity to segment the markets. UK tour operator Club 18–30, for example, uses age and lifestyle stage variables to segment the holiday market to attract young singles interested in a vibrant nightlife.

(b) Psychographic segmentation divides buyers into different groups based on social class, lifestyle, and personality characteristics. Pyschographics and lifestyle segmentation are based on personality traits, attitudes, motivations, and activities, and were discussed in more detail in Chapter 2. People in the same demographic group can have very different psychographic profiles.

(c) Geographic segmentation is the division of markets according to geographical boundaries, such as countries, provinces/states, regions, cities, or neighbourhoods. In the past, for many DMOs, market segmentation was often limited to understanding the more lucrative international tourist market. However, since the terrorist attacks of 11 September 2001, destination marketers have recognized the significance of local and provincial residents and the impact that they have on tourism receipts (Hudson and Ritchie, 2002).

(d) Benefit segmentation divides customers based on the benefits they desire, such as education, entertainment, luxury, or low cost. Customers weigh different features of a service, and these are evaluated to form the basis of benefit segmentation. Customers of Richard Branson's new Virgin Hotels, for example, will value benefits such as a social lobby scene, displays by local artists, and food from celebrity chefs.

(e) Behaviour segmentation divides the market into groups based on the various types of buying behaviour. Common bases include usage rate (light, medium and heavy), user status (former users, nonusers, potential users, first-time users and regular users of a product), loyalty status (many people stay in five-star hotels as much for the status it confers on them as for the additional comfort), buyer-readiness stage and occasions. On special occasions, people are prepared to pay more for special treatment, so many restaurants now have packages for children's birthday parties, while hotels and cruise lines have special honeymoon suites.

Table 4.2 summarizes the key characteristics of four different generational segments, the Silent Generation, Baby Boomers, Generation X, and Generation Y. The idea of generation, derived from generational theory, has been popularized in America by Strauss and Howe (1997). A generation is usually 20–25 years in length and is defined commonly as an 'aggregate of all people born over roughly the span of a phase of life who share a common location in history and, hence, a common collective persona' (Strauss and Howe, 1997: 61). Due to the same life span, each generation has gone through the same social events and external influences in their formative years, thus creating similar life experiences and perspective. These external events further help mold their core values; and these core values usually do not change significantly during the course of one's life. These generational values are termed as 'peer personality' by Strauss and Howe (1997). As a generation ages, its inner beliefs retain a certain consistency over its life cycle, like that of an aging individual. In Chapter 11, Table 11.1 summarizes previous research on these four generations and their travel behaviour, research that has explored their information sources, online information search and booking behaviour, travel interests, activities preferred and experiences sought.

In sum, the heart of any marketing plan is careful analysis of available market segments and the selection of the appropriate target markets. A common mistake within tourism and hospitality is the selection of inappropriate segments. At one time, Las

TABLE 4.2 The key characteristics of four different generational segments (Reprinted from *Tourism Management*, 37, Li, X., Li, X. and Hudson, S., 'The application of generational theory to tourism consumes behaviour: An American perspective; 147–164, copyright 2013, with permission from Elsevier)

Generations	Silent Generation	Baby Boomer	Generation X	Generation Y
Epochal events/ trends	WWI and WWII The Great Depression The Korean War	The Civil Rights movement The Women's Liberation movement The Vietnam War Landing on the moon The assassination of President John F. Kennedy	The oil crisis of 1973 The end of the Cold War The HIV-AIDS epidemic Corporate downsizing State budget cuts Emerging technology	The fall of the Soviet Union The first Gulf War The rise of the Information Age Widespread use of the Internet
Core values	Conformity equalled success They appreciate discipline, hard work, authority, loyalty and self-denial and overall are socially and financially conservative They distrust change and would prefer the status quo and a major worry to them is outliving their assets. Therefore, they tended to save money and save money now. They are also avid readers, especially of newspapers	With increased educational, financial and social opportunities, the Boomer Generation is often portrayed as a generation of optimism, exploration and achievement In addition, they are the first generation who grew up with and are strongly influenced by television. They value individual choice, community involvement, prosperity, ownership, self-actualizing, and health and wellness	This generation values the entrepreneurial spirit, loyalty, independence, creativity and information. They welcome feedback and adapt well to new situations This generation also values quality of both work and life. While Baby Boomers are working hard to move up the ladder, Generations X-ers are working hard so that they can have more time to balance work and life responsibilities	They are the most globally oriented generation. Generation Y values self-expression. They adapt rapidly, crave change and challenge, and create constantly They are exceptionally resilient, committed and loyal when dedicated to an idea, cause or product In summary, Generation Y is smart, creative, optimistic, achievement-oriented and tech-savvy. They envision the world as a 24/7 place and expect fast and immediate processing
Market share in leisure and business travel (US Travel Association, 2011)	Represent 21% of all leisure travellers and 14% of business travellers	Represent 36% of all leisure travellers and 38% of business travellers	Make up 31% of all leisure travellers and 36% of all business travellers	Make up 12% of leisure travellers and 13% of business travellers
Average number of trips taken (US Travel Association, 2011)	Take an average of 4.1 leisure trips and 6.7 business trips per year	Take an average of 4.2 leisure trips and 7.5 business trips per year	Take an average of 3.5 leisure trips and 6.9 business trips per year	Take an average of 3.9 leisure trips and 4.2 business trips per year
Other travel characteristics (domestic travel) (TIA, 2006)	Tend to take longer trips than other generations, and most likely to travel out of state and region	Generate the most travel in the United States, most likely to travel for business, and are also the most affluent travellers	Generation X is more likely to travel with children than other generations	Generation Yers are more active travellers than their older counterparts

Source: adapted from Li, Li and Hudson (2013).

Vegas tried unsuccessfully to rebrand itself as a family destination, providing pirate and circus themed hotels, funfairs, rides, amusement and games arcades, and animal attractions. Marketers in Vegas have since reverted to attracting more appropriate market segments, with the help of their successful 'What Happens in Vegas, Stays in Vegas' advertising campaign. Market segmentation is a dynamic process because customer trends are not static. It is thus important to carry out regular – preferably continuous – tracking studies to monitor changes happening in the market. One of the most recent trends in tourism and hospitality has been a 'demassification' of the market, in which a greater number of niche markets are replacing the mass ones of the past (Crawford-Welch, 1991). As a result, niche marketing is increasing, whereby products are tailored to meet the needs and wants of narrowly defined geographic, demographic, or psychographic segments. A good example is an Australian wine tourism company called Wine for Dudes, which has successfully targeted the Generation X market. The entrepreneurial company has won many different business and enterprise awards for its innovative concept, service and marketing. Its approach is chatty, cheeky and light-hearted rather than the more snobbish, sophisticated ambience of traditional wine tasting.

SWOT ANALYSIS

SWOT is an acronym for strengths, weaknesses, opportunities, and threats. A SWOT analysis provides scope for an organization to list all its strengths (those things it does best and its positive product features) and its weaknesses (problems that affect its success). These factors are always internally focused on the company itself. For hotels and visitor attractions, location may be a major strength, or the strength may lie in the skills of certain staff members. Strength may also lie in historical artifacts or architectural style, or it may reflect having a particularly favourable consumer image. Once identified, strengths are the basis of corporate positions and can be promoted to potential customers, enhanced through product augmentation, or developed within a strategic framework. Weaknesses, ranging from aging products and declining markets, to surly customer contact staff, must also be identified. Once identified, they may be subject to management action designed to minimize their impact or to remove them where possible. Weaknesses and strengths are often matters of perception rather than 'fact' and may be recognized only through consumer research. Opportunities are events that can affect a business, either through its reaction to external forces or through its addressing of its own weaknesses. Threats are those elements, both internal and external, that could have a serious detrimental effect on a business.

A SWOT analysis is usually best undertaken early in the planning process, and in large organizations a SWOT is often carried out for each division. For example, a convention hotel would conduct a SWOT on the property as a whole, but might also undertake a separate exercise for the functions area, restaurants, retail outlets and recreation facilities. To enhance their own foresight and bring to bear an independent, fresh vision, it is common practice in large market-oriented businesses for managers to commission consultants to carry out regular audits of all aspects of their business, including a SWOT analysis. Destinations will also conduct a SWOT analysis as part of a marketing plan. Myanmar's first Tourism Master Plan, for example, identified a number of strengths and opportunities for Myanmar's tourism industry to build on, constraints to overcome and risks to manage. These can be seen in Figure 4.4.

Strengths

- Tourism is a national priority
- Rapidly increasing visitor arrivals.
- Outstanding historic, natural and cultural heritage.
- Renowned friendliness of Myanmar's people.
- New destination with extensive international media exposure.
- Commitment to effective and efficient Government.

Constraints

- Lack of trained human resources.
- Insufficient public services, infrastructure, and financial systems.
- Weak regulatory environment.
- Insufficient coordination among and between the public and private sectors.
- Lack of accurate tourism information.

Opportunities

- Strategic location between the People's Republic of China and India.
- Robust market demand.
- Increase foreign direct investment and public revenue.
- Deepen regional cooperation.
- Job creation.
- Technology transfer.
- Intercultural exchange with international visitors.

Risks

- Visitor's perception of poor value for money.
- Negative economic, social and environmental impacts.
- Speed of economic reform and liberalization.
- Inappropriate metrics used to measure tourism performance.
- Global economic instability and climate change.
- Natural disasters.

FIGURE 4.4 SWOT for Myanmar's tourism industry (Source: Adapted from Myanmar Tourism Master Plan, 2013)

DIGITAL SPOTLIGHT: FROM HUMBLE TO HEDONISTIC. THE GENTRIFICATION OF ANDERMATT, SWITZERLAND

IMAGE 4.3 Andermatt (Courtesy of Heinz Baumann, Andermatt Holiday Region. Reproduced by permission)

An Egyptian-born billionaire developer, Samih Sawiris hatched a daring plan to transform humble Andermatt in Switzerland into a year-round resort. After a helicopter tour of the central Swiss mountainous area in 2005, he mapped out ski hill improvements as well as a blueprint for 25 top-notch chalets, six hotels, an indoor pool, an 18-hole golf course and a chain of 490 condominiums across 42 buildings. With a dwindling population of around 1,400, the former army town had been struggling economically, with many younger residents migrating elsewhere for job opportunities.

Sawiris's global real-estate company, Orascom Development Holding AG, kickstarted the $2 billion gentrification project by purchasing around 345 acres of developable land, on which his Swiss company, Andermatt Swiss Alps AG, is now realizing the project. Already popular with off-piste skiers, the pretty village was surrounded by a varied and challenging ski area on the 2,961-metre Gemsstock Mountain. While these predominantly Dutch, Scandinavian and local expert skiers were content to hike to fresh snow, much of the new ski infrastructure development would focus on improving the inbounds ski area, opening up the appeal to every level of skier and snowboarder.

Ecosign was responsible for the ski hill structure plan with stakeholders, Andermatt Gotthard Sportbahnen, the Sedrun Bergbahnen, the Matterhorn-Gotthard-Bahn and Andermatt Swiss Alps all working closely together. Plans included construction of a gondola and two six-seater chairlifts and extensive snowmaking installations. Work started on these aspects in summer 2015 with the first of two chairlifts opening for the 2014/15 ski season and the second for 2016/17, making it the largest Swiss ski resort development at the time.

In any resort development, community collaboration is key and this is where Sawiris excelled. At a town gathering, he got locals on board by presenting his plans to bring hundreds of jobs to the area. He worked with local farmers and town-dwellers in decision-making forums, listening to and adopting ideas for traffic rerouting, building heights, land use and financial compensation. The village voted overwhelmingly for the project in March 2007.

Breaking ground on 26 September 2009, the blueprints called for a modern design to blend with Andermatt's traditional cobblestone alleys and rustic wooden chalets. Financing for the development came from presales, from Orascom and from a $160 million personal investment by Sawiris, said Marta Falconi in a 2013 article for the *Wall Street Journal*. Falconi said it was a 'risky venture'. Competition was coming from other developments around Switzerland including nearby Lake Lucerne. 'The developer struggled one and a half years ago to keep up the project's timetable and cash flows, prompting some investors to swoop in,' said Falconi. 'One of them, Hans-Peter Bauer, a co-founder of the Swiss Finance & Property AG real-estate firm, bought 72 units for about $135 million.' Bauer, who sat on the board of Andermatt Swiss Alps, was responsible for pitching the resort to overseas investors in Singapore, Hong Kong and Russia. Unlike most Swiss resorts – which are subject to the Lex Koller law which drastically limits foreign investment – the Sawiris project in Andermatt is exempt and is targeting markets in Switzerland, Germany, United Kingdom, Italy and overseas.

Alongside ski lift redevelopment, Andermatt Swiss Alps focused on real estate development and – together with local authorities – planned improvements in water systems, roads and a train station facelift. No extra retail or restaurant facilities were planned at the initial stages although future phases would allow this. Most of the resort

(Continued)

(Continued)

was designed to be car-free, facilitated by new underground parking structures. One of the major town centre improvements was the five-star, deluxe flagship, the Chedi Andermatt Hotel launched in time for the 2013–14 ski season. Offering private ownership as well as overnight stays in 48 rooms, the high-end hotel combines traditional region values with the vision of a luxury, state-of-the-art holiday destination. 'In time for winter season 2014/15 the condominiums of the first two apartment houses of the new resort were handed over to their owners and put on the rental market,' says Markus Berger. 'Whenever the owners are not using the condos for themselves, they will be let to vacationers.' By the following ski season a total of almost 70 apartments would be available to skiers in the new Andermatt resort. Three or four further condo buildings as well as a second hotel were scheduled for completion by 2017, Berger adds: 'In summer 2016 the brand new championship standard golf course – 18 holes, par 72 – will see its official opening after having been played in two preopening seasons by hundreds of enthusiastic golfers.'

As Head of Communication for Andermatt Swiss Alps AG, Markus Berger is integral in the marketing of the ambitious project which has hit the headlines many times since the massive renovation was launched. In 2016, Berger was focusing on the launch of a new, more attractive website as well as securing wider coverage in the media. 'All the important steps are communicated via press release and shortly after seen on online platforms and in print. Of course they are all also posted and shared over social media,' he explains. In terms of digital marketing, the resort is developing an increasing range of networks. 'Facebook and Twitter are at the moment the main channels that we use,' Berger says. 'Instagram is about to kick off and we will also "feed" YouTube a bit more often. We have a weekly blog and Pinterest.' Andermatt's golf and rental properties are on Tripadvisor, he adds, and rental also gets feedback on Booking.com. A newsletter is sent out once a month as well as a bilingual (German and English) and half-yearly guest magazine *DER ANDERMATTER*, reinforced with an online version. Other marketing tools include the Andermatt Holiday Region's downloadable app that allows push-notification.

By transforming Andermatt into a highly competitive, all-season destination, Sawiris planned to create a stable, growing local community. 'This project brought new life to this place,' confirmed Andermatt Mayor, Roger Nager in an article for the *Wall Street Journal* in 2013.

Sources: Communications with Markus Berger, Head Communication for Andermatt Swiss Alps AG 2013 and 2016; Falconi (2013); Hide (2014).

CASE STUDY QUESTIONS

1. Looking at the eight steps in the marketing planning process, what steps would you say has Andermatt completed with flying colours?

2. Who were the key stakeholders responsible for transforming Andermatt into a highly competitive, all-season destination? List them in order of importance.

3. What particular segments of the travelling population would be attracted to the 'new' Andermatt?

3. FORECASTING

Because information is never perfect and the future is always unknown, no one right conclusion can ever be drawn from the evidence gathered in the SWOT process. As a result, forecasting becomes an important stage in the planning process to support a SWOT. The Myanmar Tourism Master Plan (2013), referred to above, forecast 3.01 million international visitors in 2015 and 7.48 million in 2020. Based on this high-growth scenario, tourism receipts were projected to increase from a baseline of $534 million in 2012 to $10.18 billion in 2020, with the number of tourism-related jobs rising from 293,700 to 1.49 million. Forecasting is market research-based but future-oriented, and it relies on expectations, vision, judgment and projections for factors such as sales' volume and revenue trends, consumer profiles, product profiles, price trends and trends in the external environment. Because the future for tourism and hospitality products is subject to volatile, unpredictable factors and competitors' decisions, the goal of forecasting is not accuracy but careful and continuous assessment of probabilities and options, with a focus on future choices. Forecasting recognizes that most marketing-mix expenditure is invested months ahead of targeted revenue flows. Since marketing planning is focused on future revenue achievement, it is necessarily dependent upon skill, judgment, foresight and realism in the forecasting process.

There are two main sets of forecasting techniques: qualitative and quantitative. Qualitative techniques are those that seek to estimate future levels of demand, based on detailed subjective analysis. They include sales staff estimates, senior management opinions and buyers' intention surveys. Two more sophisticated qualitative techniques are the Delphi technique and scenario planning. The Delphi technique involves obtaining expert opinions about the future prospects for a particular market without the experts actually meeting or necessarily knowing at any stage the composition of the panel. Long-term scenario planning is undertaken by larger organizations such as hotel or airline companies. This is a systematic attempt to predict the composition of the future market environment in 10–25 years' time and the likely impacts on the company.

Quantitative techniques rely on analysis of past and current data. In some instances this implies the simple projecting of future demand in terms of past trends, and in other instances unravelling casual determinants needs to be considered. A number of well-tested methods are used; however, most require a degree of statistical ability. Time-series, noncausal techniques involve the forecasting of future demand on the basis of past trends. Causal methods attempt to show, by using regression analysis, how some measure of tourism demand is influenced by selected variables other than time. Finally, computer simulations are becoming more popular – trend-curve analysis and multiple regressions are combined mathematically to generate a computer model that simulates tourism demand.

4. SETTING MARKETING GOALS AND OBJECTIVES

Goals are the primary aims of the organization, and objectives the specific aims that managers try to accomplish to achieve organizational goals. Goals can be defined in terms of sales growth, increased profitability and market leadership. Objectives are the activities that will accomplish the goals. For example, the goal of sales growth for a hotel could become an objective of a 20 per cent increase in accommodation sales and a 30 per cent increase in food and beverage sales. The goal of increased profitability could be translated into objectives of a 15 per cent increase in profits across the board, and a goal of market leadership could be translated into objectives for each city in which a hotel chain operates.

Marketing objectives at the tactical level derive logically from the previous stages of the planning process. Middleton and Clarke (2012) suggest that to be effective and actionable in practice, tactical marketing objectives must be:

(a) integrated with long-term corporate goals and strategy;

(b) precise and quantified in terms of sales volume, sales revenue, or market share;

(c) specific in terms of which products and which segments they apply to;

(d) specific in terms of the time period in which they are to be achieved;

(e) realistic and aggressive in terms of market trends (revealed in the situation analysis) and in relation to budgets available;

(f) agreed and endorsed by the managers responsible for the programmes of activity designed to achieve results; and

(g) measurable directly or indirectly.

If these criteria are not fully reflected, the objectives will be less than adequate for achieving the success of the business, and the marketing programmes will be harder to specify and evaluate. The more thorough the previous stages of the marketing plan, the easier the task of specifying precise objectives. To ensure profitability and to remain competitive in today's marketplace, it has become necessary to establish several sub-objectives. For instance, a thousand-room hotel will undoubtedly have two broad objectives: average occupancy and average room rate. By themselves, these objectives do not serve as sufficient guides for developing marketing strategies. A set of sub-objectives might therefore include occupancy per period of time, the average room rate by type of room, and annual sales by each salesperson. Each marketing support area needs to be guided by a set of sub-objectives. This includes areas such as advertising, promotion, public relations, market research and sales.

It is important to acknowledge that objectives may not always be profit-based. The main objective for Cheddar Caves and Gorge, one of Britain's oldest and most popular tourist attractions, for example, is conservation. The 300 acres in the southwest of England, are owned by the Marquis of Bath's family trust, which also owns Longleat House, and are operated through a private limited company, Longleat Enterprises Ltd. While activities have to be self-financing, the main objective is to protect the fragile environment rather than to make money. The attraction is an L-shaped 300-acre land-holding comprising the whole of the south side of Cheddar Gorge, about 50 caves (including two Showcaves which are Scheduled Ancient Monuments), Britain's highest inland limestone cliffs, a grassland plateau of great ecological significance, and various car parks, buildings and man-made attractions. More than 500,000 visitors a year spend time at Cheddar Gorge.

IMAGE 4.4 Map of Cheddar Caves and Gorge (Used with permission of Cheddar Caves and Gorge)

5. MARKETING STRATEGY: TARGETING AND POSITIONING

TARGETING

No area of the marketing plan surpasses the selection of target markets in importance. If inappropriate markets are selected, marketing resources will be wasted. High-level expenditures on advertising or sales will not compensate for misdirected marketing effort. Target markets should be selected from a previously developed list of available segments. These include segments currently served by the organization and newly recognized markets. A target market is simply the segment at which the organization aims its marketing message. Implicitly, the nonprofitable customers should be given less attention. A target market generally has four characteristics. It should comprise groups of people or businesses that are well-defined, identifiable and accessible; members should have common characteristics; they should have a networking system so that they can readily refer the organization to one another; and they should have common needs and similar reasons to purchase the product or service. One key target market for the new Virgin brand of hotels is the female business traveller. The hotels emphasize safety with separate room chambers to accept deliveries and good lighting in the corridors. On the convenience side, rooms offer extra closet space, drawers for makeup and supplies and larger showers with a bench that makes it easier for guests to shave their legs.

The family market is also a popular target market for many tourism organizations. Family travel is growing as more parents are choosing to share travel experiences with their children. Club Med is a good example. Once known for its ability to cater to young singles, it now has more than 80 family-friendly holiday villages worldwide. Portuguese-based Martinhal, profiled in Chapter 11, is another example of a company focusing on families. Co-founder Chitra Stern, saw an opportunity in young professionals with children wanting something 'more sophisticated than Disneyland'. Targeting families at the luxury end of the market, Martinhal provides everything that well-heeled parents might look for during their holiday in terms of childcare, kids' activities, food and facilities in a refined and artfully designed environment.

Other tour operators are choosing to target the Baby Boomers specifically. This sector, born between 1946 and 1964, generates the highest travel volume in North America, and is a very attractive market for the tourism and hospitality industry. Bumps for Boomers, an Aspen ski company, has successfully targeted this market, providing ski clinics just for this age group. Joe Nevin, founder of the company, first defined his target market back in 2003, deciding to focus on boomers due to their sheer numbers. 'In 1962 there were four million skier days in the US. Currently there are approximately 60 million skier days,' he says. 'That growth was fueled entirely by the boomer demographic. These are folks who started skiing when they were young, got married and introduced their families to skiing and now the children of their children are being introduced to the sport. Skiing has become a family theme full of great memories and boomers want to continue skiing into their later years and continue to make memories with their family members' (Hudson, 2011).

The LGBT tourism (lesbian, gay, bisexual and transgender) market is another segment that is growing in significance for the tourism industry. The annual economic impact of LGBT travellers is over $100 billion per year in the US alone (CMI, 2014). Around 29 per cent of LGBT participants are frequent leisure travellers, taking five or more leisure trips per year, with ten or more leisure hotel room nights per year. The ski industry has been successful in targeting this market. Whistler in Canada, for example, hosts the Whistler Pride and Ski Festival, one of the biggest gay and lesbian weeks in North America (Image 4.5 below). The event features eight days of skiing, snowboarding, parties, comedy nights and social events. Other North American resorts hosting gay ski events include Aspen and Telluride in Colorado, Stowe in Vermont, and Park City in Utah. Elsewhere, European Gay Ski Week and European Snow Pride are held each year in the French Alps, while Gay Snowhappening is held in Solden in Austria.

IMAGE 4.5 Whistler Pride parade (©Jackson photografix/GayWhistler.com)

POSITIONING

Once the market has been segmented and a target market identified, the next step in the marketing plan is positioning. Positioning is a communications strategy that is a natural follow-through from market segmentation and target marketing. Market positioning is ultimately how the consumer perceives the product or service in a given market, and is used to achieve a sustainable competitive advantage over competitors. Four Seasons Hotels and Resorts, mentioned a few times in this chapter, has always had a distinctive positioning strategy leading to global competitive success. Founder Isadore Sharp's 'Golden Rule' has given Four Seasons a remarkable record of customer service excellence for half a century. In his quest to be tops for service, Sharp's modus operandi is to 'treat others as you wish to be treated yourself' and this considerate culture has permeated all levels of Four Seasons' personnel.

Three steps are necessary to develop an effective position in the target market segment: product differentiation; prioritizing and selecting the competitive advantage; and communicating and delivering the position.

STEP 1: PRODUCT DIFFERENTIATION

Product differentiation, a phrase coined by Michael Porter, describes a technique that enables organizations to seek to gain competitive advantage by offering a product that has features not available in the offerings of competitors. Product differentiation has the potential to assist companies in gaining a competitive edge and can distinguish them from competitors by offering competitive advantages. A competitive advantage offers greater value to the consumer by providing benefits that justify a higher price. These advantages can be established through product attributes, features, services, level of quality, style and image, and price range. The key elements will shape how the consumer perceives the product. Physical attribute differentiation is achieved by enhancing or creating an image in the consumer's mind through tangible evidence. For example, Quality Inn offers a very simple physical appearance, communicating a clean, safe, cheap place to sleep. Fairmont Hotels & Resorts, on the other hand, combines an elaborate exterior with a luxurious interior to inspire feelings of comfort, relaxation and prestige.

Service differentiation is an increasingly important way of gaining competitive advantage. Service quality has been more frequently identified as a key factor in differentiating service products and building a competitive advantage in tourism. The process by which customers evaluate a purchase, thereby determining satisfaction and likelihood of repurchase, is important to all marketers, but especially to services marketers because, unlike their manufacturing counterparts, they have fewer objective measures of quality by which to judge their production (Zeithaml, Berry and Parasuraman, 1988). Service differentiation is explored in more detail in Chapter 10.

STEP 2: PRIORITIZING AND SELECTING THE COMPETITIVE ADVANTAGE

Positioning is much like a ranking system, and an organization must decide where it wants to be in the hierarchy. Some companies have an image of high quality, service and price – others, of being low budget. Neither image is better or worse. However, once the position is established, it is very difficult to change it in the consumer's mind. Therefore, companies must be very cautious in selecting the most effective combination of competitive advantages to promote and to contribute to building their positioning strategy.

It is important to promote not only one benefit to the target market, but to develop a unique selling proposition (USP), a feature of a product that is so unique that it distinguishes the product from all other products. The goal of a USP is for a company to establish itself as the number one provider of a specific attribute in the mind of the target market. The attribute chosen should be desired and highly valued by target consumers. If the marketing mix elements build the brand and help it to connect with the customer year after year, the total personality of the brand, rather than the trivial product differences, will decide its ultimate position in the market. Although it is difficult in the tourism industry to find an effective USP in such a competitive and free market, it is essential to offer something new. Package holidays tend to offer similar deals, with only minor differences. Therefore, it is important for a company to create a new good, service, or benefit that can be offered to consumers by that company alone. UK tour operator Crystal Holidays, for example, recently equipped 700 overseas personnel with iPads loaded with custom-built software enabling predeparture video calls with customers, as well as online information packs complete with in-depth advice and resort tips. This new technology also facilitates snow reports and advance ski and boot orders to eradicate lengthy queuing in rental outlets.

STEP 3: COMMUNICATING AND DELIVERING THE POSITION

The final goal of an organization in the positioning process is to build and maintain a consistent positioning strategy. The overall aim of tourism providers is to attract attention from potential customers and to delight them with product offerings that cannot be beaten by competitors. Programmes and slogans that support the organization's position must be continuously developed and promoted in order to establish and maintain the organization's desired position in the consumer's mind. Quality, frequency and exposure in the media will determine how successful the positioning strategy will be.

Tourism and hospitality providers try to differentiate their products by using branding, a method of establishing a distinctive identity for a product based on competitive differentiation from other products. Branded products are those whose name conjures up certain images – preferably positive ones – in consumers' minds. These images may relate to fashion, value, prestige, quality or reliability. Image is an important element of customer perception. If a hotel chain has an image of quality, staying at the hotel will provide benefits to business customers who want to project a successful image to their clients or colleagues. Some brands are recognized for their reliability. It is comforting for many travellers, for example, to know that a Best Western property will meet certain standards, and that selecting one will be a reliable choice, even if the traveller is unfamiliar with the specific property or region. Hotels, in particular, brand specific properties within their group to identify different categories of product. (See Chapters 5 and 8 for more information on branding.)

6. TACTICS AND ACTION PLANS

Although no single strategy will be suitable for all organizations, marketing planning provides the opportunity to understand the operating environment and to choose options that will meet the organization's goals and objectives. Planning involves selecting and developing a series of strategies that effectively bring about the required results. Among the types of strategies that can be considered are:

(a) Making good investment decisions. Selecting the best, most effective use of financial resources is crucial. This will include reviewing the product's life cycle and doing a portfolio analysis.

(b) Diversifying. While it is important to ensure that resources are allocated to those markets showing the best potential yields, the possibility of disruptions to markets must also be taken into account. Diversification can provide an important cushion.

(c) Planning for the long term. Tourism marketing campaigns can have long lead times. The cumulative effect of promotions may take a while to produce measurable results. Building effectiveness over time is just as important as generating instant results.

(d) Seizing new opportunities. Being aware of consumer trends, fads, fashions and attitudinal shifts will also help an organization to identify opportunities. Being flexible enough to respond to market developments will give an organization a strong competitive edge.

(e) Developing strategic partnerships. It is important to identify customers, suppliers, and competitors with whom it is possible to develop an enhanced working relationship. Strategic alliances offer the opportunity to increase profits for all participants.

Marketing strategies are designed as the vehicle to achieve marketing objectives. In turn, marketing tactics are tools to support strategies. Action programmes comprise a mix of marketing activities that are undertaken to influence and motivate buyers to choose targeted volumes of particular products. This part of the marketing plan shows how the organization intends to use the marketing mix. The marketing mix is the mixture of controllable marketing variables that the firm uses to pursue sales in the target market. The original four Ps of the marketing mix, introduced in the 1960s are product, place, promotion and price. Because services are usually produced and consumed simultaneously, customers are often part of the service production process. Also, because services are intangible, customers will often be looking for any tangible cue to help them understand the nature of the service experience. These facts have led service marketers to conclude that they need to use additional variables to communicate with and satisfy their customers. Acknowledgement of the importance of these additional variables has led service marketers to adopt the concept of an expanded marketing mix for services, so in addition to the traditional four Ps, the services marketing mix includes people, physical evidence, and process.

Table 4.3 shows the activities that should be included in this section of the marketing plan. A marketing mix programme or marketing campaign expresses exactly what activities will take place in support of each identified product/market subgroup on a week-by-week basis.

In 2009, recognizing that Ghana had not realized its full potential as a tourism destination, the Ghanaian government produced a tourism marketing plan, with

TABLE 4.3 Specific strategies included in the action plan

Strategies	Marketing mix elements (Ps)
Product strategies	Product Physical evidence Process
Pricing strategies	Price
Distribution strategies	Place
Advertising strategies	Promotion
Sales promotion and merchandising strategies	Promotion
Public relations strategies	Promotion
Sales strategies	Promotion
Direct marketing strategies	Promotion
Internet marketing strategies	Place Promotion
Internal marketing strategies (personnel, managing service quality, etc.)	People Process

the goal of attracting one million tourists by 2012. The action plans put in place to achieve this goal can be seen in Table 4.4, and were centred around four themes: developing its tourism proposition; building the brand inside; building the reputation of Ghana as a 'must see' destination; and improving accessibility to the country. The plan was successful – by 2012, 1,263,857 international tourists spent US$2.5 billion in the country, confirming the sector as the fourth largest export after gold, cocoa and remittances.

TABLE 4.4 The action plans for Ghana tourism (Source: Adapted from the Ghana Tourism Authority, 2009)

1. Ghana needs to develop its tourism proposition (product improvement and development).	2. Ghana needs to build the brand inside
Develop receptive facilities for use by travellers	Undertake internal marketing communications of Ghana's tourism proposition
Enforce law on establishing places of convenience at rest stops	Source and shortlist agencies
Train staff at entry points on importance of tourism and customer care	Brief agencies and hold pitching sessions
Install modern toilet facilities at tourist attractions, airports and borders	Appoint and brief the selected agency
Install tourist signage to direct tourists to attractions, using international symbols and colours	Develop a multimedia integrated communications programme
Provide disposal bins at attractions, to ensure that sites are kept clean	Make an interim presentation to GTB/GHATOF
Develop proposals to make the tourist attractions more exciting	Finalize the approval of the internal communications campaign
Conduct research and development into other attractions that deserve to be included in the directory of world heritage sites	Roll out the internal communications campaign
Improve capacity for monitoring and evaluating tourism development by establishing robust information systems	Conduct tourism outreach programs at primary, JHS and SHS schools
Conduct training and develop needs assessment for the entire industry	Lobby GES to include tourism in the curriculum of schools
Develop training policy for the industry	Develop tourism programs on television; quiz shows on radio, etc.
Develop minimum requirements for different job positions, so that service providers have the requisite professional backgrounds	Set up schools tourism website where schoolchildren can write about their experiences at tourist attractions, and post their pictures
Coordinate training of tourism personnel. This will include in-house training, external training, targeted skills, workshops, conferences, etc.	Organize familiarization visit for domestic journalists
Establish a Human Capital Monitoring Department within GTB or MOT to monitor the development of the human resources within the industry	

(Continued)

TABLE 4.4 (Continued)

3. Ghana needs to build a reputation as a 'must see' tourist destination in West Africa	4. Ghana needs to improve accessibility to the country
Organize familiarization visit for international travel journalists	Set up committee to review the online utilization of the hospitality sector, especially of hotels and tour operators
Undertake external marketing communications	Ensure that hotels and tour operators have corporate websites
Source and shortlist agencies	Participate in key industry fairs and exhibitions, e.g. ITB and WTM
Brief the agencies and hold pitching sessions	Lobby government to revise/simplify visa regime, and upgrade tourism infrastructure
Appoint and brief the selected agency	Develop an annual directory of qualified and accredited operators in the industry
Agency to develop multimedia integrated communications programme	Visit major tour operators in targeted source countries (not during exhibitions)
Interim presentation to GTB/GHATOF	Explore opportunities to get on to global online platforms such as PayPal and ixeo.com
Give final approval of internal communications campaign	
Roll out external communications campaign	
Appoint internet marketing consultant to advise on online strategy	
Review Touringghana website against SEO benchmarks	
Implement online strategy	
Development of tourism collaterals. These includes videos, photographs and high-quality brochures (for give-aways and downloads)	
Get international sports personalities like Michael Essien and Sulley Muntari to wear Ghana branded T-shirts under their club strips	
Set up representative offices in major source countries	
Set up information desks at foreign missions	
Organize tours of Ghana for information desk representatives at foreign missions and representative offices	
Develop crisis management strategy	

7. RESOURCE REQUIREMENTS

The marketing plan needs to address the resources required to support the marketing strategies and meet the objectives. Such resources include personnel, equipment and space, budgets, intra-organizational support, research, consulting and training. A common error in writing a marketing plan is developing strategies that are probably highly workable but for which there is insufficient support. Generally, the most costly and difficult resource needed to ensure the success of marketing/sales strategies in tourism and hospitality businesses is personnel. Management commonly views the addition of personnel as unnecessary, impractical, or unwise, given budgetary restrictions.

Of prime importance in analysing resource requirements is the budget. Setting a budget that provides the marketing department with sufficient resources to deliver its plan is essential. However, in most organizations, various departments compete for funds, and it is not always easy to convince management that the marketing budget should have a priority claim in limited funds. Although this is less of an issue in commercially oriented organizations, it can be a major problem in arts and entertainment organizations and nonprofit groups. The idea of spending money on marketing (which is frequently not viewed as a core activity) at the expense of collections, maintenance, acquisitions, or expanding performance programmes is often a very contentious issue.

8. MARKETING CONTROL AND COMMUNICATING THE PLAN

The final step in the planning process is to ensure that objectives will be achieved in the required time, using the funds and resources requested. In order to measure effectiveness, evaluation programmes have to be put in place, and regular monitoring needs to occur. There is little value in preparing a one-year marketing plan and including an evaluation methodology that commences towards the end of the operating year. This will not allow enough time to identify potential problems or initiate remedial action.

Because objectives have been set in quantifiable terms, regular reviews of sales' forecasts and quotas, assessments of expenditure against budget, and data collection and analysis will provide guidance on how well objectives are being met. If a problem arises, contingency plans can be activated. Effective contingency plans are considered long before emergencies or problems arise. Reacting under pressure is rarely as effective as preplanning. If, as part of the original process, alternatives are considered, it is more likely that they will be successful. The most important reason for insisting on precision in setting objectives is to make it possible to measure results. Such results for a tourism business might be flow of bookings measured against planned capacity, enquiry and sales response related to any advertising, customer awareness of advertising messages calculated by research surveys, sales response to any price discounts and sales promotions, sales response to any merchandising efforts by travel agents, consumer use of websites and flow of bookings achieved and customer satisfaction results.

Most marketing plans are written to cover a one-year action plan in detail, with references made to the longer term – traditionally three years and five years. While the corporate goals may be longer-term (often as long as 10 or 20 years), the actual objectives are usually defined in terms of a much shorter time frame. Some organizations base their marketing plans on their funding cycles. Some art organizations or government departments on three-year funding cycles prepare business and marketing plans that cover the full funding period. Even these, however, stress the importance of regular review and reevaluate their action plan sections on a 12-month basis.

Involving as many staff members as possible in the process of setting objectives and drawing up plans that communicate well is an important aspect of motivating staff at all levels and securing enthusiastic participation in the implementation process. This involvement is a subject of increasing attention in many tourism and hospitality organizations (Middleton and Clarke, 2012). It is especially important for service businesses, in which so many staff members have direct contact with customers on the premises. It is a good idea to time the stages in marketing planning so that managers and as many staff as possible in all departments can take some part in initiating or commenting on draft objectives and plans. Motivation can be damaged if objectives are continuously changed or if there is no opportunity to debate their practicality in operation. While marketing planning is conducted primarily to achieve more efficient business decisions, its secondary benefit is to provide a means of internal participation and communication, vital in creating and sustaining a high level of organizational morale.

Marketing plans must be sold to many people. Internally, these include members of the marketing and sales department, vendors and advertising agencies, and top management. Marketing plans are also important in communicating with stakeholders outside the company. Approaching banks or other investors – for example in tourism projects funded by government sources – invariably requires a business plan in which marketing is a primary component. Where money is granted, evidence of results will be required through a formal evaluation process. In terms of presenting the report, many readers, both inside and outside the organization, will be impatient and will want the conclusions immediately. The executive summary is therefore a key section of the report. Indeed, it can be assumed that some staff – and perhaps senior executives and board members – will read only the executive summary. In general, an executive summary should be between two and six pages. It should avoid the use of jargon, and it should highlight the key objectives and action aspects of the plan and budget, leaving the analysis of current situations and detailed market analyses for the main document.

CHAPTER SUMMARY

A marketing plan serves a number of purposes within any tourism organization: it provides a roadmap for all marketing activities of the firm for the future; it ensures that marketing activities are in agreement with the corporate strategic plan; it forces marketing managers to review and think objectively through all steps in the marketing process; it assists in the budgeting process to match resources with marketing objectives; and it creates a process to monitor actual against expected results. There are eight logical steps in a systematic marketing planning process:

the corporate connection, analysis, forecasting, setting marketing goals and objectives, marketing strategy, tactics and action plans, resource requirements, and marketing control and communicating the plan.

REFLECTION QUESTIONS

1. Choose a large tourism or hospitality enterprise you are familiar with and apply the BCG matrix (Figure 4.2) to the various products and services on offer. Does the organization have a balanced portfolio?

2. The chapter highlights a number of target markets growing in attractiveness for the tourism industry. Segment the tourists that your region attracts. Are there any segments of the travel market that are not being targeted? Why not?

3. Go out and find a marketing plan from a tourism organization in your area. Does it follow the eight steps of the planning process outlined in this chapter? If not, how is it different?

MARKETING IN ACTION: THE DEER HUNT FESTIVAL, WINNEBA, GHANA

Ghana may not be top of the global tourism charts as yet, but one area has plans for the near future to secure niche markets via eco- and cultural tourism based around a singular sporting event.

According to an Oxford Business Group article (2016), the World Travel and Tourism Council (WTTC) has forecast that Ghana's economy would grow by an annual average of 4.5 per cent between 2014 and 2024, with tourism and travel contributing around 3 per cent GDP in 2024. The article suggests, though, that increasingly active tourism authorities in Ghana hope to accelerate this growth well beyond the forecast.

IMAGE 4.6 Deer Hunt Festival

This is certainly the case in Winneba, Ghana, where your authors met with the Mayor, the Honourable F. K. Tagoe. Mayor Tagoe – who at the time was just three months into his first term at this coastal tourist and fishing area near to the capital Accra – echoes these proactive sentiments: 'One of my main priorities is to expand our Deer Hunt Festival which is held the first Saturday of May each year. We need a clean environment for that and we need to protect the hunting grounds for the future, as well as the lagoon that serves the grounds.' Deer hunting is actually strictly controlled throughout the year in order to ensure sustainability.

The festival, called 'Aboakyer' in the local Fante language, is a tribute to the successful migration of the Effutu people led by two brothers from the Northeastern African town of Timbuktu to the Winneba area in the central coast region of Ghana (previously known as the Gold Coast) about 300 years ago. To thank the gods at the time and ward off future calamities, hunts for human sacrifices among the royal family were conducted annually. This eventually morphed into a leopard sacrifice following a huge game hunt organized by the two bands of warriors, known as 'Asafo'. The live leopard,

(Continued)

(Continued)

caught with bare hands, would later be sacrificed to appease the deities. In time, the dangerous leopard hunt was downgraded to a deer hunt in order to spare more human bloodshed. Nowadays, it is still celebrated with many activities for both old and young in a weeklong festival, showcasing Winneba's tribal history, culture and athleticism.

The Mayor highlighted the need for the Deer Hunt Festival to be properly packaged, advertised and extended beyond its typical weeklong festivities in order to establish Winneba on the international tourism map. 'Next year we're engaging professional event organizers to attract more international attention,' he says. Increased tourist visitation for any large event can inevitably lead to burdens on infrastructure but the Mayor is confident that the hotel facilities in Winneba would be sufficient. 'And in Accra, there are first-class hotels where people can spill over,' he adds. As for access, Winneba, Ghana's third city, was planned professionally in 1923, he says, with a substantial road network: 'They need improvement now and we have a project already approved to upgrade 11 km of roads. Central government is coming to our aid on this – so there will be no potholes next time you visit!' Much of the new prosperity for the area comes from the trickledown effect of the oil industry.

The Deer Hunt Festival is a pivotal way of showcasing Ghana's historical heritage, natural beauty, culinary eclecticism and colourful traditional clothing, which is sported by the two competing warrior groups and reflected in the audience's attire, too. 'There are three advantages we have in order to show our culture to tourists,' says the Mayor. 'Firstly, Ghana, and in particular the Winneba region, has a rich and diverse culture which has been largely unspoilt by modernization. Secondly, we are very safe here – people don't commit much crime. And thirdly, knowledge – we have a fully fledged university which is number one in the region.' The Mayor hopes that, along with a professional marketing organization for the festival, these three local elements will combine to create a highly successful event. 'When visitors come we want them to adapt quickly to our way of life, eating and drinking local foods,' he adds.

Our tour guide in Winneba was Tina Yawson, Secretary for the Sister Cities' Commission. She describes some of the ancient customs involved in the Deer Hunt Festival: 'In order to recognize the first catch to be sacrificed, the people were broken into two groups. Initially there was only one group – the "Dentsefo" – so the males who had male children had to give out one or two of their children to form the other group which was named "Tuafo".' The younger group, who had their own hunting grounds, usually started ahead of the parents. Each group was given specific colours to aid identification: 'Tuafo Asafo Company used black, white, blue, grey and green. And Dentsefo Asafo Company used red, yellow, black, brown, cream, violet, purple and almost all bright colours,' Yawson explains. In typical military procedure, uniforms and regalia are inspected by a panel of elders before festival day. There is also a ceremony for displaying the captured deer which must be carried shoulder high by the winning company and brought to the 'durbar' grounds where the Chief steps on it three times to make sure it is still alive. It can then be declared as fit for sacrifice and the winner is announced.

The festivities also act as an opportunity to contract or dissolve marriages and to pave the way for other celebrations over the course of the year. Nowadays, there is also a musical party component with popular multigenre artistes performing at various venues. So far, word has spread about the signature event via media such as the BBC, Pilot Guides, Ghana News Agency, various blogs, YouTube videos and the Charlottesville, VA website which discusses the festival in an article about its Sister City programme with Winneba. Festival organizers now have the task of securing sponsorship. Their mandate reads: 'It is the wish of the Planning Committee of the annual Deer Hunt Festival that brothers and sisters, companies and corporate bodies and even individuals anywhere on the globe who will be willing to support us in the areas of advertising, marketing and rebranding of the festival, help us in promoting some of the major activities which will at the end of the day bring Winneba on to the tourism map of the world.'

Sources: Personal visit by the authors to Winneba, Ghana, 2016.

CASE STUDY QUESTIONS

1   If you were to offer advice to Mayor Tagoe as to how he could grow the Deer Hunt Festival, what would you say?

2   Draw up a SWOT analysis for the Deer Hunt Festival, drawing on the material from this case study and Table 4.4.

3   What type of tourists might be attracted to a festival like this? Where might they come from?

REFERENCES

Birnbaum, E. (2015) 'G Adventure ups its game in sustainable travel', *National Post*, 19 October. www.pressreader.com/canada/national-post-latest-edition/20151019/282355448588782 (accessed 12 December 2016).

CMI (2014) *LGBT Tourism Demographic Profile.* http://m.communitymarketinginc.com/site/communitymarketinginc/lgbt-tourism-demographic-profile#2916 (accessed 12 December 2016).

Crawford-Welch, S. (1991) 'Marketing hospitality in the 21st century', *International Journal of Contemporary Hospitality Management*, 3(3): 21–7.

Falconi, M. (2013) 'Swiss valley aims for peak of luxury', *Wall Street Journal*, 23 August: M1 andM6.

Ghana Tourism Authority (2009) *Making Tourism the Lead Sector of Ghana's Economy: National Tourism Marketing Strategy 2009–2012*.

Hide, W. (2014) 'Skiing in Andermatt: Changes afoot to a resort with awesome off-piste'. *The Guardian Travel*, 8 November. https://www.theguardian.com/travel/2014/nov/08/andermatt-skiing-switzerland-alps-sedrun (accessed 12 December 2016).

Hoeller, S-E. (2015) 'A group of fans are trying to bring the Concorde supersonic jet back', *Business Insider*, 25 September. www.businessinsider.com/concorde-jet-may-come-back-2015-9 (accessed 6 December 2016).

Hudson, S. (2011) 'Bumps for Boomers: Marketing sport tourism to the aging tourist'. In B. Garrod and A. Fyall (eds), *Contemporary Cases in Tourism: Vol. 1.* Oxford: Goodfellow Publishers Ltd, 165–89.

Hudson, S. and Hudson, L. J. (2013) *Customer Service for Hospitality and Tourism.* Oxford: Goodfellow Publishers Ltd.

Hudson, S. and Hudson, L. J. (2015) *Winter Sport Tourism: Working in Winter Wonderlands.* Oxford: Goodfellow Publishers Ltd.

Hudson, S. and Ritchie, J. R. B. (2002) 'Understanding the domestic market using cluster analysis: A case study of the marketing efforts of Travel Alberta', *Journal of Vacation Marketing*, 8(3): 263–76.

IBISWorld (2016) *Ski & Snowboard Resorts in the US.* IBISWorld, December.

Li, X., Li, X. and Hudson, S. (2013) 'The application of generational theory to tourism consumer behavior: An American perspective', *Tourism Management*, 37: 147–64.

Middleton, V. T. C. and Clarke, J. R. (2012) *Marketing in Travel and Tourism* (3rd edn). Oxford: Butterworth-Heinemann.

Myanmar Tourism Master Plan 2013–2020 (2013) Ministry of Hotels and Tourism. The Republic of the Union of Myanmar, Nay Pyi Taw.

Oxford Business Group (2016) 'Ghana's government positive about tourism'. www.oxfordbusinessgroup.com/overview/emerging-star-bold-targets-show-government%E2%80%99s-positive-intent-sector (accessed 6 December 2016).

Porter, M. E. (1980) *Competitive Strategy: Techniques for Analyzing Industry and Competitors.* New York: Free Press.

Strauss, W. and Howe, N. (1997) *The Fourth Turning: An American Prophecy.* New York: Broadway Books.

Zeithaml, V. A., Berry, L. L. and Parasuraman, A. (1988) 'Communication and control processes in the delivery of service quality', *Journal of Marketing*, 52: 35–48.

THE TOURISM AND HOSPITALITY PRODUCT

5

INTRODUCTION

This chapter begins by introducing the peculiarities of the tourism product and the idea that tourism and hospitality products are a selected group of components or elements brought together in a 'bundle' to satisfy needs and wants. The next section looks at the three levels of tourism products – the core product, the tangible product and the augmented product – and these product levels are then applied to music festivals. The role of events in the tourism and hospitality sector is the subject of the next section and this is followed by a discussion of product planning. An in-depth analysis of branding in tourism is then followed by sections on managing the service-scape and creating a memorable experience. The final part of the chapter looks at new product development and the various theoretical stages a company can follow in developing a new product or service. Case studies in this chapter focus on the Dance World Cup, the adoption of technology in museums and music-themed hotels.

LESSONS FROM A MARKETING GURU: JO ARNETT-MORRICE, DANCE WORLD CUP

Dance World Cup (DWC) has been taking place in a different country each year since 2004 when it initially attracted around 1,000 competitors. Since then, the global event has burgeoned, with up to 12,000 hopefuls – from age 4 to 25 – auditioning for the prestigious event. Competitors in a wide variety of dance genres come from as far afield as the Ukraine, South Africa, Malaysia, India and Japan to various European DWC locations. The 2016 DWC in Jersey involved 4500 competitors from 33 countries.

IMAGE 5.1 Kimberley Wyatt from Pussycat Dolls (centre) and Chloe Fenton from *Les Miserables* (left) join Jo Arnett-Morrice (right) in congratulating dancer Imogen Chambers from Harlequin Dance School (back) (Used with permission of Jo Arnett-Morice)

Jo Arnett-Morrice is an event planner and marketing expert for Dance World Cup and also manager for Team England, Team Wales, Team Scotland and, from 2017, Team Northern Ireland. As UK Team Manager, her job is to encourage dance schools across the whole of Great Britain to enter their best talent. Via a multifaceted marketing campaign, she grew her first team, Team England, from 50 to 740 participants. She uses direct marketing, word of mouth and social media strategies, including Facebook and MailChimp. As a result of integrated marketing and networking efforts, Arnett-Morrice led Team England to victory in Brighton 2013, Portugal 2014, Romania 2015 and Jersey 2016, an unprecedented record.

In 2013 she took on the role of event planner for the Brighton DWC event. With much of her preparation work focused on securing sponsorship, she brought in over $20,000. She developed a ladder for sponsors, who were all featured with hyperlinks on the DWC website. Each sponsor could also pick a particular dance genre, which would then be reflected on the printed dance programmes. In conjunction with VisitBrighton, Arnett-Morrice set up a dedicated website for the Brighton DWC with discounts at many hotel groups and local businesses. Securing media coverage and celebrity endorsement were both vital to Arnett-Morrice's marketing strategy. 'We had a press launch at Bloch with Kimberley Wyatt of Pussy Cat Dolls fame – she's also a judge on the SKY TV show, *Got to Dance*,' she explains. 'It was a joint venture with Bloch in which I chose four Team England dancers as current champions to model their dancewear.' Other celebrities who have endorsed DWC include Bonnie Lythgoe, one of the hosts of *So You Think You Can Dance*, and there have also been 'good luck' messages to the UK Teams from Arlene Phillips, a high-profile TV show dance judge and choreographer. And, in Brighton, the DWC trophy was presented to Arnett-Morrice, as manager of the winning team, by child star, Isabelle Allan, who played the young Cossette in *Les Miserables* in both the West End production and the BAFTA award-winning film starring Russell Crowe and Hugh Jackman.

One of Arnett-Morrice's biggest coups was to get the *Dance Mums* TV Reality Show to base an entire season's script on DWC. 'The finale of the first series was filmed by Shiver TV Productions at DWC Portugal,' she recounts. 'Jennifer Ellison, who played the leading lady, Roxy Hart in *Chicago* in the West End and a leading role in Andrew Lloyd Weber's film of *Phantom of the Opera*, was there as well as all the cast and crew. The whole series was developed around the children trying to qualify for DWC.' One of the stars was Chloe Fenton, a soloist in Team England, and also famous around the UK for her performances on the 10th anniversary TV show of *Britain's Got Talent*. Fenton is now Team England's mascot and is often featured on Arnett-Morrice's social media. As an ardent advocate of social media, Arnett-Morrice uses Facebook, Twitter and Instagram to leverage all the media coverage, celebrity endorsements, and footage from the annual competitions as well as other dance highlights during the year. Her UK Teams website, DWC-UK.com, is linked to dwcworld.com, the central site for the whole organization. Her masterful marketing resulted in letters from Her Majesty Elizabeth II, offering her personal congratulations to Team England for winning the Dance World Cup in Romania 2015 and Jersey 2016.

Arnett-Morrice sees each DWC event as a team-management, PR and networking opportunity. Photographic and video footage is also integral to her social media campaigns: 'When people see this and also the live streaming of the action on the website, it can encourage them to come and see it for themselves or enter the following year.' After each competition, Arnett-Morrice starts working immediately on the following year's event. 'I need to keep the momentum going year round in order to get more competitors each year as well as attracting more sponsors,' she explains. 'I also need to give regular website coverage to existing sponsors and post results and photos from the previous event.'

Another prong to her campaign is to help her teams with fundraising, without which many of the dancers and teachers could not afford to attend DWC's annual international fixtures. With her huge circle of contacts, Arnett-Morrice also works closely with the DWC management helping them to grow the business and referring new nationality teams to them. As well as working with all the UK teams, Arnett-Morrice corresponds regularly with dance teachers from other countries, maintaining a high level of international enthusiasm, awareness and cooperation. 'I have links with Slovenia and Gibraltar, for example, and I bring over dancers from these countries to other festivals that I organize during the year – competitions that they would never have thought of entering before,' she says.

Her background before working for DWC was in sales, advertising and marketing in a variety of genres from clothing to radio ads to computer games. When her own daughters were involved in the dance world, she started out as a volunteer, then took on various roles working with local dance festivals and competitions. 'I was a "dance mum" myself but I also always volunteered to help coordinate all the shows and festivals in which my daughters Lulu and Arabella were performing,' she says. 'They went on to win gold medals in Austria and silver and bronze in Brighton and they have often helped me with the admin work at festivals over the years.' Nowadays, Arabella Arnett-Morrice works as her social media assistant, particularly for Twitter and Instagram with plans to add Snapchat by 2017.

Sources: Louise Hudson attended DWC in Villach, Austria and Brighton, England; interview with Jo Arnett-Morrice in June 2016.

THE TOURISM AND HOSPITALITY PRODUCT

As the opening case demonstrates, tourism and hospitality constitutes such a wide span of products that it has to be considered in terms of sectors rather than as a single industry, as discussed in Chapter 1. These sectors include accommodations, attractions, transportation, travel organizers, events, and destination organizations, among others (see Figure 1.9). This diversity is matched by an even greater range of component features specific to each sector, which need to be considered and managed in providing individual products for particular markets. The conceptualization of tourism and hospitality products as a group of selected components or elements brought together in a 'bundle' to satisfy needs and wants is a vital image for marketing managers. Product decisions, with all their implications for the management of tourism and hospitality operations, influence not only the marketing mix, but also a firm's long-term growth strategy and its policies for investment and human resources. Product specifications largely determine the corporate image and branding that an organization is able to create in the minds of its existing and prospective customers (Middleton and Clarke, 2012).

For many years, marketing theory has differentiated between three levels of product offering (Kotler and Armstrong, 2014). The three levels can be seen as a continuum, with the product's most basic benefit at one end, and a range of add-on benefits, not directly related to the product's essential purpose, at the opposite end. These three levels are:

(1) **Core product:** the basic need function served by the generic product. The case study at the end of this chapter discusses music-themed hotels, and in this case the core product is a place to stay.

(2) **Tangible product:** these are the specific features and benefits residing in the product itself – styling, quality, brand name, design, etc. Music-themed hotels differentiate themselves by featuring designs, artifacts and memorabilia inspired by music, or by having the ability to rent musical instruments and the opportunity to meet artists.

(3) **Augmented product:** these are add-ons that are extrinsic to the product itself but may influence the decision to purchase. Augmented features may include credit terms, after-sales guarantees, car parking, etc. For music-themed hotels, add-ons may include the food and beverage service in the hotel, or the parking facilities.

Although these levels were defined with manufactured products in mind, they do apply, with modifications, to tourism and hospitality goods and services. For example, Figure 5.1 applies the three levels to music festivals. The emotional stimulation for example would be one of the core products, the bands themselves are part of the tangible product, and the weather is an augmented product. Conceptualizing the product in these three areas allows the tourism marketer to appraise the comparative advantages and consumer appeal of his or her product versus those of others. In a highly competitive market, it is unlikely that any supplier will have an advantage in the core benefits, and differentiation is instead likely to reside in the second and third levels. Most music festivals, for example, offer atmosphere and excitement for consumers, but compete with each other on the variety and quality of bands, accommodation, or the space for attendees to camp out overnight.

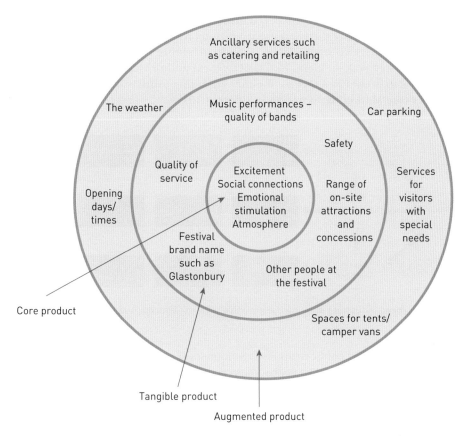

FIGURE 5.1 The Three Levels of Product – Example of a music festival (Source: adapted from Swarbrooke and Page (2002: 46)

THE ROLE OF EVENTS IN TOURISM AND HOSPITALITY MARKETING

Events play a significant role in today's society, and for tourism destinations they are important due to their tourist, social and cultural functions (Getz, 2007), as well as their role in local and regional development (Wood, 2005). Firstly and foremostly, events are a great anchor for attracting tourism, providing tourists with a prime opportunity to get to know the local culture and experience the essence of the place. During an event, visitors have a unique chance to interact with the local community, gaining a deeper experience of the ambience, customs and local culture. Events can also help in improving a place's image, creating a window for positive media coverage. Finally, for the residents themselves, events are a unique occasion to celebrate the local culture and interact within the community. All of this is exemplified in the Dance World Cup case study at the beginning of this chapter.

According to Jackson (2013), three industries in particular are shaping the growth of the events sector (see Figure 5.2). Firstly, the hospitality industry – be it hotels, restaurants or venues – has viewed events as a way of encouraging new clientele or increasing the yield of existing customers. This is the case for the World Ski and

Snowboard Festival held in Whistler, Canada every April, created to increase occupancy rates at the end of the winter season. Hotel rooms are fully booked during the event, which spans two weekends in order to maximize occupancy rates. Secondly, tourism industry stakeholders, like DMOs, local authorities or trade associations, have turned to events as a means of either attracting tourists or enhancing the stay of visitors (see Marketing in Action in Chapter 10).

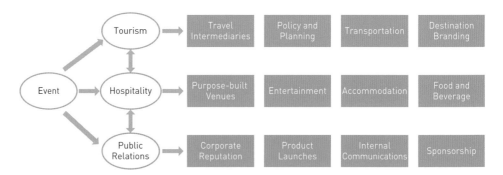

FIGURE 5.2 Three industries shaping the growth of events (Source: Adapted from Jackson, 2013, p. 7)

Finally, marketing and public relations practitioners are using events as an opportunity to achieve their objectives. The sponsorship activities of Red Bull are a good example. The Austrian brand has taken the whole concept of sponsoring sporting events to a different level. The company, makers of the highest-selling energy drink in the world, doesn't believe in signing sponsorship deals with teams to have their logos displayed

IMAGE 5.2 Boys practising during the open cyphers at Red Bull BC One Pre events at Pavillon Paul de Louvrier in Paris, France on 27 November 2014 (© Red Bull Media House)

on players' jerseys or racing cars. Instead they have 'invented' a host of sports and promoted their brand through it. Red Bull's marketing activities are mainly targeted at youth, and the brand identity is all about youthfulness, aggression and freedom. The logo of Red Bull shows two raging bulls implying power: aggression personified. Also the colour red implies aggression, too. The slogan, 'Red Bull gives you wings', signifies a sense of freedom. To ensure there is a match between the brand identity and brand image, Red Bull has launched a host of marketing initiatives, all with the aim of connecting with the youthful, adventure-seeking target audience, and driving home the message of what the brand stands for. The major marketing initiatives undertaken by Red Bull fall into two types – sponsoring teams through outright ownership, and sponsoring adventure sports and events.

PRODUCT PLANNING

The starting point in product analysis and planning is an examination of the consumer and competitive offerings in relation to the goals and product capacity of the tourism organization. The most successful products emerge when the marketing planning steps outlined in Chapter 4 are followed. Portfolio and SWOT analysis are discussed there; another useful method of analysing the tourism product is by considering its features and benefits. Features consist of the objective attributes of a tourism product; benefits are the rewards the product gives the consumer. The difference between the two is shown in Table 5.1. Hong Kong International Airport is often ranked as one of the world's best airports due, partly, to its features and, partly to, the benefits these features offer passengers. Apart from being able to shop for everything from rare white tea to cell phones, there are free plasma televisions to watch, a children's play area, wireless broadband, Internet cafés, a prayer room, a pharmacy, nap rooms, a beauty salon, shower facilities, a medical centre (complete with onsite vaccinations and X-ray machines) and displays from Hong Kong museums.

One of the most basic product analysis tools is the product life cycle (PLC) analysis (see Figure 5.3). Plotting products or services to identify what stage they are at in their PLC is a valuable way of reviewing a product's past and current position and making predictions about its future. As part of a portfolio analysis (see Chapter 4), an organization should access each good and service in terms of its position in the product life cycle. *Product development* begins when the company finds and develops a new product idea. The founder of the Sydney BridgeClimb conceived the idea nine years before it was put into action. The *introduction* phase is a period of slow sales and

TABLE 5.1 Features and benefits analysis for tourism and hospitality products

Tourism product item	Product feature	Consumer benefit
Low-cost airline	Low service	Low-cost travel
Purpose-built ski resort	All lifts near hotel rooms	Ski in, ski out facility
Museum	Interactive facilities to learn	An entertaining place
River adventure tour	Quality kayaks and rafts	Reconnecting with nature
5-star hotel	Quality beds	Comfort

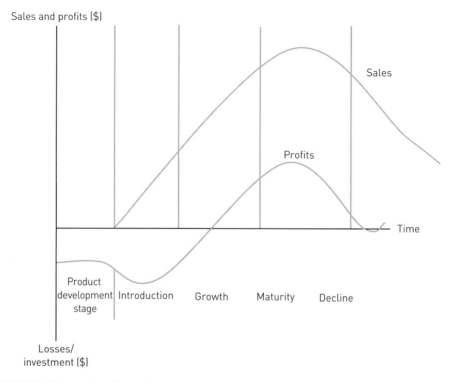

FIGURE 5.3 The product life cycle

low profits because of the investment required for product introduction. The *growth* phase is characterized by increasing market acceptance and substantial improvement in profits. The *maturity* phase is a period of slow sales but is marked by high profits as the product is well entrenched in the marketplace and has an acceptable market share. However, when sales begin to drop because competitors are moving into the marketplace, the product enters the *decline* stage. Profits and market share decline, and major costs may be involved in redeveloping, refurbishing or maintaining the product.

The PLC is not as simple as it sounds in theory and, according to one writer, its supposed universal applicability is largely a myth (Mercer, 1992). The study of the PLC pattern for a particular product has to take into account the market the product is in. For example, if a product is showing no growth or decline, it may still be very successful if the market as a whole is in decline. Another complication of the PLC is that a product that is in overall decline may be losing its customers from one market segment but increasing appeal or holding steady with another. Ski areas, for example, have been very successful in attracting an increasing number of snowboarders over the past decade, despite a drop in the number of downhill skiers. In addition, although the PLC concept is neat on paper, it is often difficult to determine what particular stage a product is at. Finally, even assuming that a product's life-cycle position can be determined, it may not be obvious what action should be taken. However, despite these problems, the PLC is a valuable concept to operationalize, since it forces the organization to analyse trends for its product in relation to the overall market and the segments within it, in order to assess future marketing requirements. Ski areas, for example, have adapted to the growth in snowboarders referred to above by changing the products they offer; most successful ski areas these days have designated snowboarding parks.

BRANDING

The practice of branding developed initially in the field of packaged goods as a method of establishing a distinctive identity for a product based on competitive differentiation from other products. Branding was commonly achieved through naming, trade marking, packaging, product design and promotion. Successful branding gave a unique identity to what might otherwise have been a generic product. This identity produced a consistent image in the consumer's mind, which facilitated recognition and quality assurance. In the nineteenth century, products such as Beecham's Pills, Cadbury's Chocolate and Eno's Salts were early users of branding. These days, the market in packaged goods is dominated by brands and, in the last few decades, branding has also been widely recognized in services marketing. A 'brand', in the modern marketing sense, offers the consumer relevant added value – a superior proposition that is distinctive from competitors' and that imparts meaning above and beyond the product's functional aspects. There is even a Museum of Brands in London where visitors can view 10,000 consumer products covering 200 years of packaging, branding and advertising.

Branding in services offers a solution to some of the problems in services marketing – in particular those of consistency and product standardization. Branding can be a way of unifying services, which is why it has been particularly developed in hotel marketing. For large hotel companies that have a wide variety of properties, grouping them into brands can:

(1) unify them into more easily recognizable smaller groups;

(2) enable each branded group to be targeted at defined market segments; and

(3) enable product delivery, including human resource management, to be focused on creating a specific set of benefits for a specific market.

Figure 5.4 shows the breakdown of branded versus nonbranded hotels by region around the world. North America – with 67 per cent of its hotels carrying a brand – leads the world in branded inventory, followed by the Asia-Pacific region, with 51 per cent of its hotel inventory branded. Europe, South America and the Middle East/Africa still favour nonbranded hotels, but that gap is narrowing as brand companies become increasingly open to alternate expansion strategies beyond the traditional franchise model.

Figure 5.5 lists the ten largest hotel brands by room count. Hilton Worldwide is the global hospitality leader with twelve distinct brands, 4,300 hotels and timeshare properties and more than 715,000 rooms in 94 countries and territories.

In the past, branding was often seen mainly as a matter of promotion and of creating the right image through advertising and publicity. But marketing managers now recognize that successful branding involves the integrated deployment of product design, pricing policies, distribution selection and promotion. The case for branding is stronger for tourism products that offer the possibility for differentiation in

FIGURE 5.4 A breakdown of branded versus non-branded hotels by region (©STR, Inc. Reprinted by permission)

	EXISTING		PIPELINE		IF 100% OPEN	
	HOTELS	ROOMS	HOTELS	ROOMS	HOTELS	ROOMS
IHG	4,840	710,295	1,221	193,772	6,061	904,067
HILTON	4,278	708,268	1,351	230,000	5,629	938,268
MARRIOTT	4,044	692,801	1,450	240,000	5,494	932,801
WYNDHAM	7,645	660,826	960	117,000	8,605	777,826
CHOICE HOTELS	6,379	505,278	510	39,000	6,889	544,278
ACCOR	3,717	482,296	800	156,188	4,517	638,484
STARWOOD	1,222	354,225	480	108,000	1,702	462,225
Best Western	3,931	303,522	447	44,441	4,378	347,963
Home Inn	2,609	296,075	401	N/R	3,010	N/R
CARLSON REZIDOR	1,092	172,234	280	50,150	1,372	222,384

FIGURE 5.5 Ten largest hotel brands by room count (©STR, Inc. Reprinted by permission)

several areas of the marketing mix. This is why branding has been particularly successful in hotel and restaurant marketing. Branding of restaurants, hotels, and airlines developed extensively in the US during the 1980s and 1990s, and companies in the rest of the world are following suit. The momentum is driven mainly by large organizations that recognize that, to remain competitive, they need to offer several products to different markets instead of relying upon a monolithic presence in one main one. Even museums and science centres are recognizing the importance of branding. Major cultural brands, such as National Geographic, BBC and Smithsonian, are expanding their reach through either licensing or exploring new types of facilities in new locations (TEA, 2015). Examples include the National Geographic branded giant screen movie theatres in science centres; BBC's collaboration with Sega on the Orbi experience centre in Yokohama, Japan; and the Museum at Prairie Fire's (Kansas City) unique content partnership with the American Museum of Natural History.

It should be recognized that a competitive brand is a live asset and not a fixture, and therefore its value may depreciate over time if starved of investment and marketing and management skill. Brand decay may begin if a brand is overstretched into new products that damage its essence, or following a merger or takeover. Marketers sometimes use the term 'brandicide' to describe the process of taking a well-known brand and extending it into a new area that will 'kill' the brand. Companies are increasingly attempting to stretch their proven expertise into new areas. Over the past 25 years, Richard Branson, for example, has diversified his Virgin brand into a far-reaching empire, encompassing mobile phone services, rail service, hotels and even wedding dresses, as well as his original record label and discount airline. Many of his companies have been successful, but others have failed, and these include Virgin Cola, Virgin Vodka, Virgin Clothing, Virgin Cars and Virgin Flowers (Russell, 2012).

The subject of destination branding, has received increased profile over the last few decades and deserves special attention (Ferguson and Bourke, 2013; Garcia, Gomez and Molina, 2012; Pike and Mason, 2011; Zenker and Martin, 2013). In an increasingly competitive global marketplace, the need for destinations to create a unique identity – to differentiate themselves from competitors – has become more critical than ever. The process of building a destination brand should begin with an analysis of the current situation. This stage should consider how contemporary or relevant the brand is to today's consumer and how it compares with key competitors. Once this market investigation is complete, the next stage is to develop the brand identity. Critical to the success of any brand is the extent to which the brand personality interacts with the target market. A brand's personality has both a head and a heart: its 'head' is its logical features, while its 'heart' is its emotional benefits and associations. Brand propositions and communications can be based around either.

The third stage in destination brand building is to communicate the vision and launch the brand. This may be done through a single announcement or as a part of huge international advertising campaign. This stage involves translating the brand personality and proposition into deliverable messages. A logotype or brand signature and a design style guide, which ensures consistency of message and approach, should also reinforce the brand values. The vision should be expressed in the brand's core values that are consistently reinforced through the product and in all marketing communications. Every execution in all media contributes to maintaining brand presence. Continuous monitoring and evaluation of the communications is the key here, in conjunction with open-mindedness and a willingness to embrace change on the part of the brand managers. Any change must be managed with the overall consistency of the brand. The secret is to evolve continually and enrich the original brand personality, building on the initial strengths to increase their appeal and broaden the market. This book describes numerous examples of destination branding campaigns, including Myanmar, Las Vegas, New Mexico and Bluffton, South Carolina.

DIGITAL SPOTLIGHT: MUSEUMS GO DIGITAL

Just as dinosaurs appear alongside modern-day people in *Jurassic Park*, museums are turning to today's technology to enhance ancient artifacts and historical concepts with youth-oriented digital gadgets. 'Museums have increasingly caught on to the idea that they need to lock in their visitors earlier. While they have long offered children's programmes – come for cookies and collage! – institutions all over the country are now devoting far more creative resources to targeting teenagers,' says American journalist, Robin Pogrebin. In an article about the new 'teenaged museum connoisseurs', Pogrebin quotes a 2014 survey of 220 museums, undertaken by the Association of Art Museum Directors, which found that about a third had docent programmes for teenagers, or teenage councils. These youthful mentors advise the staff and management and, in some cases, give tours to

IMAGE 5.3 Fly Like a Pterosaur exhibit at the American Museum of Natural History (©AMNH/ D. Finnin. Used with permission)

visitors in their own age range. In March 2015, Pogrebin said, 'the Art Institute of Chicago invited 100 teenagers to spend 24 hours at the museum reimagining aspects of its operations, like the security officers' uniforms and gallery benches'. Their reward: a midnight dance party, caffeine bar and sunrise yoga.

Increasingly, museums are looking to digital outlets and facilities to lure the younger crowd. One technique is through online museum lectures which have been gaining in popularity since the early 2000s. The Smithsonian American Art Museum in Washington was an early adopter in 2006 and, in concert with three other American museums, it went on to start ArtBabble, a website that now offers videos from 60 museums across the United States and overseas. It covers global art in six languages, encompassing an increasing variety of mediums, periods and themes. In New York, the Frick also began streaming online museum lectures in 2012. The nearby American Museum of Natural History used whole-body, motion-sensing Microsoft Kinect technology in two of its recent exhibitions – *Pterosaurs: Flight in the Age of Dinosaurs* and *Life at the Limits: Stories of Amazing Species*. In the first, visitors could 'pilot' two species of flying pterosaurs over prehistoric landscapes complete with forest, sea, and volcano in a whole-body interactive exhibit that uses motion-sensing technology. During the *Life at the Limits* exhibition, visitors could meet and interact with some of the creatures that they had encountered throughout the show. Through exploration of several virtual environments and the use of guided gestures using whole-body, motion-sensing technology, visitors could cause creatures to behave in ways consistent with some of their amazing abilities, highlighting why these creatures live life at the limits.

But this is by no means just an American phenomenon. In Poland, a successful techie tactic instated in 2011 has been attracting a whole new age group of advocates at the Sukiennice Museum in Kraków. Visitors can scan QR codes with smartphones, enabling augmented reality to act out scenes depicted on the array of nineteenth century art. More recently, in May 2016, Royal Museums Greenwich, Evergreen Exhibitions, Boeing and NASA joined to open *Above and Beyond*, a new interactive flight exhibition at the National Maritime Museum (NMM). It explores the wonder of flight and the marvels of aerospace innovation, design, and technology using fully immersive experiences to represent the impact of aerospace in our world – and beyond. Another museum in London, the New Churchill Museum, has installed £6 million-worth of high-tech facilities, including a unique electronic 'Lifeline' table which allows visitors to journey through Churchill's extraordinary life. The 18-metre-long Lifeline is a computerized filing cabinet, with a virtual file containing items relating to each year – and in many cases each month and day – of his career. Touching the strip at the edge of the Lifeline brings up contextual data, documents, films, photographs and even sound tracks that relate to his life while providing historical context.

In Rome, Italy a tribute to the 2000th anniversary of the death of its first emperor, Augustus opened in September 2014, showcasing new virtual museum technologies. The *Keys to Rome* exhibition opened in three other cities at the same time, demonstrating how virtual technology will routinely be utilized by museums in the future. Through a stream of new apps and immersive technology developed by the V-MUST.NET group, the objects exhibited in all four cities were discovered through a digital itinerary using computer graphics, movies, interaction installations, multimedia and mobile apps. And in Belgium, the Historium Museum brings fifteenth-century Bruges to life via a movie screened in various segments as visitors wander from room to room. Like a soap opera, the viewer is hooked by the love story and compelled to check out each different area in order to find out how the drama ends.

So, is all this technology and innovation managing to attract a younger clientele? Hong Kong student, Lo Shun Siu Zabrina visited the Hakone Open Air Museum in Japan in January 2016 when travelling around the world with the Semester at Sea academic programme. 'Of all the popular places I visited such as the Komagatake Ropeway that led me to the top of the mountain to see the spectacular Mount Fuji, Shinto shrines, Tokyo Tower, the bustling Shibuyu area or the sake breweries in Kobe, this museum – which I had never heard of – was the wonderland in my journey to Japan,' Lo Shun Siu said. As well as opening her eyes to various genres of art, the whimsical outdoor experience had an impact on her thinking: 'The museum expanded my imagination and understanding

(Continued)

(Continued)

of art and of how visitors interacted with the exhibition.' Featuring e-tickets on its English language website – dubbed 'in advance ticket sale at the electronic terminal of a convenience store' – the museum also offers Internet discounts. Children are given a worksheet to summarize all the art installations in easy interpretative illustrations. And there are also educational workshops which incorporate open-air sketch experiences. Back home at Hong Kong Baptist University, Lo Shun Siu's Internet-hooked peers had questioned her urge to go around the world and see things for herself: 'Two years ago my friend challenged my high hopes for travelling, saying "What is the point of going to the Louvre to look at *Mona Lisa* when you can simply Google it?" All I insisted was that I needed to *see* it with my very own eyes. It's about the experience on-site!'

Sources: Pogrebin (2015); Levere (2014); Suellentrop (2014). Visit by Dr Simon Hudson to The New Churchill Museum in July 2006. Visit by both authors to The Historium, Bruges, Belgium in 2014. Personal interviews with Zabrina Lo Shun Siu during and after the Semester at Sea Spring 2016 voyage.

CASE STUDY QUESTIONS

1. According to the material in this chapter, the servicescape can play four key strategic roles simultaneously. Is the servicescape in museums performing any of these roles?

2. How are museums adapting their environment to appeal to a younger market?

3. With reference to the material below about creating memorable experiences, what more could museums do to engage attendees emotionally?

MANAGING THE SERVICESCAPE

Because many tourism and hospitality services are intangible, customers often rely on tangible cues, or physical evidence, to evaluate the service before its purchase and to assess their satisfaction with the service during and after consumption. The physical evidence is the environment in which the service is delivered and in which the firm and customer interact, and any tangible components that facilitate performance or communication of the service. The physical facility is often referred to as the 'servicescape', and is very important for tourism and hospitality products such as hotels, restaurants and theme parks, which are dominated by experience attributes. Disney, for example, effectively uses the servicescape to excite its customers. The brightly coloured displays, the music, the rides, and the costumed characters all reinforce the feelings of fun and excitement that Disney seeks to generate in its customers. In the new Shanghai Disney Resort, design and art play a major role. The park and resort cost about $5.5 billion to build and spans an area more than 11 times the size of the original Disneyland in Anaheim, California. Visitors can choose from six themed zones, such as Fantasyland and Tomorrowland, plus two hotels and a shopping area.

The servicescape is often one of the most important elements used in positioning a tourism or hospitality organization, and according to Zeithaml et al. (2007), the servicescape can play four key strategic roles simultaneously.

1. PACKAGING

The servicescape essentially 'wraps' the service and conveys to the consumer an external image of what is 'inside'. This packaging role is particularly important in creating expectations for new customers and for newly established businesses that are trying to develop a particular image. Howard Schultz has purposefully positioned Starbucks to look and feel less like a bar or restaurant and more like a home with its comfy chairs, fireplaces, coffee smells and camaraderie. What Schultz did from the outset was create an inviting, comfortable and compelling servicescape, full of sensory pleasures designed to make his customers relax and linger. The Hard Rock Cafés are another good example of servicescape packaging. They use rock 'n' roll memorabilia both outside and inside the restaurants to establish an expectation in the mind of visitors.

2. FACILITATOR

The second role the servicescape can play is as a facilitator in aiding the performances of people in the service environment. To encourage the neat appearance of frontline staff, mirrors can be strategically places so that they can easily check their appearance before going 'on stage' to meet customers. In fast-food restaurants, strategically located tray return stands and notices on walls remind customers to return their trays. Grady and Ohlin (2009) have emphasized the importance of physical layout and design for serving guests with disabilities. They suggest that for hotels, both guests and employees should be encouraged to bring forth recommendations for improvement in physical layout and design so that reasonable modifications can be made.

3. SOCIALIZER

The design of the servicescape can also aid in the socialization of both employees and customers in the sense that it helps convey expected roles, behaviours and relationships. In Canada, lodges owned by adventure tour operator Canadian Mountain Holidays (CMH) have been designed specifically to meet the needs of heli-skiers. Each lodge has a dining room and a fully stocked lounge and is equipped with a sauna and hot tub. But the layout of the dining room is the same in each lodge. CMH has discovered over the years that, in order to encourage socialization at the dinner table, the ideal layout is four tables of 12 people – a total of 44 guests and four staff who sit at the head of each table and interact with customers over dinner.

4. DIFFERENTIATOR

The design of a physical facility can differentiate a business from its competitors and signal the market segment that the service is intended for. Airlines often employ design consultants to help them differentiate the appearance of their aircraft and employees from those of their competitors. Although some cabin staff look interchangeable, others have really distinctive uniforms that immediately identify them as employees of, for example, Singapore Airlines. In fact, Singapore Airlines has built its reputation on the beauty and hospitality of the sarong-wearing staff known in its global ad campaigns as the 'Singapore Girls'.

Consumer researchers know that the design of the servicescape can influence customer choices, expectations, satisfaction and other behaviours. Bitner (2002) has

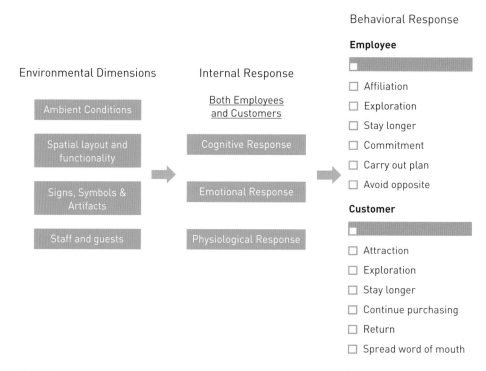

FIGURE 5.6 How the servicescape impacts consumers and employees (Source: Adapted from Bitner, 2002)

developed a comprehensive servicescape model which shows the environment and behaviour relationships in service settings. This model has been slightly adapted and presented in Figure 5.6. The model has three key elements – environmental dimensions, internal responses, and behavioural responses – all of which will be discussed in turn.

1. ENVIRONMENTAL DIMENSIONS

(A) AMBIENT CONDITIONS

Ambient conditions refer to the characteristics of the environment that pertain to the five senses. They are composed of numerous design elements that work together to create a desired environment. Even when they are not noted consciously, they may affect emotional well-being, perceptions and even attitudes and behaviours. The resulting atmosphere creates a mood that is perceived and interpreted by consumers. Ambient conditions include music, temperature, air quality, noise, smell and colour. A number of field experiments have shown the effects music can have on customers. One restaurant study showed that beverage revenue increased substantially when slow-beat rather than fast-beat music was played (Lovelock and Wirtz, 2007). Customers also spent longer in the restaurant if the slower music was playing. Scent is another ambient variable that can permeate a service environment. Howard Schultz went to great lengths to preserve the smell of coffee in Starbucks stores (Schultz, 2011).

(B) SPATIAL LAYOUT AND FUNCTIONALITY

Spatial layout and functionality create the visual and functional servicescape for delivery and consumption to take place. Spatial layout refers to the floor plan, size and shape of furnishings, counters and equipment, and the way in which they are arranged. Functionality is the ability of those items to facilitate the performance of service transactions. Between the two elements, they determine the user-friendliness of the facility to service customers well, and they not only affect the efficiency of the service operation, they also shape the customer experience. Guinness & Co. goes to great lengths to ensure that spatial layout and functionality of pubs deliver the right consumer experience. The company has created a programme that supports the launch of authentic Irish pubs by providing advice and resources for entrepreneurs opening and operating pubs, including help with site selection, décor, music and staffing.

(C) SIGNS, SYMBOLS AND ARTIFACTS

Signs, symbols and artifacts are used by service providers to guide customers clearly through the process of service delivery and to teach the service process in as intuitive a manner as possible. Customers become disoriented when they cannot derive clear signals from a servicescape, leading to anxiety and uncertainty about how to proceed and how to obtain the desired service. Examples of explicit signals include signs which can be used to give directions (to the elevators or washrooms, for example), communicate the service script (take a number), and behavioural rules (no smoking, turn off cell phones, etc.).

(D) STAFF AND GUEST BEHAVIOUR AND IMAGE

Some researchers suggest that the importance of social aspects of the servicescape are often underestimated, and that social variables such as staff behaviour and staff image are just as important as tangible elements (Tombs and McColl-Kennedy, 2003; Harris and Ezeh, 2007). These variables have therefore been added to Bitner's original model. Research has shown that the greater the customers' perceptions of staff customer orientation, staff credibility and staff competence, the more likely they are to be loyal to the service provider (Harris and Ezeh, 2007). Many customers frequent certain service establishments simply because of the type of people who patronize the place. An example is Abaco, an extraordinarily theatrical and lavish bar in the centre of Palma on the Spanish island of Mallorca. Inhabiting the restored patio of an old Mallorcan house, Abaco is filled with ornate candelabra, elaborate floral arrangements, cascading towers of fresh fruit, and bizarre artworks. It hovers between extravagant and kitsch, but the effect is overwhelming and visiting the bar is an experience in itself. Upon opening the door of this bar you are transported to a different world; it feels like you have walked into an ostentatious seventeenth-century Mallorcan house. Atmosphere is low key, with only the muted sounds of the tinkling courtyard fountain, the songbirds and classical music in the background. Since opening in 1981, Abaco remains one of Europe's most beautiful and memorable nightspots.

2. INTERNAL RESPONSES

Employees and customers in service firms respond to dimensions of their physical surroundings in three ways – cognitively, emotionally and physiologically – and these responses influence their behaviours in the environment.

(A) COGNITIVE RESPONSES

Firstly, the perceived servicescape may elicit *cognitive* responses, including people's beliefs about a place and their beliefs about the people and products found in that place. 'Handwritten' signs at Starbucks, for example, tend to attract customers by signalling a more authentic experience. One consumer study found that a travel agent's office décor affected customer anticipation of the travel agent's behaviour (Bitner, 1990). Research has shown that the servicescape has a direct influence on perceived service quality – particularly for hedonistic services like restaurants (Reimer and Kuehn, 2004).

(B) EMOTIONAL RESPONSES

In addition to influencing cognitions, the perceived servicescape may elicit emotional responses that in turn influence behaviours. The colours, décor, music and other elements of the atmosphere can have an unexplained and sometimes subconscious effect on the moods of people in the place. Servicescapes that are both pleasant and arousing have been termed 'exciting', while those that are pleasant and non-arousing, or sleepy, are called 'relaxing'. Unpleasant servicescapes that are arousing are 'distressing', while unpleasant, sleepy servicescapes are 'gloomy' (Russell, Ward and Pratt, 1981). Figure 5.7 depicts these feelings experienced in service environments.

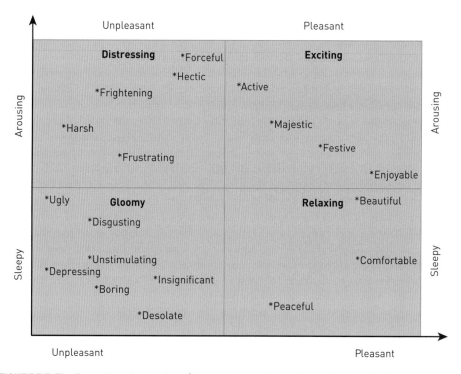

FIGURE 5.7 The Russell model of affect (Source: Adapted from Russell et al., 1981).

(C) PHYSIOLOGICAL RESPONSES

Finally, the servicescape may affect people in purely physiological ways. Noise that is too loud may cause physical discomfort, the temperature of a room may cause people to shiver or perspire, the air quality may make it difficult to breathe, and the glare of lighting may decrease ability to see and may cause physical pain. All of these physical responses will influence whether people remain in and enjoy a particular environment. Airlines are constantly looking at ways to make long-haul flying more comfortable. Thanks to new technology in Boeing's new 787 Dreamliner, flights are pressured to the equivalent of 6,000 feet in elevation, lower than the 8,000-foot mark that is typical for commercial passenger aircraft. Boeing says this (coupled with the higher humidity levels possible on the 787) should alleviate headaches, fatigue and reduce the general wear and tear travellers often feel from travelling (Mutzabaugh, 2011).

3. BEHAVIOURAL RESPONSES

The internal customer and employee responses discussed above lead to overt behavioural responses such as avoiding a crowded theme park or responding positively to a relaxing environment by remaining there and spending extra money on purchases. At Madame Tussauds waxworks museums, researchers have discovered that customers will stay longer, and have a more satisfactory experience, if they are permitted to touch the exhibits. Most museums have a strict hands-off policy when it comes to their exhibits. At Tussauds, visitors can touch, hug and even kiss the lifelike figures. 'A traditional museum would have ropes up,' said Bret Pidgeon, general manager at Tussauds in Manhattan. 'But this is the closest a lot of people are going to get to an actual celebrity. We allow our guests to get up close and personal' (Klara, 2011). Because of this, the figures – which are made in London and cost up to $200,000 – often get damaged.

CREATING A MEMORABLE EXPERIENCE

Much has been written recently about customer experiences and their important role in influencing consumer behaviour (Zeithaml et al., 2007), and companies in the tourism and hospitality sector are being admonished to create memorable experiences for their customers. Research has shown that consumer experiences are derived through a unique combination of responses to physical environment dimensions and human interaction dimensions. The physical environment has an important influence on experience of consumers in many service settings. Walls et al. (2011), for example, found that in the hotel setting, the ambience, the multisensory impact of the hotel, the space and function, and the signs and symbols were four themes that emerged from their research as key constructs of the physical environment.

Human interaction dimensions, both with employees and fellow guests, are also a key influence on the consumer experience. Studies by Lin, Huang and Chiang (2008) and Wang (2009) reinforce the impact that employees' roles have on customers' experience in a service setting. As service consumption often takes place in the presence of other customers, customer-to-customer interactions can also have a substantial impact on consumption experiences. Positive interactions among consumers, in a variety of service settings, have been shown to be important to both consumers and companies, and research shows that managerially facilitated positive customer-to-customer interactions enhance consumer satisfaction and enjoyment (Levy, Hudson and Getz, 2011).

The consumer experience is also significantly impacted by personal characteristics, and cultural differences can affect the experience of customers. Americans, for example, in a hospitality setting, are more likely to tell a friend, to return to the same place, and be motivated to increase the amount of the tip, in comparison to Asians (Manzur and Jogaratnam, 2006). Finally, the consumer experience is impacted by trip-related factors. Andersson and Mossberg (2004), for example, in studying the customer experience in a restaurant, found that customers expect evening restaurants to satisfy social and intellectual needs whereas lunch restaurants mainly cater for physiological needs.

Delivering a consistent and distinctive customer experience has always been a central concern of brand management. In the early 1900s, retail pioneers like Gordon Selfridge were similarly clear about delivering such experiences. The man who first coined the phrase 'the customer is always right' described his original vision for his new department store, Selfridges, as 'delighting them with an unrivalled shopping experience' (which included such innovations as in-store coffee shops) and training his staff in the 'Selfridges Way' to ensure a distinctively consistent level of customer service (Mosley, 2007).

NEW PRODUCT/SERVICE DEVELOPMENT

About 250,000 new products are introduced globally every year, with a typical failure rate of about 85–95 per cent (Wong, 2010). Many new ideas take years before the idea becomes reality. The BridgeClimb in Sydney is a prime example of the latter, taking nine years for the idea to become reality. Safety concerns and other issues kept the unique tourism product on hold for over a decade.

Developing new products is different from maintaining existing ones, and planning for both kinds of product will differ according to whether the products are targeted at existing markets or new ones.

According to Holloway and Plant (1992), a company has four alternatives when developing new products.

1. MARKET PENETRATION

Firstly, it can follow a market penetration strategy by modifying an existing product for the current market. Improvements to an existing product can render that product so new as to make it seen by prospective purchasers as a genuinely new product. Casinos in Macau, for example, are modifying their service offerings in order to provide new experiences for their customers. New sites include luxury shopping arcades, spas, swimming pools and ballrooms. The Venetian has a 15,000-seat arena, where the Rolling Stones performed in 2014, and SJM's planned Lisboa Palace complex strip will feature a wedding pavilion and a theatre. 'Gambling won't go out of fashion. It will just become part of a wider offering,' said Ian Coughlan, president at Wynn Macau (Wassener, 2014).

2. MARKET DEVELOPMENT

The second strategy, market development, calls for identifying and developing new markets for current products. If an existing product is launched to a new market that is unfamiliar with it, that product is also, for all intents and purposes, a new product. Hoteliers, for example, are aggressively expanding into Africa, targeting fast-growing economies like Ghana and Ethiopia. Most of Africa 'is a bit of a blank piece of paper for the hospitality industry,' said Alex Kyriakidis, chief of Marriott's Middle East and Africa division (McGroarty and Berzon, 2012). Business travellers are flocking to Africa thanks to rich stores of minerals, oil and natural gas.

3. PRODUCT DEVELOPMENT

The third strategy, product development, involves developing a genuinely new product to be sold to existing customers. The author was pleased to hear recently that Marmite (an English food paste) had developed a mini version available in a 70 g travel-friendly size for those who can't bear to board a plane without their favourite snack (along with many British travellers, he has had several of the larger sizes confiscated in the past). Another example of product development comes from the US, where in 2015, the National Football League (NFL) announced that they would be joining with two private-equity firms on a new venture to provide travel, entertainment, hospitality and on-field access at the leagues' biggest events. The venture was intended to test the power of the NFL brand as a force beyond the football field and, especially, internationally where the hospitality business at sports events is far behind the US market (Futterman, 2015).

4. DIVERSIFICATION

Diversification growth makes sense when good opportunities can be found outside the present business. Three types of diversification can be considered. Firstly, the company could seek new products that have technological or marketing synergies with existing product lines, even though the product may appeal to a new class of customers (concentric diversification). Secondly, the company might search for new products that could appeal to its current target market (horizontal diversification). Finally, the company might seek new businesses that have no relationship to the company's current technology, products, or markets (conglomerate diversification). An example of diversification comes from the Virgin Group, which has recently moved into Virgin Hotels, seeking to attract Millennial and Generation X business and leisure travellers.

APPROACHES TO NEW PRODUCT DEVELOPMENT

A company must develop new products to survive. New products can be obtained through acquisition or through new product development (NPD). There is a reasonably established approach to NPD, but Scheuing and Johnson (1989) have proposed a model for new service development (NSD), based on a review of other models and research into 66 US-based service firms. The model has 15 steps and four main stages.

The first stage (steps 1–3) of NSD focuses on how new ideas are generated and developed. The development process must begin with a precise formulation of *objectives and strategy*. A well-designed strategy drives and directs the entire innovation effort and imbues it with effectiveness and efficiency. The second step is for companies to ensure that they have organized or *structured* their plan in such a way as to enable innovation to take place. In large companies, this may involve setting up a research and development (R & D) department. The third step consists of *idea generation and screening*. New ideas can be drawn from external sources, or be generated internally through consultation and brainstorming. Often the most powerful idea source is customer feedback.

The idea generation and development stage of NSD is followed by the second stage – the 'go/no go' stage – comprising four steps (steps 4–7) that enable the company to decide whether or not it will proceed with the new development. *Concept development* requires that the surviving ideas be expanded into fully fledged concepts, especially if there is a significant service element. *Concept testing* is a research technique designed to evaluate whether a prospective user understands the idea of the proposed good or service, reacts favourably to it, and feels it provides benefits that answer unmet needs. The sixth step, *business analysis*, should represent a comprehensive investigation into the business implications of each concept. The *project authorization* step occurs when top management commits corporate resources to the implementation of a new idea. In an industry such as tourism, which consists of many small organizations, it is likely that 90 per cent of companies have just one person or department in the company to authorize all innovative projects (Jones, Hudson and Costis, 1997).

Once the go-ahead has been given, the third stage of NSD – test design – is reached, in which detailed design and implementation of the innovation is carried out (steps 8–11). At this point, the new concept is converted into an operational entity. This requires *design and testing*. For a service, this activity should involve both the input of prospective users and the active cooperation of the operations personnel who will ultimately be delivering the service. It may also be necessary to design new production *processes* or develop new equipment. This stage also includes *marketing design and testing*. To complete the test design phase, all employees should be familiarized with the nature and operational details of the new service. For instance, research into flight catering showed that 91 per cent of airlines engaged in personnel training, whereas only 68 per cent of food manufacturers did so (Jones, 1995).

The final stage of NSD is the evaluation of the new innovation, comprising four steps (steps 12–15). *Service testing* should be used to determine potential customer acceptance of the new service, while a pilot run ensures its smooth functioning. Several years ago the Marriott Corporation designed a new chain of hotels for business travellers – Courtyard by Marriott – and then tested the concept under real-world conditions, before subsequently developing the large chain that filled a gap in the market.

The next step, *test marketing*, examines the sale-ability of the new service, and a field test should be carried out with a limited sample of customers. With the delivery system and marketing in place and with the service thoroughly tested, the company should next initiate the full-scale *launch*, introducing the service product to the entire market area. Different sectors tend to evaluate their new services/products in slightly different ways. For instance, fast-food operators use market surveys, whereas food-service contractors rely more on after-sales for customer feedback. The final step, *post-launch review*, should be aimed at determining whether the strategic objectives were achieved or whether further adjustments are needed.

Sheuing and Johnson suggest that firms should not rigidly follow this model but instead consider it as a framework from which to select those activities they deem necessary for the specific development they are undertaking.

An organization also creates internal conditions that either foster or hinder innovation. Often, these are strongly influenced by the external environment. Conditions that may encourage a systematic but rigid approach to innovation are a bureaucratic culture, mature marketplace, the involvement of external consultants, and formal research and development departments. Conditions that encourage a dynamic and flexible approach to innovation are the following: growing supply chain integration; an organizational culture founded on innovation; industry association sponsorship; creative and entrepreneurial leadership; and deregulated markets. These conditions are likely to be more typical of organizations in tourism and hospitality, as there are many small, highly entrepreneurial firms operating in a largely deregulated marketplace. However, large companies can also encourage innovation. Virgin, for example, has always been innovative, largely because of the creative leadership of Richard Branson. Marriott, too, is a large corporation well known for innovation. Like Virgin, Marriott's strive for innovation comes from the top. CEO Arne Sorenson looks for continuous innovation from his employees, emphasizing the company's mission to 'define the cutting edge of the industry, from strategy through design, to deliver new products, services and experiences that differentiate its brands and drive competitive advantage' (Sorenson, 2015). The case study below highlights innovation in the hotel sector, whereby some boutique hotels around the world are differentiating themselves by providing a 'music-themed' experience.

CHAPTER SUMMARY

Tourism and hospitality products are a group of selected components or elements brought together in a 'bundle' to satisfy needs and wants. There are also three levels of tourism products: the core product, the tangible product, and the augmented product. An important part of the augmented product is the physical environment – often referred to as the 'servicescape'. This is very important for tourism and hospitality products such as hotels, restaurants and theme parks, which are dominated by experience attributes. Branding has developed as a method of establishing a distinctive identity for a product based on competitive differentiation from other products, and has been particularly successful in hotel and restaurant marketing. Developing new products is different from maintaining existing ones and planning for both will differ according to whether the products are targeted at existing markets or new ones.

REFLECTIVE QUESTIONS

1. Apart from the illustrations provided in the chapter, give some examples of businesses that are responding to consumer desires for experiences. How are they using the servicescape to deliver these experiences?

(Continued)

(Continued)

2. Holloway and Plant suggest that a company has four alternatives in developing new products: market penetration, market development, product development and diversification. Think of an example (not already given in the text) of each strategy that has been use in the tourism, hospitality or events sector.

3. Why is it do you think that companies don't always follow the new service development (NSD) steps suggested by Scheuing and Johnson?

MARKETING IN ACTION: HOTELS THAT DON'T MISS A BEAT

Hotels are constantly searching for the perfect formula to provide visitors with an addictive experience and music-themed hotels have become very popular, particularly in big cities. A perfect example is the Aria Hotel in Prague, Czech Republic, a city known for its musical history. The five-star luxury property hosts regular live concerts, and even has an on-site musicologist who will advise on which Rudolfinim seats have the finest acoustics and who's the hottest Prague Philharmonic conductor. Musical virtuosos and their fans can immerse themselves in music with the very first step they take on the property. From the Italian mosaic based on a Gregorian chant, to the surround-sound features in each room, every detail of the hotel is inspired by music.

IMAGE 5.4 The Modrophenia room at the Hotel Pelirocco in Brighton (Courtesy of Hotel Pelirocco)

Further west in Europe, the Backstage Hotel in Amsterdam is similarly decorated with a music theme, designed to resemble an off-stage hangout for rock bands. Decked out with saxophones and guitars, the hotel's piano is graffitied with the signatures of visiting performers. Over the border, the Nhow Hotel in Berlin, Germany goes one step further by providing services and facilities for musicians. Situated on the banks of the Spree, Nhow not only has its own recording studio with panoramic views of the city, it also offers a music-themed room service, delivering guitars and keyboards to guests at any time. There are two control rooms and a state-of-the-art recording booth in the studio which hosts sessions from 150 euros for a half-day.

Mexico is home to another hotel with a recording studio, the Hotel El Ganzo in Los Cabos, a trendy designer property that doubles up as an arts and culture centre. Beneath a trapdoor in the lobby lounge lies 'The Underground', a 1700-square-foot, state-of-the-art recording studio where musicians from around the world come to create, perform and record their work. Guests and locals can attend El Ganzo Sessions, a free ongoing series of live music performances, and anyone can view the entire catalogue of performances on the Hotel El Ganzo YouTube channel. Each month the hotel hosts various visual artists, filmmakers, and musicians as part of its Artist In Residence (AIR) programme. The boutique hotel's white walls double as a blank canvas, beckoning artists-in-residence to leave their colourful mark.

The Hotel da Música in Porto, Portugal, also holds weekly concerts and performances in order to enhance the hotel's music motif. In addition, vintage violins adorn the front desk, music stands act as menu holders, and the bedrooms have treble clef lamps and sheet music painted on the walls above the bed. The Evelyn in New York (formerly known as the Gershwin) similarly has music-themed bedrooms. The chandeliers are shaped like trombones and the bathroom tiles are decorated with musical notes and famous song lyrics. Rooms also come equipped with hi-tech gramophones that guests can sync up with their smartphones. The hotel is not far from Manhattan's Tin Pan Alley, which was once the centre of the American pop music industry.

Hotel BPM in Brooklyn, New York, has an even narrower focus, targeting budding DJs to its trendy 75-room property. Devised by a local hip hop hero, BPM stands for 'beats per minute'. DJ Bijal has created a hip hop playlist which streams throughout the hotel. To give wannabee DJs an edge, the hotel offers free lessons with the Scratch DJ Academy.

Some music-themed hotels are inspired by one particular artist or band. The Beatles-themed Hard Days Night Hotel in Liverpool England, for example, is named after the band's film, album and song. The hotel opened four years after initial conception in February 2008 during Liverpool's reign as European Capital of Culture. It has some 110 rooms, including the famed McCartney and Lennon suites, as well as numerous bars and restaurants. The hotel is situated adjacent to the world famous Cavern Club from where The Beatles rose to fame.

Another hotel in England, the Hotel Pelirocco in Brighton, has been inspired by local pop culture, touting itself as Brighton's original rock 'n' roll boutique hotel – with 19 individually themed bedrooms. One of them – the Modrophenia room – is a cheery allusion to the fact that Brighton is still pulling in visitors fascinated by the skirmishes between Mods and Rockers that took place on its seafront over the Whitsun Bank Holiday weekend in May 1964, and which spread to several other seaside resorts throughout that summer. The Mod room even has a shiny red Lambretta coming out of the bedroom wall. The scooter's front half is the left-hand bedside table, its back half the right. The bedspread is parka-coloured with a Royal Air Force roundel in the middle, and the melamine breakfast table is flanked by moulded bucket seats in orange plastic. The room is complete with Vespa-style tables and pop art images of original Mod, Keith Moon.

So, what explains the popularity of music-themed hotels? For Zuzana Šelová, Sales & Marketing Executive at the Aria Hotel in Prague, differentiation is the reason: 'There are so many hotels nowadays, it is a concept that gives the added value to the property. The music concept makes the story and people love stories.' Aria caters mainly to Baby Boomers who expect the best, so for Šelová, knowledgeable employees who deliver excellent personal service are the hotel's biggest asset. The Aria does tend to attract celebrities, and that in turn adds to the cachet of the place. 'Gérard Depardieu once

(Continued)

(Continued)

stayed here for two months and had a suite featuring a view into the Vrtba Garden,' says Šelová. 'As the windows are quite low, people were stopping and wondering if it's really him sitting on the window sill reading a book.'

Hans Spuijbroek, from the Backstage Hotel in Amsterdam also believes that differentiating with a music motif enables a hotel to stand out from the pack. 'Standard hotels are not the future of the global hotel industry,' he says. 'The more individual the people get, the different the demand is going to be.' However, Spuijbroek suggests that success for new entrants into this space is not guaranteed: 'The problem is that a lot of big hotel chains start new branded hotels with a music theme without having a clue what they are focusing on. There are a lot of "Hard Rock" kind of hotels popping up where you can rent a guitar.' For Spuijbroek, authenticity is critical. 'We know what our guests want because we're experienced and passionate about the added value we're supporting. The whole look and feel is real. The staff is real, no dressed up and over-trained robots. It's BackStage. You get it or you don't.' Although the hotel attracts visitors from all walks of life (kids love it, says Spuijbroek) Backstage specializes in hosting bands, artists and crews. But privacy is king according to Spuijbroek. 'What happens BackStage... stays BackStage!'

When asked why music-themed hotels are so popular today, Hotel El Ganzo's General Manager, Ella Messerli says: 'They say "music feeds the soul". That being said, travel now has become a larger experience selection and music definitely adds another dimension to the experience of visiting any part of the world.' Messerli says that his cultural-centric hotel goes beyond music with art interventions within the hotel. 'Music has become an integral part of the El Ganzo experience and makes the hotel unique since these musicians are brought in through our Artist in Residence programme,' he explains. 'Only at El Ganzo can you experience an under-the-stars performance of these carefully curated live concerts. Also our Music Director – who also runs our professional recording studio – carefully selects musicians who offer a high quality of delivery with their genre.'

El Ganzo attracts people from all over the world, Messerli adds: 'We have successfully defined a new experiential offering for a resort with art, music in a more natural surrounding of Los Cabos. Our location on the Marina, with our private, swimmable beach gives guests an opportunity to enjoy a relaxing day in the sun or a fun day of paddle boarding, kayaking or fishing. This has attracted many age groups, as well as weddings, for clients who seek a very private place with activities and a cultural offering that is unique as well as enriching. It is also so enjoyable to meet artists and musicians who discover our corner of Los Cabos for the first time, and hear from them how our natural setting stimulates their creative minds.'

Messerli's advice for hotel owners or managers around the world who are considering having a music theme is to keep it simple. 'But most importantly do it only if you get professionals to help you, and offer only quality. Any experiential offer in a hotel has to be of the utmost quality for it to be real and unique, which is what guests are looking for.'

Source: Hudson, S. (2016). "Hotels that Don't Miss a Beat." *Hotel Business Review*, January. http://hotelexecutive.com/business_review/

CASE STUDY QUESTIONS

1.   Why is it that hotels are constantly searching for the perfect formula to provide visitors with an addictive experience?

2.   What do all the music-themed hotels have in common? Is there one in particularly that looks appealing to you?

3.   What explains the popularity of music-themed hotels? Are they likely to increase in popularity?

REFERENCES

Andersson, T. D. and Mossberg, L. (2004) 'The dining experience: Do restaurants satisfy customer needs', *Food Service Technology*, 4: 171–7.

Bitner, M. J. (1990) 'Evaluating service encounters,' *Journal of Marketing,* 54(April): 69–82.

Bitner, M. J. (2002) 'Servicescapes: The impact of physical surroundings on customers and employees', *Journal of Marketing*, 56(April): 57–71.

Ferguson, S. and Bourke, A. (2013) 'Living the brand. The evangelical experiences of snowsport workers', in S. McCabe (ed.), *Handbook of Tourism Marketing*, pp. 435–6). London: Routledge.

Futterman, M. (2015) 'NFL expanding hospitality services', *Wall Street Journal*, 30 March: B3.

Garcia, J. A., Gomez, M. and Molina, A. (2012) 'A destination-branding model: An empirical analysis based on stakeholders', *Tourism Management,* 33(3): 646–61.

Getz, D. (2007) *Event Studies. Theory, Research and Policy for Planned Events*. Oxford: Butterworth-Heinemann.

Grady, J. and Ohlin, J. B. (2009) 'Equal access to hospitality services for guests with mobility impairments under the Americans with Disabilities Act: Implications for the hospitality industry', *International Journal of Hospitality Management,* 28: 161–9.

HNN (2015) 'The 2015 big brands report', *Hotel News Now*, 23 March. www.hotelnews now.com/Article/15433/The-2015-Big-Brands-Report (accessed 7 December 2016).

Harris, L. C. and Ezeh, C. (2007) 'Servicescape and loyalty intentions: an empirical investigation', *European Journal of Marketing*, 42(3/4): 390–422.

Holloway, C. J. and Plant, R. V. (1992) *Marketing for Tourism*, 2nd edn. London: Pitman.

Jackson, N. (2013) *Promoting and Marketing Events*. Oxon: Routledge.

Jones, P. (1995) 'Innovation in flight catering'. In P. Jones and M. Kipps (eds), *Flight Catering*, pp. 163–75. London: Longman.

Jones, P., Hudson, S. and Costis, P. (1997) 'New product development in the UK tour-operating industry', *Progress in Tourism and Hospitality Research,* 3(4): 283–94.

Klara, R. (2011) 'Waxing eloquent. Behind the scenes at Madame Tussauds', *USAir Magazine*, December: 42–6.

Kotler, P. T. and Armstrong, G. (2014) *Principles of Marketing*, 15th edn. New Jersey: Prentice Hall.

Levere, J. L. (2014) 'If you can't make it to the lecture', *New York Times*, 19 March. www.nytimes.com/2014/03/20/arts/artsspecial/if-you-cant-make-it-to-the-lecture.html (accessed 7 December 2016).

Levy, S., Hudson, S. and Getz, D. (2011) 'A field experimental investigation of managerially facilitated consumer-to-consumer interaction, *Journal of Travel and Tourism Marketing*, 28(6): 656–74.

Lin, M-Q, Huang, L-S. and Chiang, Y-F. (2008) 'The moderating effects of gender roles on service emotional contagion'. *The Services Industries Journal*, 28(6): 755–67.

Lovelock, C. and Wirtz, J. (2007) *Services Marketing: People, Technology, Strategy*, 6th edn, New Jersey, USA; Prentice Hall International.

Manzur, L. and Jogaratnam, G. (2006) 'Impression management and the hospitality service encounter: cross-cultural differences', *Journal of Travel and Tourism Marketing*, 20(3/4): 21–31.

McGroarty, P. and Berzon, A. (2012) 'Hoteliers fill a gap: Africa', *The Wall Street Journal*, 19 September. www.wsj.com/articles/SB10000872396390443720204578004243238970954 (accessed 7 December 2016).

Mercer, D. (1992) *Marketing*. Oxford: Blackwell.

Middleton, V. T. C. and Clarke, J. R. (2012) *Marketing in Travel and Tourism*, 3rd edn. Oxford: Butterworth-Heinemann.

Mosley, R. W. (2007) 'Customer experience, organisational culture and the employer brand', *Brand Management*, 15(2): 123–34.

Mutzabaugh, B. (2011) 'First Dreamliner fliers sing its praises', *USA Today*, 28 October: 1B–2B.

Pike, S. and Mason, R. (2011) 'Destination competitiveness through the lens of brand positioning: The case of Australia's Sunshine Coast', *Current Issues in Tourism,* 14(2): 169–82.

Pogrebin, R. (2015) 'Museums seek to lure, then lock in, teenage connoisseurs', *New York Times*, 16 March 16. www.nytimes.com/2015/03/19/arts/artsspecial/museums-seek-to-lure-then-lock-in-teenage-connoisseurs.html (accessed 7 December 2016).

Reimer, A. and Kuehn, R. (2004) 'The impact of servicescape on quality perception', *European Journal of Marketing*, 39(7/8): 785–808.

Russell, M. (2012) 'Richard Branson's fails: 14 Virgin companies that went bust', *Business Insider*, 21 April. www.businessinsider.com/richard-branson-fails-virgin-companies-that-went-bust-2012-4 (accessed 7 December 2016).

Russell, J. A., Ward, L. M. and Pratt, G. (1981) 'An affective quality attributed to environments', *Environment and Behavior,* 13(3): 259–88.

Scheuing, E. E. and Johnson, E. M. (1989) 'A proposed model for new service development', *Journal of Services Marketing,* 3(2): 25–34.

Schultz, H. (2011) *Onward*. New York: Rodale Inc.

Sorenson, A. (2015) 'How to live innovation', *LinkedIn*, 11 February. https://www.linkedin.com/pulse/how-live-innovation-arne-sorenson (accessed 7 December 2016).

Suellentrop, C. (2014) 'At play in skies of Cretaceous Era', *New York Times*, 19 March. www.nytimes.com/2014/03/20/arts/artsspecial/at-play-in-skies-of-cretaceous-era.html (accessed 7 December 2016).

Swarbrooke, J. and Page, S.J. (2002) *The Development and Management of Visitor Attractions* (2nd Edition). New York: Routledge.

TEA (2015) *Theme Index and Museum Index: The Global Attractions Attendance Report.* Themed Entertainment Association (TEA). www.teaconnect.org/images/files/TEA_103_49736_150603.pdf

Tombs, A. and McColl-Kennedy, J. R. (2003) 'Social-servicescape conceptual model', *Marketing Theory*, 3(4): 447–75.

Walls, A., Okumus, F., Wang, Y. and Kwun, D. J-W. (2011) 'Understanding the consumer experience: An exploratory study of luxury hotels', *Journal of Hospitality Marketing and Management*, 20(2): 166–97.

Wang, E. S-T. (2009) 'Displayed emotions to patronage intention: consumer response to contact personal performance'. *The Service Industries Journal*, 29(3): 317–29.

Wassener, B. (2014) 'It already dwarfs Las Vegas, and its casino boom has room to grow', *New York Times*, 26 March: B1, B7.

Wong, E. (2010) 'The most memorable product launches of 2010'. Forbes, 3 December. www.forbes.com/2010/12/03/most-memorable-products-leadership-cmo-network.html (accessed 7 December 2016).

Wood, E. (2005) 'Measuring the economic and social impact of local authority events', *International Journal of Public Sector Management*, 18(1): 37–53.

Zeithaml, V. A., Bitner, M. J., Gremler, D., Mahaffey, T. and Hiltz, B. (2007) *Services Marketing: Integrating Customer Focus Across The Firm*, Canadian Edition. New York: McGraw-Hill.

Zenker, S. and Martin, N. (2013) 'Measuring success in place marketing and branding', *Place Branding and Public Diplomacy*, 7(1): 32–41.

PRICING 6

INTRODUCTION

After a brief introduction to pricing, Chapter 6 begins by highlighting the key factors determining pricing decisions. As well as marketing objectives, these include costs, other mix variables, channel member expectations, buyer perceptions, competition, and legal and regulatory restrictions. The next part of the chapter focuses on how companies use pricing as part of their positioning of a product, employing one of three basic approaches: premium pricing, value-for-money pricing and undercut pricing. Pricing strategies for new products are the subject of the next part of the chapter, which discusses prestige pricing, market skimming, and penetration pricing. Other pricing techniques are then examined, followed by a look at the specific characteristics of the tourism and hospitality industry which affect pricing policy. Case studies focus on a ski travel agent, the marketing of riads in Morocco, and the proliferation of low-cost airlines around the world.

LESSONS FROM A MARKETING GURU: SARAH PLASKITT, SCOUT

With the enticing tagline 'Dream, Find, Book, Ski', Scout is the brainchild of Sarah Plaskitt, a former journalist and ad agency brand strategist. Her background in journalism helped her create a top-notch travel website featuring inspirational stories as well as persuasive photography. Reviews of resorts and lodging are more credible since hotels don't pay to be featured on the site. 'What makes Scout different from other ski travel agents or online booking services, is that we have been to every resort and property on Scout,' says Plaskitt, who was away 'scouting' in France when she organized a fam trip itinerary to Nozawa Onsen in Japan for your authors.

IMAGE 6.1 Sarah Plaskitt (Courtesy of scoutski.com)

With immaculate attention to detail, she provided a two-night, two-day itinerary staying at Ryokan Sakaya, a traditional Japanese boutique hotel complete with kimonos, ceremonial tea service, futons, tatami mats and indoor/outdoor onsens (hot tubs) for après ski recovery. 'Scout is a small company offering highly personalized service. We do all the uphill work for you so you can concentrate on heading downhill,' Plaskitt quips. The exquisite town winds uphill, with cobbled streets intersecting traditional buildings, housing quaint restaurants, cafés and shops. Alongside each street is a gushing hot spring, warm water from which is piped on to the streets to clear the snow naturally.

Established in 2013, Scout operates as a magazine, guidebook and boutique travel agency via the website www.scoutski.com. 'It's a one-stop shop where you can book your ski trip,' says Plaskitt. This can be anything from just a room to a full ski package with meticulously crafted itinerary and Scout Field Guide. 'Although I have some set packages on the site, most of the packages I sell are completely customized for each client,' she explains. 'To create package prices I start with the rates the suppliers give me and that can either be starting with the net rate and marking that up, or a rack rate and then I get my commission off that price. Sometimes each item that makes up a package is broken out as a cost, but other times you just give one price for the complete package.' While some customers want individual costs itemized, others don't care, she says: 'And in some cases you have a contract which stipulates that it may not be able to be broken out.' Because the company operates online, care is taken not to undersell a supplier's own price but discounting is possible when various items are packaged together.

From her background working for ad agencies in New York and Sydney, Australian-born Plaskitt decided to go it alone in order to have more control, flexibility and purpose in her career. 'I quickly decided that I wanted to focus the business online which meant I could have customers from all over the world,' she recounts. 'The heavy emphasis on original content helps Scout get discovered organically by skiers everywhere but, if I do any marketing, it tends to be focused on the US and Australian markets.'

Scout operates in an ever-expanding list of destinations in the US, Canada, New Zealand, Italy, Austria, Switzerland, France and Japan. With Japanese resorts gaining more international visitation annually, Scout turned its attention to Nozawa Onsen, Japan's oldest ski resort. Due to its rich history, authentic architecture and reinforcing relationship with St Anton, Nozawa Onsen has an appeal to skiers looking for an immersive Japanese experience.

'There's a lot of traditional ryokans – Japanese inns, like Ryokan Sakaya – and shrines, and it's not overly developed by Westerners,' Plaskitt explains. The powder snow is another of the big draws: 'Everyone's heard about it and everyone wants to try it. And it is as awesome as people say – if you get a great powder day, which is highly likely during peak season.' In fact your authors had an epic powder day there, skiing in the lightest, fluffiest, knee-deep snow all day long.

Due to its proximity by bullet train to Tokyo and Kyoto, Nozawa Onsen is often added on to a cultural city itinerary. A challenge is to get people to book in advance, says Plaskitt: 'One of the big things I'm trying to achieve with PR in the US is to educate people that they need to book really early for Japan. A lot of properties (and particularly in places like Nozawa Onsen) for key dates are booked out by June/August for the following season – and it's getting earlier every year.'

Although Scout typically operates directly with its customers and suppliers, occasionally it uses intermediaries to facilitate business. 'In a few instances I use receptive or wholesale agencies to sell me a product, even if I've been there and developed a relationship with the supplier. This could be for a variety of reasons,' says Plaskitt. 'Although it can be convenient, generally I find it doesn't save me any time and often not being in complete control of the process makes it harder. So where possible I try to go direct, which is very unusual for a smaller agency. But I prefer it that way and I believe it gets a better result for my clients.' Again for reasons of independence, Plaskitt avoids joint promotions: 'It's a very slippery slope that could see me losing independence over what I sell.'

Ultimately, it is content that is of primary importance to the former journalist. 'Making my content work hard is what I'm focusing on at the moment so that has included some SEO marketing efforts,' she explains. 'I'm also doing some Google Adwords campaigns which are great because you can be very targeted and focused on what you're selling and to whom.'

Sources: Personal visits by both authors to Ryokan Sakaya, Nozawa Onsen, Japan in January 2016; email interviews with Sarah Plaskitt.

INTRODUCTION TO PRICING

As the opening case study highlights, pricing is crucial to the successful marketing of any product or service, but it is often the least understood of the marketing mix elements. As with Sarah Plaskitt of Scout, the prices that an organization charges for its products must strike a balance between gaining acceptance with the target market and making profit for the organization. Even in not-for-profit organizations, the pricing of products and services is the key to encouraging consumption. The pricing element of the marketing mix is unique in that it is the only one that directly affects an organization's revenues, and hence its profits. The fields of finance and economics have much to contribute in setting prices, but on their own perhaps do not lead to the best pricing decisions. Other marketing mix decisions will often interact with pricing decisions. Product quality (both real and perceived) needs to be considered in light of price. Knowledge of the 'price-quality trade-off' compels decision-makers to recognize that consumers might accept a higher cost for a better quality of product. Similarly, with regard to brand image – often the consequence of marketing communications decisions – lesser-known brands might command lower prices. For example, research has shown that hotels that belong to a branded chain tend to charge higher prices and provide smaller discounts than those not attached to a well-known brand (Becerra, Santaló and Silva, 2013).

As with other elements in the marketing mix, pricing should be treated as a tool to achieve corporate and marketing objectives. If the target market has been clearly identified, and a decision has been made about where a product is to be positioned, then pricing will become easier to determine. Companies choosing to position their products in the mass market and to enter a field with many competitors will need to adopt a very careful pricing policy. Those seeking to appeal to niche markets (like Scout targeting skiers interested in Japan) may have slightly more price flexibility, since they have fewer competitors and perhaps more points of difference between their products and others in the niche. For the last decade or so, downward pressure on prices in general has been very strong, some of it caused by sluggish growth in Western economies and Japan, but there are other contributing factors such as the increasing power of retailers such as Wal-Mart, low labour costs in emerging markets like China and Vietnam, and the power of the Internet, which makes pricing more transparent (Marn, Roegner and Zawada, 2003).

FACTORS DETERMINING PRICING DECISIONS

Whatever strategy an organization adopts, clear pricing objectives should be established before price levels are set. The key factors determining pricing decisions are shown in Figure 6.1. They are as follows.

1. MARKETING OBJECTIVES

The most common objectives are profit maximization, target rate of return, market share and survival. However, for some organizations, such as national parks or museums, objectives are not only commercial in their nature, and pricing decisions are made for societal reasons. This may involve raising entry fees to reduce the social and environmental impacts of increasing numbers of visitors, as in the case of Machu

FIGURE 6.1 Factors affecting pricing decisions (Source: Adapted from Dibb et al., 1994)

Picchu in Peru, or lowering fees to encourage more access. Social motives were behind the Czech Republic's initiative to lower prices of soft drinks in restaurants in 2013 (Carney, 2013). The country's health minister was trying to put Czechs on a lower-hops diet, and in most restaurants and taverns, a mug of beer is cheaper than water. He was asking restaurants and bars, therefore, to offer at least one non-alcoholic beverage at a price lower than beer, primarily to offer teens an alternative. Other marketing objectives may include wanting to be perceived as offering outstanding value for money. At the Masters' golf tournament in Augusta, spectators can still buy lunch for half the price of any other tournament, because the original owners believed that anyone who had to travel hundreds of miles to watch a game of golf ought to be able to buy a decent meal at a decent price (Hudson and Hudson, 2013).

2. COSTS

The setting of prices should incorporate a calculation of how much it costs the organization to produce the product or service. If the company is profit-oriented, a margin will be added to the cost price to derive the selling price. This was evident in the opening case study, where Sarah Plaskitt from Scout would look at the cost of each item that makes up a ski package before adding her commission and quoting one price for the package. When pricing events, costs are a crucial consideration. The costs of putting on a musical, for example, can be extremely high. As composer Andrew Lloyd Webber says: 'On Broadway, unless you are grossing $1 million a week, you're not even in the game: you haven't even started to repay your debts. *School of Rock* is a small production but it cost $14.5 million' (Wright, 2016). These costs would explain why tickets to such events are so high.

3. OTHER MARKETING MIX VARIABLES

Pricing decisions always have an interaction with the other elements of the marketing mix. Consider the example of Canadian Mountain Holidays (CMH), which sells expensive heli-skiing holidays. The high price of this product must be reflected in other elements of the marketing mix. A high level of personal service is included as part of the promotional package, and the quality of the lodges must meet the expectations that the high price has generated in the minds of the customers. Distribution of the holidays takes place via an exclusive channel system of overseas agents, reflecting the high-quality image and resulting high price. In fact, research has show that businesses in the top quintile of relative service quality realize on average an 8 per cent higher price than their competitors (Gale, 1992). The case study below about riads in Morocco explains how the Madada Mogador boutique hotel in Essaouira can charge a premium price all year round because of a consistent high quality.

4. INTERMEDIARIES

A marketer must consider the intermediaries in the distribution channel when pricing a product or service. Travel intermediaries like Scout, for example, will expect to earn commissions for their efforts. However, some stakeholders in the travel industry, such as airlines, car rental companies, and international hotel chains, have been quick to grasp the potential of marketing and selling their services online. They have recognized an opportunity to bypass agents and sell their basic products and services directly to the customer. Increasingly, package holiday tour operators are including direct sales via the Internet in their sales strategy, thus bypassing the travel agent.

5. BUYER PERCEPTIONS

The prices set for travel products and services must reflect customers' perceptions in the target market. The key is whether customers perceive that the price they have paid represents good value for money and matches their quality expectations. In tourism and hospitality, consumers expect a high level of service and special features if a high price is being charged. For example, after paying $10,000, a CMH heli-skier can expect lodges to contain a fully stocked bar, a sauna and jacuzzi, and even a resident qualified massage therapist. High prices may deter tourists, though, and this was the case for Cirque du Soleil, the operator of avant-garde circus events, which reported that revenues of its European tours fell by 37 per cent in 2013 due to a sharp drop in the number of shows it hosted. The Canadian company was juggling with increased competition and the economic downturn, which was a particular problem as tickets to Cirque shows are perceived to be expensive (Sylt, 2015). Business tourists are also price sensitive. Event planners, for example, are finding that smaller cities are emerging as appealing alternatives for business events to the typical destinations like Orlando and Las Vegas. 'The entire meeting experience will be cheaper for the attendee,' said Reggie Aggarwal, CEO for Cvent, an event-management portal. 'But also people are looking for different experiences. That's why we are seeing a rise of regional alternatives' (Jones, 2015).

6. COMPETITION

In competitive markets, organizations will be trying to win customers from competitors in two ways. Price competition involves offering the product or service at a lower price than the price charged by the competition. In a very competitive marketplace, organizations are likely to resort to intense price competition to sell goods and services. Nonprice competition, on the other hand, is concerned with trying to increase market share or sales by leaving the price unchanged but persuading target customers that their offering is superior to that offered by the competition. Such a strategy is more typical in oligopolistic markets, in which there are few competitors. It is important for tourism organizations, including destinations, to monitor the prices charged by competitors. Tripadvisor recently compiled a list of the most expensive and the best value destinations for a three-day city break for British travellers. The website's TripIndex survey compared the cost of a three-night break during June to August, taking into account typical costs for two people. The top three best value destinations were Hanoi in Vietnam, Warsaw in Poland and Sharm el Sheikh in Egypt. The most expensive cities to visit were Cancun in Mexico, Zurich in Switzerland and New York (Kynaston, 2015).

7. LEGAL AND REGULATORY ISSUES

There may be legal and regulatory restrictions that control the ways in which an organization fixes prices. For example, Robben Island in Cape Town, the political prison where Nelson Mandela was incarcerated for 18 years, is subsidized by the government, and is put under pressure to keep prices low to encourage people to visit. Since the prison and island were opened to the public in January 1997, the number of annual visitors has risen from 100,000 in the first year to over 300,000 by 2015. With its poignant history, designation as a World Heritage Site in 1999, environmental attributes – including the beautiful backdrop of prosperous Cape Town, a full view of Table Mountain, the colourful international harbour, and its abundant wildlife – Robben Island will always remain an important tourist destination as well as a tangible symbol of South Africa's divided history (Hudson, 2008). In addition to regulatory restrictions, legal boundaries are often placed on the practice of price fixing and collusion. Additionally, there are a number of organizations, quasi-governmental and industrial, that exercise some influence on pricing policies and strategies, a fact that marketing managers must bear in mind.

CONTRIBUTIONS OF ECONOMICS TO PRICING

Economists contend that producers of a commodity are more likely to provide that commodity if the price for it in the marketplace is high. This is coupled with the suggestion that buyers are more likely to purchase more of the commodity if prices are low. From this comes the idea that the quantity produced and consumed and the price acceptable to each party will be in equilibrium at some point. This is shown in Figure 6.2.

Unfortunately, this simplistic model is unlikely to be useful as a mathematical way of determining prices because it assumes that certain conditions need to be present for the process to occur. One of these is the assumption that consumers have perfect knowledge, and know all the prices from all the producers. Although the use of the Internet is increasing, the likelihood of such wide consumer knowledge occurring is small in the travel industry. Although the model may not help pricing decisions in a mathematical or graphical way, it does not mean that the concept is completely redundant. For instance, if a tourism organization has a feeling that the market is undersupplied, it may tend to increase prices. This is happening in some developing countries like Ghana, where hoteliers are able to charge premium room rates due to low supply and high demand. Similarly, if a buyer senses that the market is oversupplied, the buyer may try to negotiate lower prices – as happens often in the hotel market after a terrorist attack (Chazan, 2015).

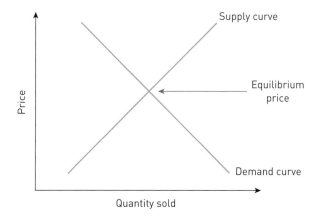

FIGURE 6.2 The interaction of supply and demand

The raising and lowering of prices generally has an effect on the level of sales. The analysis of buyers' reactions to price change employs the concept of the elasticity of demand. This is represented by the formula:

$$\text{Price elasticity of demand} = \frac{\% \text{ change in quantity demanded}}{\% \text{ change in price}}$$

If demand increases in line with price cuts then the product or service is said to be elastic. But if demand remains relatively unaltered by price changes, the product or service is said to be inelastic. In the tourism and hospitality industry, many products are elastic – as prices fall, demand increases. However, there are many occasions when this is not true. Business travel is often inelastic, and popularity or fashion may render a destination or restaurant inelastic. Demand for the Burj Al Hotel in Dubai, for example, would seem to be inelastic. The hotel can charge very high prices, as business travellers are willing to pay a high price for such luxury. Boasting seven stars, the Burj Al Hotel caters to the millionaires and billionaires of the world with its luxurious and spectacular facilities. It provides exclusivity, security and privacy for celebrities, in particular, and international businessmen for a high price tag – around US$600 for a basic room per night and US$8,000 for the Royal Suite.

Figure 6.3 shows two demand curves – one for an elastic product, and one for an inelastic product. As with knowledge of the state of supply and demand, managers are not often in a position to know mathematically the value of elasticity for a product. They may not have access to all price and quantity data, or the service may be new and there may therefore be no historical data from which to derive the slope of the demand curve.

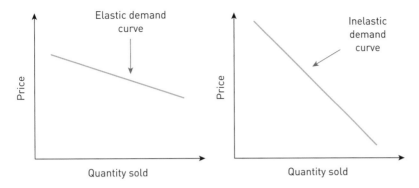

FIGURE 6.3 Elastic and inelastic demand curves

In setting prices, a company will want to know what levels of demand it is likely to experience at different prices. This can be done in two ways. The first method is often called willingness to pay (WTP) assessment. Research has shown, for example, that demand for space travel is fairly elastic; in willingness-to-pay surveys, demand increases significantly when the price falls. The difficulty with this method is that what people say they will do does not always translate into actual behaviour when the product is launched. A second way of assessing demand at different prices is test marketing, although it is difficult to control all the factors apart from price that will influence consumer decisions in different areas.

PRICING AND POSITIONING

Generally, companies use pricing as part of their positioning of a product, employing one of three strategic approaches: premium pricing, value-for-money pricing, and undercut pricing (Dickman, 1999). Any of these policies can be seen as 'fair-pricing' policies. A fair price can be defined as one that the customer is happy to pay while the company achieves a satisfactory level of profit. Thus a premium-pricing policy is acceptable, provided that the customer receives the benefits appropriate to the price. Only when companies are able to force up prices against the consumers' will, such as in the case of monopolies, can it be said that fair pricing is inoperative. A monopoly is a supply situation in which there is only one seller.

1. PREMIUM PRICING

In premium pricing, a decision is made to set prices above market price, to reflect either the image of quality or the unique status of the product. The product may be new, or it may have unique features not shared by competitors, such as the Burj Al Arab Hotel in Dubai. No expense was spared on the hotel's design or its rococo furnishings fit for a sheik's palace. It is shaped like a ship's sail soaring over 341 metres high, making it the tallest hotel in the world. The lobby is a massive atrium, stretching several hundred feet up, making it one of the largest in the world. Gold pilasters and enormous aquariums surround the escalators.

Alternatively, a company itself may have such a strong reputation that the brand image alone is sufficient to merit a premium price. The Four Seasons Hotel chain follows this strategy in setting prices. Promoted as upscale, full-service hotels,

Four Seasons will, on occasion, raise prices to the highest level in the area. Others may use premium pricing in order to generate publicity. A good example is the $5,000 FleurBurger, sold at Fleur restaurant in Las Vegas. The burger is the creation of chef Hubert Keller, and contains Wagyu beef, foie gras, shaved black truffles and truffle sauce. It's served on a brioche truffle bun. The price also includes fries and a bottle of vintage 1995 Chateau Petrus, which has a price tag of around $2,500.

IMAGE 6.2 Fleur restaurant in Las Vegas (©MGM Resorts International. Used with permission)

2. VALUE-FOR-MONEY PRICING

In value-for-money pricing, the intention is to charge medium prices and emphasize that the product represents excellent value for money at this price. Organizations with well-established reputations for service generally do well with such a pricing strategy. According to *Travel & Leisure* magazine, guests staying at properties in the Fairmont Hotels & Resorts collection are consistently maximizing the value of their dollar by receiving exceptional service, unique offerings, and renowned hospitality at an affordable price. For many 'medical tourists', having surgery in a foreign country represents excellent value for money, and it has become increasingly common for residents of industrialized countries to make long-haul trips to certain developing countries to take advantage of their less expensive, yet high quality, medical facilities and services. The rapid rise in this new industry is attributable to the high costs of medical care in developed countries, in conjunction with the comparative ease and affordability nowadays of international travel, rapidly improving technology and standards of care worldwide, and the proven safety records of medical care in many developing countries around the world (Bookman and Bookman, 2007).

3. UNDERCUT PRICING

Sometimes called 'cheap value' pricing, the objective in undercut pricing is to undercut the competition by setting lower prices, and the lower price is used as a trigger for immediate purchasing. Unit profits are low, but satisfactory overall profits are achieved through high turnover. This strategy is often used by organizations seeking a foot in or rapid expansion into a new market. For example, no-frills airline carriers are expanding their services to include longer routes, and are entering the market with very low prices. In 2014, in a move that could deliver a devastating blow to major full-service airlines, European budget carrier Ryanair announced a plan to offer $10 tickets for flights between London and New York. Big airlines typically charge about $500 for one-way flights between the two cities. The price announced by the Dublin-based company is incredibly low, even if it does not include fees for using airport facilities. Michael O'Leary, Ryanair's chief executive, claims such rock-bottom prices are nothing new for his company, pointing out that it already offers some European services for less than 1 euro (Nikkei Asian Review, 2014).

PRICING STRATEGIES FOR NEW PRODUCTS

At the core of pricing is the consumer's perception of price in relation to quality and value for money. This perception can be influenced by the way in which a company charges for its services. When a new product enters the market, it is vital to obtain market share and create the desired image for the product in the consumer's eyes. New products face unique problems. If the product is truly new – something never before available in the marketplace, like space tourism – it will be extremely difficult for consumers to develop a sense of what price is appropriate. If there are no similar products with which to compare it, they may either undervalue the innovation or perhaps overvalue it. Detailed research on price sensitivity, clearly outlining the unique features of the new product and researching the best way to communicate this information to consumers, will be important.

Three strategies commonly used for the introduction of new products are prestige pricing, market skimming and penetration pricing.

1. PRESTIGE PRICING

This method sets prices high in order to position a product at the upper or luxury end of the market. For example, tourism and hospitality operators that wish to be seen as top-end operators or establishments must enter the market with high prices to reflect this quality image. The product itself will need to deliver this quality level (in terms of décor, menu, locations, fittings, etc.). A coach company introducing a new luxury vehicle with airline-style seats, individual light and air-conditioning controls, panoramic windows, onboard catering, and amenities can price the transportation as a prestige product. If consumers value these attributes, they will pay the additional premium price. In 2016, Reykjavik's Secret Solstice festival was promoting what it called 'the world's most expensive festival ticket' (Norwegian, 2016a). The $1million package for six included transportation by private jet, VIP access to the Artists' Bar, special concerts in a volcano-glacier-lava field, luxury accommodation, a private evening at the Blue Lagoon, helicopter and plane tours, and a personal dining experience with one of Iceland's top chefs.

IMAGE 6.3 The Secret Solstice festival, Iceland (Courtesy of secretsolstice.is)

2. MARKET SKIMMING

This policy of 'skimming the cream' calls for setting high prices at the launch stage and progressively lowering them as the product becomes better established and progresses through its life cycle. The policy takes advantage of the fact that most products are in high demand in the early stage of the life cycle, when they are novel or unique or when supplies are limited. Demand can be managed by setting very high prices initially to attract those prepared to meet them, and gradually reducing the price to meet different market segments' price elasticities. The particular value of this policy is that it provides a high inflow of funds to the company when the marketing costs are highest. Operators in the space tourism market are currently following this strategy. If the product anticipates a very short life cycle – as in the case of major events such as the World Cup football tournament, where organizing and marketing costs must be recovered quickly – market skimming is a sensible policy to pursue.

3. PENETRATION PRICING

This strategy is the opposite of market skimming, as prices are set at a very low initial level. If an organization is trying to achieve maximum distribution for the product in the initial stages, it will probably price at a lower level to obtain maximum sales and market share. This method is commonly used in the marketing of fast-moving consumer goods, when rapid distribution-stocking is essential to the success of the product. If the market is price sensitive (such as in the fast-food sector), penetration pricing is an efficient way to gain a quick foothold. The intention is to set low prices only until this market share has been established and then to raise prices gradually to market levels. Of course, a company may choose to offer a service complete free of charge in order to establish a competitive advantage. Norwegian, one of the largest low-cost carriers in Europe, followed such a strategy when it became the first airline to offer free wi-fi on its European routes in 2011. By April 2016, more than 19 million passengers had logged on, with one-third of passengers logging into a social media site within five minutes (Norwegian, 2016b).

DIGITAL SPOTLIGHT: RITZY RIADS IN ESSAOUIRA, MOROCCO

IMAGE 6.4 Cooking class at Madada Mogador (Courtesy of Christine Dadda)

When an Air France stewardess had a vision for a high-quality boutique hotel in the beachy-chic resort of Essaouira, Morocco, she did not at first appreciate the barriers she would face in terms of language, the local system of baksheesh, and a lack of confidence in her business savvy. 'In 2000 a notary said to me "Why are you buying in Essaouira? You're going to lose your money." In the mind of Moroccans, Essaouira was just a very small village with nothing there.' But Monaco-born, Christine Dadda was way ahead of the curve. She saw the potential for gentrification and growth in the beautifully designed medina and glorious sandy coastline. It took a visit from the King of Monaco to speed up her acceptance by local businessmen: 'Prince Albert came to stay here. He's a family friend as I'm originally from Monaco, one of the 6500 Monaco passport holders in fact. He came and gave me a good benediction and after that I had no trouble with administration. Before I was just a former Air France flight attendant who bought a house here.'

She now owns the oceanfront Madada Mogador boutique hotel nestled behind the city ramparts and overlooking the port and beaches from its stylish rooftop lounge and dining area. Chic, high-ceilinged rooms at Madada Mogador feature oversized Moroccan ceramics and basketwork, colourful art, huge light fixtures, sumptuous bed linen all in subtle shades of mocha. Extra touches include: fresh roses in rooms; a cell phone to contact the hotel or make reservations; a morning news sheet updating news from guests' home countries; top-quality toiletries made from patchouli oil and orange blossom. Because of these high standards, Dadda commands a set price year round: 'My prices are based on quality-service-location-human hospitality and I have only one price the same all year because all these things are the same quality all year, too,' she explains. The weather in Essaouira helps as it is warm and sunny for most of the year. She also runs a ritzy restaurant called La Table Madada which features haute cuisine cookery workshops (L'Atelier Madada), and an interior design concept store, Le Comptoir Oriental by Madada where African and oriental antiques are juxtaposed with modern Moroccan pieces in Dadda's signature fashionable fusion.

Media exposure has been responsible for the Madada's continued success. 'Madada is on Facebook and has its own website, of course, but it has also been in over 30 magazine articles – French magazines, Japanese, Russian. And I also advertise in the town magazine,' says Dadda. The seaside retreat has attracted rich and famous celebrities over the years. Jimi Hendrix was there, Orson Welles made *Othello* there (and now has a

(Continued)

(Continued)

hotel and public garden named after him), Catherine Deneuve visited, and the actors from *Kingdom of Heaven* were there while filming in 2016. 'Also, one of the people in government, André Azoulay, the right-hand man of the King Mohammed VI of Morocco, was born here and comes back every weekend with his family and he promotes it,' Dadda adds.

Wander a little further into the heart of Essaouira's medina, and you will find, hidden behind an immense wooden door, the Riad Dar Maya – a tranquil haven from the retail racket of Essaouira's old town. It is run by Gareth Turpin, a Brit who fell in love with the area during a visit in 2006 when he stayed at the Madada Mogador. Bored with his suit-and-tie lifestyle, he pooled a legacy and the proceeds of a London house sale to buy first a villa to live in and secondly the site to build his small hotel. Run as a bed-and-breakfast, it is artfully built around an open-air quad with all balconies opening on to the cool courtyard with its subtly seeping water wall and cooling tall plants. 'It was just a piece of land so we built from the foundations up,' says Turpin. Opening in April 2013, the Riad Dar Maya has been approximately 80 per cent booked ever since. 'There is some seasonal change – for example, we are busier at Christmas, Easter, August and during the Gnaoua World Music Festival. But we have blue skies most of the year so it is consistent,' says Turpin.

His boutique B&B is always booked up in advance for Essaouira's signature music festival which runs in May or June depending on the dates of Ramadan. Covered by French TV channels, the Gnaoua Festival features a broad range of world music stars – including, in the past, Annie Lennox – over various downtown and beach stages. The rest of the year, Turpin works with different websites, including Mr and Mrs Smith which specialized originally in English boutique hotels and more recently expanded internationally. 'These are very select and carefully curated,' Turpin explains. He also uses Booking.com, Splendor, Tablet Hotels, Fleewinter and Tripadvisor for direct bookings. 'With all these sources, our five rooms can each be occupied by different nationalities some weeks. At the moment the biggest percentage is Brits, but it was the French originally,' he says. Locally, newletters such as *Made in Essaouira* help publicize the Riad Dar Maya which has also been featured in the *Telegraph*, *Guardian*, *Times*, and by *Condé Nast Traveler*.

One of the great advantages of setting up business in Morocco was the low cost of property and renovations: 'Prices are much lower compared to the UK, and especially compared to London,' says Turpin. 'For example, you can pick up a smallish riad for 200,000 euros already renovated. Prices in Essauouira for renovations are about 600–700 euros per square metre.' This meant that, with the help of a French architect, he could design a top-notch property with careful attention to details for the artsy interior décor.

Sources: Hudson, S. (2016). "Ritzy Riads Putting Morocco on the Map." *Hotel Business Review*, October. http://hotelexecutive.com/business_review/4879/ritzy-riads-putting-morocco-on-the-map

CASE STUDY QUESTIONS

1. With reference to the factors determining pricing decisions discussed at the beginning of the chapter, how do accommodations in general set their prices?

2. What pricing strategies are the two riads profiled in this case study following?

3. The end of the chapter looks at the specific characteristics of the tourism and hospitality industry which affect pricing policy. Do any of these apply to the riads in Morocco?

OTHER PRICING STRATEGIES AND TECHNIQUES

PROMOTIONAL PRICING

Promotional pricing is used by companies when they temporarily sell products below their normal list price (or rack rate). Usually this is done for a short period of time, often to introduce new or revamped products. Promotional pricing is used in the restaurant sector in these situations. The assumption is made that consumers will buy other items at normal price levels along with the promotionally priced items. Promotional pricing is often used in conjunction with product-bundle pricing (see below).

PRODUCT-BUNDLE PRICING

When a company groups several of its products together to promote them as a package, it is using product-bundle pricing. An example would be a hotel offering a weekend special that includes a room, dinner in a restaurant, valet parking, room-service breakfast, and late checkout for a set price. In some cases the package will include products that customers might not normally buy (such as the valet parking); this is often done to improve usage during slow periods. Package tours are a popular type of product bundling (Naidoo, Ramseook-Munhurrun and Seetaram, 2011). Wholesalers package airfare, ground transport, accommodation, sightseeing tours and admission to attractions and, because of their bulk purchasing power, they can negotiate significant discounts. These companies can then offer packages to customers that work out to be considerably cheaper than buying the individual components separately. Bundling, therefore, offers cost advantages to the company as well as convenience to the consumer. Research on bundling in the tourism sector has shown that transparent pricing, that is itemization of individual package components and discounts, is actually preferred by consumers if it reduces uncertainty or simplifies the decision process. Nontransparent pricing is more effective if savings are not shown or the price is higher than the alternative, in which case the itemized components complicate the decision process without providing useful information (Tanford, Baloglu and Erdem, 2012).

PRICE SPREAD AND PRICE POINTS

Organizations in tourism and hospitality try to offer a price spread – a range of products that will suit the budget of all target markets. A holiday park, for example, may offer campsites with tents, standard cabins, ensuite cabins and family units, each different from the other in terms of size, location, types of fittings and furnishings. Table 6.1 shows the range of prices offered by Banff Mount Norquay, a ski resort in Canada that charges by the hour. The range of prices that an organization can set is virtually unlimited. However, research in the restaurant sector has suggested that if the price spread is too wide, consumers will tend to order from among the lower-priced items (Carmin and Norkus, 1990).

Price points are the number of 'stops' along the way between the lowest-priced item and the highest-priced item. Price points vary among industry sectors and types of business. In a restaurant, it is possible to create a menu with a wide range of dishes and to allot a different price to each dish. Restaurants will generally pick several price points and group dishes around those prices. There may be several dishes

TABLE 6.1 Range of prices at Banff Mount Norquay (as of November 2015)

Regular	Adult (18+)	Youth (13–17)	Child (6–12)	Senior (65+)
Full day (9 am–4 pm)	65.00	50.00	25.00	50.00
Afternoon (12 pm–4 pm) (tickets on sale from 11.40 am)	55.00	40.00	16.00	40.00
All inclusive (Ski/Tube/Sightsee)	75.00	60.00	30.00	60.00
Night skiing (Fri. and Sat. 5 pm–10 pm *8 Jan.–27 Feb. 2016*)	25.00	22.00	14.00	22.00
Last hour	20.00	15.00	10.00	15.00
Sundance Magic Carpet	17.00	13.00	10.00	13.00
Hourly tickets	Adult (18+)	Youth (13–17)	Child (6–12)	Senior (65+)
2 hours	43.00	30.00	13.00	30.00
3 hours	52.00	37.00	15.00	37.00
4 hours	55.00	40.00	17.00	40.00
Multi-day: Number of days	**2**	**3**	**4**	**5**
Adult	115.00	160.00	215.00	265.00
Youth/senior	85.00	120.00	155.00	190.00
Child (6–12)	35.00	45.00	60.00	75.00

priced at $10–$13, then several priced around $19–$20, then others at $23–$28. The idea here is to simplify costing and menu planning, and to create points of comparison for the consumer.

DISCRIMINATORY PRICING

Organizations often alter prices to suit different customers, products, locations and times. This discriminatory pricing allows the organization to sell a product or service at two or more prices, despite the fact that the product costs are the same. For example, many restaurants charge higher prices in the evening than they do at lunchtime, even if the food is identical, because of demand differences. Ski resorts may charge more for a weekend ski pass than during the week if the majority of their customers drive up on a Saturday or Sunday. These are examples of 'time-based' discriminatory pricing, but a market may also be segmented to encourage increased participation from special groups, such as senior citizens or students. In this case, the groups would be offered special concessions, as seen in Banff Mount Norquay's cheaper prices for children, students, and seniors (see Table 6.1). The market must be capable of being segmented if discriminatory pricing is going to be an effective strategy. Segments will have highly distinct sensitivities, and being able to price differently to the various segments is key to success in maximizing profits (Hiemstra, 1998). Care should also be taken to ensure that the strategy is legal and that it does not lead to customer resentment.

DISCOUNTING

From time to time, most businesses will need to consider discounting their standard prices. Many tourism organizations engage in volume discounting – offering special rates to attract customers who agree to major purchases. Hotels and airlines, for example, offer special prices (or upgrades) to corporate clients to encourage volume business, and loyalty programmes frequently offer discounts to ensure that travellers use a particular brand. The discount will often reflect the level of overall demand. Airlines and hotels traditionally discount during slow periods and low seasons. A discounted price is only a wise move if it increases demand, brings new users, or increases consumption by regular users. Organizations that discount key products but don't lower costs to offset the discount are taking an economic risk unless the discount is only for a very short period or is designed to overcome a very specific problem. There is also the risk that discounting may not lead to increased demand (Naidoo et al., 2011).

In recent years, ski resorts have joined forces to provide passes that allow visits to multiple ski areas at a discount. The Epic Pass in Colorado started the momentum when it connected all of the Vail Resorts under one pass. Since then a number of others have followed suit, including the Powder Alliance Pass, the Mountain Collective Pass, and the White Mountain Superpass. 'From a consumer point of view, you're always looking for the best value, and I think that's why these passes are trending,' says Snowbasin Marketing Manager, Jason Dyer (Krichko, 2013). Snowbasin, a Utah resort, joined Stevens Pass (Washington), Crested Butte (Colorado), Bridger Bowl (Montana), and eight other big-name western resorts on the Powder Alliance Pass in 2013. The Alliance had grown to 36 resorts by the 2014/15 season. Such partnerships on lift tickets started back in the 1990s in Canada. 'Resorts of the Canadian Rockies was the first in the Canadian ski industry to introduce multi-resort passes and loyalty cards, providing guests with the greatest benefit in flexibility, savings and variety of terrain,' says Matt Mosteller, RCR's Senior VP Marketing & Resort Experience. The group owns Kicking Horse, Fernie, Kimberley and Nakiska, bundled in the RCR Rockies Season Pass. Similarly the RCR Rockies Card covers all four resorts, giving three days skiing at each and discounts at partnering resorts in Alberta and British Columbia. While this may seem like taking away business from the parent resort, Mosteller thinks it adds wow factor: 'Offering guests multi-resort discount cards like the RCR Rockies Card provides them with the most choice, based on snow, ease of access, variety of terrain, flexibility and convenience based on their schedule and time, with the huge benefit of savings or free days' (Hudson and Hudson, 2015).

YIELD MANAGEMENT

Yield is the profit that is made on the sales of goods and services; it is calculated based on the number of customers, how much they spend, and the number of products they buy. Yield management is the practice of developing strategies to maximize opportunities for the sale of an organization's perishable products, such as airline seats, hotel rooms, and tour seats, and therefore improving its long-term viability. More simply, it has been defined as 'lowering the price … according to expected demand, and relying heavily on computers and modeling techniques' (Lundberg et al., 1995). It was initiated by the airline industry in the 1980s as a way to increase revenue from existing routes and aircraft. Computer technology made it possible for airlines to predict the number of seats that would be sold on a given flight – called the load factor. By analysing costs, and also determining the price sensitivity of various types of airfares, airlines discovered that offering seats at a variety of special fares could boost load and revenues.

Many have argued in favour of yield-management techniques, using price to balance the market conditions of supply and demand. Duadel and Vialle (1994), for example, distinguished between 'spoilage', the under-utilization of resources, and 'spill', selling too cheaply early, with the result that later, higher-yielding demand has to be denied. Others suggest that marketers who apply yield management in their firms should take into account price perceptions of clients and that pricing decisions should be made by properly communicating changes in prices and the reasons behind them (Rondan-Catalun and Rosa-Diaz, 2014).

The practice of yield management is now common in other sectors of tourism, from hotels to ski resorts. Different rates are offered for certain groups of customers, and restrictions are placed on the use of these rates by other groups. Even theatres use yield management techniques to maximize revenue. The Koubu Kaburenjo theatre in Kyoto, for example, uses a simple three-tier approach to pricing tickets during the Cherry Blossom Festival (Hudson, 2008). The premium-priced tickets enable viewers to sit on reserved seats on the first floor or the front of the second floor. They are also invited to attend a geisha tea ceremony 40 minutes before the performance. This includes green tea in exquisite cups with Japanese cake as well as a take-home souvenir dish. They also have the opportunity to walk around the authentic Japanese style garden. First-class tickets give patrons reserved seats – either on the second floor or on the designated seating area without chairs at the sides of this floor. They get a close-up appreciation of the dancers and musicians and a clear view for photos. The cheapest, second-class tickets are for the free seating area without chairs on the third floor. Here viewers either kneel barefoot on cushions on raised deck areas or perch on narrow wooden benches.

ALL-INCLUSIVE PRICING

Another popular strategy is all-in pricing or all-inclusive pricing. This type of pricing was used originally in holiday camps in the UK, where customers were provided access to every entertainment facility in the camp for a single price. The strategy proved highly successful, and Club Med built on this model for its chain of holiday resorts around the world. Club Med now advertises 'total all-inclusive' holidays, so that consumers pay for no extras whatsoever. Today, tourists are very familiar with booking all-inclusive holidays in destinations like the Caribbean and Mexico. Theme parks also normally adopt the all-inclusive strategy by charging just one fee for the use of all their attractions.

OFF-SET PRICING

A contrasting strategy involves charging a low basic entrance fee and recouping prof-its through add-ons, which require that customers pay for each individual attraction. Organizers at the Calgary Stampede have used this strategy for the fun fair set in the middle of the Stampede grounds. Guests pay a small entrance fee but then have to pay for all of the rides. The Calgary Stampede is an annual rodeo, exhibition and festival held each year in July. The ten-day event, which bills itself as 'the Greatest Outdoor Show on Earth', attracts over one million visitors per year and features one of the world's largest rodeos, a parade, midway, stage shows, concerts, agricultural competitions, chuckwagon racing and First Nations' exhibitions. This pricing strategy is sometimes called off-set pricing or bait pricing, in which an operator such as an attraction will set a very low entry charge, possibly even a 'loss leader' at below cost, in order to attract visitors who then find themselves facing extra charges for every event. Casino hotels provide an example of bait pricing. Prices are often extremely reasonable for rooms, food and drink because profits are reaped through gambling on the premises.

TOURISM AND HOSPITALITY CHARACTERISTICS THAT AFFECT PRICING POLICY

Although some of the following points have already been referred to in this chapter, a separate discussion of the particular features of the tourism and hospitality industry that affect pricing is warranted here.

1. HIGH LEVEL OF SEGMENTATION IN THE INDUSTRY

The tourism industry is highly segmented, with varying elasticities of demand in the segments. These demand segments may be associated with different income levels, age groupings, seasonality, and types of pleasure or business. Groups are also not homogeneous in their demands. Some may be business travellers with expense accounts and others may be pleasure travellers spending their own funds.

2. VARIABILITY OF DEMAND

Different product offerings also face much variability in the level of demand within customer segments associated with different days of the week, holidays, different seasons of the year, and normal fluctuations in local personal or business situations. For hotels, this variability causes difficulty in forecasting normal room demands for an individual property, and requires that each day of the year be projected and priced differently. Some hotels have responded to this variability by offering customers the opportunity to 'pay what you want' in a bid to fill up beds. In 2014, for example, five hotels in Paris were allowing guests to pay only what they think their stay was worth (Orr, 2014). This is not a new strategy for those in the leisure industry. At the Edinburgh Festival in 2014, the comedian Lewis Schaffer gave audience members the option to prepurchase tickets for £5, or to give what they felt at the end of the show. Interestingly, in Freakonomics, the successful pop-economics book, the authors discuss Paul Feldman who set up a bagel business in an office based on the honour system. He discovered that people are more likely to pay better when the weather is nice. By that logic, the hotels in Paris should at least do well over the summer!

3. PERISHABLE NATURE OF THE PRODUCT

The tourism product is perishable, i.e. it cannot be stored and sold at a later date. In addition, suppliers may not wish the surplus to be sold through the same channel as the standard product, as this may affect future demand and pricing. This is why outlets exist that allow the supplier to remain anonymous. For example, the Internet provides an outlet for tour operators and airlines to offload surplus holidays or flights at reduced margins without changing their main brochures.

4. HIGH FIXED COSTS

High fixed costs in major tourism sectors exacerbate the perishable nature of the business of selling holidays, seats, or hotel rooms. This means that an organization saves little by not filling to capacity. In the hospitality sector, for example, variable costs associated with the rooms department account for only one-fourth of total room department income, while fixed costs associated primarily with paying for the building and overhead expenses account for a large share of the remaining revenue. This feature gives strong incentive to rent rooms at relatively low rates rather than leaving them vacant.

5. COST FLUCTUATIONS

For many operators in the tourism industry, there is a high probability of unpredictable but major short-term fluctuations in cost elements such as oil prices and currency exchange rates. A tour operator running packages to various European and South American destinations may, according to exchange rates and the general climate of tourism in each country, have to vary its prices.

6. VULNERABILITY TO DEMAND CHANGES

The industry is vulnerable to demand changes resulting from unforeseen economic and political events. As mentioned in Chapter 1, the global recession which started in 2007 had long-lasting impacts for tourism in many countries, although some did benefit from an increase in domestic tourism (Papatheodorou, Rosselló and Xiao, 2010). By 2016, though, most parts of the world had recovered from the recession, and trends in consumer habits and a rise in disposable income worldwide has led to a rapid increase in the luxury travel market; in North America, luxury travel produces almost a trillion dollars in annual sales.

7. HIGH LEVEL OF CUSTOMERS' PSYCHOLOGICAL INVOLVEMENT

Customers display a particularly high level of psychological involvement in choosing vacation products, in which price may be a symbol of status as well as value (Laws, 1998). They are, therefore, likely to invest considerable care in their choice. In the packaged holiday market, where the tour operators or travel agents emphasize prices rather than destination attributes in their promotions, the customers' attention is likely to be focused on comparing prices rather than on what each destination offers, potentially resulting in a reduced commitment to the resort visited. Under these conditions, there is more likely to be a mismatch between the tourists' holiday expectations and their destination experiences, resulting in dissatisfaction and complaint.

8. SEASONAL DEMAND

One of the most common ways of setting holiday price differentials is the seasonal banding that is typical of tour operators' brochures – and familiar to all who purchase all-inclusive holidays – in the form of price and departure date matrices. Seasonality of demand leads to differing price expectations. Commercial business demand for some hotels often declines in high summer. This leads to domestic consumers anticipating lower rates and higher availability in mid-week. Conversely, many tour operators and airlines are able to increase prices in high summer when demand is at its peak. An interesting pricing strategy was set by the Eden Roc Resort & Spa in Miami in the 1990s. The resort charged guests the same amount in dollars as the day's highest temperature. The idea was to give guest no cause for complaint even in the event of a cold snap!

9. TACTICAL PRICE-CUTTING AND PRICE WARS

If supply exceeds demand, there is near certainty of price-cutting by major competitors. This leads to the high possibility of price wars being provoked in sectors such as transport, accommodation, tour operating and travel agencies, in which short-term profitability may disappear. The case study at the end of the chapter explains how airlines based in the Persian Gulf have shaken up the North American market by offering high-quality service at lower prices, leading to downward pressure on prices.

10. LOW PRICES

Price competition in many sectors has led to an industry characterized by low prices. Low prices have not only stimulated demand for holidays currently on offer, but have also altered the timing of demand – for example, by extending the holiday season – and have changed the demographic profile of holidaymakers to include all age groups and most socioeconomic groups of society. A lower price provides an increased access to the product, bringing the product to a new group of potential purchasers that have different behavioural characteristics. One example of this is the way in which cruise holidays are now promoted to a broader market on the basis of reduced prices.

11. FIXED CAPACITY

Even though demand may be highly variable and unpredictable, in many sectors of the industry supply available in the short run tends to be relatively fixed. For a hotel, for example, it takes a long time to expand a building or to build a new one. Adding part-time or seasonal labour may be useful in better serving guests during periods of peak occupancy, but it can add little to available room inventory. As a result, pricing policies are largely restricted to allocating existing supplies among competing demands. This restriction adds importance to effective no-show policies.

12. THE CUSTOMER'S TOTAL PURCHASES

Some sectors of the industry have to consider the customer's total purchases when considering prices and profits. Hotels should not consider room rates and restaurant prices separately. Selling a room cheaply to a guest who will use the restaurant and bars extensively may be more profitable than selling it to someone who pays full rate for the room but purchases nothing else. For example, mixed-offering destinations like those owned by Intrawest or Vail Resorts do not have to concern themselves too much with visitors not skiing, as they can earn huge profits from selling other on-snow activities, as well as earn revenue from the restaurants and retail units.

13. RELIANCE ON THE INTERNET

Many travel consumers have 'empowered' themselves by learning the routines of Internet research and making vacation transactions online. They are also increasingly aware of their ability to exercise more control over their purchases, and a large percentage of hotel customers attempt to negotiate lower prices on their rooms. In general, consumers have become more self-reliant, and the most adventurous are building their own holidays, many of them encouraged to make online purchases with Internet-only discount rates. Social media is also having an increasing influence on pricing strategies for travel providers as consumers rely more and more on such platforms for their information (Noone, McGuire and Rohlfs, 2011).

14. LATE BOOKING

Price reductions for late booking are a widespread holiday industry response to its unsold capacity, and are typically promoted by operators shortly before departure. It is now typical to see last-minute discounts; online-only offers; discounted pricing for groups; incentive rates for travel agents, tour operators, and reservation agents; and a variety of packages at different price points, including such add-ons as meals, activities, and transportation.

CHAPTER SUMMARY

The key factors determining pricing decisions are marketing objectives, costs, other mix variables, intermediaries, buyer perceptions, competition, and legal and regulatory restrictions. The analysis of buyers' reactions to price change uses the concept of elasticity of demand. If demand increases in line with price cuts, the product is said to be elastic. But if demand remains relatively unaltered by price changes, then the product is said to be inelastic. Generally, companies use pricing as part of their positioning of a product, employing one of three strategic approaches: premium pricing, value-for-money pricing and undercut pricing. Three strategies commonly used for the introduction of new products are prestige pricing, market skimming and penetration pricing. Other pricing techniques include promotional pricing, product-bundle pricing, price spread and price points, discriminatory pricing, discounting, yield management, all-inclusive and off-set pricing.

REFLECTIVE QUESTIONS

1. When would a tour operator introduce a new travel tour with premium pricing? When might it use undercut pricing?

2. Look online at hotel websites in your area and find examples of product-bundle pricing. Explain how they work. Try to calculate the savings that the bundle offers.

3. Explain the differences between prestige pricing, market skimming and penetration pricing, using examples from a sector of tourism and hospitality apart from hotels.

MARKETING IN ACTION: LOW COST AIRLINES TAKE OFF

'No-frills' is the latest buzzword for the airline industry around the world where cut-price companies such as Ryanair are taking it to the extreme. The Dublin-based airline, the second biggest international carrier in the world, is spearheading the move towards very basic, cheap continental travel with no complementary food and beverage services, very low luggage allowances, tight cabin space, high charges for excess baggage, and other surcharges for extras, such as wheelchair service. Also, cut-price flights often use smaller, secondary airports, sometimes situated far from city centres (Ryannair frequently uses Stansted instead of Heathrow). There are also compensation limitations if flights are delayed: passengers may not be eligible for food and accommodation since most cut-price airlines are not part of the EU's Passenger Service Commitment.

IMAGE 6.5 Low-cost airline Norwegian reaching 500,000 UK passengers on its ground-breaking low-cost long-haul flights to the US (Source: Norwegian.com)

Despite the disadvantages and potential discomforts of cheap travel, price is the bottom line and passengers are vying for seats sometimes offered as low as $25 for one-way European flights. This only covers the flight taxes and service charges so basically the seats are sold for free. There are about 60 low-price airlines within Europe, including Geneva-based Flybaboo. Many have recently failed in this volatile, cut-throat market – such as JetGreen, Duo, JetMagic, V Bird and Volareweb.com.

Similar price-cutting has also been happening throughout India, Asia and the Middle East. SpiceJet, an Indian low-fare airline, competes with Kingfisher Airlines Ltd and Air Deccan for the lucrative domestic market. Within India, with its increasingly prosperous emerging middle class, there has been a shift from train travel to the quicker and more efficient air travel. Air travel demand continues to rise, with around 100 million people choosing air over travel by land, thanks to low fares and also improved in-flight amenities and service. This has been partly due to government deregulation but also to the fierce competition between airlines which has transformed the industry from its original reputation for poor service to an efficient and comfortable option. Low-cost air travel is mainly distributed via the Internet in India. SpiceJet sells about 70 per cent of its seats on the Internet and also reduces its overheads by utilizing its aircraft for a full 12 hours per day as well as aiming to fill up each flight with at least 80–90 per cent loads.

In Southeast Asia, likewise, a fierce price war erupted in the budget airline market during the 2000s, in sharp contrast to its traditional high-price flights. To gain market share and capture public attention, low-cost carriers offered one-way tickets from Singapore to popular destinations such as Bangkok for less than US$1 each. The lowest

(Continued)

(Continued)

price was 59 cents which Tiger Airways offered for one-way tickets to three different Thai destinations. In retaliation, Thai Air Asia offered a 29-cent ticket to Bangkok, delighting consumers who would normally pay around US$250 return for Singapore to Bangkok flights.

Finally, in the Middle East, the region's air transportation sector is becoming increasingly segmented, as new start-up airlines emerge to challenge the incumbent Middle Eastern carrier Emirates, for a share of the global aviation pie. Low-cost carriers, like Air Arabia and Jazeera Airways, launched in 2003 and 2005 respectively, were prompted by the success of low-cost pioneers in North America and Europe, as well as the opportunity to offer a wide choice of prices and options on intraregional flights compared to legacy rivals. Three Middle East airlines – Emirates, Qatar Airways and Etihad Airways – are even challenging American domestic airlines for market share. In 2014, they increased their number of US flights by 47 per cent across 11 US cities. As well as offering 'old-fashioned service' with hot towels, flying nannies, onboard showers and first-class bars, these Gulf competitors are taking over the lion's share of Airbus and Boeing orders, putting most of the industry's long-haul international growth in their hands. Rivals complain that the government-owned Gulf airlines have huge financial advantages that create an uneven playing field.

In more recent years, discount airlines have started to bring lower prices to longer-distance services. The largest discount airline in the Philippines, Cebu Pacific Air, for example, is planning to invest around $4 billion by 2021 in Airbus passenger jets in order to meet the growing demand for cheaper flights from Filipino expats living all over the world. In an article in the *Nikkei Asian Review*, the airline's plans to expand its medium-haul operations, including flights to Japan, were outlined: 'Recently, Cebu Pacific announced it will start operating four flights per week to Australia and three to Kuwait, possibly in September. The prices will be about 30 per cent lower than those of competing services.' This trend among budget carriers to shift their focus from domestic flights to international services is being driven by deteriorating earnings in the short haul market, the article maintained: 'The companies' traditional strategies for sales and profit growth are starting to lose effectiveness amid ever-intensifying competition.'

Norwegian Air is a good example of a low-cost carrier that has expanded aggressively across the world, and as a result of the new low fares they brought into the US, domestic carriers have lowered their prices to compete. A Norwegian Air ticket from San Francisco to Copenhagen with a layover in London can often be cheaper than a sole ticket from San Francisco to London. Norwegian gets away with charging rock-bottom prices by taking advantage of low operating costs and charging passengers via an à la carte model. Passengers who book air passage on the airline get just that; baggage, seats and food all cost extra. Conversely, a legacy airline such as American, Delta or United usually provides all of that bundled together with their international fare. In April 2016, Norwegian reached 500,000 UK passengers on its low-cost long-haul flights to the US (see picture above). Norwegian first launched the flights from Gatwick Airport in July 2014. As of May 2015, Norwegian was offering low-cost flights to seven US destinations from the UK – New York, Los Angeles, Boston, San Francisco Oakland, Orlando, Fort Lauderdale and Puerto Rico – with fares from £135 one way.

According to Grant Martin from *Forbes*, for travellers, the spread of the international low-cost carrier is only good news. 'Frugal travelers now have an ultra low-cost approach to crossing the Atlantic without the comforts or ancillary fees associated with legacy carriers. But the rest of the consumer base also profits by the competitive fares that the legacies are forced to publish. In the end, everyone gets across the ocean for a few dollars less.'

Sources: Matthews (2013); Bagri (2014); McCartney (2014); Srivastava (2016); Park (2006); Martin (2014).

CASE STUDY QUESTIONS

1. Pick three of the airlines profiled in this chapter and discuss the different pricing strategies they are following.

2. What are the key factors that influence the price of a flight ticket?

3. Do some background research – are the Middle East airlines – Emirates, Qatar Airways and Etihad Airways – still challenging American domestic airlines for market share?

REFERENCES

Bagri, N. T. (2014) 'A peacock replaces a worn airport in Mumbai', *New York Times*, Business, 15 January: B5.

Becerra, M., Santaló, J. and Silva, R. (2013) 'Being better vs. being different: Differentiation, competition, and pricing strategies in the Spanish hotel industry', *Tourism Management*, 34: 71–9.

Bookman, M. Z. and Bookman, K. R. (2007) *Medical Tourism in Developing Countries*. New York: Palgrave Macmillan.

Carmin, J. and Norkus, G. (1990) 'Pricing strategies for menus: Magic or myth?' *Cornell Hotel and Restaurant Administration Quarterly*, 31(3): 50.

Carney, S. (2013) 'Brewing controversy over proposal to make water cheaper than beer', *Wall Street Journal*, 24 January: A1&10.

Chazan, D. (2015) 'Upmarket Paris hotels lose out after terrorist attacks', *Daily Telegraph*, 28 October. www.telegraph.co.uk/news/worldnews/europe/france/11960730/Upmarket-Paris-hotels-lose-out-after-terrorist-attacks.html (accessed 7 December 2016).

Dibb, S., Simkin, L., Pride, W. M. and Ferrell, O. C. (1994) *Marketing: Concepts and Strategies*, 2nd edn. London: Houghton-Mifflin.

Dickman, S. (1999) *Tourism and Hospitality Marketing*. Oxford: Oxford University Press.

Duadel, S. and Vialle, G. (1994) *Yield Management: Applications to Air Transport and Other Service Industries*. Paris: Institut du Transport Aerien.

Gale, B. (1992) 'Monitoring customer satisfaction and market-perceived quality', *American Marketing Association Worth Repeating Series*, Number 922CSO I. Chicago: American Marketing Association.

Hiemstra, S. J. (1998) 'Economic pricing strategies for hotels'. In T. Baum and R. Mudambi (eds), *Economic and Management Methods for Tourism and Hospitality Research*, New York: Wiley, pp. 215–32.

Hudson, S. (2008) *Tourism and Hospitality Marketing: A Global Perspective*. London: Sage.

Hudson, S. and Hudson, L. J. (2013) *Customer Service for Hospitality and Tourism*. Oxford: Goodfellow Publishers Ltd.

Hudson, S. and Hudson, L. J. (2015) *Winter Sport Tourism: Working in Winter Wonderlands*. Oxford: Goodfellow Publishers Ltd.

Jones, C. (2015) 'Business meetings branch out to smaller cities', *USA Today, Money*: 3B.

Krichko, K. (2013) 'Combination Ski Passes are Sweeping the Ski World'. GrindTV. com. 29 August. www.grindtv.com/skiing/combination-ski-passes-are-sweeping-the-ski-world/#YUM10tKL32k1eqp4.97 (accessed 12 December 2016).

Kynaston, N. (2015) 'World's cheapest and most expensive cities for a mini-break revealed', *Mail Online*, 16 June. www.dailymail.co.uk/travel/travel_news/article-3126265/World-s-cheapest-expensive-cities-mini-break-revealed-Hanoi-Vietnam-offering-best-value-money-Cancun-Mexico-worst-London-New-York-not-far-behind.html (accessed 7 December 2016).

Laws, E. (1998) 'Package holiday pricing: Cause of the IT industry's success, or cause for concern?' In T. Baum and R. Mudambi (eds), *Economic and Management Methods for Tourism and Hospitality Research*, pp. 197–214. New York: Wiley.

Lundberg, D. E., Krishnamoorthy, M. and Stavenga, M. H. (1995) *Tourism Economics*. New York: Wiley.

Marn, M. V., Roegner, E. V. and Zawada, C.C. (2003) 'The power of pricing', *McKinsey Quarterly*, February.

Martin, G. (2014) 'International low-cost airlines drive transatlantic fares into the ground', *Forbes,* 30 October. www.forbes.com/sites/grantmartin/2014/10/30/international-low-cost-airline-drive-transatlantic-fares-into-the-ground/#4b4d83f77033 (accessed 7 December 2016).

Matthews, C. (2013) 'Heathrow chief has high hopes for growth', *Financial Times*, National News, 12 August: 3.

McCartney, S. (2014) 'Now landing: Touch challengers', *Wall Street Journal*, Personal Journal, November 6: D1.

Naidoo, P., Ramseook-Munhurrun, P. and Seetaram, A.K. (2011) 'Marketing the hotel sector in economic crisis. Evidence from Mauritius', *Global Journal of Business Research*, 5(2): 1–12.

Nikkei Asian Review (2014) 'Budget carriers take price war to long-haul segment', *Nikkei Asian Review*, 23 June. http://asia.nikkei.com/Business/Trends/Budget-carriers-take-price-war-to-long-haul-segment (accessed 7 December 2016).

Noone, B. M., McGuire, K. A. and Rohlfs, K. V. (2011) 'Social media meets hotel revenue management: Opportunities, issues and unanswered questions', *Journal of Revenue and Pricing Management*, 10(4): 293–305.

Norwegian (2016a) 'Get online', *Norwegian In-Flight* Magazine, 41 (May): 5.

Norwegian (2016b) 'nth degree', *Norwegian In-Flight* Magazine, 42 (June): 13.

Orr, G (2014) 'Honesty box hotels: You decide how much you pay', *Independent*, 22 July. www.independent.co.uk/travel/hotels/honesty-box-hotels-you-decide-how-much-you-pay-9622062.html (accessed 7 December 2016).

Papatheodorou, J., Rosselló, A. and Xiao, H. (2010) 'Global economic crisis and tourism: Consequences and perspectives', *Journal of Travel Research*, 49(1): 39–45.

Park, K. (2006) 'Flying high on low costs', *The Hindu Business Line*, 12 March: 11.

Rondan-Catalun, J. F. and Rosa-Diaz, I. M. (2014) 'Segmenting hotel clients by pricing variables and value for money', *Current Issues in Tourism*, 17(1): 60–71.

Srivastava, T. (2016) 'Fare war heats up summer skies, Air India offers tickets at Rs 1,499', *Hindustan Times*, 22 May. www.hindustantimes.com/business/fare-war-heats-up-summer-skies-air-india-offers-tickets-at-rs-1-499/story-9jnGCerzp2afmoYD7gFr5M.html (accessed 7 December 2016).

Sylt, C. (2015) 'Cirque du Soleil tour revenue tumbles to £40m', *Telegraph*, 22 February. www.telegraph.co.uk/finance/newsbysector/retailandconsumer/leisure/11428511/Cirque-du-Soleil-tour-revenue-tumbles-to-40m.html (accessed 7 December 2016).

Tanford, S., Baloglu, S. and Erdem, M. (2012) 'Travel packaging on the Internet: The impact of pricing information and perceived value on consumer choice', *Journal of Travel Research*, 51(1): 68–80.

Wright, C. (2016) 'The amazing technicolor comeback', *Hemispheres*, July: 45–56.

DISTRIBUTION 7

INTRODUCTION

Chapter 7 begins with an introduction to the nature and types of distribution channels and then describes various marketing intermediaries in the tourism and hospitality sector. A discussion of the emerging sharing economy precedes a section on channel organization, that has a particular focus on alliances and franchises. The final two sections of the chapter look at designing the distribution system and channel management. Case studies in the chapter discuss a tour operator in Russia, the sharing economy in India, and the National Brotherhood of Skiers' Annual Summit.

LESSONS FROM A MARKETING GURU: FROM RUSSIA WITH LOVE, ELENA ULKO

With their reputation as difficult customers in the tourism industry, it comes as no surprise that one Russian tour company is going *against* the grain by specializing in customer service. Ulkotours, Russia & Scandinavia, a member of the American Society for Travel Agents (ASTA), runs private shore tours for cruise passengers in the Baltics. The company, based in St Petersburg, also sets up tailor-made tours for air and train passengers, specializing in city itineraries such as Moscow, Tallin, St Petersburg, Stockholm, Helsinki and Berlin.

IMAGE 7.1 Elena Ulko with her team at Ulkotours (Photo courtesy of Elena Ulko)

How it differs from other – bigger – operators is in its personalized service message and delivery both to customers and B2B. The website (http://ulkotours.com/) reads like an invitation to come on a family vacation with founder and CEO, Elena Ulko, whose smiling photographs dominate the site and advertising messages. Ulko says her intention is to create a strong personal connection with customers: 'I have included personal information for the clients to know that I am a real person standing behind Ulkotours and from personal experience I know that it creates an emotional attachment when you visualize the person you're communicating with and when you are able to obtain some personal information about the person you are dealing with.'

Ulkotours is also a founding member of the Baltic Cruise Association, working closely with other operators and sectors of the tourism industry. Since 2012 the company has grown substantially, offering tours in increasingly more destinations around the Baltics. 'It all has been done with only one purpose – to make Ulkotours a one-stop shop and minimize search time for our clients,' says Ulko. 'Selling Baltic destinations is not something that brings a lot of profit for us (I'd rather say it only creates more work) but it's something that brings clients who buy these tours together with other St Petersburg private tours.'

As a member of ASTA, Ulkotours is able to reach out to a network of over 22,000 US travel agents, cruise line and tourist board personnel. Ulko attends a variety of travel shows, specifically for travel agents and relationship-building. She has thereby expanded her network of agents, providing them with free brochure and catalogue delivery and conducting face-to-face presentations in their offices. At the same time, she has branched out to encompass online intermediaries, too. 'Travel agents are the easiest to work with, because they also offer a very similar personalized travel approach and most of them have been on our tours, so they feel confident in referring their clients to us, or reselling our tours directly to their clients,' she explains. 'Each agent knows his/her client needs and it's very easy for us to set up a tour for them.

They don't ask too many questions because most of them have already experienced a tour with us, so they are able to handle most questions themselves. They also recommend specific guides to their clients, usually those that they had been on tour with previously, so guides are always very excited to work with such referral customers.' Online intermediaries, however, pose different challenges but Ulko has solved this more impersonal relationship by travelling to meet the agents involved. 'There is a very large travel agency in California, where we had been working with a single agent, at first, who had found us online and sent in a request on behalf of her clients,' she explains. 'After I had flown into Los Angeles to meet everyone in their office in person and tell them about Ulkotours and about the services that we provide, our sales with the agency increased considerably and now we regularly arrange tours for their private clients and groups as well.'

Since 2014, Ulkotours has been working with major online tour platforms such as Viator.com and, in order to cope with the flow of bookings and to ensure tour quality, had to launch a new department responsible for automated bookings. But this brings its own array of problems: 'One of the main inconveniences of working with such online intermediaries is that there is no customer communication involved and most of them offer closed loop communication through supplier extranet. Often, tour platforms are not fully developed in the way we would want them to be, so there's a lot of information missing from bookings and a lot of essential details need to be somehow obtained or communicated to the client after the booking has been placed,' says Ulko. Booking blips – such as customers failing to realize that they need to submit further information to complete a reservation – often occur, which ultimately gives Ulkotours more work rather than streamlining the process.

The impact of the sharing economy has not yet had a negative impact on bookings. 'We have not really noticed any substantial decrease in sales or requests for accommodations and transport services because people who go with us prefer that we arrange everything together as a package for them,' Ulko explains. 'We have had several cases of clients cancelling private transfers and choosing to go with a taxi or Uber, but such cases are extremely rare.'

In a savvy cross-marketing project, Ulkotours has another office based in the US St Petersburg in Florida. 'When I was taking client calls while in the US, all of the clients asked if they were talking to the US office or Russian office,' says Ulko. When she told them she was in the US with her family but was usually based in Russia, the conversation would invariably lead to the clever connection between the Florida St Petersburg and the Russian one. 'We would then talk about the weather and kids going to school... and voila, next day comes their tour booking,' says Ulko.

It is all very well connecting emotionally with customers when trying to close the initial booking sale, but there is still the task of continuing that connection both during their visit and afterwards. Ulko works hard to perpetuate this personal connection by meeting with clients during their tours, giving them welcome gifts and posing for photos with them. After their holiday, communication continues with picture sharing, feedback and client referrals. Business is booming, confirming Ulko in her 'personal attention' strategy.

Sources: Interview with Elena Ulko (2012, 2016); Matthews (2011).

THE NATURE AND TYPES OF DISTRIBUTION CHANNELS

The opening case study highlights the significance of the distribution system, the purpose of which is to provide an adequate framework for making a company's product or service available to the consumer: in this instance Ulko Tours, offering specialized vacations to Russia and Scandinavia. In the tourism industry, distribution systems are often used to move the customer to the product, and the true rationale behind a company's distribution system can be traced back to its specific needs and wants. Figure 7.1 shows that each distinct distribution participant in the tourism sector has a unique set of needs and wants. The motivation for developing an effective distribution network, therefore, is to help the different members meet their individual needs. By choosing to combine the activities of the various members, participants in the distribution system can work together to identify opportunities to fulfil each other's needs.

A distribution channel is a method of delivery used by a supplier, carrier, or destination marketing organization. There are two different types of distribution channels that a firm can use to deliver its product. The first and most simple form of distribution is a direct distribution channel, a channel through which a company delivers its product to the consumer without the outside assistance of any independent intermediaries. In such a case, the service provider is solely responsible for the delivery of its product. Most bed-and-breakfasts use a direct distribution channel to market products to potential customers. They perform all of the necessary channel functions on their own, without relying on any assistance from outside intermediaries. The second type of distribution channel used to deliver a product is an indirect channel. In this case, the service provider makes use of independent intermediaries to help facilitate the distribution if its product.

It is important to acknowledge that distribution as a marketing term can also refer to the physical location (the 'place' component of the marketing mix), as consumption of the core service requires a physical location. Operational requirements may set tight constraints for the distribution of some tourism services. Airports, for example, are often inconveniently located relative to travellers' homes, offices or destinations. Because of space, noise and environmental factors, finding suitable sites for the construction of new airports is a complex task. The need for economies of scale may be another restriction on choice of locations. Also, many tourism services require a fixed, geographic location that severely restricts distribution. By definition, ocean beach resorts have to be on the coast and ski resorts have to be in the mountains. In fact, physical location is critical to the ski industry. In the US, 67 per cent of ski resorts are within 74 miles or easy commuting distance to major metropolitan areas (Hudson and Hudson, 2015).

MARKETING INTERMEDIARIES

Marketing intermediaries are channels of distribution that include travel agents, tour operators, travel specialists and the Internet. Their purpose is to help the service provider complete the six different functions listed above. Through the use of channel intermediaries, a company is able to expand the strength of its distribution network and to reach a much larger portion of its target market. As a result, the combined marketing efforts of the entire distribution network will lead to an increase in the number of customers using the service, thus boosting overall revenues.

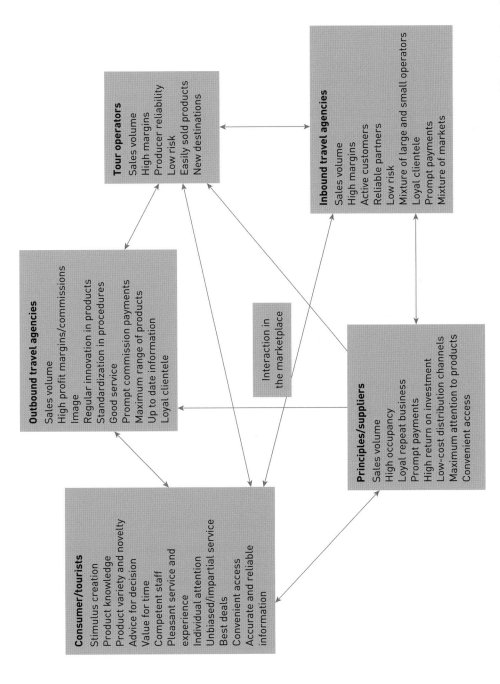

Consumer/tourists

Stimulus creation
Product knowledge
Product variety and novelty
Advice for decision
Value for time
Competent staff
Pleasant service and
experience
Individual attention
Unbiased/impartial service
Best deals
Convenient access
Accurate and reliable
information

Outbound travel agencies

Sales volume
High profit margins/commissions
Image
Regular innovation in products
Standardization in procedures
Good service
Prompt commission payments
Maximum range of products
Up to date information
Loyal clientele

Tour operators

Sales volume
High margins
Producer reliability
Low risk
Easily sold products
New destinations

Interaction in
the marketplace

Principles/suppliers

Sales volume
High occupancy
Loyal repeat business
Prompt payments
High return on investment
Low-cost distribution channels
Maximum attention to products
Convenient access

Inbound travel agencies

Sales volume
High margins
Active customers
Reliable partners
Low risk
Mixture of large and small operators
Loyal clientele
Prompt payments
Mixture of markets

FIGURE 7.1 Needs and wants of tourism distribution channel members (From: *Tourism Distribution Channels: Practices, Issues and Transformations*, Buhalis, D. and Laws, E. ©2001 Cengage Learning. Reproduced with permission of Cengage Learning EMEA Ltd.)

TRAVEL AGENTS

Travel agents offer the tourism customer a variety of services, including everything from transportation plans and tour packages to insurance services and accommodation. They are the most widely used marketing intermediaries in the tourism industry. An agency will earn a commission for each sale, the amount depending on the type of product sold. The modern tradition of holiday packages started with the Industrial Revolution and the spread of railways. In July 1841, a Baptist cabinet-maker called Thomas Cook booked a party of 500 on a train from Leicester, England to a temperance rally in Loughborough. The future travel agent negotiated a price that included entertainment in local private gardens.

Today, the travel agency market is very competitive. Barriers to entry are low and, as a result, there are many new entrants, which is especially true for the rapidly growing segment of online agents. Independent travel agents are under pressure not only from e-agents but also from direct selling by tour operators. They, therefore, seek to differentiate themselves, adding value to the product in order to justify their role in the value chain and help retain market share. Travel agencies perform four distinct functions that pertain to a company's distribution system.

1. DISTRIBUTION AND SALES NETWORK

Travel agents are a key player in the distribution and sale of a company's product under an indirect distribution system. Travel agents essentially act as tour brokers that bring the buyers and sellers of travel products together. The agents have access to an extensive network of suppliers and customers and are able to help facilitate interaction between the two by identifying the particular needs of each group.

2. RESERVATIONS AND TICKETING

Making reservations and issuing tickets are two of the more traditional roles of travel agents. Through the use of a global distribution system (GDS) such as Galileo, Abacus, or Sabre, travel agents can place reservations in numerous locations throughout the world. However, with the arrival of ticketless travel systems in the 1990s, the role of travel agents in issuing tickets (particularly airline tickets) is slowly diminishing.

3. INFORMATION PROVISION AND TRAVEL COUNSELLING

Travel agents have a wealth of information at their disposal. They possess an extensive knowledge of tourism destinations and are well equipped to offer advice to the inexperienced traveller. Whether a customer is looking for a quick flight across the country or planning a major expedition around the world, travel agents can provide valuable assistance in planning a trip.

4. DESIGN OF INDIVIDUAL ITINERARIES

The person-to-person nature of the travel agent business allows the travel agent to gain an in-depth understanding of customers' travel needs. By identifying what specific needs are, the agent can put together a personalized itinerary that best suits those needs. Travel agents can arrange trip components including transportation, accommodation, insurance, activities and tours, all with the intent of satisfying the traveller's particular needs and expectations.

Despite the benefits that travel agents can provide to a company's distribution system, the emergence of new and cheaper distribution tools such as the Internet has placed the future role of travel agents in doubt. But while traditional agents have lost market share to online purchasing, expert advice from travel advisors is likely to remain a vital service in the tourism marketplace. America's largest travel agency company, Travel Leaders Group, for example, promotes the fact that the company delivers a high-touch, personal level of travel expertise to leisure and corporate clients (see www.travelleadersgroup.com). The company, led by founder and chairman Mike Batt, has more than 6,500 company-owned, franchised and affiliated travel agencies throughout the US, Canada, the UK, Ireland and Australia. The company caters to time-poor leisure travellers and companies looking to manage expenses but still willing to pay a premium over online booking options for personal service and support.

TOUR OPERATORS

Tour operators, like Ulkotours profiled above, are organizations that offer packaged vacation tours to the general public. These packages can include everything from transportation, accommodation, and activities to entertainment, meals and drinks. Tour operators typically focus their marketing efforts on the leisure market, which represents the dominant buying group of travel packages. The tour operating sector has become increasingly concentrated. In Europe, for example, about 70 per cent of the market is currently monopolized by the five largest companies, which all have their corporate seats in either Germany or the UK. In 2015, Germany's DER Touristik became Europe's third-largest tourism group behind TUI and Thomas Cook with the takeover of Kuoni's European tour operators by parent company Rewe. DER Touristik was expecting annual revenues of about €7 billion (and some 7.7 million customers) in 2015. In comparison, TUI had group revenues of some €18.7 billion and Thomas Cook about €10.7 billion in 2014 (FVW, 2015).

In the 1990s, these large tour operators followed a strategy of vertical integration. By controlling the value chain from sales and packaging through to transportation and hotels, tour operators sought to secure strategically their market share and shore up low profit margins in their core business with more profitable activities in downstream areas of the value chain. But a slowing and changing tourism market has exposed the lack of flexibility in this model. The 'de-packaging' of travel – with customers building their own trips piece by piece in Internet platforms – has struck a blow at the heart of traditional tour operator products.

Tour operators have the ability to bring in large volumes of customers. They receive discounted rates from the various service providers in exchange for providing a large number of guaranteed visitors. Tour operators traditionally made their profits by providing low-margin travel packages to a large number of consumers, but with the rising use of the Internet as a distribution mechanism, some are choosing to restrict their offerings to only a select number of specialized travel packages. G Adventures in Toronto, for example, has chosen to target young, adventurous individuals interested in purchasing travel packages to the developing world, while Canadian Mountain Holidays (CMH) in Canada focuses on offering up-market heli-skiing packages in the Canadian Rockies.

CONVENTION/MEETING PLANNERS AND CORPORATE TRAVEL MANAGERS

Convention and meeting planners are important intermediaries for the business travel sector, and plan and coordinate their organizations' external meeting events. These planners work for associations, corporations, large nonprofit organizations, government agencies, and educational institutions. Some combine the task of convention planning with that of corporate travel management, whereas other organizations split up the tasks. The private sector is also involved in the marketing of conventions and exhibitions. An example is Reed Exhibitions, one of the world's leading organizers of trade and consumer events, conferences and meetings, ranging across 43 industry sectors – from aerospace and aviation to beauty and cosmetics to sports and recreation. Every year the company runs over 500 events in more than 30 countries, bringing together over 7 million participants. With 3800 employees in offices around the globe, Reed says that the company is not just about organizing trade shows. Its role is that of a relationship broker – identifying, targeting, attracting and matching the needs of buyers and suppliers.

IMAGE 7.2 London Book Fair (©Reed Exhibitions. Reproduced by permission)

TRAVEL SPECIALISTS

Travel specialists are intermediaries that specialize in performing one or more functions of a company's distribution system. Hotel representatives, for example, specialize in providing contact with a hotel's customers in order to identify their specific accommodation needs. Advertising agencies can also act as specialists, performing the promotional aspect of a company's distribution system. By using travel specialists in its distribution system, a company can designate particular functions to the interme-diaries that are best equipped to perform them. Focusing on one specific operation within the distribution channel allows the travel specialist to perform effectively the function at hand in the best possible way.

An example of a travel specialist is PGA Tour Experiences, the licensee and fulfil-ment arm of the PGA golf tour. It serves as the tour operation side of the PGA, providing golf vacations, instructional centres and corporate events and tournaments, all emulating the lifestyle of golf's top professionals. The company handles travel and accommodation, VIP tournament tickets and golf bookings, working with brand partners like MasterCard and The World Golf Village to create golf travel experiences. The 'Hall of Fame Experience' package, for example, includes a four-night stay at the Renaissance Resort World Golf Village, two rounds of golf, club fitting, tickets to the Hall of Fame and IMAX theatre, and a breakfast and lunch. Prices in 2016 started at $245 per person.

Other examples of specialist intermediaries are motivational houses and junket representatives. Motivational houses provide incentive travel, offered to employ-ees or distributors as a reward for their efforts. Incentive trips usually involve staying in high-class accommodation in resort areas, but not necessarily in warm destinations: winter sports incentives are becoming increasingly popular in North America, too. Junket representatives serve the casino industry as intermediar-ies for premium players. Junket reps maintain lists of gamblers who like to visit certain gaming areas such as Las Vegas, Reno or Atlantic City, and they work for one or two casinos rather than the whole industry. Junket reps are paid a com-mission on the amount the casino earns from the players or, in some cases, on a per-player basis.

ONLINE INTERMEDIARIES

Tourists are turning in increasing numbers to the Internet to help them plan and book their travel, in part because of the convenience and time-saving opportuni-ties (Amaro and Duarte, 2015). Stakeholders in the travel industry, such as airlines, car rental companies, and international hotel chains, have been quick to grasp the potential of marketing and selling their services online. These travel companies are adopting both organic (internal) and acquisitive growth strategies. Many traditional companies have developed their own websites and interactive divisions, while others are acquiring Internet companies.

Online travel agencies (OTAs) have also seen tremendous growth over the last decade, with gross bookings exceeding $150 billion in 2013, representing 38 per cent of the global online market and 13 per cent of the global travel market (Forbes, 2015). The online travel sales figure is estimated to be growing at 12 per cent annually. OTAs have 15 per cent of total hotel sales in the US with around $19 billion of gross bookings and are expected to grow 5–6 per cent over the next two years. OTAs' customer segments span across business, leisure, and group. OTA websites play multiple roles, acting as marketing engines, booking engines, and search engines, as well as existing as an execution platform for customers. The global leaders in this space include Priceline and Expedia, which individually sell more than 22 million and 12 million hotel room nights per month, respectively. The world's largest travel review platform, TripAdvisor receives 315 million monthly unique visitors, on its website (Forbes, 2015).

The OTA sector is becoming increasingly consolidated. In 2015, Expedia purchased Orbitz Worldwide for about $1.3 billion, further solidifying the American market for online travel booking to two companies, Expedia and the much bigger Priceline Group (de la Merced, 2015). In the same year Expedia acquired Travelocity and Wotif.com of Australia. Despite the current dominance of Priceline and Expedia among specialists in online travel booking, other companies like Google and Amazon are trying to move in on the two companies' turf. 'We're in the business of travel distribution,' said Dara Khosrowshahi, Expedia's chief executive. 'And in that business, the players in that are diverse and there's always new players that are coming in. Competition is fierce' (de la Merced, 2015). TripAdvisor has also recently added a 'Book with TripAdvisor' option, which might provide direct competition to the big online booking brands and gain a portion of their market share.

There has been a growing body of research related to online travel marketing. Lee, Guillet and Law (2013), for example, looked at the challenges facing hotels in this new digital era, concluding that they must find ways to make the most effective possible use of available technology and distribution channels, and perhaps even form consortia to share information about third-party distribution channels. Koo, Mantin and O'Connor (2011) looked at the airline sector, analysing factors that affect an airline's online distribution strategy. They found that airlines are less likely to use OTA platforms if they have a large loyal consumer base or if the OTA platform is highly competitive. Finally Aslanzadeh and Keating (2014) focused on consumer satisfaction with online travel services, and found that excellence in offline service is associated with a favourable view of an agent's online presence. That is, the consumers' view of the website was improved by the availability of live chat or video chat interactions.

Paraskevas et al. (2011) have discussed the importance of search engine marketing (SEM), a form of online marketing whereby marketers and webmasters use a range of techniques to ensure that their webpage listing appears in a favourable location in search engines' results pages. They note that travel industry firms have developed three main SEM techniques: (1) organic search engine optimization (SEO); (2) paid placement or 'pay-per-click' (PPC); and (3) paid inclusion.

Organic SEO involves designing a webpage to meet the search engines' requirements so that the page is listed in the highest possible position. SEO involves the key design features such as keywords, content and link popularity. Search engines value the visible descriptive body copy of a webpage more than the invisible copy (tags) or flash animations. Search engines also value links from authoritative sites or links from websites sharing the same focus as the site under evaluation. Payment involves bidding for specific search keywords, where the actual placement will depend on other bidders' offers for the same keywords, and also on the number of referrals (PPC) that the website receives from the sponsored link. Finally, paid inclusion puts a website in the organic results list (noted as a sponsored link), without, however, guaranteeing any particular ranking.

DIGITAL SPOTLIGHT: SHARING ECONOMY IN KERALA, INDIA

The sharing economy, primarily driven by Millennials, is now taking over every demographic, worldwide. Its growth has been so astronomical that hotels everywhere, concerned about the unexpected competition, are urging local authorities and governments to curb its progress with taxation and prohibitive laws.

IMAGE 7.3 Author Simon Hudson with K. P. Francis from the Francis Residence

In Kerala, India the Airbnb concept is echoed in the pervasive 'Homestay' trend. Homestays here tend to be smaller, unique properties with a few rooms, managed and tended by devoted homeowners. Around the cobbled and quaint streets of Fort Cochin, Kerala, there's a vast variety of homestays on offer including The Francis Residence. Owner K. P. Francis is the ultimate 'host with the most'. Around a central indoor garden feature, he has designed his modernized homestay with opulent bedrooms, top-end ensuite bathrooms and flower-filled balconies, emulating the five-star hotels he used to manage. 'Hospitality is a passion with me,' says Francis who worked for the Taj Group for 15 years and then moved on to work as general manager for Fort Cochin's The Malabar House for eight years. With the help of his wife, he artistically presents lovingly created meals according to the dietary requirements and culinary whims of his clientele, calling this 'food from the heart'. He also helps orientate guests around the city and area.

While running his own homestay, he still works as a consultant for top-notch hotels such as the Tea Bungalow and other hospitality businesses around Fort Cochin, a fount of ideas for upgrades. 'There are around 200 homestays in the area,' says Francis. 'So my wife, Rosy and I have to differentiate ourselves with an authentic experience but also a very high standard. There are many people, who are fed up with five-star hotels, but are looking for that kind of quality. With many years of experience in hospitality, I am able to specialize in customization and individual attention. This way we get to know our guests and they become like family.' Featuring predominantly seafood dishes, his wife Rosy runs cooking classes at the homestay for visiting groups of up to 20 people. The operation is all serviced by a website (www.francisresidence.com) as well as by word-of-mouth recommendations from Francis's huge circle of friends and acquaintances in the hotel business.

(Continued)

(Continued)

On nearby Princess Street, Fort Cochin's oldest street, historian Christopher Walton runs the Walton's Homestay. Reminiscent of Charles Dickens's Old Curiosity Shop, Walton's overstocked office area combines a bookstore and historical archive with the meticulously managed homestay. Walton gives his guests the historical background to explore the Portuguese, Dutch and British architecture, religion and commerce of the city from his own knowledgeable perspective. And his daughter, Charlotte Walton – an MBA from Mahatma Gandhi University – professionally frames and displays all the glowing reports about the homestay in the media. With a chirpy bird song in the background, their trendy website features a Sam Walter Foss poem which has inspired Walton. 'We have a Facebook page which we keep updating on our regular progress for our guests and clients,' says Walton. 'We depend mostly on word of mouth and guests' recommendations.' He says that he favours open and sincere communication with guests 'from the word go' from the very first email exchanges. 'The reason being that via direct communication with clients and customers, we get to know their requirements of stay which can be taken care of,' he explains. 'This way, guests do not arrive at our home as strangers. We hope by then to have initiated a rapport with our guests, through emails or telephone.'

Cherai Beach is a popular seaside retreat for Fort Cochin locals and visitors, many of whom are on *Eat, Pray, Love* style quests or seeking out spa and yoga experiences. Brighton Beach House is a more humble homestay right on the beach, run by Krish Brijesh and his wife, Divya. Since 2006, the couple - both university graduates and IT professionals from Bangalore - has been providing basic accommodation in a family-oriented compound coupled with great fresh homemade food and solicitous service at the rustic seaview restaurant. Brijesh says that their customers are mainly from Europe and bookings are often made a year ahead. Customer find them through word of mouth, Tripadvisor and Lonely Planet. Most visitors book one, two or even three week stays between November and April, combining the beach with trips to Munnar's tea plantations, Fort Cochin's heritage sites and Alleppey's houseboat attractions.

Checking his email and social media at least four times per day, Brijesh says that Facebook is an important resource, too, notching up more than 600 `Likes' per year. He keeps it updated continually, recently adding pictures of dolphins jumping out of the water right in front of Brighton Beach House. Going from corporate life to small business held a few challenges but he learnt from talking to visitors and scouring the Internet for tips. For example, he didn't know basic things like finding a good cook, or arranging a room. He learnt from YouTube how to tuck in bed sheets properly. With no plans to expand on his success, his mantra is `less is more'. He doesn't want to build up another floor as some people have suggested, as he doesn't want guests to lose their privacy or tranquility with too many people in the space. Providing love, care, good food and nature in a simple homestay framework are enough, he says, leaving travellers with more money to spend on experiences around the area.

Sources: Personal visit by both authors to Fort Cochin, Kerala in 2016 including interviews with K. P. Francis, Christopher Walton and Krish Brijesh.

THE SHARING ECONOMY

As the Digital Spotlight highlights, the sharing economy is having a disruptive influence on the travel industry. Such collaborative consumption describes the shift in consumer values from ownership to access. Together, entire communities and cities around the world are using network technologies to do more with less, by renting, lending, swapping, bartering, gifting and sharing products on a scale never before possible (McAlpine, 2014). Travel-oriented peer-to-peer (P2P) websites are rapidly expanding, allowing travellers to rent lodging, cars, sports equipment and more from other individuals. Since August 2008, over 25 million guests have chosen to sleep in one of the 800,000 Airbnb listed properties. The ridesharing app Uber is signing up over 1100 new ridesharing partners every month in Australia (Allen, 2015).

The current valuations of these peer-to-peer models are over $75 billion (Allen, 2015). They do not own the cars, the houses, or the helicopters. What the companies own is the software – and the algorithms – that help match potential private buyers and sellers (Allen, 2015). Their software models are based on self-regulation mechanisms such as insurance for guests and hosts, a secure payment system, and reputation-based accountability. For consumers, these companies are attractive because they offer lower prices, better accessibility, great flexibility, ease of use, and 'a user focused mission' including transparency and interactive communication (Clark, 2014; ITB, 2014). As Allen (2015) suggests, riding with Uber and hosting with Airbnb are tangible experiences through which individuals can realize the immense benefits of free markets absent from government control.

Rigorous studies that attempt to estimate empirically the impacts of the sharing economy have not yet emerged, although a recent study of the impact of Airbnb in Texas found evidence that the sharing economy is significantly changing consumption patterns, and that Airbnb's entry into the Texas market has had a quantifiable negative impact on local hotel revenues, particularly lower-end hotels (Zervas, Proserpio and Byers, 2014). The sharing of information online with complete strangers is also having an influence on travel decisions (Martin, Rosenbaum and Ham, 2015), especially in the realm of online reviews. In fact, the sharing economy has led to the phenomenon of 'two-way reviews' on services like Uber and Airbnb, where customers themselves are rated in addition to businesses (Euromonitor, 2015).

The regulatory, legal and tax framework associated with the sharing economy has received a fair amount of attention. As PWC (2015) says, the right balance of solutions needs to be built from the bottom up, where local authorities can quickly trial and experiment with new models. Not surprisingly, this is more easily done when both sides work together. For instance, Airbnb worked with Amsterdam's local council to pass an 'Airbnb-friendly law' in February 2014 which permits residents to rent out their homes for up to 60 days a year, provided that the owner pays the relevant taxes. In the US now, Airbnb is voluntarily collecting and remitting taxes on behalf of hosts and guests in a growing number of states including South Carolina, Florida, North Carolina, Alabama and Oregon.

Cohen and Muñoz have analysed hundreds of sources of data on 36 different sharing business startups, and identified six key dimensions of sharing-economy business models, each of them with three distinct decisions that can be made by sharing startups (see Figure 7.2). Four of the dimensions in their 'Sharing Business Model Compass' – transaction, business approach, governance model and platform type – offer business model decision choices roughly on a continuum from more market-based sharing (i.e. platform capitalism) towards commons-based sharing (i.e. platform cooperatives). While the other two dimensions – technology and shared resources – have decisions, which are not influenced by market or commons orientations. The authors suggest that if one assumes that all sharing business models contain the six dimensions addressed in the Compass, and that all sharing startups must choose just one option within each dimension, this leads to a total possible of 729 unique business models in the sharing economy.

A 2014 survey of US consumers, found that 19 per cent of the total US adult population had engaged in a sharing economy transaction, and that trust, convenience and a sense

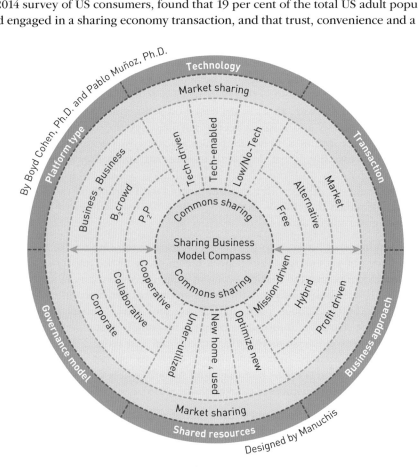

FIGURE 7.2 The sharing business model compass (Reprinted with kind permission of Boyd Derek Cohen)

There are two main forms of the vertical marketing system: alliances and franchises. Both carry with them advantages and disadvantages. Which form an organization chooses depends on which one best matches that company's specific goals.

ALLIANCES

An alliance is a partnership formed when two or more organizations combine resources through a contractual agreement that allows them to overcome each other's weaknesses by benefiting from each another's strengths. In this form of distribution channel, each organization shares everything from information to resources to strategies, but the key advantage to alliances is increased distribution. Those organizations joined through the alliance will enjoy access to new markets through new and diversified sales locations. A good example is the cooperation in South Africa's Greater Kruger National Park conservation area. Kruger, itself, has pulled down fences delineating its lands, allowing animals freedom to roam in and out of the national park and the bordering private reserves. At Motswari Private Game Reserve, one of six camps in the Timbavati area just west of Kruger, cooperative marketing is just part of day-to-day business. The four-star operation links with its neighbours in a concerted marketing effort to attract international and domestic tourists.

Cooperation in marketing initiatives is also coupled with a cooperative approach to game spotting. All guides within the Timbavati area alert the others about animal sightings, kills, and activities, making their successes available to everyone.

Another example of an alliance in the tourism sector is the Adventure Collection, a group of nine adventure companies that have joined together to form an alliance based on the principle that each company is deeply committed to the environment and culture through which it takes its guests. In fact, the companies in the Adventure Collection have agreed to uphold rigorously certain strategic principles of responsible travel. The alliance has a website and blog (see www.adventurecollection.com), and prints a collective brochure that is sent to guests of all nine companies. The companies also combine itineraries to create new trips in order to give travellers more choices. The nine companies in the collection are Backroads, Bushtracks Expeditions, GeoEx, Lindblad Expeditions, Micato Safaris, Natural Habitat Adventures, Nols, OARS, and Off the Beaten Path.

Increasingly, destinations are collaborating in order to create a competitive advantage for the region in which they operate. A good example comes from British Columbia, Canada, where in 2006, seven ski resorts came up with the concept of the Powder Highway to showcase snow sports in the entire Kootenay Rockies region. 'When we first set out to brand the Powder Highway, we did it to place ourselves as a cohesive region within BC that could compete with areas like Banff and Whistler and the big American snow resorts,' said Anne Pigeon, vice-president of marketing and director of operations at Whitewater Ski Resort near Nelson, BC at the time. 'It's been very successful for the region. As a collective we're able to saturate the market in a way that an individual resort can't do' (Milner, 2013).

Ashley Tait, former director of sales and marketing for Revelstoke Mountain Resort, said that though the Kootenay Rockies resorts compete for customers, the Powder Highway brand supports all of them. 'It's about identifying our region, so that collectively we promote tourism in our area and across the province,' she said. 'We market internationally with the Canadian Tourism Commission, nationally with Destination BC, and regionally with Kootenay Rockies Tourism and the Powder Highway. We're competitive in a supportive environment.'

Kathy Cooper, CEO of Kootenay Rockies Tourism, said the Internet has been a powerful factor in marketing the Powder Highway. 'A shift has taken place from traditional marketing in newspapers, magazines and consumer shows to web-based marketing that has grown significantly even in the last four to five years,' Cooper said. 'The Powder Highway website is a one-stop shop for information on all the winter activities.' The site is a specific landing spot for information about the complete Powder Highway product; it provides snow reports, information about the terrain and the nearby communities, and blog posts from enthusiastic visitors (Milner, 2013).

FRANCHISES

Franchises are businesses that are established when a franchiser grants a franchisee the right to engage in offering, selling, or distributing its goods or services under its marketing format. Franchising has become increasingly popular in tourism and hospitality, particularly in the hotel and restaurant sector. The Hard Rock brand is a good example of a successful franchise operation, and the owners, the American Indian Seminole Tribe, has expanded its commercial operation overseas by buying the British-owned chain of Hard Rock Café restaurants and casinos. The Florida tribe was the first native band in the casino business to expand internationally on such a large scale. The tribe had already partnered successfully with Hard Rock in hotel, gambling, and entertainment complexes in Tampa and Hollywood, Florida. With venues in 68 countries, including 163 cafes, 23 hotels, 11 casinos, and five live concert venues, Hard Rock International (HRI) is one of the most globally recognized companies.

Most investors in hotels today require some type of chain affiliation before they will consider becoming involved in a hotel project. They believe that the benefits of having an established brand image, a central reservations system, coordinated marketing, and a frequent traveller programme are worth the cost of associating with a hotel chain. Hotel companies that have an established brand give independent lodging owners the right to use their brand logo, reservations system, and other programmes by either granting a franchise or actually taking over the property's management through a management contract. Globally, franchising has become the most popular method of obtaining brand identity because the hotel owner does not have to relinquish operational control. Normally the franchisee will pay a fee to purchase a full-service franchise, as well as paying an annual percentage of sales. For example, in the car rental business, Thrifty Car Rental franchisees pay a monthly fee of five per cent of their gross revenue from rental and parking activities, which helps pay for headquarters' support and for select programmes for franchises. There is also an advertising fee, but many services are provided to franchisees for free. Many people in the world of franchising claim that the relationship between franchiser and franchisee is one of the most important and challenging aspects of the business.

DESIGNING THE DISTRIBUTION SYSTEM

Tourism, hospitality and events organizations must decide how to make their services available to their selected target market by choosing their distribution mix strategy. This can be a complex decision. They must select a mix that will provide them with the maximum amount of exposure to potential travellers as well as ensure that the strategy chosen aligns with the company or destination image. In addition, the strategy should maximize control over sales and reservations and should work within the organization's budget.

An organization can consider three broad distribution strategy choices:

INTENSIVE DISTRIBUTION

In this case the organization maximizes the exposure of its travel services by distributing through all available outlets or intermediaries. This strategy is most useful for an organization that is trying to obtain high market coverage. An example of a tourism organization that uses this strategy is the TUI Group, the world's leading tourism group, operating in around 180 destinations across the globe, and providing services along the entire tourism value chain for its 30 million customers. The group includes 1,800 travel shops and online portals in Europe, five tour operator-airlines flying more than 140 medium- and long-haul aircraft, over 300 hotels in its own portfolio under premium brands such as Riu and Robinson, and a cruise fleet of 13 ships. In financial year 2014/15, the TUI Group with its 76,000 employees turned over 20 billion euros.

EXCLUSIVE DISTRIBUTION

Here the organization deliberately restricts the number of channels that it uses to distribute its product or service to its customers. Because only a limited number of intermediaries are given the right to distribute the product, the result is often a strengthening of the company's image and an increase in the status of those who purchase the product. This strategy is an effective method for prestige tourism products and is used by companies like Canadian Mountain Holidays (CMH), the heli-skiing operator in Canada mentioned previously. When CMH began marketing in Europe during the late 1960s and early 1970s, Europeans had no knowledge of Canadian heli-skiing opportunities. Rather than following the normal route of mass-media advertising, CMH chose to place no advertisements at all. Instead, the company found one person in each nation to be the CMH agent, and this person had to know the product and its market intimately. Although the distribution system has become more sophisticated over the years, these agents still work in Europe and bring in nearly half of the business.

SELECTIVE DISTRIBUTION

In this strategy between intensive and exclusive distribution, a company uses more than one but less than all of the possible distribution channels. The Rocky Mountaineer in Canada employs selective distribution, using sales representation in over 20 countries to sell over a half-million tours each year. Since its inception in 1990, the British Columbia-based, family-owned business has grown to become the largest privately owned luxury tourist train company in the world and has welcomed nearly two million guests onboard. Marketing is heavily directed towards the international customers that make up much of Rocky Mountaineer's customer base. More than one-third (36%) of its business comes from Australia, while the UK and US account for approximately a quarter each. The average Rocky Mountaineer customer is married with a higher than average household income, and these passengers spend around $2,500 on their trip (Powell, 2015).

Before an organization begins to design its distribution strategy, it is important that it considers the following five factors:

(1) **Market coverage.** The amount of market coverage should be considered in coordination with the organization's goals and objectives, as this factor will directly impact the particular distribution mix that is best for the company.

(2) **Costs.** Only the most cost-effective distribution methods should be implemented, and they should make effective use of the organization's budget.

(3) **Positioning and image.** The distribution strategy chosen should be consistent with the position and image that the company wants to achieve and maintain.

(4) **Motivation of intermediaries.** Intermediaries should be provided with appropriate incentives in order to motivate them to sell the product or service to consumers. The Quebec City Convention Bureau, for example, hosts about 700 tour operators and 400 meeting planners on custom itineraries each year. These trips provide an excellent promotional forum for giving intermediaries a first-hand appreciation of the facilities and services being offered.

(5) **Characteristics of the tourism organization.** Each organization has unique characteristics and needs that are specific to its operations. These needs must be considered when designing the distribution strategy. For example, if an organization operates in a manner that requires it to communicate directly with the consumer in order to be successful, then it must develop its distribution strategy to meet those needs.

Cruise lines have a carefully planned distribution strategy. These companies have traditionally used exclusive distribution, but are gradually moving towards selective distribution. A large percentage of cruises are sold through traditional travel agencies, and, in today's economy, suppliers are reluctant to jeopardize these firmly established, reliable relationships, despite the agency commissions involved. In fact, according to a new Phocuswright report, travel agents' share of US cruise sales grew to 66 per cent in 2015, up from 65 per cent in 2014 and from 59 per cent in 2013. Changing cruise industry dynamics is an important factor in the renewed strength of the travel agency distribution channel, Phocuswright said. After surviving several tough years, cruise industry revenues grew three per cent in 2014, and in this healthier sales environment, bolstered by smarter ship deployment and sales of inclusive packages, cruise lines are discounting less. Instead, they're focusing on attracting more spend from repeat cruisers, Phocuswright observed. In doing so, they're selling more complex itineraries and pushing bundled packages, both of which lend themselves more readily to sales through offline channels, including travel agents, than through OTAs and supplier websites or apps (Phocuswright, 2016).

DISTRIBUTION CHANNEL MANAGEMENT

Once the tourism organization has decided on its distribution mix strategy, it must implement and manage the chosen distribution channel. Channel management includes selecting and motivating individual channel members and evaluating their performance over time.

SELECTING CHANNEL MEMBERS

Tourism organizations must share information and work closely with the members of their distribution system. It is critical, therefore, that an organization selects the best suited channel members in order to ensure an effective distribution system. Motswari safaris, referred to earlier, has selected certain tour operators to distribute its safari packages, based on their geographic position and their ability to reach key international markets. When selecting channel members, the service provider should determine the characteristics that distinguish the most valuable marketing intermediaries from the others. Evaluation criteria may include such aspects as a channel member's number of years in business, the services and products it already carries, its past growth and financial history, its level of cooperativeness, and its reputation and image.

MOTIVATING CHANNEL MEMBERS

After an organization has selected its distribution channel members, it must continually motivate these members to perform their best. Three incentives are commonly used to motivate a company's intermediaries. The first one is financial, and includes commissions and bonuses. The second incentive often used in the tourism industry is the provision of educational trips for intermediary staff, during which they can experience the supplier's product for themselves. Such 'familiarization trips' are common in the travel agency sector. Canadian Mountain Holidays, mentioned above, uses both these methods to motivate international agents. Another incentive, again quite common in travel agencies, is to provide intermediaries with reduced-price holidays. This type of incentive gives intermediaries greater knowledge of the product and enthusiasm for selling it to consumers.

EVALUATING CHANNEL MEMBERS

Tourism organizations must constantly monitor each channel member's performance in order to ensure the success of the channel as a whole. Performance can be measured through the generation of sales, customer delivery time, and/or the success of combined promotional efforts among intermediaries. Channel members who perform well should be recognized and rewarded, and assistance should be provided to those who are struggling to meet the company's goals and objectives. The organization should also 'requalify' its channel members periodically and replace the weaker members that harm the overall effectiveness of the distribution system. One reason that Best Western likes to renew contracts annually is so that it can maintain control over the distribution channel. The company has also implemented a 'quality assurance process,' whereby a quality inspection team will use the same criteria to review every one of the member hotels around the world. Finally, the Best Western website gives customers the opportunity to provide online feedback regarding service quality.

CHAPTER SUMMARY

This chapter discusses various influences on the distribution of tourism and hospitality products. One of these is the sharing economy which is having a disruptive influence on the travel industry. Traditionally, there are two different distribution channels that the service provider or principal can pursue: direct or indirect channels. In a direct channel, a company delivers its product to the consumer without the outside assistance of any independent intermediaries. In an indirect channel, the supplier makes use of several marketing intermediaries such as travel agents, tour operators, convention and meeting planners, travel specialists and online intermediaries. There are two types of marketing system – conventional and vertical – and there are two main forms of vertical marketing systems: alliances and franchises. When designing its distribution system, a company can choose from intensive, exclusive distribution or selective distribution. Before an organization begins to design its distribution strategy, it is important that it considers market coverage, costs, positioning and image, motivation of intermediaries, and the characteristics of the tourism organization itself. In order for the company to ensure the effective execution of its distribution strategy, it must select individual channel members, motivate these members and monitor their performance over time.

REFLECTIVE QUESTIONS

1. How does the tourism and hospitality industry's distribution system differ from that of other industries?

2. Choose a company within the tourism/hospitality sector that you are familiar with and explain how it uses its distribution strategy to attract customers to its product/service. Do you think that the company is using the most effective distribution channel available to it? What do you recommend that the company do to improve its distribution system?

3. Why do you think the sharing economy has grown so much in the last few years? What are your experiences using it?

MARKETING IN ACTION: NATIONAL BROTHERHOOD OF SKIERS ANNUAL SUMMIT

The scene: a brand new onhill restaurant and après ski facility with Prosecco patio heated by trendy tabletop firepits. The clientele: exuberant skiers and snowboarders relaxing in designer gear, sampling appetizers, quaffing beer and Italian champers, dancing to professional DJ music. Could be a chi-chi ski resort anywhere in the world, possibly Europe with such a heady level of animation. But it was actually Elk Camp at Aspen Snowmass in February 2013 when the National Brotherhood of Skiers (NBS) brought high-spirited African American attitude to the trendy town's newest venue.

The fun-loving fanfare was all to celebrate the 40th Anniversary Summit of the NBS, established back in 1973 when black skiing was truly a minority sport.

IMAGE 7.4 Skiers from the National Brotherhood of Skiers enjoying après-ski at the Spider Sabich Cabin, Aspen Snowmass (photo courtesy of the authors)

Contradicting typical skiing ethnic demographics for the week, the 3,000-strong cohort of black skiers and snowboarders from all over America held court on the snow-deluged slopes of Snowmass, in the chic shops and in hotels, condominiums and private homes dotting the extensive ski in/out resort.

Taking a break from their home hills of Mammoth, Big Bear and Tahoe were 11 Californian ski clubs including the All Seasons Ski Club, Oakland; Camellia City Ski Club, Sacramento, Fire and Ice Ski from San José; Snowbusters from Pasadena; and Winter Fox and Bladerunners from Los Angeles. Lenore Benoit, membership director for Winter Fox Ski Association based in LA, joined the club after moving from New York in 1990. 'One of the ladies at my new company befriended me and told me about Winter Fox. She said it was a great way to meet people as well as learn to ski,' said Benoit. She enjoys the club's year-round activities including camping, house boat trips, watersports, river rafting, concerts, wine tastings and, of course, several ski trips. 'I'd never been to Aspen so it was just an awesome experience to come here and see the beauty and the amazing runs,' she added. The social scene was particularly important to her: 'Each trip I get to see people I haven't seen for a while. They have become like family through the NBS. We meet skiing and then stay in touch, it's just a beautiful thing.'

Fellow Fox, Ida Cochrane is a past president of the club and member since 1980. A veteran with the NBS, she has seen numbers fluctuate at yearly summits which reached a peak at Vail in 1993 when there were 4,000 registrants and another 2,000 hangers-on. Every summit has its 'renegades', nonmembers who tag along for the party. Averaging 20 ski days per season, Cochrane meets up with friends from all over the States at NBS events including ski buddy, Georgia Odom who moved to Texarkana, Texas, but reconnects annually under the Winter Fox banner: 'I have never missed a season, I'm afraid if I stop I'll never start again,' she said at the mid-week picnic on the piste. 'My motto is as long as I can walk, I can ski.'

Odom has skied the Italian, French, Austrian and Swiss Alps as well as resorts from New Mexico to Canada. After taking instruction courses in North America, Italy and France, she is an accomplished skier who feels a resurgence of youth during every Summit. 'I also join in with all the happy hours and really enjoy myself – you would think I was 30 years old,' she said. After skiing the Aspen Snowmass area six times, it had become

(Continued)

(Continued)

her firm favourite resort: 'It's easy to get to and the lodging is mostly ski in/out. You don't need a car and everything is walkable. And the runs are wide open,' she enthused.

The whole week of the 2013 NBS Summit, the party pulse was so persuasive that it made Snowmass locals and other tourists eager to join in the après action. 'I worked security one night and saw so many nonmembers who wanted to join in all the fun,' said Darryl Joseph, a member of the Jazz Ma Tazz ski club from New Orleans. 'The resort staff were dancing more than us!' NBS sponsors, Diageo had brought DJ Ike T and DJ B-Sharp from New Orleans to emcee the week's activities. Apart from the après ski, Joseph's main focus on NBS trips is the sport: 'I am back on skis after surgery. I've been skiing three years and injury hasn't stopped me. I think Snowmass is wonderful, very welcoming, the mountain is great and the weather has been fantastic,' he said. But it was the strength in numbers that was particularly gratifying for him: 'When I ski outside the organization I don't see many African Americans. So it's great that once or twice a year I get to see so many African Americans enjoying skiing together.'

Original founders, Ben Finley and Arthur Clay were centre stage that week, presiding over the opulent opening ceremony on the Westin Snowmass patio. Clay has been skiing since 1965 when he said he was often the only black skier on the slopes. Bringing together 350 skiers from 13 black ski clubs for the first NBS summit in Aspen, he has since helped develop the organization to encompass 60 clubs from 43 cities over 25 states. 'It's a big family reunion,' said Clay, who had to overcome considerable trials and tribulations to keep the NBS alive. 'A lot of people have told me over the years you can't do this. But it is doable, although there's a lot of administration.'

Featuring team colours and cheers, dances, prayers, national anthem, torchlight ski and fireworks, the opening ceremony heralded a host of diverse on and off snow activities throughout the week. As well as ski and snowboard races, piste picnics, happy hours, concerts and comedy, there were also special events for tag-along nonskiers including a movie screening, gospel fest and shopping spree.

With over 3,000 members, the nonprofit, volunteer-run association is one of the largest ski organizations within the industry. The Summit itself is the largest gathering of skiers and riders among all US ski conventions. Although serious ski-related issues are addressed – such as introducing the sport to underprivileged inner city youth – it is all about a shared love of skiing, snowboarding and socializing for most participants. The group next met in Sun Valley, Idaho in 2014; returned to Aspen Snowmass in 2015; met at Heavenly Valley, Lake Tahoe, California in 2016; and planned to reconvene at Keystone, Colorado in 2017.

Sources: Both writers attended the 40th Anniversary Summit and interviewed (and skied and partied with) the participants in February 2013.

CASE STUDY QUESTIONS

1. If you were organizing the next group summit, what particular marketing intermediaries would you use to attract more black skiers and snowboarders?

2. What are the advantages for a resort like Aspen in hosting a large event like this?

3. What special considerations do destinations need to think of when hosting events of 3,000 plus people?

REFERENCES

Allen, D. (2015) 'The sharing economy', *IPA Review*, 67(3): 25–7.

Amaro, S. and Duarte, P. (2015) 'An integrative model of consumers' intentions to purchase travel online', *Tourism Management*, 46: 64–79.

Aslanzadeh, M. and Keating, B.W. (2014) 'Inter-channel effects in multichannel travel services: Moderating role of social presence and need for human interaction', *Cornell Hospitality Quarterly*, 55(3): 265–76.

Belk, R. (2014) 'You are what you can access: Sharing and collaborative consumption online', *Journal of Business Research*, 67: 1595–1600.

Botsman, R. and Rogers, R. (2010) *What's Mine is Yours: The Rise of Collaborative Consumption*. New York: HarperCollins.

Buhalis, D. and Laws, E. (2001) *Tourism Distribution Channels: Practices, Issues and Transformations*. New York: Continuum.

Clark, J. (2014) 'Making connections via peer-to-peer travel', *USA Today*, 31 January: 8B.

Cohen, B. (2016) 'Making sense of the many business models in the sharing economy', *co.exist*, 4 June. www.fastcoexist.com/3058203/making-sense-of-the-many-business-models-in-the-sharing-economy (accessed 7 December 2016).

de la Merced, M. J. (2015) 'Expedia to acquire Orbitz as travel sites consolidate', *New York Times*, 13 February: B3.

Ert, E., Fleischer, A. and Magen, N. (2016) 'Trust and reputation in the sharing economy: The role of personal photos in Airbnb', *Tourism Management*, 55: 62–73.

Euromonitor (2015) *Top 10 Global Consumer Trends for 2015*. London: Euromonitor International. www.siicex.gob.pe/siicex/documentosportal/alertas/documento/doc/810395732radDD19D.pdf (accessed 7 December 2016).

Forbes (2015) 'Competition is shaking up the online travel market', 5 January. www.forbes.com/sites/greatspeculations/2015/01/05/competition-is-shaking-up-the-online-travel-market/#2beb603a5846 (accessed 7 December 2016).

Forno, F. and Garibaldi, R. (2015) 'Sharing economy in travel and tourism: The case of home-swapping in Italy', *Journal of Quality Assurance in Hospitality and Tourism*, 16(2): 202–20.

FVW (2015) 'DER Touristik turns European with Kuoni deal', 23 June, *FVW*. www.fvw.com/european-tour-operators-der-touristik-turns-european-with-kuoni-deal/393/144748/11245 (accessed 7 December 2016).

Hamari, J., Sjöklint and Ukkonen, A. (2015) 'The sharing economy: Why people participate in collaborative consumption', *Journal of the Association for Information Science and Technology*. doi: 10.1002/asi.23552.

Hudson, S. and Hudson, L. J. (2014) *Golf Tourism*, 2nd edn. Oxford: Goodfellow Publishers Ltd.

Hudson, S. and Hudson, L. J. (2015) *Winter Sport Tourism: Working in Winter Wonderlands*. Oxford: Goodfellow Publishers Ltd.

Huxley, L. (2016) 'Tui Specialist Group companies to operate under new Travelopia brand', *Travel Weekly*, 11 May. www.travelweekly.co.uk/articles/61587/tui-specialist-group-companies-to-operate-under-new-travelopia-brand (accessed 7 December 2016).

ITB (2014) *ITB World Travel Trends Report 2014/15*, IPK International, Germany. www. itb-berlin.de/media/itbk/itbk_dl_en/WTTR_Report_A4_4_Web.pdf

Koo, B., Mantin, B. and O'Connor, P. (2011) 'Online distribution of airline tickets: Should airlines adopt a single or a multi-channel approach?' *Tourism Management*, 32: 69–74.

Lee, H, Guillet, B. D. and Law, R. (2013) 'An examination of the relationship between online travel agents and hotels: A case study of choice hotels international and Expedia.com', *Cornell Hospitality Quarterly*, 54(1): 95–107.

Martin, D., Rosenbaum, M. and Ham, S. (2015) 'Marketing tourism and hospitality products worldwide: Introduction to the special issue', *Journal of Business Research*, 68(9): 1819–21.

Matthews, L (2011) 'Ulkotours set to help Russia become a major travel and tourism market', PRWeb. www.prweb.com/printer/8609955.htm (accessed 7 December 2016).

McAlpine, T. (2014) 'The sharing economy', *Cues*, 37(12), December. https://www.cues. org/article/view/id/The-Sharing-Economy (accessed 7 December 2016).

Milner, M. (2013) 'Powder Highway welcomes the world', *Kootenay Business*, November. http://kootenaybiz.com/tourism/article/powder_highway_welcomes_the_ world (accessed 7 December 2016).

Paraskevas, A., Katsogridakis, I., Law, R. and Buhalis, D. (2011) 'Search engine marketing: Transforming search engines into hotel distribution channels', *Cornell Hospitality Quarterly*, 52(2): 200–8.

Phocuswright (2016) *U.S. Online Travel Overview Fifteenth Edition*. Sherman CT: Phocuswright.

Powell, C. (2015) 'Rocky Mountaineer's new marketing track', *Marketing Magazine*, 17 September. www.marketingmag.ca/brands/rocky-mountaineers-new-marketing-track-156787 (accessed 7 December 2016).

PWC (2015) *The Sharing Economy: Consumer Intelligence Series*. Delaware: PricewaterhouseCoopers. https://www.pwc.com/us/en/technology/publications/assets/ pwc-consumer-intelligence-series-the-sharing-economy.pdf (accessed 7 December 2016).

TUIgroup.com (2016) 'Strategy and equity story'. https://www.tuigroup.com/en-en/ investors/tui-group-at-a-glance/strategy-and-equity-story (accessed 7 December 2016).

Zervas, G., Proserpio, D. and Byers, J. W. (2014) 'The rise of the sharing economy: Estimating the impact of Airbnb on the industry', Boston University School of Management Research Paper Series No. 2013-16. http://questromworld.bu.edu/platformstrategy/ files/2014/07/platform2014_submission_2.pdf (accessed 7 December 2016).

THE ROLE OF ADVERTISING AND SALES PROMOTIONS

8

INTRODUCTION

Chapter 8 begins with a description of the types of promotional tools used by those in the tourism, hospitality and events sectors. This is followed by an outline of the communication process. The chapter then discusses the rise of integrated marketing communications (IMC) as a result of the recognition that advertising can no longer be crafted and executed in isolation from other promotional mix elements. Consideration is then given to the communication techniques of advertising and sales promotion. The case studies in this chapter focus on the Lopesan Group in Spain, Brand USA's efforts to sell America as a tourism destination, and how Brazil has attempted to leverage its two recent sporting mega-events – the 2014 World Cup and the 2016 Summer Olympics.

LESSONS FROM A MARKETING GURU: EUSTASIO LOPEZ, THE LOPESAN GROUP, GRAN CANARIA, SPAIN

A few years back, your authors visited three Lopesan resort hotels in the Canary Islands to observe their operations and find out more about visionary hotel entrepreneur, Eustasio Lopez. Everything is top-notch at the Lopesan Costa Meloneras Resort, Spa & Casino, part of Lopez's vision to create an upmarket enclave in the sandy south of the island of Gran Canaria, incorporating five-star hotels, beach, restaurants, shopping malls, golf course, conference centre and entertainment facilities. Since 2000 Lopez has built several huge, high-class hotels in the resort and also taken over existing properties to revamp and reinvent.

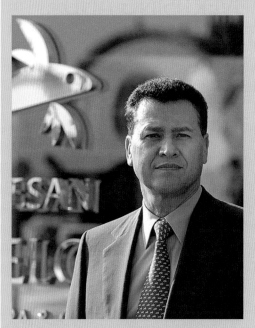

IMAGE 8.1 Eustasio Lopez (©The Lopesan Group. Reproduced by permisssion)

It was a massive undertaking, but Lopez is unfazed by scale. His signature hotel, the four-star Costa Meloneras, comprises 1,250 rooms amidst opulent décor and lavish landscaping featured prominently by Condé Nast magazine. It is the company's cash cow, with high occupancy almost year round. Nearby, the five-star, 570-room Villa del Condé is modelled after his hometown of Aguimes, including all the buildings that a typical Canary village would incorporate as well as a gigantic, central cathedral which is actually the hotel reception. The African-themed Baobab cost 110,000,000 Euros to build, and exudes Africa with jungle foliage, rivers, bridges, thatched roofs, bamboo furniture, animal pelts and wood-posted balconies, emulating the architecture in rotunda-style villages.

Naturally customer service is high on Lopez's list of priorities and the first inkling of this is when waiters deliver cooled cocktails at check-in. According to Lopesan's quality control manager, Pablo Lorenzo, Lopez holds to the Spanish saying 'there's no second chance for a first impression'. His aim is to make guests feel as if they have stepped into a different planet. 'The president wanted to promote a different conception of Canary Island tourism in this area,' says Lorenzo. 'I think his vision is a bit like Vegas, not for the casinos, but he would like a very big resort with thematic variety, hence the African and colonial themes.'

The Lopesan mandate is to give more value for money and attract a high-class segment of tourism to Gran Canaria, a destination which, since the 1960s, has typically promoted cheap package deals. Exceptional service doesn't stop at reception though. Once in their rooms, Lopesan guests find televisions already tuned into the correct language channel for them. Later, if they order a particular drink on their room key card, the next day the waiters will already know their favourite tipple. 'This makes a customer feel special,' explains Lorenzo, who says that innovative ideas come from both customer and staff feedback. If guests return more than three times, they are considered 'repeaters' and will be greeted in their rooms with complementary drinks and fruit.

But all this luxury and top service doesn't sell itself. Lopesan has to create marketing plans and campaigns to communicate its facilities and message to the world. When Russian tourism numbers began to burgeon, Lopesan specifically targeted this newer tourism market through the Internet. In 2014 the company improved the online experience for this important audience by publishing the Russian version of its website. Initially a partial version of the whole site, it encompassed all the necessary information on the most popular tourist destinations under the Lopesan umbrella in countries like Spain, Germany, Austria and the Dominican Republic. A contact form was included in Russian to answer any questions about reservations or payments. The chain already had Spanish and German websites, too.

Another way the company communicates with customers is via a news section on its website (www.lopesan.com/en/news/p/1) which keeps followers apprised of its latest achievements with in-house copy on interesting initiatives. One of the key events promoted through this site was a Hollywood movie filmed on Lopesan's turf. In a savvy marketing move, Lopesan secured the filming of *Wild Oats*, starring an array of Hollywood movie stars, at the Costa Meloneras Resort, Spa & Casino. As well as hosting key personnel, it allowed filming on the premises – while still operating as a hotel resort – and also staged a presentation and press conference there in 2014.

Film tourism is a hot destination-marketing topic these days and Lopez was quick to seize the opportunity to leverage the film and its celebrities via the media. Locally, *La Provincia, Diario de Las Palmas,* covered the high profile visit, focusing heavily on Demi Moore, who was brought in at the last minute to replace Sarah Jessica Parker. The article said that filming was expected to last for about a month, involving 150 extras alongside the movie stars. And many other international news articles emanated from this strategic press conference, including one in the Norwegian publication, *See and Hear,* which called Gran Canaria one of the Norwegians' most popular holiday destinations. They were particularly interested in Demi Moore who played scenes in the resort's Corallium Spa and the Casino Costa Meloneras. Giving even more celebrity cachet to the Maspalomas/Meloneras area, the article also mentioned Norwegian singer, Jahn Teigen who has stayed there.

Europapress.es covered the event in a story entitled 'Hollywood moved to Gran Canaria', citing the difficulties of combining filming with a full hotel. It also said that the historical landmarks, climate and natural landscapes of the island may have been the reason for setting the film there – significant marketing messages for the resort and the whole area. The film's general location was also mentioned in the UK's *Daily Mail* although the hotel wasn't specifically mentioned. Google has a host of photos under the heading 'Demi Moore in Gran Canaria' including promo shots of the Lopesan hotel. The film's own website – www.imdb.com/title/tt1655461 – included fun facts about the island such as: 'Las Palmas de Gran Canaria, the capital of Gran Canaria, where the movie takes place, was ranked as the city with the best climate in the world in a 1996 scientific study called "Pleasant Weather Ratings" by Thomas Whitmore, director of research on climatology at Syracuse University, New York.'

Sources: Personal visit by both authors, 2011.

MARKETING PROMOTION TOOLS

As seen in the opening case study, effective communication with target customers is carried out by a variety of methods, referred to as 'marketing communications'. In many people's perception, marketing is promotion, for promotion is the highly visible, public face of marketing. However, promotion is only one element of the marketing mix, its role being to convince potential customers of the benefits of purchasing or using the products and services of a particular organization. Organizations use marketing communications – promotional tools used to communicate effectively with customers – for many reasons other than simply launching new products. They may, for example, be trying to encourage potential customers to try their product at the same time as encouraging their existing customers to purchase or use the same product again. Or, as in the opening case, communications may be used just to keep customers informed of latest developments and news from the company, keeping it current and trending.

Together with marketing, marketing communications dramatically increased in importance in the 1980s and 1990s, to the extent that effective, sustained communication with customers is now seen as critical to the success of any organization, whether in the private, public, or not-for-profit sector, from international airlines to events to tourism destinations and attractions. Promotions decisions will be determined by the overall marketing plan, as illustrated in Figure 8.1. Chapter 4 explains how marketing objectives are derived from the strategic tools of targeting and positioning. The marketing mix is then used to achieve these objectives, and promotions are just one part of this marketing mix.

The blend of promotional elements outlined in Table 8.1 is known as the promotional mix, and promotional management involves coordinating all the elements, setting objectives and budgets, designing programmes, evaluating performance, and taking

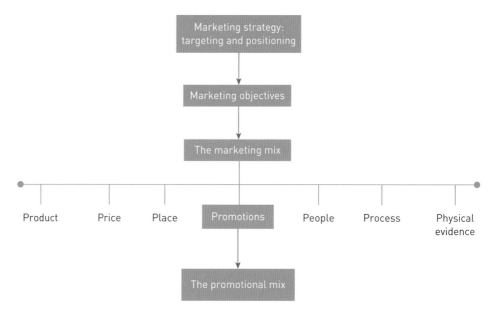

FIGURE 8.1 The role of promotions in the marketing strategy

corrective action. Promotion can be a short-term activity but, considered at a strategic level, it is a mid- and long-term investment aimed at building up a consistent and credible corporate or destination identity. Promotion, when used effectively, builds and creates an identity for the product or the organization. Brochures, advertisements, in-store merchandising, sales promotions, and so on, create the identity of the company in the mind of the consumer, and all aspects of the promotional effort should therefore project the same image to the consumer.

Internet marketing has been covered in Chapter 3, and public relations and personal selling will be discussed in Chapter 9. This chapter discusses the first two tools listed in Table 8.1 – advertising and sales promotion. It is worth clarifying that promotion management deals explicitly with the promotional mix. In contrast, marketing communications is an all-encompassing term (and activity) that includes communication via any and all of the marketing mix elements. How a product is packaged, priced, and distributed all communicates an image to a customer just as much as how the product is promoted.

TABLE 8.1 The promotional mix used in tourism and hospitality

Promotional tool	Tourism and hospitality application
Advertising	Television, newspapers, magazines, billboards, Internet, brochures, guidebooks
Sales promotion	Short-term incentives to induce purchase. Aimed at salespeople, distributors such as travel agents, and consumers. Can be joint promotions. Include merchandising and familiarization trips
Public relations	All non-paid media exposure appearing as editorial coverage. Includes sponsorship of events and causes
Personal selling	Meetings and workshops for intermediaries; telephone contact and travel agents for consumers
Word of mouth	Promotion by previous consumers to their social and professional contacts
Direct marketing	Direct mail, telemarketing, and travel exhibitions
Internet marketing	Direct email marketing, Internet advertising, social media, customer service, selling, and market research

THE COMMUNICATION PROCESS

The communication process that takes place between the sender and receiver of a message is outlined in Figure 8.2. The diagram presents a scenario in which the message is prepared in a symbolic form by the sender (a cruise line, for example) for the prospective audience, perhaps as a visual representation. This process is referred to as 'encoding'. The message is then transmitted by way of a suitable medium such as a television advertising campaign. The receiver sees the message and decodes it: 'decoding' is the method by which the message is filtered or internalized. The major concern of the sender at this stage is that the message is not distorted in the process by what is termed 'noise'. For example, a television advertisement promoting a cruise holiday that followed a news item referring to a cruise ship attacked by pirates (as happened off the coast of Africa in 2005) would fail to convey a convincing message. Likewise, the message might be distorted by clutter, which means the audience may see an excessive number of commercial messages that just get in the way of the advertiser's intended message.

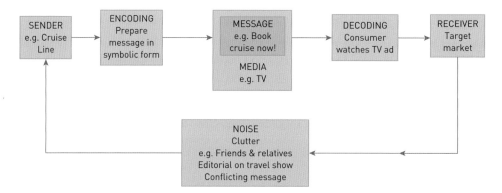

FIGURE 8.2 The communication process

HOW COMMUNICATION WORKS

There are a number of models that show how communication works, particularly in advertising. The models developed invariably assume that customers follow a number of predetermined stages, commencing with awareness and progressing to purchase. The most commonly cited model is that first proposed by Strong (1925), called the AIDA model (attention, interest, desire and action). The idea of this model is that communication should first attract the receiver's attention, then engage the receiver's interest, then create in the receiver a desire for the product or service, and then inspire action in the receiver. For example, in the print advertisement for the 'Bond is GREAT' campaign below (see Figure 8.3), the picture of actor Daniel Craig grabs the reader's attention. This visual image works with the print copy (*Tailored: Live the Bond Lifestyle in Britain*) to gain the reader's interest and to provoke the desire in him or her to visit the website and inspire action to enter the competition. Of course, the influence of advertising differs significantly depending upon the stage of the decision-making process and upon the tourism products under consideration (Park, Nicolau and Fesenmaier, 2013). But though undoubtedly over-simplistic, the AIDA model is a memorable and useful checklist of the aims of advertising, and it provides a framework for other, more complex theories. All of the models of communication that have been developed are known as 'hierarchies of effects models', as they assume a progression from one stage to the next (see Table 8.2).

All the hierarchies of effects models have as their basis the assumption that an effective advertisement makes the receiver think about the product, feel positively towards it, and do something to purchase it. Lavidge and Steiner (1961) label these the cognitive, affective and conative stages of the response. The cognitive stage involves the rational, conscious part of the brain; the affective stage involves the emotions; and the conative stage, a resulting change in behaviour. Rogers argues that the effect of advertising is to interest the consumer enough to evaluate the

TABLE 8.2 Hierarchies of effects models

Type of effect	Strong (1925)	Lavidge and Steiner (1961)	Rogers (1962)	Broadbent and Jacobs (1984)	Colley (1961)	Wells et al. (2006)
Cognitive	Attention	Awareness	Awareness	Problem Recognition	Awareness	Perception
		Knowledge		Information search	Comprehension	Learning
Affective	Interest Desire	Liking Preference Conviction	Interest Evaluation	Attitude Intention	Conviction	Persuasion
Behavioural	Action	Purchase	Trial	Behaviour Adoption	Action	Behaviour

merits of the product and then to give it a trial before adopting it (Rogers, 1962). Broadbent and Jacobs (1985) go further in saying that it is often the trial and not the advertisement that convinces the customer to change an attitude towards a product. Colley (1961) presents the DAGMAR model (defining advertising goals for measured advertising results), which begins with awareness, moves to comprehension, then to conviction, and ends with action. Finally, Wells, Burnett and Moriarty (2006) suggest that there is a set of categories of typical effects that advertisers hope to achieve. The first category is perception, which means the advertiser hopes the ad will be noticed and remembered. Then there are two categories of effects that are focused either on learning, which means the audience will understand the message and make the correct associations, or on persuasion, which means the advertiser hopes to create or change attitudes or touch emotions. The last major category of effects is behaviour: getting the audience to try or buy the product or perform some other action.

INTEGRATED MARKETING COMMUNICATIONS (IMC) IN TOURISM

Perhaps one of the most important advances in marketing in recent decades has been the rise of integrated marketing communications (IMC) – the unification of all marketing communications tools, as well as corporate and brand messages, so they send a consistent, persuasive message to target audiences. This approach recognizes that advertising can no longer be crafted and executed in isolation from other promotional mix elements. As tourism markets and the media have grown more complex and fragmented, consumers find themselves in an ever more confusing marketing environment. Tourism marketers must address this situation by conveying a consistent, unified message in all their promotional activities. IMC programmes coordinate all communication messages and sources of an organization. An IMC campaign includes traditional marketing communication tools, such as advertising or sales promotion, but recognizes that other areas of the marketing mix are also used in communications. Planning and managing these elements so they work together help to build a consistent brand or company image.

TABLE 8.3 An IMC campaign plan

Steps in the campaign	Details
1. Situation analysis	Product and company research Consumer and stakeholder research Industry and market analysis Competitive analysis
2. SWOT (strengths, weaknesses, opportunities, and threats) analysis	Internal strengths and weaknesses External opportunities and threats Problem identification
3. Campaign strategy	Objectives Targeting Positioning
4. Message strategy	Message development research The creative theme Tactics and executions
5. Media plan	Media mix Scheduling and timing
6. Other marketing communications activities	Sales promotion Direct marketing Public relations
7. Appropriation and budget	Based on the cost of reaching the target market
8. Campaign evaluation	Measure the effectiveness of stated objectives

Table 8.3 outlines an IMC communications campaign plan, and it can be seen that such a plan considers a variety of communications tools – not just advertising. VisitBritain followed this type of strategy to achieve its promotional objectives in the recent 'Bond is GREAT' campaign. The national tourism organization launched the campaign in conjunction with the release of the 24th James Bond film *Spectre*, using a mix of outdoor billboards, print, digital and social media. The official website included items like an exclusive behind-the-scenes video that illustrated the pivotal part that London played in the film. The website also offered 360-degree experiences of places such as Blenheim Palace, Camden, Westminster Bridge and City Hall. Advertisements promoted a competition for a chance at living like Bond for a spell (see Figure 8.3). Contestants had to describe their best Bond adventure to win a prize that included a chauffeur-driven Aston Martin, an exclusive afterhours Champagne tour of Madame Tussauds and a stay at a luxury Radisson Blu Edwardian Hotel in London. VisitBritain's Chief Executive Officer, Sally Balcombe said: 'We know that the link between tourism and film is a potent one. Recent films have demonstrated that

they deliver a real increase in visitor numbers with just under half of our potential visitors to Britain wanting to visit places they have seen featured in films or TV so we are doing everything we can to capitalize on this "set-jetting" phenomenon. That's why we are working hard to encourage and inspire more people to holiday in Britain through our "Bond is GREAT Britain" campaign, leading to a measurable increase in international visitor numbers and visitor spend across the nations and regions of Britain' (Zaldivar, 2015).

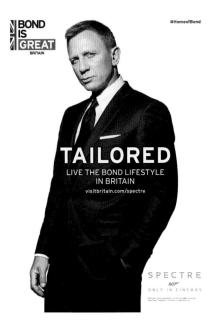

FIGURE 8.3 'Bond is GREAT' advertisement (©VisitBritain. Reprinted with permission)

Another good example of an integrated marketing communications campaign was the 'True' winter campaign launched by the New Mexico Tourism Department (NMTD) in 2013. The idea behind the campaign was to dispel the misconceptions that New Mexico is a dry and arid state: 'We are showing that New Mexico has snow and also an abundant offering of skiing and snowboarding as well as snow-shoeing, sleigh rides and snowmobiling,' said Rebecca Latham, NMTD Cabinet Secretary (Hudson and Hudson, 2015). The creative campaign was disseminated via multimedia: 'We're using a little bit of everything, really targeting print in AFAR, Food Network magazine, Texas Monthly, Southwest, and Outside magazine (see Figure 8.4). So we have some really targeted messages based on what the appeal of the publication is. We also do broadcasts, 30-second TV commercials, and also cinema advertising in our main target markets. In New York City and Chicago we do transit advertising, on subway trains and taxi cabs. And we have beautiful, larger than life dioramas in the airports. And closer to home we have billboards within the state of New Mexico,' Latham explained. This was backed up with a wide-scale social media presence on Facebook, Twitter, Instagram and Pinterest plus 15-second digital ads on targeted websites.

FIGURE 8.4 New Mexico print ad in *Outside Magazine* (Courtesy of New Mexico Tourism Department)

PUSH AND PULL PROMOTIONAL STRATEGIES

One final factor to consider in the promotional strategy will be the position of the organization in the distribution channel. For example, does a retailer (i.e. the travel agent or the venue) carry out its own promotion for the travel product, or does the producer (i.e. the tour operator or destination organization) have to promote the product in order to bring the public into the travel agency to buy it? This is known as the choice between push and pull promotional strategies. A push strategy calls for using the sales force and trade promotion to push the product through channels; the producer promotes the product to wholesalers, the wholesalers promote to retailers, and the retailers to consumers. In contrast, a pull strategy calls for spending a large amount on advertising and consumer promotion to build up consumer demand; if successful, consumers will ask their retailers for the product, the retailers will ask the wholesalers, and the wholesalers will ask the producers. The two strategies are contrasted in Figure 8.5.

The choice of strategy will depend on the degree of influence each member of the distribution channel has on the consumer's decision process and on the relative power of the producer's and the retailer's brand names. In most cases, a combination of the two strategies will be used, with each player in the channel marketing itself to the

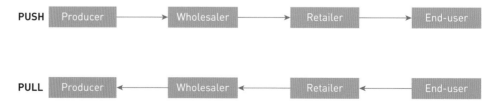

FIGURE 8.5 Push and pull promotional strategies

others and providing support for joint promotions. Carnival Cruises might use a pull strategy to entice consumers to purchase cruise vouchers as gifts using advertising and promotion, whereas a push strategy will be used to promote the idea through the distribution channel using virtual sales kits for travel agents available on the cruise line's travel agent Internet portal.

DIGITAL SPOTLIGHT: SELLING AMERICA TO THE WORLD WITH 'BRAND USA'

IMAGE 8.2 The original 48 plates by Scott Hanson (©DiscoverAmerica.com. Reproduced by permission)

In response to a 36 per cent decline in international visitor share, the Travel Promotion Act of 2011 established Brand USA to oversee the first global marketing effort to promote the US as a travel destination. Formed as the Corporation for Travel Promotion, the public–private entity commenced operations in May 2011. Funded through a $14 fee on tourists from the 37 countries whose citizens don't require a visa to visit the country, the organization is allowed to use up to $100 million a year, provided it obtains matching contributions from the tourism private sector.

Brand USA engaged marketing agency, JWT, to determine the perceptions of the US around the world. Through several roundtable sessions with international planners, and a quantitative research study among 3,000 travellers, JWT discovered that America was perceived as unwelcoming, overly familiar, brash and arrogant. Essentially, America had become 'middle-aged', neither as attractive as the historical destinations of Europe, nor as appealing as the newcomers of the East. JWT also set out to uncover

(Continued)

(Continued)

existing traveller's motives for visiting the US. Using an innovative research technique designed to tap into respondents' deepest feelings about the US, visitors were asked to write 'America's postcard', telling Americans about their experiences there. Their sentiments revealed that people love the freedom of America where everything is larger than life, and they see it is country full of diversity where anything is possible.

These insights helped inform JWT's approach to bringing the US brand to life with a new identity and promise. The creative task was to establish a perceptual shift away from a brand personality of being brash and unwelcoming, to being fresh, unexpected, welcoming, with a sense of freedom and possibility. The brand promise was therefore 'The United States of Awesome Possibilities Welcomes Everyone', and the key message of the initial marketing campaign was 'Discover This Land, Like Never Before'. The intention of this call to action was to remind the world's travellers that the US was a land of possibilities and limitless experiences. Marketers identified four experience pillars to help frame and balance the messaging – the great outdoors, urban excitement, indulgence, and culture. These pillars were used as a guide to help create messaging across all of the marketing platforms. A new logo was created – an arrangement of dots that fastened together to harmonize the letters 'USA' – the concept grounded in the ideals of diversity and unlimited possibilities. Underneath the three letters was 'DiscoverAmerica.com'.

After four rounds of creative testing in 13 international markets, it was decided to use the universal language of music as a cornerstone of the campaign. Rosanne Cash, daughter of American music legend Johnny Cash, composed an original song, 'Land of Dreams', to serve as the heart of the campaign. The song was merged with visuals that show typical USA landmarks (for new travellers) as well as more off-the-beaten-path locales and experiences (for those who perceived America to be hackneyed). The intention, according to Brand USA, was to produce an anthem that shows 'America the destination' while simultaneously emanating a feeling of freedom and limitless possibilities.

The new campaign, with a fully integrated marketing strategy, was unveiled in April 2012 via a mix of 15, 20 and 60 second television spots, combined with digital, billboard and print advertisements, a robust online presence and social media strategy. The new website, DiscoverAmerica.com, acted as a visitors' information portal for trip planning, and country-specific Facebook, Twitter and YouTube pages sought to engage consumers with unique promotions. A media budget of $12.3 million was allocated for the first three months of the campaign, with advertising starting in the UK, Japan and Canada, and then spreading to Brazil, South Korea, China, India, Germany, Mexico, India and Australia. In selecting the overseas markets for its targeted campaigns, Brand USA relied on six criteria: annual volume of visitors; total annual tourism revenue; year-over-year growth on travel volume and tourism revenue; cost of buying media in the country; travellers' ease of entry into the US; and infrastructure, including the availability of representative firms and social media in the country. Brand USA also targeted the travel trade. Industry-specific pages were set up on Twitter and Facebook to engage the trade in customized initiatives, such as the Brand USA Megafam whereby 100 agents from the UK and Ireland were brought to the US to experience seven different itineraries. A 'FAM Photo Competition' was also set up for agents to upload photographs from recent trips, encouraging peer-to-peer engagement.

Brand USA looked towards branded entertainment as another innovative way of reinforcing the new brand values. A website was launched in London to encourage confidential television ideas from producers. An advisory board then met to evaluate submissions and the potential to create the programmes in partnership with the producers. Preference was given to submissions that: encompassed the four experience pillars referred to above; covered multiple destinations; would be broadcast in a number of countries in addition to the UK; and engaged the viewer beyond television to additional online content. Building on this initiative a new broadcast/production programme was launched at the 2014 IPW conference in Chicago. This allowed broadcast and production media from Australia, Canada, UK and Ireland to participate in face-to-face appointments with US destinations to find out more about filming in the US. The idea was to encourage producers to feature the USA as a premier destination and leverage the new brand promise.

In a preliminary report released in September 2012, Brand USA said that intent to visit climbed 13 points in Canada, 17 points in the UK, and 11 points in Japan as a result of the initial marketing campaigns. Campaign awareness in launch markets averaged 25 per cent. In the first eight weeks of the campaign, the *Land of Dreams* song was downloaded 20,000 times, 99 per cent of social media sentiments were positive, and the Brand USA YouTube channel had received over 500,000 views. Brand USA reported that its website had more than 467,000 page views in June 2013, compared with about 77,000 in April 2012.

Source: Hudson (2014).

CASE STUDY QUESTIONS

1. In what way was Brand USA's campaign an integrated communications campaign (IMC)?

2. What measures are Brand USA using to evaluate the campaign? What additional measures could be used to measure success?

3. Take a look at Brand USA's website (www.thebrandusa.com). What efforts are they currently engaged in to attract tourists to America?

TOURISM AND HOSPITALITY ADVERTISING

Advertising can be defined as paid nonpersonal presentation and promotion of ideas, goods, or services by an identified sponsor, using mass media to persuade or influence an audience. Advertising is a key marketing tool in the tourism, hospitality and events sectors industries. These industries require potential customers to base buying decisions upon mental images of product offerings, since they are not able to sample physically alternatives. As a result, advertising is a critical variable in the tourism marketing mix, and it covers a wide range of activities and agencies. Its role reflects that of promotion in general, which is to influence the attitudes and behaviour of audiences in three main ways: confirming and reinforcing, creating new patterns of behaviours, or changing attitudes and behaviour. Thus tourism and hospitality companies use images to portray their products in brochures, posters and media advertising. Destinations do the same, attempting to construct an image of a destination that will force it into the potential tourist's list of options, leading ultimately to a purchase decision.

DEVELOPING AN ADVERTISING PROGRAMME

The process of developing an advertising programme includes six important stages. These are illustrated in Figure 8.6 and discussed below.

1. SETTING THE OBJECTIVES

In planning and managing advertising, a key factor is the setting of objectives. An advertising objective can be defined as a specific communication task to be accomplished with a specific target audience during a specific period of time. In general terms, advertising has four major tasks: informing, persuading, reminding and selling. However, advertising in tourism and hospitality can have many uses. These might include creating awareness; informing about new products; expanding the market to new buyers; announcing a modification to a service; announcing a price change; making a special offer; selling directly; educating consumers; reminding consumers; challenging competition; reversing negative sales trends; pleasing intermediaries; recruiting staff; attracting investors; announcing trading results; influencing a destination image; creating a corporate image; soliciting customer information; improving employee morale; and contributing to cooperative/partnership advertising ventures. For the 'Bond is GREAT Britain' campaign, described above, the objective was to capitalize on the 'set-jetting' phenomenon, and encourage and inspire more people to holiday in Britain through the campaign, leading to a measurable increase in international visitor numbers and visitor spend. In the Brand USA campaign, outlined in the Digital Spotlight, the objective was to bring the US brand to life with a new identity and promise, and create a perceptual shift away from a destination brand personality of being brash and unwelcoming, to being fresh, unexpected, welcoming, with a sense of freedom and possibility.

FIGURE 8.6 The process of developing an advertising programme

2. SETTING THE BUDGET

Ideally, the advertising budget should be calculated on the basis of the objectives set in the first stage of the process. The media plan must reach sufficient numbers in the target market to produce the size of response that will achieve the sales target. Several methods can be used to set the advertising budget. The objective and task method involves developing the promotion budget by (1) defining specific objectives,

(2) determining the tasks that must be performed to achieve these objectives, and (3) estimating the costs of performing these tasks. Using this method requires considerable experience of response rates and media costs, as well as confidence in the accuracy of predictions. Cautious managers prefer to base the advertising budget on what they know from previous experience they can afford to spend. This is often referred to as the affordable method. The percentage of sales method involves setting the promotion budget at a certain percentage of current or forecasted sales or as a percentage of sales price.

In tourism and hospitality, the percentage of gross sales generally set aside for marketing is somewhere between 4 and 12 per cent, advertising being allocated about a quarter of this amount. Cheddar Gorge in the UK, for example, an international centre for caving and rock climbing, spends about 10 per cent of gross turnover on marketing and publicity. The actual percentage will vary according to the product's position on the product life cycle (see Chapter 5), and new products will require more advertising to launch them into the market. The budget size for communications can have a tremendous range. For example, the Las Vegas Convention and Visitors Authority spent $60m on their original 'What Happens in Vegas Stays in Vegas' advertising campaign. New Mexico Tourism Department has an annual budget of around $10m, whereas Tourism Queensland spent just $1m on the 'Best Job in the World' campaign to promote Hamilton Island (see Chapter 3).

Another way of setting the budget is the competitive parity method, which sets the promotion budget at the level needed to achieve parity or 'equal share-of-voice' with competitors. It may seem unwise to spend significantly less than competitors if you are aiming for a similar share of the same market. In the hotel business the advertising expenditure for the average hotel is 1 per cent of sales, but for limited-service hotels, advertising expenditure is higher, representing 2 per cent of sales.

3. ADVERTISING AGENCY DECISIONS

Since advertising is usually considered the most important tool in the marketing communications mix, companies must decide carefully whether they are going to do the work themselves or hire an outside agency. Only very small businesses, such as guesthouses or local visitor attractions, are likely to undertake their own advertising without professional help. At the very least, advertising agencies can help with the purchase of advertising space at discounted rates. Most advertising agencies enjoy working on tourism and hospitality accounts as they involve intrinsically interesting products, and may welcome the account as a stimulating break from their usual subject matter.

The best advertising agencies create value for their clients, as seen in the Brand USA case study. Brand USA engaged marketing agency, JWT, to create a new image for America as a tourist destination. JWT is one of the world's best-known marketing communications agencies. Headquartered in New York, JWT is a global company with more than 200 offices in over 90 countries, employing nearly 10,000 marketing professionals. An agency can clearly interpret what the customer wants and then communicate information about the client's product so meaningfully, so uniquely, and so consistently that customers reward that product with their loyalty. An agency can add perceived value to the product of its client by giving the product a personality, by communicating in a manner that shapes basic understanding of the product, by creating an image or memorable picture of the product, and by setting the product apart from its competitors.

There are two main types of advertising agency: the full-service agency and the specialized agency. In advertising, a full-service agency is one that provides the four major staff functions: account management, creative services, media planning and buying and account planning (which is also known as research). A full-service advertising agency will also have its own accounting department, a traffic department to handle internal tracking on completion of projects, a department for broadcast and print production, and a human resources department. However, tourism and hospitality organizations often use the services of a specialized agency. This type of agency will specialize in certain functions (e.g. writing copy, producing art, media buying), audiences (e.g. minority, youth), or industries (e.g. health care, computers, leisure), or in certain marketing communication areas, such as direct marketing, sales promotion, public relations, events and sports marketing, and packaging and point-of-sale.

4. MESSAGE STRATEGY

The message strategy is the fourth stage in the process of developing an advertising programme. Studies have shown that creative advertising messages can be more important than the number of dollars spent on the message. Creative strategy plays an increasingly important role in advertising success. Developing a creative strategy requires three message steps: generation, evaluation and selection, and execution. The intangibility of services makes advertising difficult for tourism and hospitality marketers. Before buying services, consumers have problems understanding them, and after purchase, they have trouble evaluating their service experiences. Various strategies have been proposed to overcome these problems. One is to present vivid information and evoke strong emotions. Advertisers of top-notch resorts, for example, often try to build a mood or image around the resort, such as beauty, love or serenity, creating an emotional relationship between the resort and potential visitors.

Over the years, researchers have explored message strategies in advertising in various sectors of tourism and hospitality. Research on advertising for destinations, for example, has shown that travellers tend to show more positive attitudes towards cognitive language in city-level utilitarian destination advertisements, whereas they tend to show more positive attitudes towards affective language in attraction-level hedonic destination advertisements (Byun and Jang, 2015). This implies that marketers can more effectively promote their destinations by matching advertising language with destination type. In a study of destination television commercials, Pan (2011) suggested that something old (i.e. something familiar to viewers), something new (i.e. something that cannot be seen or done in the viewer's immediate environment), and something white and something blue (i.e. clean and pristine) should be included when developing promotional tourism videos. Research on advertising in the cruise sector has shown that expert consumers have more favourable attitudes than novice consumers towards cruise advertising (Martin and Vincent, 2014).

Hotel marketers are realizing the importance of touching emotions and getting into the consumer psyche, and have begun to focus on promoting experiences as opposed to physical attributes. In 2011, Ritz Carlton ran a campaign called 'Let us stay with you', replacing the usual hotel-chain request to 'Please say with us'. The switch was intended to convey that the memories of a visit to a luxury Ritz Carlton property will last longer than another fluffy bathrobe. Mark Miller, chief strategic officer at the Ritz Carlton creative agency said the new campaign takes an emotional approach to encourage travellers to evolve from 'measuring a stay in the number of days to measuring a stay in the number of memories, so you get your memories' worth, not just your money's worth' (Elliott, 2011). Oriental-Express Hotel took a similar tack the same year with a campaign that carried the theme 'Embark on a journey like no other'. The campaign was centred on video clips of a fictional family, the Astorbilts, whose behaviour is contemporary, valuing experiences over material possessions.

Other marketers are using nostalgia as the message strategy to attract tourists. Nostalgia has become a big driver in destination choice, especially for Baby Boomers (Hudson, 2010). Not only have tourists become more interested in history, but the scale, richness, and diversity of the history they are interested in has also expanded enormously in the past 30 years. Nostalgia tourism provides an alternative to the present by recourse to an imagined past, a version of reality that people carry around in their heads. A consequence of this emergence in nostalgia tourism is the increasing desire to revisit a specific country or city with a sentimental association instead of discovering somewhere new. A good example of a destination capitalizing on this trend is the Space Coast in Florida. In 2016, a major theme of the Space Coast Office of Tourism's $3.88 million marketing campaign was the beach vibe of decades past, and how tourists could recapture those memories (Berman, 2016). One key tag line in the marketing campaign was 'Cocoa Beach: Still Cool.' A major campaign strategy was to curate nostalgic images and stories, and relate them to current Space Coast experiences. Memories from decades ago of a trip to Cocoa Beach and Ron Jon's; a Saturn or space shuttle launch; low-key Indialantic or amazing surf at Sebastian Inlet were recalled by nostalgic visuals, compared to current beauty and family images. The key message was that Cocoa Beach, Melbourne and its nearby beaches, and Titusville offer families the opportunity to reconnect and rediscover the authentic Florida beach town vibe.

5. MEDIA STRATEGY

The media plan section in an advertising plan includes media objectives (reach and frequency), media strategies (targeting, continuity and timing), media selection (the specific vehicles), geographic strategies, schedules and the media budget. The range of advertising media available to today's advertiser is increasingly bewildering and is becoming ever more fragmented. While these changes offer the prospect of greater targeting, they also make the job of the media planner more difficult. Table 8.4 provides a reference guide to the range of the main advertising media and lists their major advantages and disadvantages. All these media outlets are referred to as the media mix – created by media planners by selecting the best combination of traditional media vehicles (print, broadcast, etc.); nontraditional media (Internet, cell phones, unexpected places like the floors of stores); and marketing communication tools such as public relations, direct marketing and sales promotion to reach the targeted stakeholder audiences.

Given cost constraints, media planners usually select the media that will expose the product to the largest target audience for the lowest possible cost. The process of measuring this ratio is called efficiency – or cost per thousand (CPM). To calculate the CPM, two figures are needed: the costs of the unit (e.g. time on TV or space in a magazine) and the estimated target audience. The cost of the unit is divided by the target audience's gross impressions to determine the advertising dollars needed to expose the product to 1,000 members of the target.

$$\text{CPM} = \text{cost of message unit} / \text{gross impressions} \times 1000$$

For example, if the show *Globe Trekker* has 92,000 target viewers, and the cost of a 30-second announcement during the show is $850, the CPM will be $9.42 (CPM = $850 / 92 000 × 1000 = $9.24).

There are many components to the media mix, and how an organization blends them depends on a number of factors, particularly the nature of the product or service and the target audience. For example, tour operators and major destinations rely heavily on television advertising, but niche players such as special interest operators tend to focus their advertising in specialist publications.

TABLE 8.4 The advantages and disadvantages of the major advertising media

Media type Print media	Advantages	Disadvantages
Local press	High market coverage Short lead time Easily laid out Frequency/immediacy Relatively inexpensive Allows for repetition of ads Creates local image	Audience reads selectively Short life span Low attention Media clutter Poor reproduction quality
National press	Large circulation Many creative options for layout Appeals to all income levels Relatively cheap for national coverage Frequency allows repetition Allows audience/geographical selectivity	Audience reads selectively Short life span Poor reproduction Low attention Clutter
Consumer magazines	Large circulation High pass-on readership High-quality reproduction and colour Relatively long life and read in leisurely fashion Well-segmented audience High information content Allows sales promotion inserts	Expensive Distant copy dates Clutter

Media type Print media	Advantages	Disadvantages
Specialist trade journals	Well-segmented audience Short lead times Potential for high information content ads	Clutter Competitors' ads may be featured
Circulars	Low production and distribution costs Blanket coverage in target areas	Poor image Distribution abuse Short attention span
Inserts in free press and magazines	Relatively cheap Good for direct response ads	Short life span May be seen as having a poor image
Posters	Cheap Target specific areas/groups Longevity (especially on public transport – buses, etc.)	Short exposure time Poor image Clutter Audience segmentation difficult
Broadcast media		
Television	Opportunity for high creativity and impact (sound, visual, etc.) Good for image Appeals to all income levels Relatively cheap for national coverage Frequency allows repetition Allows audience/geographical selectivity High attention gaining	Relatively high production and airtime costs Short life span Clutter Fleeting attention
Commercial radio	Large localized audience Gains local recognition Flexible deadlines Well-segmented audience Allows repeat messages	Production can be expensive Allows audio message only Clutter Short life span Fleeting message Low attention; audience high distraction
Cinema market	Possibility to segment audience or mass market Allows frequent exposure Potential for high creative impact of colour and visuals – large screen and sound	Relatively high production and air time costs Competitors' ads may be featured Fleeting message Difficult to establish audience profile
Out of home		
Billboards	High impact Low cost and large readership Longevity Ability to create awareness	Brief exposure Limited message – unsuitable for complex ads Needs large-scale distribution Creativity needed for impact

(Continued)

TABLE 8.4 (Continued)

Media type Print media	Advantages	Disadvantages
Transit	Can be targeted to specific audiences with high frequency Allows for creativity Can provide detailed information at a low cost	Brief exposure Image factors
Other media		
Direct mail	Allows tracking Prepared mailing lists Allows audience/geographical selectivity High information content	Relatively high production costs of creating and maintaining databases Potential for poor image
Exhibitions/ trade fairs and shows	Large target audience Reach large numbers of customers simultaneously Good for attracting new, maintaining existing customers	Costs of set-up and staffing can be expensive Clutter
Sponsorship and events company to build credibility and time-consuming to build relation-ships and links with partners	Possibility to reach attractive segments or mass market of control over others' actions	Relatively costly Transience of celebrity and lack Allows benefit from reflected success Potential for unusual, attention-grabbing activity
Difficult to evaluate impact Point-of-sale displays, in-store merchandising	Relatively inexpensive Reinforces ad message Incentive for trade location to stock product	Builds company recognition Reaches customers already likely to purchase
Ambient media		
	Good coverage Good segmentation potential Many creative options	Creativity a constant challenge Targeting can be difficult Impact wears off quickly
Internet		
	Global impact Immediacy Many creative options for design Possibility of direct response and audience profiling	Short life span Creativity and Web design costs Low attention Targeting can be difficult

While tourism and hospitality advertising makes use of all of the main media, the key vehicles are print (mainly brochures) and electronic media. Today, an increasing number of companies are focusing on digital advertising. Holiday Inn Express, for example, has recently brought its longtime 'Stay smart' campaign into the twenty-first century by making it largely digital. Jennifer Gribble, vice president for Holiday

Inn Express, Americas, at Intercontinental, said the brand was taking a digital slant with the new advertising because its 'target guest is a working professional who is connected digitally 24/7. The digital approach is the best way to reach our guests, who have an on-the-go lifestyle' (Levere, 2014a).

One of the fastest growing sectors of media is ambient advertising. This approach includes place-based advertising and uses new, unexpected ways of getting messages across. Examples of ambient advertising include ads on the back of grocery receipts, gas pumps, in elevators, ATM screens, seatbacks and tray tables in planes, shop floors, washroom walls, toilet paper, pizza boxes, welcome mats and on tickets. In 2014, Virgin Hotels introduced a 'rumor campaign' meant to be a teaser campaign for its new hotels (Levere, 2014b). In addition to a preliminary website, some rumours were printed on red doormats (red is Virgin Group's signature colour) that were placed outside competing hotels around Chicago. Ambient tactics might involve live advertising. Golden Palace Casino, for example, advertised on the back of professional boxers using large tattoos between 2001 and 2002. By the end of 2002, the casino had 'sponsored' more than 25 boxers, paying each an average of $5-$10,000. As a result, Golden Palace saw a tremendous upswing in media attention, traffic and brand recognition. Then, once the novelty factor ran out, the company looked at alternative ways of advertising.

6. CAMPAIGN EVALUATION

Managers of advertising programmes should regularly evaluate the communication and sales objectives of advertising. The campaign evaluation stage is often the most difficult in the advertising cycle, largely because, while it is relatively easy to establish certain advertising measures (such as consumers' awareness of a brand before and after the campaign), it is much harder to establish shifts in consumer attitudes or brand perception. Despite such uncertainties, the evaluation stage is significant not only because it establishes what a campaign has achieved but also because it will provide guidance as to how future campaigns could be improved and developed.

There are many evaluative research techniques available to marketers to measure advertising effectiveness. Memory tests are often used, and are based on the assumption that a communication leaves a mental residue with the person who has been exposed to it. Memory tests fall into two major groups: recall tests and recognition tests. In a traditional recall test, a commercial is run on a television network and the next evening interviewers ask viewers if they remember seeing the commercial. This type of test, in which the specific brand is mentioned, is called 'aided recall'. Alternatively, the interviewers may ask consumers what particular ads they remembered from the previous day, and this is known as 'unaided recall'. If the commercial fails to establish a tight connection between the brand name and the selling message, the commercial will not receive a high recall score. Another method of measuring memory, called a recognition test, involves showing the advertisement to people and asking them whether they remember having seen it before.

The persuasion test is another evaluative research technique used to measure effectiveness after execution of a campaign. In this technique, consumers are first asked how likely they are to buy a particular brand. Next, they are exposed to an advertisement for the brand. After exposure, researchers again ask them what they intend to purchase. The researcher analyses the results to determine whether intention to buy has increased as a result of exposure to the advertisement. Persuasion tests are expensive and have problems associated with audience composition, the environment, and brand familiarity. However, persuasion is a key objective for many advertisers, so even a rough estimate of an advertisement's persuasive power is useful.

As the Digital Spotlight highlighted, Brand USA measured its success based on improvements and increases to two key areas: awareness and image of the US as a travel destination; and travellers' intent to travel to the US. The New Mexico True winter campaign, referred to above, also had a positive impact on tourism. Said Rebecca Latham, NMTD Cabinet Secretary: 'Shortly after New Mexico True campaign launched, we did a Return On Investment (ROI) study and saw that for every $1 spent, $3 was returned on the tax base level, so we know we have a 3:1 ROI. We look at the money that's being spent while people are vacationing here and the taxes that are coming back to us as a result of the dollars being spent. Let's say if someone saw a New Mexico True ad and then travelled here as a result of the advertising and let's say they spent $200 while here, it's the percentage of that that goes back into the state tax level.' Total visitor spending since 2010 has also increased by 24 per cent and the amount of overnight leisure trips has gone up 37.5 per cent: 'That is three times the national average,' said Latham. The change in perception – and resulting leisure travel increase – has emanated from New Mexico's target 'fly markets': Dallas, Houston, Denver, Phoenix, San Diego, Chicago and New York City. 'We know that in the past two years we have seen record-breaking tourism growth as a result of the New Mexico True campaign,' she added (Hudson and Hudson, 2015).

INTERNATIONAL ADVERTISING AND THE GLOBAL VERSUS LOCAL DEBATE

In 2015, global expenditure on advertising worldwide was about US$570 billion (eMarketer, 2015). Of all the elements of the marketing mix, decisions involving advertising are those most often affected by cultural differences among country markets. Consumers respond in terms of their culture, value systems, attitudes, beliefs and perceptions. Because advertising's function is to interpret or translate the qualities of products and services in terms of consumer needs, wants, desires and aspirations, the emotional appeals, symbols, persuasive approaches and other characteristics of an advertisement must coincide with cultural norms if the ad is to be effective. A few years ago, Australia's 'Where the Bloody Hell Are You?' global campaign was met with concern and criticism from consumers and media outlets alike; complaints ranged from the use of the words 'bloody hell' to worries about age-appropriateness and a scene in which one actor is taking a swig of beer. However, not only was Tourism Australia prepared for the backlash, but frankly it welcomed it. 'The campaign is creating a "talkability" that marketers can usually only dream about,' said Scott Morrison, managing director of Tourism Australia. 'More than 180 destinations advertised on UK television last year to attract tourists and only one of them, Australia, is now getting this type of reaction,' he said. Even the British Prime Minister at the time Tony Blair asked *'Where the bloody hell am I?'* when speaking in the Australian Parliament and suffering from jet lag.

Reconciling an international advertising campaign with the cultural uniqueness of markets is the challenge confronting the global marketer. A classic Harvard Business

Review article by Theodore Levitt ignited a debate over how to conduct global marketing. He argued that companies should operate as if there were only one global market. He believed that differences among nations and cultures were not only diminishing but should be ignored because people throughout the world are motivated by the same desires and wants. Other scholars like Philip Kotler disagreed, pointing to companies like Coca-Cola, PepsiCo, and McDonald's, arguing that they did not offer the same product everywhere.

The outcome of this debate has been three schools of thought on advertising in another country:

(1) **Standardization.** This school of thought contends, like Levitt, that differences between countries are a matter of degree, so advertisers should focus on the similarities of consumers around the world.

(2) **Localization.** The localization or adaptation school of thought argues that advertisers must consider differences between countries, including local culture, stage of economic and industrial development, stage of life cycle, media availability and legal restrictions.

(3) **Combination.** The belief here is that a combination of standardization and localization may produce the most effective advertising. Some elements of brand identity or strategy, for example, may be standardized, but advertising executions may need to be adapted to the local culture.

The reality of global advertising suggests that a combination approach will work best, and most companies or destinations tend to use the combination approach or even lean towards localization. The Digital Spotlight showed how Brand USA developed country-specific Facebook, Twitter and YouTube pages in order to engage international consumers with unique promotions. Starbucks has also adapted its products and services (and thus its advertising) for international markets, offering more tea in the Far East, stronger coffees in Europe, and gourmet coffees in the US. The company has, however, standardized its product name, logo, and packaging to maintain brand consistency even though there is variation in its product line. 'We remain highly respectful of the culture and traditions of the countries in which we do business,' says Howard Schultz, chairman and chief global strategist. 'We recognize that our success is not an entitlement, and we must continue to earn the trust and respect of customers every day' (Moffett and Ramaswamy, 2003). Today, the company has more than 24,000 retail stores in 70 countries. The largest market for Starbucks is China where the company has 2,000 stores in 90 Chinese cities.

SALES PROMOTIONS

Whenever a marketer increases the value of its product by offering an extra incentive to purchase the product, it is creating a sales promotion. In most cases, the objective of a sales promotion is to encourage action, although it can also help to build brand identity and awareness. Like advertising, sales promotion is a type of marketing communication. Although advertising is designed to build long-term brand awareness, sales promotions are primarily focused on creating immediate action. Simply put, sales promotions offer an extra incentive for consumers, sales reps, and trade members to act. Although this extra incentive usually takes the form of a price reduction, it can sometimes be additional amounts of the product, cash, prizes and gifts, premiums, special events, and so on. It may also be a fun brand experience. Furthermore, a sales promotion usually has specified limits, such as an expiration date or a limited quantity of the merchandise.

The use of sales promotion is growing rapidly for many reasons: it offers the manager short-term bottom-line results; it is accountable; it is less expensive than advertising; it speaks to the current needs of the consumer to receive more value from products; and it responds to marketplace changes. Sales promotions can also be extremely flexible. They can be used at any stage in a product's life cycle and can be very useful in supporting other promotional activities. In 2014, seven out of ten marketers expected their companies to increase spending on social media in response to shrinking television audiences and stale print ads (Sass, 2013). Tactical promotional techniques designed to stimulate customers to buy have three main targets: individual consumers, distribution channels and the sales force. Table 8.5 highlights the sales promotion objectives

TABLE 8.5 Sales promotion objectives and techniques used in tourism and hospitality

	Objectives	Techniques
Customer	Sell excess capacity – especially as the delivery date approaches Shift the timing of product purchases/peaks and troughs Attract and reward regular/loyal customers Promote trial of products (new users) Generate higher consumption per capita Increase market share Defeat/pre-empt competitors' promotions	Price cuts/sale offers including Internet Discount vouchers/coupons Disguised price cuts Extra product Additional services Gifts Competitions Passport schemes for regular customers Prize draws Point-of-purchase displays and merchandising materials Contests, sweepstakes and games
Distribution channels	Secure dealer support and recommendations Achieve brochure display and maintain stocks Support for merchandising initiatives Improve dealer awareness of products Build room value Increase room rate	Extra commission and overrides Prize draws Competitions Parties/receptions Trade and travel show exhibits Educational seminars Recognition programmes Flexible booking policies
Sales force	Improve volume of sales through incentives Improve display in distribution outlets Achieve sales 'blitz' targets among main corporate accounts Reward special efforts	Bonuses and other money incentives Gift incentives Travel incentives Prize draws Visual aids

for each target market, along with typical techniques used to achieve these objectives in the tourism and hospitality industry. As the table shows, many tools can be used to accomplish sales promotion objectives. Some of the main tools used are discussed below, including samples, coupons, gift certificates, point-of-purchase displays (often referred to as merchandising), patronage rewards, contests, sweepstakes and games.

SAMPLES

Sampling involves giving away free samples of a product to encourage sales, or arranging in some way for people to try all or part of a service. As many tourism and hospitality services are intangible, sampling is not always a straightforward process. However, restaurants and bars often give customers free samples of menu items or beverages. Sampling for the travel trade often comes in the form of familiarization trips. A familiarization trip (commonly referred to as a 'FAM trip') is a popular method used to expose a product to intermediaries in the channel of distribution. For example, a hotel might have a group of travel agents visit the facility to familiarize them with the features and benefits. If travel agents are impressed with a facility during a FAM trip, they will convey their enthusiasm to customers, and bookings will increase. The trips are free or reduced in price and can be given to intermediaries by suppliers, carriers or destination marketing groups. As the Digital Spotlight noted, as part of the Brand USA campaign, marketers organized a 'Megafam' whereby 100 agents from the UK and Ireland were brought to the US on a familiarization trip to experience seven different itineraries. A 'FAM Photo Competition' was also set up for agents to upload photographs they had taken on recent familiarization trips in the US. Travel agents had the option to 'like' their favourite photos, encouraging peer-to-peer engagement (Hudson, 2014).

COUPONS

Coupons are vouchers or certificates that entitle customers or intermediaries to a reduced price on a good or service. Inmar, a company that operates intelligent commerce networks, said that 2.84 billion coupons were redeemed in 2014 in the US alone. Growth in redemption for digitally discovered coupons has been accelerating significantly for the last several years, with redemption for load-to-card coupons increasing significantly. More than 70 per cent of US adult digital coupon users redeemed a coupon or code on a mobile device for online or offline shopping in 2014 (see Figure 8.7). The convenience these offers provide shoppers, and the flexibility they afford both retailers and manufacturers, is enhancing their position in the marketing mix. Companies issue coupons to encourage people to sample new products, to make impulse purchases and to foster brand loyalty. Coupons are used extensively in the tourism and hospitality industries, especially among restaurants, hotels, rental car companies, tourist attractions and cruise lines. Online coupons, in particular, have a fast and wide adoption in the tourism industry (Sigala, 2013). Research has also shown that a significant number of travellers are fond of online deals and promotions because such tools make them feel as though they are being smart shoppers (Christou, 2011). But despite their advantages, many marketing professionals feel that too much promotional use of coupons creates a commodity out of a differentiated product. Overuse has also led to coupon wars and other forms of price discounting, all the while detracting from the intrinsic value of a company's product or service.

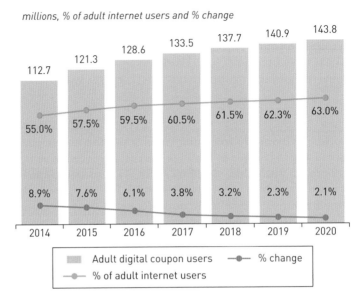

millions, % of adult internet users and % change

FIGURE 8.7 1. US Digital Coupon Users and Penetration, 2014–2020

Note: ages 18+; internet users who redeem a digital coupon/code via any device for online or offline shopping at least once during the calendar year; includes group-buying coupons

(Source: ©eMarketer. Reprinted with permission)

GIFT CERTIFICATES

Gift certificates are vouchers that are either selectively given away by the sponsor or sold to customers, who in turn give them to others as gifts. Cruise companies often promote the sale of gift vouchers for cruise vacations over holiday periods. Carnival Cruise Line, for example, launched its first-ever gift card programme in 2012. The Carnival Gift Card is a prepaid gift card similar to a gift certificate that can be used as payment towards a cruise booking on any of Carnival's ships, prepurchased shore excursions, or spa experiences. Carnival Gift Cards can be purchased online at www.carnivalgiftcards.com, onboard Carnival's fleet or at approximately 9,000 retail locations. The gift card may be redeemed on Carnival.com, GoCCL.com, by calling Carnival (1-800-CARNIVAL), or onboard. The company promotes the gift card as more convenient than cash or a paper gift certificate.

POINT-OF-PURCHASE DISPLAYS

Point-of-purchase merchandising is a technique used to promote a product at locations where it is being sold. The value of point-of-purchase merchandising has long been recognized in retailing and is making rapid inroads in restaurants, hotels, car rental companies and travel agencies. In the food and beverage industry, menus and wine and drink lists are the key tools. In fact, many restaurants now put their menus on the Internet for customers to view; many wineries now offer free or very low-cost tasting in order to entice customers to purchase; and hotels also use a wide variety of merchandising techniques, including in-room guest directories, room-service menus, elevator and lobby displays and brochure racks. In the travel agency business, brochures, posters, and window and stand-up displays are fairly common forms of sales promotion. A few years ago, Club Med designed a floor display for travel agents that featured a beach chair with a surfboard on one side and a pair of skis on the other to show that Club Med has both snow and sun destinations.

PATRONAGE REWARDS

Patronage rewards are cash or other prizes given to customers for their regular use of a company's products or services. The intent of such rewards is to encourage loyalty and to create a positive change in the behaviour of the consumer. Examples are the frequent flyer plans that award points for miles travelled. Many hotel chains also have frequent stay programmes, and some restaurants have frequent diner programmes. One of the most dominant trends of loyalty programmes in general is the coalition model. Businesses in various industries have turned single-brand loyalty programmes into corporate-wide programmes across different brands, partnering with other businesses in order to offer customers added value. For example, airlines are partnering with hotels, rental cars, restaurants as well as credit card companies and offering loyal customers more opportunities to earn points and benefits.

CONTESTS, SWEEPSTAKES AND GAMES

Contests are sales promotions in which entrants win prizes based on some required skill that they are asked to demonstrate. Sweepstakes are sales promotions that require entrants to submit their names and addresses. Winners are chosen on the basis of chance, not skill. Games are similar to sweepstakes, but they involve using game pieces, such as scratch-and-win cards. The use of contests, games and sweepstakes has been shown to increase advertising readership. These promotional tools can be useful in communicating key benefits and unique selling points, and can be targeted at both consumers and members of the trade. An example of a contest in the tourism industry – the Sugar Bowl's 'Rep Your Shop' Facebook contest – is described below.

JOINT PROMOTIONS

There has also been an increase in joint promotions, where two or more organizations that have similar target markets combine their resources to their mutual advantage. This collaboration can reduce the cost of the incentives offered, and it may be a one-off joint promotion or a long-term campaign such as a trade association campaign using an 'umbrella' brand name. An example of a joint promotion comes from California where Sugar Bowl Resort partnered with ski and snowboard shops to cut through the clutter with a clever combination of traditional and online media. The target market was ski shops and their fans. Sugar Bowl's 'Rep Your Shop' Facebook contest ran for three weeks in February 2013. The resort's fans voted for their favourite Northern Californian ski and snowboard shops, and one voter was chosen to receive five free tickets and five meal vouchers. The winning shop received 20 lift tickets to reward employees and could also brag about being the most popular shop in the region. Sugar Bowl partnered with its most loyal vendors and reached out to their customers as well as their own visitors, promoting the contest via Facebook, Twitter, e-blasts, newsletters, text messages and radio. The shops themselves promoted the competition in their stores and on Facebook. As a result of the competition, Sugar Bowl's fan base grew more than 13 per cent.

FIGURE 8.8 Sugar Bowl's 'Rep Your Shop' Facebook contest

Other ski resorts are also forming partnerships with major brands for mutual benefit. In January 2015 Whistler Blackcomb announced a three-year retail and marketing alliance with Oakley, manufacturers of men's and women's sunglasses, athletic apparel, goggles, watches and accessories. The agreement put Oakley products on a large number of resort employee ambassadors involved with Whistler Blackcomb Snow School, the retail division and Whistler Heli-Skiing. The partnership also resulted in a variety of Oakley brand and marketing touch points throughout Whistler Blackcomb Resort, both on the mountain and in Whistler Blackcomb's retail shops in the village. 'We are excited to bring Oakley on board as our newest corporate partner,' said Stuart Rempel, Senior Vice President of Marketing and Sales at Whistler Blackcomb. 'The Oakley brand is synonymous with high-performance eyewear which is critical for an optimal guest experience at Whistler Blackcomb whether you are skiing, riding or downhill mountain biking on our mountains.' Alexandre Langevin, Oakley Canada Marketing Director said: 'It is an honor to be an official partner of Whistler Blackcomb. We are excited to share our passion for winter and summer sports with such an iconic resort. Whistler Blackcomb is key in the development of so many Oakley international athletes. Our objective is to provide the best brand experience to consumers in this sporting mecca' (Snowboarder, 2015).

CHAPTER SUMMARY

In marketing communications, the blend of promotional elements is known as the promotional mix. This includes advertising and sales promotions, both of which are discussed in this chapter.

Advertising can be defined as any paid form of nonpersonal presentation and promotion of ideas, goods, or services by an identified sponsor, using mass media to persuade or influence an audience. Sales promotion are more short-term and offer the manager short-term bottom-line results; and the ability to respond to marketplace changes. Many tools can be used to accomplish sales promotion objectives; these include samples, coupons and sweepstakes. Perhaps one of the most important advances in marketing in recent decades has been the rise of integrated marketing communications (IMC) – the recognition that advertising can no longer be crafted and executed in isolation from other promotional mix elements.

REFLECTIVE QUESTIONS

1. Find an example of an advertisement from a tourism or hospitality organization. What message strategy is it employing? How effective is the ad, and what changes would you make to improve its effectiveness?

2. What are the main factors that determine an airline's choice of advertising media? If possible, obtain details or examples of advertising from specific airlines to support your answer.

3. Do you think sales promotions create loyalty or encourage switching to competitors' products? Use examples from your own experience.

MARKETING IN ACTION: LEVERAGING EVENTS TO CHANGE A DESTINATION IMAGE: THE CASE OF BRAZIL AND THE 2014 WORLD CUP

Two years in advance of the 2014 FIFA World Cup, Brazil launched a rebranding video campaign directing the tourism focus on to dance and sport. Designed to raise the profile of the World Cup, it was also intended to boost long-term tourism beyond the six million visitors notched up in 2013. Announced by Vinicius Larges, Brazil's Minister for Tourism, the campaign emphasized the warmth of the Brazilian people, showing them dancing, playing and greeting. Ads were placed on YouTube, Facebook, TripAdvisor, Expedia and several airlines. Part of the video offering was named 'House', designed to make people feel that Brazil was a homey, comfortable place to visit. The 'Dance' segments segued dance movements with soccer moves against a scenic backdrop, and the 'Encounters' video depicted Brazil as an inviting business and leisure destination. Broadcast in 220 countries, reaching over a billion people, the World Cup was an ideal opportunity to teach the world about Brazilian culture.

IMAGE 8.3 The Maracanã Stadium, Rio de Janeiro, Brazil – host of the 2014 World Cup final (©visit.rio/Alexandre Macierira. Reproduced by permission)

An article in the UK's *Mirror* newspaper in August 2014 reported that the campaign was a resounding success, with 95 per cent of football fans who visited saying that

(Continued)

(Continued)

they would return for a vacation. The number of international visitors 'surpassed all expectations', according to Embratur, the Brazilian Tourism Board. 'More than one million visitors poured into the samba nation's 12 host cities to see the greatest show on earth – beating the predicted 600,000 by more than 65 per cent,' said journalist, Jeremy Armstrong. 'The World Travel & Tourism Council, an industry forum, predicts Brazil will get 6.4 million international tourist arrivals in 2014, and that this number will more than double to 14.2 million come 2024.'

But this success did not come without challenges along the way. When Adidas, the official sponsor of FIFA and the World Cup since 1970, released their World Cup T-shirts for Brazil 2014, they triggered considerable controversy and eventually had to pull them out. The reason for outrage was the sexualized representation of Brazilian women. One T-shirt presented an attractive woman in a bikini with open arms, which left an impression that she was inviting men to come to Brazil for the women rather than the football.

The Brazilian authorities complained about this non-PC sexual representation of Brazil and Brazilian women. President Flavio Dino of Embratur, the agency responsible for marketing Brazil abroad, said in a letter sent to Adidas: 'The Brazilian people and especially the Brazilian women deserve that respect. Companies should never treat the bodies of Brazilian men and women as tourist attractions.' One reason for intense governmental campaigning to shed the country's reputation as a destination for sex tourism was the general goal of establishing a positive image about the country, which the FIFA World Cup, because of its global appeal, sporting connotations and guarantee of media coverage, could help develop. Secondly, the reason for a very strong reaction by the Brazilian government was the actual problem of sex tourism in Brazil. Brazil has always been a popular tourist destination due to its exotic wildlife, pristine beaches and raucous festivals like the Rio Carnival. But the country has also been known as a destination for sex tourism, an image and situation that the government wanted to change.

In line with its rebranding mandate, Embratur has been trying hard for many years to prevent the sale of products that link Brazil's image to sexual appeal. For example, in 2012 the Ministry of Tourism asked 2100 websites linking prostitution and pornography to Brazil to remove official travel branding. Additionally, Brazil has been running prevention ads for many years to deter sex tourists from visiting the country. Prevention ads are used by marketers to discourage unwanted behaviours – the opposite of normal behavioural responses sought through advertising. Deterring actions or behaviours is a complicated process that involves counter-arguing by presenting negative messages about an unwanted behaviour and creating the proper incentives to stimulate the desired behaviour.

After the 2004 tsunami, Brazil unwillingly replaced Thailand as the number one sex tourism destination. In response, Embratur and the Brazil Ministry of Tourism, worked together to develop marketing programmes to deter sex tourism. The Sustainable Tourism and Childhood Program was created to combat sexual exploitation tourism in Brazil. Tactics included television ads that were shown in Brazil as well as on certain airlines within the country. An example is an ad that begins with the usual pictures of beautiful beaches and spectacular Brazilian icons such as the Amazon and Iguassu Falls. However, the closing shot is of the rear view of a little girl, swinging happily in a playground while the narrator talks about the prison sentences for child sex abuse. The ads brought to the forefront the March 2005 campaign to eradicate sexual abuses of children and adults, which was inaugurated during carnival season to create maximum impact.

Print ads were also used in the campaign, placed in selected magazines and newspapers throughout Brazil. They were distributed via travel operators and federal police officials at Brazilian air and seaports. With an emphasis on improving the international image, postcards of scantily clad women were banned. Traditionally, Brazil has sold millions of postcards of women, usually in tiny bikinis. In a press statement, tourism secretary Sergio Ricardo said: 'Postcards that exploit photos of women in skimpy wear suggest sex tourism, a practice that stigmatizes us with undignified labels.' The World Tourism Organization (WTO) was also involved in this collaborative project, and details of the campaign were easily accessible on the WTO website. Despite the radical move, retailers actually reported that sales were not affected as tourists bought more scenic postcards instead.

Sources: Hudson (2008); Shankman (2014); Juricic (2015); Baran (2013); Armstrong (2014).

CASE STUDY QUESTIONS

1. Why did marketers think that the World Cup was an ideal opportunity to teach the world about Brazilian culture? Do you?

2. Find one of the advertisements or commercials referenced in this case and provide a critique of it based on the material in this chapter.

3. What are the dangers of promoting a destination image through a major event or through celebrities?

REFERENCES

Armstrong, J. (2014) 'Brazil World Cup tourism triumph as 95% of fans say they will return to the samba nation for a holiday', *The Mirror*, 31 August. www.mirror.co.uk/lifestyle/travel/usa-long-haul/brazil-world-cup-tourism-triumph-4126879 (accessed 9 December 2016).

Baran, M. (2013) 'Brazil launches tourism campaign around World Cup', *Travel Weekly*, 23 October. www.travelweekly.com/South-America-Travel/Brazil-launches-tourism-campaign-around-World-Cup (accessed 9 December 2016).

Berman, D. (2016) 'New Space Coast tourism campaign to push beach nostalgia', *Florida Today*, 21 January. www.floridatoday.com/story/news/local/2016/01/20/new-space-coast-tourism-campaign-push-beach-nostalgia/78993322 (accessed 9 December 2016).

Broadbent, S. and Jacobs, B. (1985) *Spending Advertising Money*. London: Business Books.

Byun, J. and Jang, S. (2015) 'Effective destination advertising: Matching effect between advertising language and destination type', *Tourism Management*, 50: 31–40.

Christou, E. (2011) 'Exploring online sales promotions in the hospitality industry', *Journal of Hospitality Marketing & Management*, 20: 814–29.

Colley, R. H. (1961) *Defining Advertising Goals for Measuring Advertising Results.* New York: Association of National Advertisers.

Elliott, S. (2011) 'Luxury hotels market the memories they can make', *New York Times,* 14 September: B3.

eMarketer (2014) 'US mobile users turn to smartphones, tablets to redeem coupons', *eMarketer,* 2 May. www.emarketer.com/Article/US-Mobile-Users-Turn-Smartphones-Tablets-Redeem-Coupons/1010801 (accessed 9 December 2016).

eMarketer (2015) 'Total media ad spending growth slows worldwide', *eMarketer,* 15 September. www.emarketer.com/Article/Total-Media-Ad-Spending-Growth-Slows-Worldwide/1012981 (accessed 9 December 2016).

Hudson, S. (2008) *Tourism and Hospitality Marketing: A Global Perspective.* London: Sage.

Hudson, S. (2010) 'Wooing zoomers: Marketing tourism to the mature traveler,' *Marketing Intelligence and Planning,* 28(4): 444–61.

Hudson, S. (2014) 'Selling America to the world: The case of Brand USA,' *Journal of Destination Marketing and Management,* 3(2): 79–81.

Hudson, S. and Hudson, L. J. (2015) *Winter Sport Tourism: Working in Winter Wonderlands.* Oxford: Goodfellow Publishers Ltd.

Juricic, T. (2015) 'Responsible tourism at sports mega events – responsible by whom?' *The Fair Traveller,* 16 June. http://welcome.thefairtraveller.org/responsible-tourism-at-sports-mega-events-responsible-by-whom (accessed 9 December 2016).

Lavidge, R.C. and Steiner, G.A. (1961) 'A model for predictive measurement of advertising effectiveness', *Journal of Marketing,* October: 59–62.

Levere, J.L. (2014a) 'Hotel chain tries funny to sell free breakfast', *New York Times,* 3 September: B4.

Levere, J.L. (2014b) 'A whisper campaign started over the Virgin Group's new hotels', *New York Times,* 7 October. www.nytimes.com/2014/10/08/business/media/a-whisper-campaign-started-over-the-virgin-groups-new-hotels.html?_r=0 (accessed 9 December 2016).

Martin, B.A.S. and Vincent, A. (2014) 'Effects of knowledge, testimonials, and ad copy on cruise advertising judgments', *Tourism Analysis,* 19: 769–74.

Moffett, M. H. and Ramaswamy, K. (2003) *Planet Starbucks A.* Thunderbird Global School of Management.

Pan (2011) 'The role of TV commercial visuals in forming memorable and impressive destination images', *Journal of Travel Research,* 50(2): 171–85.

Park, S., Nicolau, J. L. and Fesenmaier, D. R. (2013) 'Assessing advertising in a hierarchical decision model', *Annals of Tourism Research,* 40: 260–82.

Rogers, E. M. (1962) *The Diffusion of Innovations.* New York: Free Press.

Sass, E. (2013) 'Most marketers will spend more on social media in 2014', *MediaPost Publications.* www.mediapost.com/publications/article/213850/most-marketers-will-spend-more-on-social-media-in.html (accessed 9 December 2016).

Shankman, S. (2014) 'Brazil launches global tourism campaign before the World Cup', *Shift,* 12 May. https://skift.com/2014/05/12/brazil-launches-global-tourism-campaign-before-the-world-cup (accessed 9 December 2016).

Sigala, M. (2013) 'A framework for designing and implementing effective online coupons in tourism and hospitality', *Journal of Vacation Marketing,* 19(2): 165–80.

Snowboarder (2015) 'Whistler Blackcomb and Oakley today announce three-year strategic alliance'. 6 January. www.snowboarder.com/news/whistler-blackcomb-oakley-announce-three-year-strategic-alliance/#OJHHfl6MuTPAIvGx.97 (accessed 12 December 2016).

Strong, E.K. (1925) *The Psychology of Selling.* New York: McGraw-Hill.

Wells, W., Burnett, B. and Moriarty, S. (2006) *Advertising Principles and Practice,* 7th edn. Englewood Cliffs, NJ: Prentice Hall.

Zaldivar, G. (2015) 'VisitBritain drops dazzling 'Bond is GREAT' campaign ahead of *Spectre* release', *Travel Pulse,* 9 October. www.travelpulse.com/news/entertainment/visitbritain-drops-dazzling-bond-is-great-campaign-ahead-of-spectre-release.html (accessed 9 December 2016).

PUBLIC RELATIONS AND PERSONAL SELLING

9

INTRODUCTION

This chapter focuses on two important communication techniques – public relations and personal selling. The first part of the chapter provides an overview of public relations and a discussion of the main public relations techniques used in tourism and hospitality and how they can be measured. Personal selling is the focus of the second part of the chapter, which discusses the roles and objectives of personal selling, the sales process, and the roles of a sales manager. Case studies look at an incentive and conference travel agency in Tenerife, cooperative marketing in the Stellenbosch wine region of South Africa, and how Hawaii is promoting itself through film and television.

LESSONS FROM A MARKETING GURU: TEN OUT OF TEN FOR TENERIFE'S MARCOS VAN AKEN

Running an incentive and conference travel agency in Tenerife – part of the Spanish-owned Canary Islands off the northwest coast of Africa – involves daily customer service dilemmas for Marcos Albornoz Van Aken. As Director of Sales & Operations for Ten Travel DMC, he is in charge of both wooing businesses and keeping delegates happy during their visits. 'We make personal service an absolute priority in an age when, despite social media and new technologies governing the interaction with clients, the personal, tangible, on the ground security is an added value not every company is willing to invest in. Clients love "hands on" personnel and this is what we are all about.'

IMAGE 9.1 Marcos Van Aken, Ten Travel (Courtesy of Marcos Van Aken, Ten Travel DMC)

Owned by John Lucas Sr, the company began 35 years ago with a package holiday focus but quickly diversified into the corporate group and incentive travel market. 'Business and incentive travel require a very high level of specialization. We segmented into that and were approached over time by various cruise companies, too. We aim for the top end of the market,' explains Van Aken, who, although born in Tenerife, studied for his Masters degree in Hotel Management at the University of Surrey, England. 'Times have changed enormously in a relatively short space of time. I can still remember using the Telex, then the good old fax; email has definitely changed the way we approach clients and it has also changed the perceived idea of efficiency. I am of the opinion that quick response nowadays drives profits; it is not about who has the most thorough information or detailed information; it is about who can get it faster.'

Van Aken spends a considerable amount of his time solving problems for customers. A dilemma presented itself when a German company wanted red-carpet treatment for their clients at the airport. 'They insisted on them leaving the plane and getting on to the coach without touching a suitcase,' Van Aken remembers. This was particularly sensitive in the light of the 9/11 terrorist attacks. Although he appreciated the desire for this kind of top end service, he marvelled at the amount of paperwork, lobbying and money it required for him to make it happen: 'I can understand why the client wanted the service: he wanted his guests to be taken directly to the cocktail area at the hotel and while they were having cocktails, the luggage would be delivered to their rooms.'

Van Aken thinks that this type of service is what quality is all about, making something difficult happen smoothly. 'Often the client does not have the technical know-how and does not want to know either. He/she wants things to work and is not really bothered how,' he explains. 'We organized a large gala dinner recently at a banana plantation location. The complexity is enormous because the venue requires intensive AVL rigging and also generators for sound, lighting and catering to be able to work. We had a main generator to take us through the event but also included a backup generator just in case. We ended up needing the backup due to unstable working of the main generator. This was built into the costs without the client knowing; on the night no-one noticed we used the backup!'

Although Ten Travel employs multiple staff members, freelance personnel and regular tour guides, the key accounts are Van Aken's personal responsibility. As middleman between tourism and business industries, he is in a prime position to elevate service standards in Tenerife. Part of his job is to make sure that the service levels seen on inspection visits are translated literally to the galas and conferences when guests eventually arrive. He has the perfect multicultural background for this, with a Dutch mother and Spanish father, British and German schooling, two years travelling in South America and South East Asia and experience in the hotel industry. 'That's my edge,' he says. 'I speak five languages which gives me the means to reach the Dutch market as well as UK, German and Spanish businesses; relating to clients in their own language creates empathy and ultimately profits. I constantly strive to be ahead of trends in tourism and strive to improve on my leadership skills. As far as I am concerned a leader is a manager of change nowadays.'

Before joining Ten Travel in 2003, Van Aken worked in hotel management where he was exposed regularly to the minutiae of conferences and business events. He believes in providing a wow factor for his clients who often have a limited conception of what Tenerife is all about. 'Most of the time they think it is 99 per cent sun and beach,' he says. Surprising his clients mainly consists of taking them away from the coast to inland destinations including mountain biking and hiking components in diverse landscapes and national parks. He tries to go beyond the usual tourist trip to Tenerife's volcanic park at Mt Teide, for example: 'We go up in the cable car and then on to a lodge where you stay overnight. Then there's a two-hour walk at four o'clock the next morning to make it to the top for sunrise. We are also organizing yoga sessions at 3500 m altitude overlooking the seven Canary Islands from the highest point in Spain. That's the kind of thing that will take people over the edge and say wow that was different.'

In the Digital Age, customer relations have changed in regard to the format used to execute client interaction, he maintains: 'We are constantly available through social media but I still find that the personal approach gives you the edge and that has not and will not change over time. We are in the business of making people feel good. A PC, tablet or phone cannot do that; a person can. Listening is crucial to understanding clients' business requests and demands; homing in on those specific requests with creative, profitable solutions is what keeps our company in the market generating profits.'

Source: Interview with Marcos Van Aken, June 2016.

INTRODUCTION TO PUBLIC RELATIONS

The field of public relations (PR) is growing. In the US alone, the PR industry is comprised of more than 7,000 companies bringing in estimated annual revenues of $11billion, and offering a diverse range of services from media relations to event management (Pozin, 2014). There are many types of media available to PR specialists, and these fit into three broad categories: owned, paid and earned media. Owned media is defined as communication channels that are within the organization's control, such as websites, blogs or email; while paid media refers mostly to traditional advertising, discussed in Chapter 8. Earned media, on the other hand, is generated when content receives recognition and a following outside of traditional paid advertising, often from publicity gained through editorial influence. Critically, earned media cannot be bought or owned, it can only be gained organically, hence the term 'earned'. Since most of this earned media is gained through PR activities, this section will mainly focus on PR and its various techniques. PR is broader in scope than publicity, its goal being for an organization to achieve positive relationships with various audiences (publics) in order to manage effectively the organization's image and reputation. Its publics may be external (customers, news media, the investment community, general public, government bodies) and internal (shareholders, employees).

The three most important roles of PR and publicity in tourism and hospitality are maintaining a positive public presence, handling negative publicity and enhancing the effectiveness of other promotional mix elements (Morrison, 2002). In this third role, PR paves the way for advertising, sales promotions and personal selling by making customers more receptive to the persuasive messages of these elements. Ultimately, the difference between advertising and public relations is that public relations takes a longer, broader view of the importance of image and reputation as a corporate competitive asset and addresses more target audiences.

PUBLIC RELATIONS TECHNIQUES

A variety of PR techniques are available to tourism and hospitality organizations. Those are highlighted in Figure 9.1 and discussed below.

FIGURE 9.1 Selected public relations techniques available to marketers

PRESS RELEASES AND PRESS CONFERENCES

A press release or news release is a short article about an organization or an event that is written in an attempt to attract media attention, which will then hopefully lead to media coverage. They may be planned a long time in advance or they may be opportunistic. When Hawaiian extreme surfer Garrett McNamara shattered an apparent world record in 2013 by catching an estimated 100-foot wall of water off Portuguese fishing village of Nazaré, Portugal's tourism office immediately capitalized on the opportunity to promote the country's emerging surf scene. 'We have 450 miles of clean Atlantic coastline, (and) some surfing beaches that are out of this world,' said a press release sent out immediately after the jaw-dropping spectacle.

Preparing press releases is probably the most popular and widespread public relations activity. To be effective, the release must be as carefully targeted as an advertising media schedule. It should be sent to the right publications and be written in a style that those publications would use. The headline should give a clear idea of the subject. The release should then open with a paragraph that summarizes the main points of the news story by stating who did what, when, why and where. The style should be that of a news report, and the story must be genuinely interesting to the publication's readers. Ideally, it should tell them something new that is happening and should contain a strong human angle. Other useful contents of a press release include a photograph and quotations, and it is essential to provide a contact name and telephone number in case journalists require further information. An example of a press release is below and is the official announcement of a partnership between Botswana and the world's largest travel show, ITB Berlin. The press release includes quotations from both Botswana's tourism minister and a representative from ITB, as well as contacts for further information. ITB is discussed in more detail below.

FAM TRIPS

As mentioned in the previous chapter, a familiarization trip, often referred to as a FAM trip, is a tour offered to media on behalf of an organization to get the media familiar with their destination and services. A FAM trip is a great way for the organization to get positive publicity and for the media to have an opportunity to write a story about an organization they *fully* understand and have experienced. Such FAM trips can be targeted towards certain publications/journalists, or specific regions or countries. Lake Tahoe Visitors Authority (LVTA), for example, hosted three FAM trips in the 2012–13 season for Australians – not just writers, but also key travel agents representing travel Scene, Harveys World Travel, Navigator Travel, Campas Tara Travel and Travel 2. These visits resulted in exposure worth $620,000 in the *Sun Herald*, *Sydney Morning Herald*, *The Age* and *Women's Health Magazine*, with an additional exposure valued at $1,600,000 (Hudson and Hudson, 2015).

FAM trips may also have a specific objective in mind. An example is a FAM trip which was organized by UK tour operator Mark Warner in 2016. The company took eight travel agents to its Lakitira Beach Resort in Kos, Greece, in the wake of thousands of migrant people, mainly from Syria, coming ashore the previous summer amid heavy media coverage. Agency sales manager Julie Franklin said the trip was organized to win back the 'lost confidence' of consumers who had chosen to stay away in 2016

ITB Berlin • 9 to 13 March 2016

 Messe Berlin

March 10, 2016

Botswana: the official partner country of ITB Berlin 2017

First partner country ever from Southern Africa – official announcement of partnership between Botswana and the World's Leading Travel Trade Show® at ITB Berlin on 9 March 2016

In 2017 Botswana will be the official partner country of ITB Berlin. On 9 March 2016, at a press event at ITB Berlin, an agreement between the world's leading travel trade show and Botswana was signed by Tourism Minister H.E. Tshekedi Khama II and Dr. Christian Göke, CEO of Messe Berlin GmbH.

According to Tourism Minister Tshekedi Khama of Botswana, "The Botswana Tourism Organisation has taken the opportunity to become the partner country of ITB Berlin 2017 in order to share Botswana's nature conservation achievements with the rest of the world and to raise general awareness of this country. Botswana's role as the partner country of the world's largest travel trade show will ensure the long-term attention of the global tourism industry. It will not only place the spotlight on Botswana's tourism successes but will also focus attention worldwide on our potential for economic development. In the past Botswana has achieved great success that has remained largely unnoticed around the world. Botswana will also benefit from this year's fiftieth anniversary of ITB Berlin. Numerous activities and events will give us the opportunity to market and promote our country as a tourism destination and to improve our returns on investment."

"Botswana is Africa's best-kept secret", says David Ruetz, head of ITB Berlin. "Two contrasting natural features characterise this country: the Kalahari Desert and the Okavango Basin with its many animal species, large forests, and innumerable streams that empty into small lakes. Particularly during the rainy season, visitors on trips and safaris can marvel at the unique fauna and flora. The diverse cultural heritage of the country, the warm hospitality shown by its people as well as sustainable tourism make Botswana an unrivalled holiday destination in southern Africa. The fact that almost 40 per cent of the country's surface area has been declared a national park, wildlife or nature reserve is testimony to the exemplary efforts undertaken to actively preserve nature."

In 2016 Botswana celebrated 50 years of independence. Often referred to as one of the last remaining gems of Africa, the country was quick to realise its potential as a tourism destination. The Republic of Botswana has been exhibiting at ITB Berlin every year since 1984, in an aim to make people around the world aware of its special attractions. Next to the diamond industry, the most important branch of the economy, the tourism sector currently already accounts for five per cent of GDP.

At ITB Berlin 2017 Botswana, the partner country of the show, will be organising the opening event on 7 March 2017, and from 8 to 12 March 2017 will be entertaining visitors to ITB Berlin with a wide-ranging programme of events.

About ITB Berlin and the ITB Berlin Convention

ITB Berlin 2016 will take place from Wednesday to Sunday, 9 to 13 March. From Wednesday to Friday ITB Berlin is open to trade visitors only. Parallel with the show the ITB Berlin Convention, the largest event of its kind, will be held from Wednesday, 9 to Saturday, 12 March 2016. More details are available at www.itb-convention.com. ITB Berlin is the global travel industry's leading trade show. In 2015 a total of 10,096 companies and organisations from 186 countries exhibited their products and services to 175,000 visitors, who included 115,000 trade visitors.

Join the **ITB Press Network** at www.linkedin.com.
Become a **fan of ITB Berlin** at www.facebook.de/ITBBerlin.
Follow ITB Berlin on www.twitter.com/ITB_Berlin.
Get the latest updates from the Social Media Newsroom at http://newsroom.itb-berlin.de/en.

You can find **press releases on the internet** at www.itb-berlin.com under the section heading Press / Press Releases. Make use of our information service and subscribe to our **RSS feeds**.

Press contacts:
Messe Berlin
Emanuel Höger
Press Spokesman and
Press and Public Relations
Director
Corporate Communication
Messe Berlin Group
https://twitter.com/pr_messeberlin

ITB Berlin / ITB Asia:
Astrid Zand
Press Officer
Messedamm 22
14055 Berlin
phone.: + 49 30 3038-2275
fax: + 49 30 3038-912275
zand@messe-berlin.de
www.messe-berlin.com

Additional information:
www.itb-berlin.com
www.itb-convention.com

Management board:
Dr. Christian Göke (CEO), Dirk Hoffmann (CFO)
Chairman of the Supervisory Board: Peter Zühlsdorff
Commercial Register: Amtsgericht Charlottenburg (District Court)
HRB 5484 B (Commercial Code)

FIGURE 9.2 Press release from ITB Berlin, 2016 (©Messe Berlin GmbH. Reprinted with permission)

because of safety concerns during the ongoing humanitarian situation (Parry, 2016). Sarah Jarvis, a travel agent who was on the FAM, said that seeing the destination first-hand had helped to dispel negative news coverage she had witnessed. 'It was my first time visiting Kos and from what I had seen portrayed in the media you got the impression that there were no tourists on the island, that it was overcrowded with refugees, and that the resorts would be ghost towns,' she said.

TABLE 9.1 A checklist for putting a FAM trip together (Source: Adapted from Lutz, 2014)

Checklist	Explanation
Plan ahead	There is never a great time to give comp rooms or ski passes, etc., but most destinations are seasonal and factor in the cost of FAM trips to their overall marketing and public relations budget. So if you can, pick a relatively low occupancy week
Gather media lists	You need to prioritize as to who is a priority to invite and why. You need to be strategic about every invitation that will go out. Established and trusted travel writers make great guests, because they can write multiple stories on your destination which may be picked up by two or more publications
Seek help from your local CVB	The local visitors' bureau is a great resource for media lists, verifying reporters' backgrounds, and other information. They may also help you with providing fillers, such as access to city sites and venues, or partnering restaurants, which will make your press trip a full experience. CVBs can also assist with transportation contacts and more
Decide what expenses to cover	You should research what the norm is for your area by asking your CVB, and then make your decision. Naturally, room, tax and breakfast should be included for everyone, as well as access to amenities. Your itinerary should include airport transfers for those flying, and parking passes for those who are driving
Create an interesting itinerary	Most journalists will want to have a variety of memorable experiences to write about. You should welcome this opportunity to 'sell' your destination. Be creative and informative in your descriptions
Send the invitations	Send out invitations 6-8 months in advance and track the RSVPs. Online invitations are effective and acceptable these days. Once the media RSVP, you can send a more detailed itinerary about the press trip
Block the right rooms	You must be willing to give up several VIP guestrooms out of your block in order to accommodate the press. The media are used to being wowed and you need to provide that extra touch, which will make their stay at your property unforgettable. Remember, the good ones are getting numerous offers and only have a finite amount of time. So be grateful that they want to spend time with you
Establish goals of FAM trip	Discuss with your team what you are looking to accomplish from this expense. Once you strategically determine the goals of the trip, it will be easier to track its success and consider repeating another in the future
Research media	There are several online sources where you can research more about the arriving guests. Information is crucial to understanding more about them, and you can customize their stay accordingly. For instance, if you read in a writer's profile that s/he is a vegetarian, you can let the chef know in advance. These are the things that your guests will remember
Welcome gifts	These can make quite an impact so put some thought into these gifts. Make sure you provide a welcome letter, a press kit with contact information, along with any CVB materials, such as lift tickets, free passes, etc. in a separate gift bag
Dedicate one PR professional as the main contact	The PR specialist will be the best and most informed contact for the press to ask questions and give tours. The PR contact also has experience in suggesting angles and pointing out special features to the media. The PR contact is also the most appropriate for any media follow-up questions after the FAM trip, as well as facilitating requests for photos and setting up interviews
Continue to nurture the relationship	Finally, after the FAM trip is over, the publication date of each article may vary depending on editorial calendars, but make sure to maintain the relationship with each writer. These are opinion leaders of the travel industry and the more reason you give them to talk about your destination, the more vacations you will eventually sell, and the better your image will become through editorial endorsement

Lutz (2014) suggests that the key to organizing a successful press trip is to make sure that all aspects of the trip are planned properly to the last detail. She offers a checklist to keep in mind when thinking of putting a FAM trip together (see Table 9.1).

TRAVEL EXHIBITIONS AND ROAD SHOWS

Many tourism and hospitality organizations attend travel trade shows, exhibitions, or conventions. Generally, these occasions bring all parts of the industry (suppliers, carriers, intermediaries, and destination marketing organizations) together. Exhibiting at a trade show is similar to putting together a small promotional mix. Some exhibitors send out direct mail pieces (advertising) to intermediaries, inviting them to visit their booths. The booth displays (merchandising) portray the available services and may be tied in with recent advertising campaigns. Representatives working the booth hand out brochures and business cards and try to develop sales leads (personal selling). They may also give away free samples or vouchers (sales promotions). When the trade show is over, exhibitors often follow up with personalized mailings (direct mail) or telephone calls (telemarketing).

The travel industry's leading trade show is ITB Berlin. In 2016, 10,000 exhibiting companies from 187 countries and regions met with 120,000 trade visitors in the 26 exhibition halls. Business conducted during the trade show rose from 2015's figure of 6.7 billion euros to around seven billion. The travel trade show that was held for the first time in Berlin in 1966 has now evolved into an international success: ITB Asia has been held annually in Singapore since 2008, and from May 2017, ITB China will be taking place annually in Shanghai in cooperation with that country's major tour operators and travel agents. Parallel to ITB Berlin is the ITB Convention, the world's largest convention for the global travel industry. In 2016, the 200 convention events were attended by over 26,000 visitors. The main themes at the convention, which is regarded as the 'think tank' for the international industry, were 'Travel 4.0' and the complete digitalization of all the various business processes of travel companies. Due to the evident willingness of many travellers to spend, the subject of luxury travel also attracted a great deal of interest. Discussions also took place about the opportunities and risks facing tourism as a consequence of the influx of refugees to Europe. More than 5,000 accredited journalists from 80 countries, as well as around 380 bloggers from 30 countries, reported from ITB Berlin.

HOSTING AND SPONSORING EVENTS

Players in the tourism sector can also draw attention to themselves by arranging or sponsoring special events. Golf events, for example, are often branded with a destination's name in conjunction with specification of the type of event. The Abu Dhabi Golf Championship is a good case in point, and has played a pivotal part in the city's marketing strategy to boost its golf tourism (Hudson and Hudson, 2014). For entities hosting major events, securing a title sponsor is critical, defined as 'the right to share the official name of a property, event or activity in exchange for payment to the current property, event, or activity owner' (Clark, Cornwell and Pruitt, 2009: 170). In general, event sponsorship is the financial support of an event (e.g. a car race, a theatre performance, a festival or a marathon road race) in return for advertising privileges associated with it. Sponsorships are usually offered by the organizer of the event on a tiered basis, which means that a lead sponsor pays a maximum amount

IMAGE 9.2 Delegates at ITB Berlin, 2014 (Courtesy of ITB Berlin image gallery)

and receives maximum privileges, whereas other sponsors pay less and receive fewer privileges. Investment in sponsorships is mainly divided among three areas: sports, entertainment and cultural events. The opening case study in Chapter 5 described how organizers of the Dance World Cup secured sponsorship from Bloch Europe, who specializes in dancewear and shoes.

Sporting events attract the lion's share of sponsorship revenue. For example, the London 2012 Olympics attracted over £100 million from just the top four to six main sponsors. Events can also be used to restore a poor destination image. Avraham (2014) found that hosting events is a popular strategy among marketers of places that suffer from an immediate or a prolonged image crisis. Kaplanidou et al. (2013) distinguished between 'hard' structures with an event-hosting impact and 'soft' structures. The hard structures include sports and culture infrastructure-related projects, performance halls, construction of roads, bridges, parking spots and many more developments. The soft structures are mainly intangible benefits such as governance reforms, positive media coverage, attracting opinion leaders and self-image improvement. Avraham suggests that we can add to the list of 'soft' structures the repair of the negative image of places that experienced an immediate or prolonged image crisis.

CAUSE-RELATED MARKETING

Cause-related marketing (CRM) is discussed in more detail in the final chapter, but is corporate philanthropy organized to increase the bottom line (Hudson, Miller and Peloza, 2006). CRM is a rapidly expanding trend in marketing communications, and is growing at a time when the public is increasingly cynical about big business. It is basically a marketing programme that strives to achieve two objectives – improve corporate performance and help worthy causes – by linking fundraising for the benefit of a cause to the purchase of the firm's products and/or services.

SOCIAL MEDIA

Social media has been discussed in detail in Chapter 3, but platforms such as Facebook, YouTube and Twitter have emerged as important channels for responding to a crisis (Schroeder et al., 2013; Grundy and Moxon, 2013), or for generating earned positive media. A good example of the latter comes from Canadian airline WestJet, which on a weekend in November 2013 set up interactive video screens in airport departure lounges in Toronto and Hamilton, allowing two planeloads of Calgary-bound guests to scan their boarding passes and speak to Santa. Santa, clad in WestJet royal blue/purple, asked passengers what they would like for Christmas, and answers were recorded by hidden cameras. Mostly, children wanted straightforward gifts – a toy train, a Barbie doll, an Android tablet. Some adults made humble requests: socks, underwear, scarves. One asked for a diamond ring, another for a car. While those passengers were in the air, WestJet volunteers in Calgary spent four frantic hours buying and wrapping gifts. When the planes touched down four hours later, those 357 separate presents came out of the baggage carousel, while more hidden cameras recorded their shocked amazement. Then WestJet, with the help of Toronto-based production company Studio M, packaged the footage from 19 different hidden cameras into a slick five-minute, 26-second ad. The video launched on YouTube on Monday morning, and was soon 'trending' on Twitter (Hudson and Hudson, 2013).

At the time of writing, the *Christmas Miracle* video had received over 45 million views on YouTube. Richard Bartrem, WestJet's vice president of communications and community relations, said the company had expected perhaps 800,000 views from the video. But even in the few short days after *Christmas Miracle* went live, it had topped 13 million views, been seen in more than 200 countries and made the news in the UK, Australia, Japan, Poland and Malaysia. 'We're pretty thrilled,' he said. 'For a traditional commercial, you could spend well into the mid-six figures for the production alone' (Bender, 2013). The incredulous looks on the faces of the passengers, adults and children alike, when their dream gifts come off the carousel, are the real power of the video. 'Fun is part of our DNA!' said Robert Palmer, WestJet's manager of public relations. 'This was very much a reflection of our corporate identity. We like to have fun with our guests, and on social media' (Hudson and Hudson, 2013).

PUBLICATIONS

Companies rely extensively on communication materials to reach and influence their target markets. Publications such as annual reports, brochures, and company newsletters and magazines can draw attention to a company and its products, and can help build the company's image and convey important news to target markets. Heli-ski operator Canadian Mountain Holidays, for example, published the first ever sustainability report for the heli-skiing sector in 2004 as a way of sharing successes and challenges and to increase accountability to staff, guests and other stakeholders. The report was updated with Volume 2 in 2007, and Volume 3 in 2010.

Audio-visual materials, such as films and DVDs, are also often used as promotion tools. Many DMOs use videos to promote their destinations. Some send promotional videos directly to consumers as well as to members of the travel trade. In Myanmar, when marketers launched their new branding campaign in 2013 at the World Economic Forum on East Asia, delegates were given a USB key with several films on it about the country, including its new television commercial (see Chapter 1 for more details on the campaign). Others are using current technology to showcase their promotional videos. With a new Smart TV app, Walt Disney Parks and Resorts has made available 40 videos on the different types of experiences one can expect at the theme parks.

WINNING OR SPONSORING AWARDS

In many industries, for example the car industry, it has become common practice for companies to promote their achievements. Automotive awards presented in magazines such as *Motor Trends* have long been known to carry clout with potential car buyers. And the winning of prestigious awards has become increasingly important in tourism and hospitality sectors as well. For individual operators, the winning of an award is a campaign opportunity: most of the awards in the tourism industry promote best performance and are often an indication of quality. Winning organizations can therefore use the third-party endorsements in their advertising to build credibility and attract customers. They can, therefore, provide excellent publicity for winners. UK tour operator Scott Dunn Travel, for example, has won numerous awards, including the 'Best Ski Operator' in the Telegraph Travel Awards, 2015–16, and the Condé Nast Traveler Readers' Travel Award for Favorite Specialist Tour Operator in 2011 and 2104. Founder Andrew Dunn says awards give the company 'collateral for the next 12 months or so' for marketing, advertising and online clout' (Hudson and Hudson, 2015).

CELEBRITY ENDORSEMENT

Encouraging celebrities to use or endorse tourism and hospitality products can result in considerable media coverage, and can therefore help to promote that particular product. Richard Branson built Virgin Atlantic Airways with the help of a strong public relations campaign that included inviting as many rock stars as possible to fly on his airline. Celebrity endorsement is also critical for events, as the case study in Chapter 5 about the Dance World Cup highlighted. Destinations, too, can benefit from celebrity endorsements. Vail Resorts has a sponsorship deal with Olympic gold medalist and World Alpine Ski Champion Lindsey Vonn. Vonn appears at select consumer events and ski shows in the US and Europe, and promotes the popular Epic Season Pass, which offers skiing and snowboarding at all Vail-owned Resorts. Restaurants, too, are looking to celebrity endorsement to boost their visibility. In the US, for example, Texas Roadhouse and other restaurant chains are increasingly sponsoring up-and-coming musicians in order to stand out from competitors (Jargon and Smith, 2012). Texas Roadhouse has teamed up with Candy Coburn; Cracker Barrel Old Country Store Inc. is promoting country singer Josh Turner; and LongHorn Steakhouse has been sponsoring country stars like Darius Rucker and Kenny Chesney for many years. Some restaurants give away concert tickets and have musicians perform at restaurant events, and others sell CDs by the artists recorded exclusively for the chains. While it is difficult to quantify the effect of such alliances, Texas Roadhouse says it has raised the chain's profile among country music lovers.

A recent survey of UK social media users showed 33 per cent of all users follow celebrities (Pozin, 2014), and research has shown that celebrity endorsement is even more important in emerging markets, where a celebrity endorsement will strongly affect decisions to buy one brand over another (HSBC, 2010). Tina Maze, the most successful female ski racer in Slovenian history, has been a great ambassador for skiing in Slovenia. Maze, who regularly wins on the World Cup ski circuit, is five-time winner of best Slovenian athlete, a high-fashion model and a pop star with Slovenia's most watched YouTube music video (Hudson and Hudson, 2015).

PRODUCT PLACEMENT AND BRANDED ENTERTAINMENT

Product placement is the insertion of brand logos or branded merchandise into movies and television shows, and it is another promotional tactic available to marketers. Branded entertainment, on the other hand, is a relatively new term to describe a more contemporary, sophisticated use of product placement, and has been defined as 'the integration of advertising into entertainment content, whereby brands are embedded into storylines of a film, television programme, or other entertainment medium' (Hudson and Hudson, 2006: 492). In the area of tourism marketing, industry practitioners have primarily focused on the traditional use of product placement to reach target markets. Destinations concentrate on product placement as an opportunity to gain exposure, aware that placing a destination in a film or television is the ultimate in tourism product placement (Morgan and Pritchard, 1998). Spain, for example, is encouraging Indian filmmakers to use its colourful fiestas and historic monuments as settings for their films in an attempt to grab a bigger share of India's fast-growing overseas tourism market. This is after the coming-of-age movie Zindagi Na Milegi Dobara – shot extensively in Spain in 2011 – doubled the number of Indian visitors. India's ambassador to Spain, Vikram Misri, said the film 'was singlehandedly responsible for making Spain a household name in India and increasing tourism from India' (Guardian, 2016).

Although tourism marketers have not traditionally incorporated an integrated branded entertainment approach, there are signs that some tourism organizations are moving away from traditional product placement, to strategic branded entertainment in order to attract tourists through the medium of film and television. A good example of a branded entertainment initiative comes from Las Vegas, where it was no accident that the MGM's Aria Hotel played a central role in the 2013 movie *Last Vegas*. MGM strategically 'engineered' the movie to take place in its new hotel, a marketing ploy that benefited the Aria and the film directors, who both wanted to showcase the 'New Vegas'. The architecture depicted in the film had to feel hip, upscale and beyond the expectations of the four main characters in the movie, played by Robert DeNiro, Michael Douglas, Morgan Freeman and Kevin Kline (Mlife, 2013).

As the Digital Spotlight in Chapter 8 described, Brand USA used three media platforms to promote the country, partnering with television, film and digital content producers to present engaging stories that would attract international tourists (Hudson and Tung, 2015). One of those initiatives was a partnership with MacGillivray Freeman Films to produce a documentary film for IMAX and large-screen theatres. The movie, entitled *National Parks Adventure,* showcases the country's national parks. Narrated by Oscar-winning actor Robert Redford, the movie features more than 30 of America's national parks, including Grand Canyon, Yosemite and Yellowstone. The film represents a $12.5 million investment from Brand USA, but the organization expects $45 million worth of marketing impressions to be generated by its worldwide rollout to hundreds of global theatres. 'Brand USA's charge is to increase international tourism to the US, so the international audience is a huge focus for us,' said Tom Garzilli, senior vice president of global sponsorships for Brand USA. 'National Parks Adventure will be shown in giant-screen cinemas in several different countries including China, England, Germany, Australia, India, Japan, France and many more' (Sheivachman, 2016).

IMAGE 9.3 *Last Vegas* (courtesy of MGM Resorts International. Reproduced by permission)

MEASURING THE IMPACT OF PUBLIC RELATIONS EFFORTS

The application of evaluation research remains weak in public relations, with practitioners most commonly citing lack of budget and lack of time as the main reasons for not undertaking research. However, Macnamara (1999) suggests that even if adequate budget and time were available, many practitioners would still not be able to undertake either evaluative or formative research, due to lack of knowledge on the research process. He has proposed a Macro Model of PR Evaluation that breaks PR activity into three stages. The model suggests that each PR project or programme is constructed from a series of inputs; outputs are then produced; and finally outcomes are achieved.

Inputs include the story list and copy for a newsletter or blog, information for a news release, Tweets, speaker list and programme for an event and design and contents for a website. Outputs are the physical communication materials or activities produced such as printed publications, news releases, DVDs, events, or social media activity. Finally, outcomes typically sought in public relations are increased awareness, attitudinal change or behavioural change. The list of evaluation methods shown in Figure 9.3 is far from exhaustive but illustrates that a range of techniques, tools and research instruments is available to evaluate inputs, outputs and outcomes. The most common is media monitoring, and social media monitoring has recently joined the evaluation of press clippings and media broadcasts under this umbrella. Advertising value equivalency (AVE) is another often used technique to measure PR value, although the method has come under fire in recent years (Likely and Watson, 2013). The Lake Tahoe Visitor's

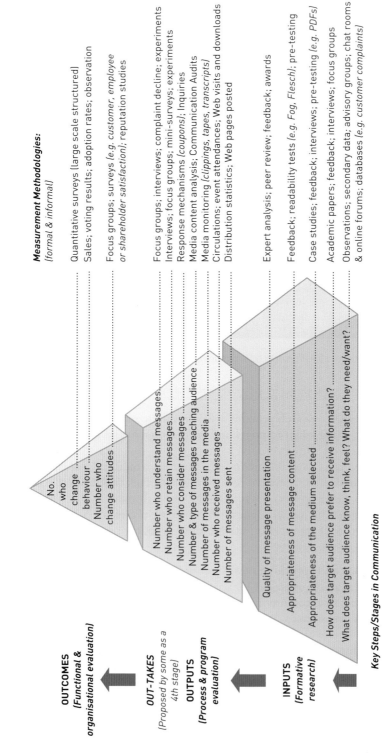

Measurement Methodologies:
(formal & informal)

Quantitative surveys (large scale structured)

Sales; voting results; adoption rates; observation

Focus groups; surveys *(e.g. customer, employee or shareholder satisfaction)*; reputation studies

Focus groups; interviews; complaint decline; experiments
Interviews; focus groups; mini-surveys; experiments
Response mechanisms *(coupons)*; Inquiries
Media content analysis; Communication Audits
Media monitoring *(clippings, tapes, transcripts)*
Circulations; event attendances; Web visits and downloads
Distribution statistics; Web pages posted

Expert analysis; peer review; feedback; awards

Feedback; readability tests *(e.g. Fog, Flesch)*; pre-testing

Case studies; feedback; interviews; pre-testing *(e.g. PDFs)*

Academic papers; feedback; interviews; focus groups

Observations; secondary data; advisory groups; chat rooms & online forums; databases *(e.g. customer complaints)*

No. who change behaviour
Number who change attitudes

Number who understand messages
Number who retain messages
Number who consider messages
Number & type of messages reaching audience
Number of messages in the media
Number who received messages
Number of messages sent

Quality of message presentation

Appropriateness of message content

Appropriateness of the medium selected

How does target audience prefer to receive information?

What does target audience know, think, feel? What do they need/want?

OUTCOMES
(Functional & organisational evaluation)

OUT-TAKES
(Proposed by some as a 4th stage)
OUTPUTS
(Process & program evaluation)

INPUTS
(Formative research)

Key Steps/Stages in Communication

FIGURE 9.3 The Macro Model of Evaluation (Used with kind permission of Jim Macnamara)

Authority (LTVA) uses such a method to evaluate its PR initiatives. The LTVA retains Weidinger Public Relations (WPR) to execute a comprehensive national and regional media communications plan, and in 2012–13 advertising equivalency reached 5–10 times the LTVA's PR budget investment, translating into $1.5 million value and a circulation of 51 million readers.

One problem with both media monitoring and advertising equivalency is that they tend not to measure the quality of coverage. Media content analysis is therefore employed at times to evaluate qualitative criteria such as whether media coverage reaches key target audiences, whether it focuses on the main issues, and whether it contains the organization's message. Often PR specialists will calculate a publicity value as well as advertising value equivalency. Such publicity value is defined in the industry to be a multiplication of three times the advertising value, and may reflect either positive or negative publicity as indicated by Slant. Slant is a subjective evaluation of an article, typically using a table of 10 with 5 as neutral and 1–4 slant trending from 'very negative to 'negative'; and 6–10 trending from 'positive' to 'very positive'.

Measuring the impact of social media campaigns will be discussed further in Chapter 11, but certainly it is a new science. Brands that conduct social media interactions with consumers in a meaningful way are beginning to see a positive return (Cruz and Mendelsohn, 2010), but there are too few research studies that can support this claim. Figure 9.4 shows the difference between measuring traditional media and social media from a PR perspective according to Ketchum Global Research & Analytics.

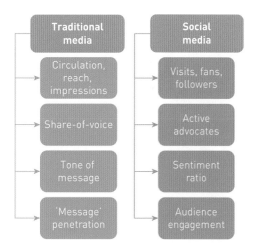

FIGURE 9.4 Measuring traditional media and social media from a PR perspective (©Ketchum, Inc. Reprinted with permission)

Finally, how should marketers be measuring the effectiveness of product placement branded entertainment? In a recent study of practitioners' attitudes towards these practices, Um and Kim (2014) found a fair degree of scepticism about the ability to gauge the effect on viewers from a single branded entertainment initiative. For the practice of product placement, academics suggest that message impact should be assessed at recall, persuasion, and behavioural levels (Balasubramanian, 1994). Among practitioners, measuring placement's effectiveness is still a rough-and-ready art, but unaided recall and brand recognition are the two most popular means of assessing placements (Karrh, McGee and Pardun, 2003). However, a recent study by Hang (2014) suggests that brand recall/recognition alone may underestimate brand placement impact, and that marketers should use multiple methods to measure branded entertainment effectiveness.

Among the more original measurement tools is that of Rentrak Branded Entertainment, a US-based specialist in branded entertainment measurement. Rentrak's measurement method allows real-time measurement of an integration's effectiveness on the basis of 19 different treatment levels. Rentrak produces a proprietary Media-Q and associated integration value that compares the effectiveness of the integrations to a traditional 30-second advertisement where a Media-Q of 1.0 is equivalent to the value of a 30-second spot. The evaluation also includes a best-practices qualitative review of the integration and suggestions as to how the integration can be enhanced upon. That being said, there are still some critics who question the high investment that branded entertainment requires, and it is critical that a more formalized measurement model be established to allow accountability (Russell and Belch, 2005; Um and Kim, 2014).

DIGITAL SPOTLIGHT: COOPERATIVE MARKETING IN STELLENBOSCH, SOUTH AFRICA

One of the top tourism attractions in South Africa is the Stellenbosch wine area. In its beautiful undulating countryside and quaint, historical town, there's a wide range of top-notch restaurants, cafés, curio shops, galleries, boutiques, museums, culinary and wine tours, and an array of annual cultural, food, wine, sports and music festivals.

The Stellenbosch Local Economic Development (LED) strategy is a multistakeholder effort in support of private sector development, aiming to unite economic stakeholders to cooperate in improving the economic future of the area. The question 'What is required to achieve 8 per cent real GDPR growth in the Stellenbosch municipal economy?'

IMAGE 9.4 Hanli Fourie from Bites and Sites at Brampton, guiding a wine tasting and food pairing tour (©Mouton Photography. Reproduced by permission)

was answered in a June 2014 report which highlighted a wide variety of initiatives including establishing free wi-fi throughout the region and investing in cutting-edge fibre optic and communications infrastructure. Other plans involved increasing the role of Stellenbosch University in economic development, providing small business incubator space, mentorship network, transport improvements, and a tourism development framework to involve the whole area. Tourism opportunities were outlined for different sectors including agri-tourism, eco-tourism, microtourism business funding, art, culture, heritage, sport and outdoor music tourism, events and conference tourism. The Stellenbosch Wine Routes were considered a key factor in the overall strategy.

Professor Nick Vink, Chair, Department of Agricultural Economics at Stellenbosch University, looks back to 1971 when the Stellenbosch Wine Route was first established by a concerted local effort to increase visitation. 'The wine industry has always had a particular fascination for the domestic tourist market. This tourism offer has also made us a popular destination for foreign tourists,' he recounts. A central office in the historic old town and an active website (www.stellenbosch.travel) enable the Stellenbosch Tourism and Information Office to interact cooperatively with visitors and local suppliers. 'The main tourist experience of the town is its history and the University and, of course, both are inextricably intertwined with the wine industry,' Vink explains. 'Second, South Africa's biggest liquor company, Distell, has its head office in Stellenbosch, so they actively advertise a range of venues – the Bergkelder vinoteque for fine wines, JC le Roux for sparkling wines and Van Rijn Brandy Distillery among others.'

The Stellenbosch Wine Routes is very active in promoting the 'producer cellars' (estate wineries). Apart from their Internet presence, there are maps and brochures on the wine route at every conceivable venue, Vink explains, including the farms, the restaurants, the hotels and B&Bs. The wine routes are divided into subroutes for some of the more important wards such as Simonsberg and Helderberg, which do their own publicity. All of the wine farms have their own websites and most sell wines both on site and online. In addition, there are numerous private promoters including SA Venues, MyDorpie.com and ShowMe.com. A convenient way to explore the wine routes is by the Stellenbosch Vinehopper (http://vinehopper.co.za). The 'hop on, hop off' buses visit various different wineries over three separate routes. Owner Raino Bolz says he focuses more on marketing than PR: 'Our marketing efforts entail printing brochures that are visible in all the guesthouses in Stellenbosch and Cape Town. We also visit travel agents and operators regularly to promote our products. We also attend international travel shows to promote our tours.' Tripadvisor, Facebook and Twitter are his main tools.

Around town, 'Foodies on Foot' tours are run by Bites and Sites (www.bitesandsites.co.za), combining historical and contemporary culture with cuisine. Hanli Fourie set the company up in 2010 inspired by 'Savor Seattle'. Culinary highlights include Schoon de Compagnie bakery and bistro, famous for its cheese and charcuterie platter as well as fresh breads and homemade ice cream. Decked out in red aprons, the guides also supervise dried meat purchases at the authentic Eikeboom Butchery, which is then paired with wine tastings at the Brampton Wine Bar. Awarded a 2015 Tripadvisor Certificate of Excellence, the company is very active on Facebook, Instagram and Twitter. 'Tripadvisor is proving to be a wonderful marketing tool,' says Hanli. 'It is free and gives credibility. We get quite a number of queries through Tripadvisor and in future guests will be able to book our tours directly from the Tripadvisor site.' She posts photos and information twice weekly and regularly updates the company website. Print advertising is the least effective marketing tool, according to Hanli, although she does advertise through brochures and the Cape Town Tourism booklet. 'We also supply guests with a print-out detailing our social media handles and request that they write Tripadvisor reviews,' she says.

(Continued)

(Continued)

Part of her PR strategy is responsible tourism. A member of Unashamedly Ethical, the company includes a detailed 'Responsible Tourism' segment on its website with commitments to social, economic and environmental responsibility. It also exploits media coverage on the site with articles and photos about the tours by food writers, bloggers, adventure travellers and cookery book authors. Many of these articles have emanated from journalist visits set up by Stellenbosch Wine Routes and Stellenbosch 360 Tourist Info. 'We also connect with local food, tourism, and responsible travel role players, promote them on social media and try to build good relationships to further our shared goal of building a better South Africa through the wonderful opportunities that these industries offer,' says Hanli.

While many tourists come to Stellenbosch just on a day trip from Cape Town, others stay overnight to experience more of the hospitality and hedonism of the area. A relatively new hotel, 107 Dorpstraat Boutique Hotel, opened as a small B&B and winebar in 2015. General Manager, Suzaan Groenewald supervises a very personal service, with cooked breakfasts, free wi-fi, advice and help in booking wine tours with Vinehopper and Uber taxis. The hotel vaunts its blend of history, luxury and technology via a combination of Tripadvisor, Pinterest, Facebook, Twitter, LinkedIn, and Google+ marketing. In terms of PR, Groenewald is happy to offer discounts to visiting media, as well as publicizing promotions through social media. 'We also use Booking.com, Expedia, Agoda and other booking sites like these for special promotions,' she says. She also sends out special rates to local businesses and travel companies. Following their visits she reinforces the relationship with 'thank you' letters and special 'regular returner discounts'.

Sources: Personal Visit to Stellenbosch by both authors March 2016; Stellenbosch Municipality (2014).

CASE STUDY QUESTIONS

1. Why do you think it is important that businesses in the Stellenbosch region have a coordinated public relations strategy?

2. Look at the PR techniques listed earlier in the chapter. What more could the Stellenbosch region do to attract publicity?

3. Take a look at www.stellenbosch.travel. What is the tourism industry in Stellenbosch currently doing to attract visitors?

PERSONAL SELLING

Personal selling is a personalized form of communication in which a seller presents the features and benefits of a product to a buyer for the purpose of making a sale. The high degree of personalization that personal selling involves usually comes at a much greater cost per contact than mass communication techniques. Marketers must decide whether this added expense can be justified, or whether marketing objectives can be achieved by communicating with potential customers in groups. Some tourism and hospitality organizations favour personal selling far more than others, as for them the potential benefits outweigh the extra costs. Many case studies in this book (Dance World Cup in Chapter 5; Ulkotours in Chapter 7; Marcos Van Aken in this chapter) have stressed the importance of personal selling in marketing. Certainly, in the meetings and convention business, the industry is still driven by personal relationships. Jason Outman, Executive Director for the Columbia Metropolitan Conventions & Visitors Bureau in South Carolina, is a great believer in personal selling: 'From the DMO world, advertising brings awareness, but it is the personal selling that makes the sale. Clients want to know what is unique about a destination. What the local hot spots are. What will their attendee experience consist of? This can't all be explained in an 8.5 x 11 advertisement. Personal selling allows the DMO to dig deep and find out what the hot buttons are and address them individually. It allows us to truly show all that the destination has to offer.' Outman believes that another benefit to personal selling is the opportunity to inform or dispel any stereotypes: 'For instance, many of the Columbia CVB clients don't realize that we have an airport or even a convention centre. While our advertisements focus on the region offering fun attractions or great culinary options, we can't address these misperceptions. Personal selling gives us the opportunity to inform the client about all that the city has to offer, address any stereotypes, and personally lay out how their meeting can fit. This is a major advantage to personal selling.'

Outman also suggests that personal selling helps build relationships that advertisements cannot. 'DMO's are dealing with clients that are booking conferences several years in advance. A sales manager may contract the business in 2016, but the convention doesn't come to the city until 2020,' he says. 'We don't want to be thought of as a destination that is just booking business and then moving on to the next group. We want to make sure our client knows we truly value them, and want their convention to be a success. Personal selling allows us to learn more about the client as an individual. We learn about their family and friends, their extracurricular activities. We spend time with them on site visits and over dinner. We build a friendship that goes beyond the contracting of business. This allows us to keep touch with the clients prior to their convention, but it also keeps us at the top of their mind if they are looking to find a location for another meeting they have. Only personal selling can provide this type of relational building.'

ROLES OF PERSONAL SELLING

While the salesperson's job is to make a sale, his or her role goes well beyond this task. Personal selling plays a number of important roles in the tourism and hospitality industry, six of which are discussed below.

1. GATHERING MARKETING INTELLIGENCE

The salesperson must be alert to trends in the industry and to what the competitor is doing. Competitive knowledge is important when the salesperson faces questions involving product comparisons, and information on competitor's promotions can be very useful for the marketing department. Data collected by the salesperson is often reported electronically to the company's head office, where managers can retrieve the information and use it appropriately at a later date.

2. LOCATING AND MAINTAINING CUSTOMERS

Salespeople who locate new customers play a key role in a company's growth. Salespeople can identify qualified buyers (those most likely to purchase travel services), key decision-makers (those who have the final say in travel decisions), and the steps involved in making travel decisions. This important information can be gathered effectively through inquiries by salespeople and from sales calls to an organization.

3. PROMOTING TO THE TRAVEL TRADE

Many organizations find personal selling to be the most effective communication tool in promoting to key travel decision-makers and influencers in the travel trade, such as corporate travel managers, convention or meeting planners, tour operators and retail travel agents. The purchasing power of these groups is impressive, which justifies the added expense of personal selling. As mentioned above, at ITB Berlin, the travel industry's leading trade show, 10,000 exhibiting companies from 187 countries and regions met with 120,000 trade visitors in 2016.

4. GENERATING SALES AT POINT OF PURCHASE

Personal selling can significantly increase the likelihood of purchase and the amount spent by customers at the point of purchase. Reservations staff at hotels and car rental desks have a great opportunity to up-sell (sell upgraded accommodations or cars), and staff in restaurants and travel agencies can have a major influence on the purchase decision of the customer. Increased sales are a result of the proper training of service and reservations staff in personal selling techniques.

5. USING RELATIONSHIP MARKETING

Sales representatives provide various services to customers: consulting on their problems, rendering technical assistance, arranging finance and expediting delivery. These representatives are very important for building relationships with customers and maintaining their loyalty. Careful attention to individual needs and requirements is a powerful form of marketing for tourism and hospitality organizations. Key customers really appreciate the personal attention they receive from professional sales representatives and reservations staff. This appreciation normally results in increased sales and repeat use, and the focus is on creating and keeping long-term customers. This is just one part of a process that has become known as 'customer relationship management' (CRM).

6. PROVIDING DETAILED AND UP-TO-DATE INFORMATION TO THE TRAVEL TRADE

Personal selling allows an organization to pass on detailed information to the travel trade and provides an opportunity to deal immediately with a prospect's concerns and questions. This is especially important for an organization that relies on travel trade intermediaries for part or all of its business. Tour operators, for example, should have regular contact with travel agents in order to update them on changes in the marketing environment.

OBJECTIVES OF PERSONAL SELLING

Although sales objectives are custom-designed for specific situations, there are general objectives that are commonly employed throughout the tourism and hospitality industry.

1. SALES VOLUME

Occupancy, passenger seats or miles, and total covers (restaurant seats) are common measures of sales volume within the industry. An emphasis on volume alone, however, leads to price discounting, the attraction of undesirable market segments, cost cutting and employee dissatisfaction. Some sectors, such as exclusive resorts, unique adventure holidays, and upper-end cruises, restrict prospecting to highly selective segments, believing that price and profits will take care of themselves. Others may establish sales volume objectives by product lines to ensure a desired gross profit. This system is the basis for yield management (see Chapter 6).

2. CROSS-SELLING, UP-SELLING, AND SECOND-CHANCE SELLING

Cross-selling occurs when a seller offers a buyer the opportunity to purchase allied products that go beyond the obvious core products. Cross-selling is now integral to virtually every segment of the travel industry, travel insurance being one of the most profitable cross-sells in the industry. Good opportunities exist for tourism companies, such as hotels and resorts, to upgrade price and profit margins by selling higher-priced products such as suites through up-selling. A related concept is second-chance selling, in which a salesperson may contact a client who has already booked an event such as a three-day meeting. The salesperson may try to sell additional services such as airport limousine pick-up, or try to upgrade rooms or food and beverage services.

3. MARKET SHARE

Some sectors of the tourism industry are more concerned with market share than others. Airlines, cruise lines, major fast-food chains, and rental car companies, for example, are often more focused on market share than are restaurants, hotels and resorts. As a consequence, salespeople are sometimes required to measure market share or market penetration and are held accountable for a predetermined level of either or both.

4. PRODUCT-SPECIFIC OBJECTIVES

Occasionally, a sales force will be charged with the specific responsibility of improving sales volume for specific product lines. This objective may be associated with up-selling and second-chance selling, but may also be part of the regular sales duties of the sales force. Such objectives might be to sell more hotel suites, holiday packages to Mexico, honeymoon packages or more premium car rentals. A common approach used to encourage the sale of specific products is to set objectives for them and to reward performance with bonuses or other incentives.

THE SALES PROCESS

The sales process consists of the following seven steps (see Figure 9.5).

1. PROSPECTING AND QUALIFYING

Prospecting is the process of searching for new accounts. It has been said that there are three truisms about prospecting: most salespeople don't like to prospect; most salespeople do not know how to prospect; and most companies are inept at teaching or training salespeople to prospect. There are two key elements to successful prospecting. The first is to determine positioning strategy, i.e. to whom you should prospect. The second is implementing a process to find and ultimately contact those prospects on a one-to-one basis.

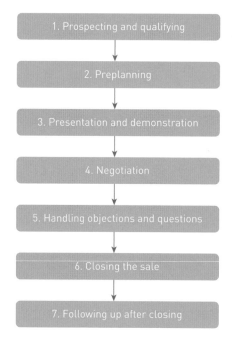

FIGURE 9.5 The sales process

2. PREPLANNING

A successful sales call, made either by telephone or in the field, requires careful preplanning and preparation. There are two elements to preplanning a sales call: the pre-approach and the approach. In the pre-approach stage, a salesperson needs to learn as much as possible about the prospect in order to be able to establish a rapport during the sales call and to have the foundation on which to build the sales presentation itself. The approach then follows and involves all the activities that lead to the sales presentation. These include arranging the appointments with prospects, establishing rapport and confidence at the start of a sales call, and checking preliminary details prior to the sales presentation. Sales representatives have three principal objectives in their approaches: to build rapport with the prospect, to capture a person's full attention and to generate interest in the product.

3. PRESENTATION AND DEMONSTRATION

The salesperson now tells the product 'story' to the buyer, often following the AIDA formula of gaining attention, holding interest, arousing desire and inspiring action. Companies have developed three different styles of sales presentation. The oldest is the canned approach, which uses memorized sales talk that covers the main points.

The formulated approach identifies early the buyer's needs and buying styles and then uses an approach formulated for this type of buyer. It is not canned but follows a general plan. The need/satisfaction approach starts with a search for the customer's real needs by encouraging the customer to do most of the talking. This approach calls for good listening and problem-solving skills. According to experts, there are certain words that make listeners take notice, such as discover, money, guaranteed, love, proven, safe, own, best, good, easy, health, new, results, save and free (Brooks, 2002).

4. NEGOTIATION

Much of selling to the travel trade involves negotiation skills. For meeting planners and hotel groups, for example, the two parties need to reach agreement on the price and other terms of the sale. The hotel salesperson will be seeking to win the order without making deep concessions that will hurt profitability. Although price is the most frequently negotiated issue, other factors may be taken into account, and numerous bargaining tools exist. Sales force members should be taught to negotiate using services or bundled services as the primary negotiating tool rather than price. For the hotel salesperson, negotiations should begin with rack rates, and price concessions should be given only when absolutely essential. Other negotiating tools, such as upgrades, airport pick-up, champagne in rooms, etc., should be employed. A hotel might package these amenities into bundles of services and brand them with names such as the Prestige Package, in order to entice buyers into making a booking.

5. HANDLING OBJECTIONS AND QUESTIONS

When most sales presentations are completed, prospects ask questions and raise one or more objections. Objections come in all forms, even through body language. Resistance can be psychological (e.g. preference for an established hotel) or logical (e.g. price). There are several effective ways to handle objections. One is to restate the objection and to prove diplomatically that it is not as important as it seems. Another is the 'agree and neutralize' tactic or the 'yes, but' approach. In this approach, sales representatives initially agree that a problem exists, but go on to show that the problem is not relevant or accurate. No matter which approach is used, objection must be met head-to-head.

6. CLOSING THE SALE

Closing means getting a sales prospect to agree with the objectives of the sales call, which normally implies making a definite purchase or reservation. Closing the sale can be the most important stage of the sales process, but many salespeople are not comfortable about asking for the order or do not recognize the opportune moment to wrap things up. A sales call without a close is unsuccessful, and every salesperson must ask for the business or at least some commitment to continue the dialogue. Knowing when and how to close are the keys to success. As with objections, this again requires careful attention to the prospect's words and body language. Closing techniques include actually asking for the order, offering to help the secretary write up the order, asking whether the buyer wants A or B, asking how the buyer would like to pay, or by indicating what the buyer will lose if the order is not placed immediately.

7. FOLLOWING UP AFTER CLOSING

A salesperson's work is not finished until all the required steps and arrangements are made to deliver the promised services. In some cases, such as the organization of major association conventions or the planning of incentive travel trips, this 'delivery' work is extensive. However, the follow-up is essential if the salesperson wants to ensure customer satisfaction and repeat business. 'Follow up or foul-up' is the slogan of many success-ful salespeople. It is often advisable to give buyers some kind of reassurance that they have made the right decision. This reduces the buyers' level of cognitive dissonance – a state of mind that many customers experience after making a purchase, in which they are unsure whether they have made a good or bad decision. An important part of post-sale activity also involves immediate follow-up after prospects or their clients have actually used the services. Many travel agents use this effectively by telephoning clients soon after their trips to find out what they liked and did not like.

SALES MANAGEMENT

Sales management is the management of the sales force and personal selling efforts to achieve desired sales objectives. A sales manager has five key roles to play: recruit-ing salespeople, training them, motivating and rewarding them, sales planning, and sales performance evaluation.

1. RECRUITING SALESPEOPLE

A sales manager's first job is to hire competent people to fill available positions. In tour-ism and hospitality, it is uncommon for field sales representatives to be hired without sales experience. The more established practice is for entry-level people to be order takers, who are eventually promoted to sales representative positions. Hiring sales-people from competitors and related outside organizations is also common. Research has shown that no one set of physical characteristics, mental abilities, and personality traits predicts sales success in every situation. Salespeople's success depends more on the actual tasks assigned to them and the environment in which they operate. Most customers say they want salespeople to be honest, reliable, knowledgeable and helpful. Companies should look for these traits when selecting candidates. Another approach is to look for traits common to the most successful salespeople in the company. A study of super-achievers found that super-sales performers exhibited the following traits: they were risk-taking, had a powerful sense of mission, had a problem-solving bent, cared about the customer, and engaged in careful planning (Garfield, 1986).

2. TRAINING SALESPEOPLE

Sales training programmes are very important to the continuation of success in per-sonal selling. Increasingly, sales training is taking place via the Internet, with many travel companies moving training online. The cruise sector is no exception, with Carnival's training, for example, including completing a five-chapter online course for each of the three levels of training. Besides basic cruise knowledge and general travel know-how, topics in these types of courses include the anatomy of a cruise ship, pre- and post-cruise experiences, and cruise marketing and selling. Other train-ing programmes concentrate on the individual cruise lines, finding cruise deals and different types and lengths of cruises.

3. MOTIVATING AND REWARDING SALESPEOPLE

The majority of salespeople require encouragement and special incentives to work at their best level. This is especially true of field selling, as the nature of the job makes it open to frequent frustration: sales reps usually work alone, their hours are irregular, and they are often away from home. Even without these factors, most people operate below capacity in the absence of special incentives, such as financial gain or social recognition. Sales managers, therefore, need to understand motivation theories and to provide financial and nonmonetary incentives to keep sales-force motivation at its peak. Financial incentives include salary and commissions, as well as fringe benefits such as paid vacations, insurance programmes and medical programmes. Often bonuses are given when predetermined volumes of sales and profits, or sales quotas, are achieved. In the tourism industry, free travel is a very important fringe benefit, especially for travel agency and airline staff. Nonmonetary compensation and motivators are reward/recognition programmes and job advancement opportunities. Sales promotions can also be used to motivate a sales force. However, they tend to work best in achieving short-term objectives and are not advisable over the long term. Sales managers at hotels, for example, can win incentive trips or reward points by meeting predetermined targets.

4. SALES PLANNING

The heart of sales planning is the sales plan, usually prepared annually and containing a detailed description of personal selling objectives, sales activities and the sales budget. These selling objectives are frequently set as forecasts of unit or sales volumes or some other financial target derived from expected sales levels. This sales forecast is very useful to others outside the sales department and is a key planning tool for the entire organization. Expected sales levels influence the allocation of personnel and financial resources in many other departments. But the selling objectives may also be nonfinancial, such as the number of sales calls, new sales prospects converted to customers or the number of enquiries answered successfully.

The sales department budgets are another part of the sales plan. Typically these will include the sales forecast, the selling expense budget, the sales administration budget, and the advertising and promotion budget. Given the relatively high cost of personal selling, this budget plays a key role in planning and controlling the sales effort. Finally, the sales plan will include the assignment of sales territories and quotas. Sales quotas are performance targets set periodically for individual sales representatives, branch offices, or regions. They help sales managers motivate, supervise, control, and evaluate sales personnel. The sales manager is likely to use a combination of past territory performance and market indices to allocate quotas for each territory.

5. EVALUATING SALES PERFORMANCE

The final function of sales management is the measurement and evaluation of sales performance. 'Sales analysis' is the term used most frequently for the evaluation of performance. This analysis can be done by considering total sales volume or by looking at sales by territory or customer groups. One of the most important methods of evaluation is to judge actual results against sales forecasts and budgets.

CHAPTER SUMMARY

The field of public relations (PR) is growing, with the media available to PR specialists fitting into three broad categories: owned, paid, and earned media. The main techniques used in PR are press releases, FAM trips, travel exhibitions, events, sponsoring causes, social media, publications, winning awards, celebrity endorsement and product placement. Personal selling is a personalized form of communication that involves a seller presenting the features and benefits of a product or a service to a buyer for the purpose of making a sale. The sales process consists of seven steps: prospecting and qualifying, preplanning, presentation and demonstration, negotiation, handling objections and questions, closing the sale, and following up after closing.

REFLECTIVE QUESTIONS

1. How important are public relations and publicity to tourism and hospitality organizations? Give examples to support your answer.
2. You have just won a tourism award and would like to publicize your achievements. Write a press release for the local newspaper in an attempt to get them to run a story relating to your win.
3. Which do you think is the most important step in the sales process? Explain your answer.

MARKETING IN ACTION: 'LIGHTS, CAMERA, ACTION...!' PROMOTING HAWAII THROUGH FILM AND TELEVISION

Nearly 8.3 million visitors came to Hawaii in 2014, spending $14.7 billion, according to the Hawaii Tourism Authority (HTA). On average 205,044 visitors were in the state on any given day in 2014, an increase of 1.1 per cent from 2013. 'By increasing visitor arrivals and spending to the majority of the Hawaiian Islands, we have been able to grow the benefits of tourism statewide, reinforcing our efforts to diversify Hawaii's tourism economy by distributing visitors across the state,' says Ron Williams, HTA's CEO.

One example of the diversification of Hawaii's tourism product is the growing significance of film tourism. The film industry itself has been important to the state since the 1930s when *White Heat* was filmed on Kauai. Hawaii's most prosperous film-production year was 2010 when production comprised of ten feature films (including the fourth installment of *Pirates of the Caribbean*, and *Battleship*), TV shows *Hawaii Five-0* and *Off the Map*, international commercials, and a steady stream of other smaller projects. Although Kauai is popular with filmmakers for its natural, versatile beauty, Donne Dawson, Hawaii's film commissioner, says Oahu brings in the most production work because it has more infrastructure, including the Diamond Head Film Studio. It is also home to the majority of Hawaii's film crew members and it has a mix of urban, suburban and beautiful natural locations. But, Dawson says, there is an effort to share the wealth. 'We are trying to build the film industry statewide and we have diversity to offer across the island chain,' she explains.

IMAGE 9.5 Author Simon Hudson with Semester at Sea students in Kualoa Ranch, January 2015

Hawaii's most valuable movie customers are the ones that live there full-time, such as CBS's *Hawaii Five-0*, which serves as a veritable live-action brochure for the state's $14 billion-a-year tourism industry. And when tourists come to Honolulu, they often get to see the series in action, as happened when producers shut down the main drag in the city to shoot sequences for the season 4 finale and the season 5 opener. 'We had literally hundreds of spectators there excited by the fact that a little bit of their vacation involved *Hawaii Five-0*,' says Honolulu film commissioner, Walea Constantinau.

Along with the immediate economic benefits from the production itself, including hotel costs, catering, and hiring of local crew and equipment, there are long-lasting economic ripples. 'We're still feeling the effects of *Jurassic Park*,' says Sue Kanoho, executive director of the Kauai Visitors Bureau. 'It's important to tie the destination to the actual place it's filmed. The idea is to get your name out there when the film is released, again when it comes out on DVD, then the actual product, a visit (by movie viewers) to the island. So there is a triple opportunity.'

Marketers in Hawaii have been quick to capitalize on the film tourism phenomenon. Two Hawaii film tour companies recently made a list of the nation's ten most popular film tours on TripAdvisor. One of those listed was Kualoa Ranch on the island of Oahu. Established in 1850, Kualoa is a 4,000-acre working cattle ranch, and is located on the northeastern side of Oahu in the Hawaiian countryside, 22 miles from Honolulu. Ancient Hawaiians considered Kualoa one of the most sacred places on the island of Oahu. It was the residence of kings, a place of refuge and sanctuary – a *pu'uhonua* – and a training ground for Hawaiian royalty who were instructed in the arts of war, history and social traditions. In 1850, King Kamehameha III sold approximately 622 acres of land at Kualoa to Dr Gerritt P. Judd. Dr. Judd had previously been a missionary doctor who arrived in Hawaii in 1828 and who served as personal advisor to King Kamehameha III, translating medical journals into the Hawaiian language. Later, additional acreage in the Hakipu'u and Ka'a'awa valleys was purchased by Dr. Judd's son, Charles Hasting Judd. This purchase increased the size of the estate to the 4,000 acres it is today and is now owned by the Morgan family, Dr. Judd's descendants. In 1927 it was named Kualoa, which means 'long back' in Hawaiian, referring to the Ranch's beautiful valleys and mountain peaks.

Kualoa has been the site of many Hollywood films such as *Jurassic Park*, *Windtalkers*, *Pearl Harbor*, *Godzilla*, *Tears of the Sun* and *50 First Dates*. TV shows including the old and

(Continued)

(Continued)

new *Hawaii Five-0*, *Magnum P.I.* and *LOST* have also been filmed there. However, filming at first played a very minor role at Kualoa Ranch, says John Morgan, president of Kualoa Ranch. '*Mister Roberts* was the first film shot at the ranch in the 1950s,' Morgan says. 'We became more active in filming in the 1970s, but it was a relatively small portion of our operations. Of late, filming is much more important due to the revenue it can generate and the relatively low cost attached to it for us,' Morgan explains. 'Kualoa's strengths are the natural beauty and culture of the place.'

Kualoa Ranch's terrain has also represented Africa, Ireland, the Amazon, Mexico, the lost city of Atlantis and other faraway destinations. The ranch has welcomed film crews from Japan, Korea and Australia and hopes to attract Bollywood productions in the future. When Nicolas Cage filmed *Windtalkers*, Kualoa was also the site of some pretty realistic battles, says Morgan. 'There were 272 major explosions – the most of any in Hollywood history in one day,' he explains. 'They had the whole valley rigged up with wires and explosives so that they could get the first 20 minutes of the film in one take. It opened craters all over the place, and they had actual medics running through the set.'

More recently, use of the ranch as a film set and for movie tours has become a more significant part of their business. Mao Lefiti, who works as Operations Coordinator at the ranch, says that the two activities related to film – hosting production and running movie tours – are equally important. 'As a ranch first and foremost we have had to diversify our operations beyond agriculture. Although movie production does bring in continued business, we actually still run movie tours daily while films are being shot.' If there is filming at the ranch, Lefiti says the ranch makes an effort to leverage this for publicity purposes. 'We are currently working on an attraction from *Jurassic World* (the Indominus Rex Cage), and we always make it a point to highlight the different movies filmed here.' Lefiti says that the tourists that come on the movie tours are of all ages and from all over the world: 'Tourists of all walks of life come and, due to our proximity to East-Asian Pacific countries, we have lots of Korean and Japanese visitors. The tour itself has changed a little over the years, adding little bits and pieces as new films add more viewpoints throughout the tour.'

Sources: Personal visit by the authors to Kualoa Ranch in January 2016.

CASE STUDY QUESTIONS

1. Name three other destinations around the world that are attracting film tourists and explain why.

2. Take a look at Kualoa Ranch's website (www.kualoa.com) and describe how the ranch is currently leveraging this 'film tourism' phenomenon.

3. Referring to the material on product placement earlier in the chapter, explain how Hawaii could measure the effectiveness of this 'destination placement'.

REFERENCES

Avraham, E. (2014) 'Hosting events as a tool for restoring destination image', *International Journal of Event Management Research*, 8(1): 61–75.

Balasubramanian, S.K. (1994) 'Beyond advertising and publicity: hybrid messages and public policy issues', *Journal of Advertising*, 23(4): 29–47.

Bender, A. (2013) 'The Real 'Christmas Miracle' of WestJet's viral video: Millions in free advertising', *Forbes*, 12 December. www.forbes.com/sites/andrewbender/2013/12/12/the-real-christmas-miracle-of-westjets-viral-video-millions-in-free-advertising/#485d6901e04d (accessed 9 December 2016).

Brooks, B. (2002) 'Prospecting: How to stay in the mind of your prospect and win', *Home Business,* 40: 42.

Clark, J.M., Cornwell, T.B. and Pruitt, S.W. (2009) 'The impact of title event sponsorship announcements on shareholder wealth', *Marketing Letters*, 20(2): 169–82.

Cruz, B. and Mendelsohn, J. (2010) 'Why social media matters to your business', *Chadwick Martin Bailey*. www.cmbinfo.com/cmb-cms/wp-content/uploads/2010/04/Why_Social_Media_Matters_2010.pdf (accessed 9 December 2016).

Garfield, C. (1986) *Peak Performers: The New Heroes of American Business*. New York: Avon.

Grundy, M. and Moxon, R. (2013) 'The effectiveness of airline crisis management on brand protection: A case study of British Airways', *Journal of Air Transport Management*, 28: 55–61.

Guardian (2016) 'Spain courts Bollywood productions to attract more Indian tourists', *The Guardian*, 20 June. https://www.theguardian.com/world/2016/jun/19/spain-courts-bollywood-productions-to-attract-more-indian-tourists (accessed 9 December 2016).

Hang, H. (2014) 'Brand-placement effectiveness and competitive interface in entertainment media', *Journal of Advertising Research*, 54(2): 192–9.

HSBC (2010) *Golf's 2020 Vision*. The HSBC Report. http://golfnetworkadmin.gamznhosting.com/site/_content/document/00017543-source.pdf (accessed 12 December 2016).

Hudson, S. and Hudson, D. (2006) 'Branded entertainment: A new advertising technique, or product placement in disguise?' *Journal of Marketing Management*, 22(5–6): 489–504.

Hudson, S. and Hudson, L. J. (2013) *Customer Service for Hospitality and Tourism*. Oxford: Goodfellow Publishers Ltd.

Hudson, S. and Hudson, L. J. (2014) *Golf Tourism*, 2nd edn. Oxford: Goodfellow Publishers Ltd.

Hudson, S. and Hudson, L. J. (2015) *Winter Sport Tourism: Working in Winter Wonderlands*. Oxford: Goodfellow Publishers Ltd.

Hudson, S., Miller, G. and Peloza, J. (2006) 'Approaches to cause related marketing'. In *Cause Related Marketing,* pp. 41–52. Hyderabab, India: ICFAI University Press.

Hudson, S. and Tung, V. W. S. (2015) 'Appealing to tourists via branded entertainment. From theory to practice'. *Journal of Travel and Tourism Marketing*, 33(1): 123–37.

ITB Berlin (2016) 'Botswana: the official partner country of ITB Berlin 2017', ITB Berlin, 10 March. www.itb-berlin.de/Presse/Pressemitteilungen/News_24711.html?referrer=/de/Presse/Pressemitteilungen (accessed 9 December 2016).

Jargon, J. and Smith, E. (2012) 'Restaurant chains, singers team up to sharpen brands', *Wall Street Journal*, 25 September. www.wsj.com/articles/SB10000872396390443589304577633822110333762 (accessed 9 December 2016).

Kaplanidou, K. K., Karadakis, K., Gibson, H., Thapa, B., Walker, M., Geldenhuys, S. and Coetzee, W. (2013) 'Quality of life, event impacts, and mega-event support among

South African residents before and after the 2010 FIFA World Cup', *Journal of Travel Research*, 52(5): 631–45.

Karrh, J. A., McKee, K. B. and Pardun, C. J. (2003) 'Practitioners' evolving views on product placement effectiveness', *Journal of Advertising Research*, 43(2): 138–49.

Ketchum (2013) 'The principles of PR measurement', presented by Ketchum Global Research & Analytics. www.ketchum.com/principles-measurement (accessed 9 December 2016).

Likely, F. and Watson, T. (2013) 'Measuring the edifice: Public relations measurement and evaluation practices over the course of 40 years'. In K. Sriramesh, A. Zerfass and J-N. Kim (eds), *Public Relations and Communication Management: Current Trends and Emerging Topics*, pp. 143–62. New York: Routledge.

Lutz, D. (2014) 'Organizing a Successful Press FamTrip', *Hotel Executive*. http:// hotelexecutive.com/business_review/841/organizing-a-successful-press-famtrip (accessed 9 December 2016).

Macnamara, J. R. (1999) 'Research in public relations: A review of the use of evaluation and formative research', *Asia Pacific Public Relations Journal*, 1(2): 107–34.

Macnamara, J. R. (2012) *Public Relations: Theories, Practices and Critiques*. Australia: Pearson.

Mlife (2013) Lights! Camera! Aria! *Mlife,* 11(4): 72–6.

Morgan, N. and Pritchard, A. (1998) *Tourism Promotion and Power – Creating Images, Creating Identities*. Chichester: John Wiley & Sons.

Morrison, A. M. (2002) *Hospitality and Travel Marketing*, 3rd edn. Albany, NY: Delmar Thomson Learning.

Parry, T. (2016) 'Kos wows agents on a Mark Warner fam', *TTG Media*, 26 May. https://www.ttgmedia.com/news/news/kos-wows-agents-on-a-mark-warner-fam-5008 (accessed 9 December 2016).

Pozin, I. (2014) '5 measurements for PR ROI', *Forbes.com*, 29 May. www.forbes.com/ sites/ilyapozin/2014/05/29/5-measurements-for-pr-roi (accessed 12 December 2016).

Russell, C.A. and Belch, M. (2005) 'A managerial investigation into the product placement industry', *Journal of Advertising Research*, 45(1): 73–92.

Schroeder, A., Pennington-Gray, L., Donohoe, H. and Kiousis, S. (2013) 'Using social media in times of crisis', *Journal of Travel & Tourism Marketing*, 30(1–2): 126–43.

Sheivachman, A'. (2016) 'Brand USA brings new 3D documentary to a global audience', *Skift*, 16 February. https://skift.com/2016/02/16/brand-usa-turns-to-nature-documentaries (accessed 9 December 2016).

Stellenbosch Municipality (2014) *Local Economic Strategy and Action Plan*, June. www.stellenbosch.gov.za/documents/socio-economic-data/1604-led-stratetgy-and-projects-jun-2014/file (accessed 12 December 2016).

Um, N-H. and Kim, S. (2014) 'Practitioners' perspectives on branded entertainment in the United States', *Journal of Promotion Management*, 20(2): 164–80.

10

INTRODUCTION

Chapter 10 focuses on the critical role of customer service, and begins by tracking the history of service, providing a definition of the term. The next part of the chapter describes the service-profit chain, and this is followed by sections on creating a service culture, and converting guests into apostles. The final two sections of the chapter look at managing service promises and the art of service recovery. Case studies look at customer service inside the Pestana Hotel Group, Vail Resort's digital strategy, and customer service at high-profile sporting events in Britain.

LESSONS FROM A MARKETING GURU: DIONISIO PESTANA, PESTANA HOTEL GROUP

Dionísio Pestana is the President & Chairman of Pestana Hotel Group, founded in 1972 by his father, Manuel Pestana. From humble beginnings with just one 300-bedroom hotel on the island of Madeira, Pestana is now Portugal's biggest international tourism and leisure group, ranking 10th in Iberia, 31th in Europe and 125th in the world. The family-owned brand now comprises eight different sectors – Hotels & Resorts, Pousadas de Portugal (boutique inns in converted monuments, palaces, convents and castles), Holiday Ownership, Gaming (Madeira Casino and São Tomé Casino), Travel, Golf and Residence, Industry and International Business Centre of Madeira.

IMAGE 10.1 Dionisio Pestana (©Copyright Pestana Hotel Group. All rights reserved)

Spreading worldwide since 1985, Pestana owns 88 four- and five-star hotels in 15 countries in Africa, South America, North America and Europe. Added to this are 15 Holiday Ownership (timeshare) units, six golf courses, three real estate ventures, two casinos, an air charter company and one tour operator, employing more than 7,000 collaborators worldwide. 'Over the last three decades, we have been investing in the hotel and tourism industry in a structured, sustainable way,' says Pestana. 'In 43 years we have witnessed the birth and growth of the Pestana Hotel Group and its consolidation not only as Portugal's leading hotel chain but also as one of the largest in the world.'

Whether in England, Brazil, Cuba, Venezuela or at home in Portugal, it's all about top-notch quality for Pestana: 'On the 1st of September 2003, the Pestana Hotel Group took on the management and destinations of Pousadas de Portugal. The inclusion of this second hotel brand under the Pestana umbrella represented an added responsibility and reinforcement of our commitment towards quality tourism in Portugal,' says Pestana. Pestana's tentacles have also reached Germany, Spain, Argentina, Uruguay, Colombia, Morocco, Mozambique, South Africa, Cape Verde, Sao Tome and Principe and the US. But diversification and growth has not lead to any diminishing of the original high standards. 'The growth and verticalization of our business activity have been marked by our permanent attention to our clients' needs,' he explains. 'We take pride in the fact that we continually provide refined, attentive, quality service.'

Customer service is paramount throughout the Pestana network. 'These principles form an unconditional part of our service standards. Our aim in applying them is to continue to exceed the expectations of all those who, every day, choose to honour us with their choice,' says Pestana. Continued growth is a strong indication of the success of Pestana's tight control on customer service quality. Even during the fall-out period from the 2008 economic recession, the group reached 2.6 million customers in 2011, an increase of nine per cent over the previous year. Room nights followed the same upward momentum, increasing 8 per cent from 2010 to 2011 to a total of 1.6 million. Online sales grew by 13 per cent and occupancy rates reached 81 per cent during high season and 30 per cent during low season.

Customer service standards are set in regard to regular customer feedback and highly personalized customer contact via satisfaction questionnaires, TripAdvisor and Holiday Check. Many Pestana properties also have a transparency mandate, allowing customers to view the internal services including equipment, hygiene and safety conditions. Also, the group has its' own satisfaction measurement index, PGSI – Pestana Guest Satisfaction Index – an index that combines online reviews with customer questionnaires and feedback in order to achieve high standards in service quality provided. This is a critical aspect, Pestana says, since it allows the company to improve its service based on accurate feedback from customers. In order to measure, manage and monitor these data, Pestana Hotel Group signed an agreement with one of the most prestigious brands in the market, ReviewPro.

In Brazil, the group instituted a customer service platform, eBuzz Connect, which monitors and manages the feedback from guests on social networking sites including TripAdvisor, Booking, Expedia and various blogs. This enabled them to gauge their positioning compared to their competition, and also facilitated the setting of objectives. Initial results garnered 146 comments answered in the first three months, followed by a 10 per cent improvement in the positioning of the Pestana Rio.

Pestana's latest goals are to add more than 3,000 room keys from up to 20 new projects currently in development and to reach the symbolic goal of 100 hotels by 2020. The group also expects to reinforce its brand presence in 20 countries, investing 70 million Euros in Portugal and almost 100 million Euros at the international level. At the same time, Pestana wants to diversify the business model, seeking out more lease and management contracts. In 2016, The Pestana Hotel Group was elected Trusted Brand in the prestigious *Readers Digest* study which surveyed 13,200 Portuguese people. Great emphasis was placed on the group's quality of service as well as perception of customers' needs. It has also won awards with World Travel Awards, Publituris Travel Awards, Condé Nast Hot List, TripAdvisor, Expedia, Zoover, Thomas Cook, TUI and Luxair Tours.

Sources: Interviews with Pedro Lopez and João Pedro Ferradeira August 2016.

DEFINING CUSTOMER SERVICE

Many attempts have been made to define customer service. Perhaps the most comprehensive definition comes from Lucas (2009: 6) who defines customer service as 'the ability of knowledgeable, capable, and enthusiastic employees to deliver products and services to their internal and external customers in a manner that satisfies identified and unidentified needs and ultimately results in positive word-of-mouth publicity and return business'. What this definition does not consider is that customer service may not always be satisfactory and can also lead to bad word-of-mouth and a loss of business. In addition, customer service is more than the interaction between employees and internal or external customers. It also relates to the physical infrastructure in a retail space or hospitality servicescape. Disney, for example, a truly customer-focused organization, has two peepholes in its hotel room doors – one at the usual height, and another at a child's level. The definition of customer service used in this chapter therefore builds on that of Lucas and is as follows: *Customer service is the practice of delivering products and services to both internal and external customers via the efforts of employees or through the provision of an appropriate servicescape.*

The modern concept of customer service has its roots in the Craftsman Economy of the 1800s, when individuals and small groups of manufacturers competed to produce arts and crafts to meet public demand. Customized orders were taken for each customer, and the customer care was highly individualized. During that era, customer service differed from what it is today by the fact that the owners of businesses were also motivated frontline employees working face-to-face with their customers and they had a vested interest in providing good service and in succeeding (Lucas, 2009).

As the era of mass production gradually evolved early in the twentieth century, it became more and more difficult to cater to the needs of individual customers. The explosion in the demand for goods after the Second World War further reduced the importance of customer service, as the power of suppliers surpassed that of the consumer. This balance shifted in the 1970s as the dominance of Western manufacturers was challenged by Asia and the increased competition caused producers to improve the quality of their products and services. The economic boom of the 1990s again increased the power of the suppliers, who, while not completely reverting to lower standards of service, were able to be more selective in which customers to serve, and of what levels of service to provide.

Today, businesses have changed dramatically as the economy has shifted from a dependence on manufacturing to a focus on providing timely, quality service (Lucas, 2009). The service economy has been in full swing for some time now, driven by increased technology, globalization, deregulation and changing consumer behaviour among other factors. Customer service is therefore more important than ever before, especially during difficult economic times, when customers are looking to increase value for money and are less forgiving of mediocre service (Miller, 2011).

THE SERVICE-PROFIT CHAIN

Customer satisfaction and loyalty are the keys to long-term profitability, and keeping the customer happy is everybody's business. Becoming customer-centred and exceeding customer expectations are requirements for business success in the tourism, hospitality and event sectors (Starmer-Smith, 2016). Well-publicized research shows that companies can increase profits from 25 to 85 per cent by retaining just 5 per cent more of their customers (Reichheld and Sasser, 1990), and research indicates that merely 'satisfying' customers is no longer enough to ensure loyalty (Heskett, Sasser and Schlesinger, 1997).

Consumers worldwide are willing to spend more on service excellence. One study found that seven in ten Americans are willing to spend an average of 14 per cent more with companies they believe provide excellent customer service (AMEX, 2014). This is slightly more than the previous two years. Another study from AMEX (2011) found a similar willingness in other countries (Australia and Canada, 12%; Mexico, 11%; UK, 10%; France, 9%; Italy, 9%; Germany, 8%; and Netherlands, 7%). In India, consumers would spend 22 per cent more for excellent customer service. Another study found that the value of great customer service in the US economy is a staggering $267.8 billion per year (STELLA Service, 2010). This figure was calculated based on the average spend per person per year with each type of company. Value is the extra percentage that people are willing to spend if they know they will receive great service. If the consumers surveyed received great customer service, 70 per cent would use the same company again, and 50 per cent would make recommendations to family and friends. In the hospitality sector, the study found that consumers are willing to spend 11 per cent more for great service, higher than most other sectors. In fact, hotel guests spend 17 per cent more on ancillary purchases than those who are merely pleased with a hotel's service.

The logic connecting employee satisfaction and loyalty to customer satisfaction and loyalty (and ultimately profits) is illustrated by the service profit chain (see Figure 10.1). The chain suggests there are critical linkages among internal service quality: employee satisfaction/productivity; the value of services provided to the customer; and ultimately customer satisfaction, retention, and profits. The model implies that companies that exhibit high levels of success on the elements of the model will be more successful and profitable than those that do not.

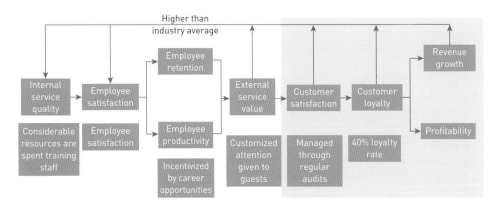

FIGURE 10.1 The service profit chain (Source: Adapted from Heskett et al., 1997)

In Figure 10.1 the profit chain is applied to the Lopesan resort hotel group featured in Chapter 8. The chain begins with internal service quality where human labour is of critical importance to the hotel industry. Efforts need to be made internally to enhance the professional skills of employees and motivate them to satisfy the specific needs and wants of guests. This is evident at Lopesan where the group spends considerable resources training its 3500 staff. The theory is that employee satisfaction will lead to increased productivity and higher retention levels, which will in turn increase the value of hotel services for customers, resulting in satisfaction and loyalty. Staff retention at Lopesan is higher than average, with 50 per cent of staff on fixed contracts. They are also paid higher wages than other competitors and are incentivized by career opportunities and financial bonuses. The resulting external value for customers comes in the form of exceptional service. From the minute customers arrive at the hotel they are treated like valued guests; waiters deliver cooled cocktails to anyone waiting to check in at reception, and once in their rooms, Lopesan guests find televisions already tuned into the correct language channel for them. Later, if they order a particular drink on their room key card, the next day the waiters will already know their favorite tipple. Satisfied guests tend to make repeat visits and share their positive experiences with other potential guests, leading to greater profits and the growth of hotel enterprises. At the Lopesan hotels, a 40 per cent loyalty rate contributes to higher than average occupancy, and a healthy balance sheet, completing the profit chain for the Canary Island's hotel group.

To understand the financial value of building long-term relationships with customers, companies sometimes calculate lifetime values. The lifetime value of a customer is a calculation that considers customers from the point of view of their potential lifetime revenue and profitability contributions to a company. This value is influenced by the length of an average lifetime, the average revenues generated in that time period, and sales of additional products and services over time. Starbucks, for example, has a customer lifetime value of $14,099 (Dragan, 2015), and Snowsports Industries America (SIA) says that a skier beginning at the age of ten has a lifetime value to the industry of $72,758 (see Table 10.1).

TABLE 10.1 Lifetime value of a skier/snowboarder starting at the age of ten (Source: Snowsports Industries America, 2012)

	Skis	Boots	Bindings	Apparel	Accessories	Lifts tickets	Food/ beverage	Lodging
Retail price	$358	$283	$164	$218	$34	$71	$34	$203
Units/Year	0.2	0.2	0.2	0.1	1	10	10	4
Years	35	35	35	35	35	35	35	35
Total ($)	$2,506	$1,981	$1,148	$763	$1,190	$24,850	$11,900	$28,420
Avg/Year								$2,079
TOTAL								$72,758

CREATING A SERVICE CULTURE

In order to provide top-notch customer service, tourism and hospitality providers need to establish a strong service culture. A service culture is a culture that supports customer service through policies, procedures, reward systems, and actions. A services marketing programme is doomed to failure if its organizational culture does not support servicing the customer. Such a programme requires a strong commitment from management. If management expects employees to have a positive attitude towards customers, management must have a positive attitude towards the customer and the employees. All organizational leaders are crucial in transmitting and preserving the culture (Ford and Heaton, 2001). Four Season's service culture is driven by Chairman and CEO Isadore Sharp; Walt Disney was the inspiration behind customer service at Walt Disney Parks and Resorts; and Richard Branson spends considerable time and money focusing on customer service. Finally, Starbucks, the brainchild of Howard Schultz, owes much of it success to Schultz's attention to customer service. 'The real reason for our success is that our partners have often exceeded the expectations of customers with their warm and caring attitude,' he said recently. Speaking about the company's expansion into Asia, he said: 'In China, we have 30,000 people working for Starbucks and they feel that they are being treated with great respect. That is what we want to show our customers' (Wen, 2016).

For companies without a strong service culture, the switch to a customer-oriented system may require changes in hiring, training, reward systems and customer complaint resolution, as well as empowerment of employees. It requires that managers spend time talking to both customers and customer-contact employees. Benchmark tourism and hospitality organizations like Starbucks, therefore, spend considerable effort teaching a culture value system so that when a situation with a customer arises that is not discussed in the training manual or can't be done by the book, the employee who has learned the culture will know how to do the right thing at that moment, will want to do the right thing, and will be empowered to do so by the organization (Ford and Heaton, 2001). At The Montage, Deer Valley in Utah, the unique service culture is instilled and maintained through intensive training. All 720 employees (called associates) go through multiday education followed by a long training period called 'Montage Mores'. Dan Howard, former Public Relations Manager for the hotel says 'No two Montage hotels look anything alike but they "feel" identical – the same messaging, the same style of hospitality. Our goal is to provide comfortable luxury – I think this is uniquely American' (Hudson and Hudson, 2013).

IMAGE 10.2 Montage Deer Valley, Utah (Image compliments of Montage Deer Valley and Barbara Kraft)

Certainly, establishing a service culture may be easier in some parts of the world. In Japan, for example, a high standard of customer service is the norm. The Japanese word for 'customer' translates as 'the invited' or 'guest', showing the status they give to their customers. In France, however, customer service excellence is harder to come by. In fact, in mid-2013, the Paris tourism board launched its 'Do You Speak Touriste?' education initiative to encourage cultural understanding and a kinder, gentler approach for the French who frequently deal with tourists. Asked whether the campaign had succeeded, tourism board spokesperson Veronique Potelet said: 'We know that work remains to be done, but the situation certainly is not catastrophic' (Nehring, 2015).

Training for a service-oriented culture will also require more than a single programme or class. Even before customer service training, new hires should have an initial training session that sets the tone for the employee's experience and begins to build a foundation for service. Once the value system is taught, training can be more specific. Ritz Carlton employees, for example, are trained based on certain specific standards. Each new recruit to the company receives a high level of continuous training and feedback, and is introduced to the Ritz Carlton Gold Standards. Printed on a card that every employee carries around, the Gold Standards illustrate the company's credo, the employee promise and rules for behaviour towards guests and fellow members of staff. These rules explain, for example, the exact vocabulary that should be used to greet guests and guidance on personal appearance. Furthermore, they form a social contract between the institution and everyone that works there. The credo is summed up simply as 'We are ladies and gentlemen serving ladies and gentlemen.'

Ritz Carlton tends to train internally, but some resorts and destinations may look externally for customer service training. Steamboat Springs, a resort town in Colorado, brought in a consultant to give the whole town customer-service training. The impetus for the dramatic move came after the town saw in surveys a significant decrease in responders saying they would recommend Steamboat Springs to friends and colleagues. Management consultant, Ed Eppley, was brought in to design the training programme, initially involving four four-hour sessions over the space of a month, teaching the very latest in customer service culture and using many Disney examples of 'going the extra mile'. 'Saying you want to create customer service experiences that are greater than your competitors is easy,' says Eppley. 'Creating a culture that supports that and rewards your people for doing so takes a tremendous effort' (Mount, 2014).

Outside consultants (People 1st Training Company) were also employed to bring UK service standards up to scratch before the 2012 London Olympics and, as the end-of-chapter case study shows, customer service training is just as critical for events. Events have unique human resource needs and challenges, especially because of their usual reliance on volunteers (Getz, 2007). Hanlon and Stewart (2006) conducted a study of staffing for a major sporting event. They concluded their study by making recommendations for tailored human resource practices, and these are summarized in Figure 10.2. The left-hand side of the model has each of the five main human resource stages, and in the middle are nine special features of major sport event organizations. Tailored event mainstream human resource strategies were identified for each of the five human resource stages and these are listed on the right-hand side of Figure 10.2. The authors recommended that managers be provided with documented guidelines and procedures that reflect the tailored and sport-specific processes required to meet the challenges faced by sport event managers.

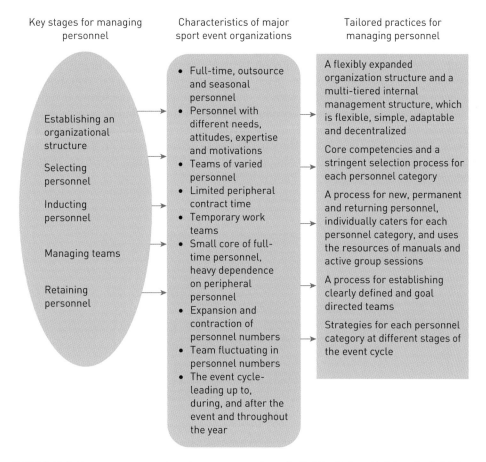

Key stages for managing personnel	Characteristics of major sport event organizations	Tailored practices for managing personnel
Establishing an organizational structure	• Full-time, outsource and seasonal personnel • Personnel with different needs, attitudes, expertise and motivations	A flexibly expanded organization structure and a multi-tiered internal management structure, which is flexible, simple, adaptable and decentralized
Selecting personnel	• Teams of varied personnel	Core competencies and a stringent selection process for each personnel category
Inducting personnel	• Limited peripheral contract time • Temporary work teams	A process for new, permanent and returning personnel, individually caters for each personnel category, and uses the resources of manuals and active group sessions
Managing teams	• Small core of full-time personnel, heavy dependence on peripheral personnel	A process for establishing clearly defined and goal directed teams
Retaining personnel	• Expansion and contraction of personnel numbers • Team fluctuating in personnel numbers • The event cycle-leading up to, during, and after the event and throughout the year	Strategies for each personnel category at different stages of the event cycle

FIGURE 10.2 Management practices for event organizers (©2017 by Robert N. Miranda, Publisher. All rights Courtesy of Cognizant Communication)

One important management function at most large events is corporate hospitality. Corporate hospitality can be defined as any event for the benefit of an organization entertaining clients or staff, or prospective clients, at the organization's expense (MDB, 2009). The activity can be an effective way of establishing networking opportunities and consolidating customer relationships. Often, an outside consultant will be used to organize corporate hospitality activities, especially for the larger events. An example is Jet Set Sports, one of the biggest suppliers of hospitality for the Winter Olympics. The US-based company started with the 1984 Games in Sarajevo. Founder, Sead Dizdarevic, a Croatian native, saw an opportunity ahead of those Games to make the most of his language skills and knowledge of the region to create travel packages for US Olympic sponsors. His new venture saw him entertaining 5,000 clients in Sarajevo, from a past generation of Olympic sponsors like Merrill Lynch, American Express, Sport Illustrated, Kraft and General Foods. Many Olympics later, Dizdarevic and Jet Set Sports counts more than ten times that number of customers for its services that now include Summer and Winter Olympics. The corporate programme Jet Set ran in Sochi in 2014, for example, catered for about 30,000 guests. In addition to arranging accommodations and transport for companies, Jet Set took over a restaurant in Sochi and brought in five Michelin-calibre chefs from around the world.

CONVERTING GUESTS INTO APOSTLES

As mentioned above, merely 'satisfying' customers is no longer enough to ensure loyalty. There is little or no correlation between satisfied (versus highly satisfied) customers and customer retention. Each customer should become so delighted with all elements of their association with a company that using a competitor is unthinkable. In a sense these customers become 'apostles' for their favourite brands. A popular model that explains these behavioural consequences of customer service is the *Apostle Model*, developed at the Harvard Business School. Based on satisfaction and loyalty, this approach segments customers into four quadrants: *Loyalists*, *Hostages*, *Mercenaries*, and *Defectors* (see Figure 10.3).

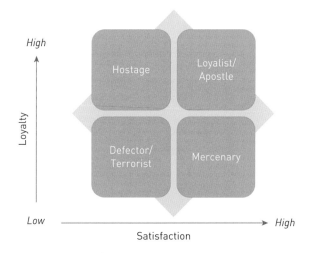

FIGURE 10.3 The Apostle Model (Source: Adapted from Jones and Sasser, 1995).

Defectors are those who have low satisfaction and low loyalty. A subsegment comprises the *Terrorists*, with the lowest satisfaction and loyalty scores. In addition to the costs associated with losing them, these customers are so unhappy that they speak out against a brand at every opportunity. *Hostages* are customers who have low satisfaction, but still report high loyalty. This typically is due to lack of competition or high switching costs. Customers in this category feel 'trapped'. Brands in this category often win business simply due to their location (when no suitable alternatives are nearby) or because of the strength of their loyalty club. However, these customers exhibit 'false loyalty' – acting loyal even when they are just waiting for a chance to jump ship. *Mercenaries* are those who have high satisfaction, but low loyalty. These customers are often price-sensitive and will switch easily when they have the opportunity.

Loyalists are customers who have high satisfaction and high loyalty. Subsegments of loyalists are *Apostles*, who have the highest satisfaction and loyalty scores. Some 80 per cent of Starbucks' revenues come from *Apostles* who visit their stores an average of 18 times a month. These types of customers are loyal because they love a business, and they value customized treatment. In the travel industry in general, requests for customized and personalized vacations are rising sharply, aided by technology and increasingly expectant and discerning consumers. So, leading resorts and hotels are attempting to customize the experience for guests to make individual customers feel unique and to make them believe that the hotel has singled them out for special attention.

In Colorado, Vail Resorts is always looking for ways to exceed expectations and drive loyalty. 'We have a programme called Epic Wishes,' says Ashley Lowe, Senior Manager of Communications. 'Staff are empowered to seek out guests who mention on social media that they're coming to visit, and we find a unique experience to offer them to enhance their Epic Vacation. Examples include providing birthday cake, giving rides in grooming cats to kids, and offering a woman who injured herself on her first day of skiing a free spa treatment and dinner' (Hudson and Hudson, 2015). Lowe acknowledges that these initiatives need to come from the top. She points to one General Manager, Jonathan Fillman, of Mountain Thunder Lodge in Breckenridge, who routinely writes hand written notes to his guests, and encourages his staff to as well. When a recent guest commented on TripAdvisor that it was his seventh stay at Mountain Thunder Lodge and he loved it, Jonathan sought him out, discovered he was still staying at the property, and asked him how he could make his stay better. 'The gentleman said he was going to hike a 14'er the next day and asked Jonathan if he knew how to get there. Jonathan replied, "Do I know how to get there? I'll take you there!" Jonathan picked the guest up at 4am the next morning and did the full hike with him.' The Digital Spotlight below focuses more on customer service at Vail Resorts.

At the Grand America in Salt Lake City, Director of Guest Experience Annie Fitzgerald says that creating loyalty starts with each individual employee. 'We ensure all employees are empowered to make each guest's stay exceptional and a personalized experience. If our employees learn something about our guests that will enhance their stay, we will recognize and deliver. For example, if we learn upon arrival that a couple is celebrating an anniversary, we will deliver a cake and card wishing them a Happy Anniversary, likewise with honeymoon couples who receive chocolate covered strawberries and a card. We recognize birthdays and we love taking care of guests who bring their children. We often provide balloons or small welcome toys for the little ones.' The Grand America also has a 'Grand Ambassador' whose role is to ensure that all repeat guests are recognized appropriately. 'Our operating system will track all of our guest preferences, and our Ambassador then reviews all reservations and prepares for these requests,' says Fitzgerald. Requests can range from a preference for a special room or view, to the type of linens a guest requires to be comfortable. 'All of these things make the Grand America truly a home away from home and ensure the retention of our guests.'

Just along the road, at the Stein Eriksen Lodge, Deer Valley, the staff uses every bit of personal information they can as an opportunity to create a memorable experience for guests. 'Every guest receives a personal escort to their room,' says Hotel Manager, Dan Bullert. 'And this enables the staff to develop a personal contact with the guest and possibly obtain information for which the hotel can then take the experience a step further. For instance, a guest made reference to their favourite TV show, *Downton Abbey*; the team then felt inclined to put together a nice card in reference to the show along with the times and where to find it on the channel lineup. Along with the card was a chips/salsa amenity to enjoy while watching the show' (Hudson and Hudson, 2015).

DIGITAL SPOTLIGHT: VAIL RESORTS, TOP OF THEIR GAME

In the old days of communicating customer service, something so insignificant as a ski-lift pass would not really have provided managers with much opportunity. It used to be a scrap of paper, attached to a jacket with a metal or plastic clip, flapping in the wind

and getting caught on tree branches and other obstacles, but needing to be visible to lift attendants. However, with modern 'smart card' technology, ski resorts all over the world now use lift passes for all manner of conveniences, including automatic access to ski lifts (keeping the pass inside a pocket) and doubling it up as a resort credit card.

IMAGE 10.3 EpicMix Photo (Courtesy of Vail Resorts).

An early adopter in the US was Vail Resorts, which has continued to investigate every nuance of smart card technology. 'One of our biggest developments for the 2014–15 ski season was the introduction of Express Ticketing,' says Robert Urwiler, Chief Information Officer for Vail Resorts. 'Express Ticketing gives our guests the ability to buy tickets on their mobile device right up to the minute that they need them. If they already have ticket media, the product is loaded automatically. If not, we have express lanes set up at ticket windows where guests can quickly pick up their media by simply showing the confirmation bar code on their mobile phone.' Benefits are two-fold. Firstly, it helps optimize ticket window lines by giving people the means to move themselves through the process very quickly. And, secondly, it provides more complete customer information than a resort might get through a traditional ticket window transaction. 'In addition to Express Ticketing and other technology feature introductions and improvements across the resorts, we continue to make advancements in the sophistication and use of our CRM and Predictive Analytics capabilities,' Urwiler adds. 'The objective of these efforts is to drive more focused and targeted guest interaction across communication channels. We are constantly looking for better ways to engage our past, current and future customers with targeted and relevant messages delivered at the appropriate time and place. Ultimately, this helps drive business.'

The radio frequency-enabled EpicMix card is a hands-free season or day pass which can also be linked with a credit card for spending on-mountain or around the resort. The hard card media can be used year after year, rather than necessitating replacements every season. Furthermore, all hard card media can be linked to the free EpicMix ski app, enabling the user to capture on-mountain activity and share it directly from the app on Facebook and Twitter. EpicMix allows guests to track their vertical feet, days skied, competitive pins earned, Leaderboard status, photos taken by professional on-mountain photographers, race medals earned and even track progress in Ski and Snowboard School. Going a step further, EpicMix introduced two revolutionary brands during the 2014/2015 season – EpicMix Guide and EpicMix Challenges. EpicMix Guide provides customized run itineraries for guests based on location, ability level and desired duration while EpicMix Challenges allows guests to compete against themselves, friends and the community.

Epicmixers can share accomplishments individually or chose to share a compilation of their day's achievements directly to social media from the free EpicMix iOS or Android app. The strategy behind all this has several advantages. 'Overall, our business objective for EpicMix is to create an unobtrusive digital companion to our guests' skiing and riding experience with a focus on recording their on-mountain experiences,' says Urwiler. 'This gives our guests the ability to relive their experiences digitally and to share those experiences socially. This, in essence, helps to create hundreds of thousands of brand advocates for Vail Resorts on social media while also helping to drive our CRM efforts through a better understanding of guest behaviour.'

Since the launch of EpicMix in 2010/11, the innovative idea captured the attention of prominent travel and ski journalists resulting in many articles in magazines and newspapers including the prestigious travel section of the *Los Angeles Times* (written, incidentally, by your author, Louise Hudson), *Skiing* magazine and Denver's *Huffington Post*. Furthermore, the app has secured Vail Resorts coverage in more unusual outlets for a ski company such as *Mashable*, *CNET*, *Wired*, *Popular Mechanics*, *FastCompany*, and other tech-focused publications. Stacey Pool, Sr. Director, Digital Experience for Vail Resorts, says that by far the most successful generation of EpicMix has been EpicMix Photo, which resonates with every guest, both destination and local. 'We're always watching the different social platforms where our guests seem to be engaging and trying to figure out a way for those guests to share EpicMix content in those platforms,' she adds. Understanding the demographic, target market and appropriate content is crucial to the company's social media strategy. 'We want the content to speak to our guest and inspire them to take action, whether that's engaging with us on these social platforms, sharing our content with others, or clicking through into our sites,' says Pool. The predominant focus in 2015 was on Twitter, Facebook and Instagram. 'As the different platforms evolve, and there starts to be real-time streaming within some of the new social platforms, we want to adapt our strategy to fill in any possible gaps along the customer journey,' she explains.

Vail Resorts is recognized worldwide as a pioneer in the field of social media marketing, combining indirect marketing with customer service and added value. Ski resorts have traditionally charged for photographic services on the hill and usually don't provide any action shots. Vail Resorts saw the value in advertising spin-offs of providing photos for free in order to encourage skiers and snowboarders to send out more professional-looking tweets and Facebook photos of themselves. Vail was also the first ski hill to use its lift pass system as an app. The company has created its own resort blogs about EpicMix with information as well as testimonials from consumers. 'As a company we are very fortunate to have a tech-savvy CEO who has a real passion

(Continued)

(Continued)

for leveraging technology to facilitate a better guest experience while driving our business,' Urwiler concludes.

Sources: Personal visits by the authors to Vail, Breckenridge, Park City, Beaver Creek and Keystone. Interviews with Robert Urwiler and Stacy Pool, April 2015.

CASE STUDY QUESTIONS

1. For the customer, what are the advantages of having the EpicMix app?

2. What about for Vail Resorts?

3. Think of three more ways the EpicMix app could be improved to increase customer satisfaction.

MANAGING SERVICES PROMISES

A major cause of poorly perceived service is the difference between what a firm promises about a service, and what it actually delivers. To avoid broken promises, companies must manage all communications to customers, so that inflated promises do not lead to overly high expectations. This difference between what is promised and what is delivered can cause customer frustration, perhaps driving the customer to the competition. As Jim Knight, Senior Director of Training for Hard Rock International, says: 'The worst mistake a business can make is to over-promise and under-deliver.' Zeithaml et al. (2007) suggest that there are four strategies that are effective in managing service promises (see Figure 10.4).

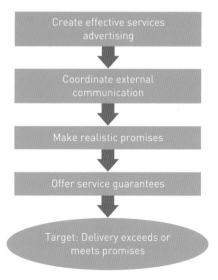

FIGURE 10.4 Four strategies that are effective in managing service promises (©McGraw-Hill Education. Reprinted with permission from Zeithaml et al., 2007)

How to create effective advertising is discussed in Chapter 8, and a challenging aspect of managing brand image is the unification of all marketing communications tools, as well as corporate and brand messages, so they send a consistent, persuasive message to target audiences. When Westin Hotels partnered with New Balance to lend fitness gear to guests, they used a variety of communication materials to promote the new service. The campaign, run by the New York office of Bartle Bogle Hegarty, included print ads, billboards and in-hotel marketing materials on key cards and on mirrors in guest rooms. A commercial was also shown online, on seat back video screens on Delta airplanes and in about 10,000 elevators in office buildings through the Captivate Network, a Gannett company. The ads were introduced in travel trade journals such as *Meetings and Conventions* and *Successful Meetings*, and they also appeared in many publications including *The Wall Street Journal*, *The New York Times* and *Runner's World*.

The Internet is increasingly used by hospitality marketers to set expectations. British luxury travel company Scott Dunn, for example, has an attractive website that promises to craft something special for each customer. This type of one-on-one service has led to more than 70 per cent repeat business through loyalty and referral. 'If you're part of the DNA of the company, you understand the importance of the guest,' says founder Andrew Dunn. 'What makes us different is that nothing is too much trouble. We've always undersold and over-delivered and provided you do that, you manage people's expectations and they wax lyrical as you exceed their expectations. It's then all about having the right people working with you' (Hudson and Hudson, 2015).

Companies must also make realistic promises. To be appropriate and effective, marketing communications about customer service must accurately reflect what customers will actually receive in service encounters. Customer expectations can be influenced by explicit and implicit promises from the service provider, and if expectations are not met then customers will become frustrated and are likely to complain. Research shows that the best way a company can stand out and exceed consumer expectations for customer service is simply 'deliver promised value at the right price' (AMEX, 2014). Figure 10.5 indicates the best ways a company can stand out and exceed customer expectations. Consumers are also looking for ease in doing business – both online and off. They want personalized service (as mentioned above), and products/services that meet their individual needs.

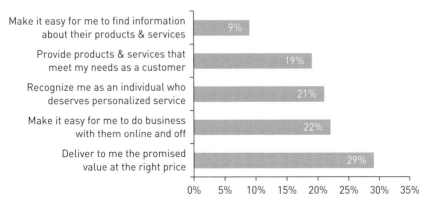

FIGURE 10.5 How to stand out and exceed customer expectations (©American Express Company. Used with permission)

Making realistic promises means there needs to be effective internal communication in an organization. Managers must pay significant attention to the communication of marketing strategies and objectives to employees, so that they understand their own role and importance in the implementation of the strategies and in the achievement of the objectives. Because service advertising promises what people *do*, frequent and effective communication across functions – horizontal communication – is critical. If internal communication is poor, perceived service quality is at risk. If company advertising and other promises are developed without input from operations, contact personnel may not be able to deliver service that matches the image portrayed in marketing efforts.

Communication mechanisms may come in the form of company meetings, training sessions, newsletters, emails, annual reports, or videotapes. Fairmont Hotels & Resorts distributes a bi-monthly newsletter in each hotel as well as a company-wide newsletter to keep staff up to date on new company procedures. Southwest Airlines created a 'Culture Committee' whose responsibility is to perpetuate the Southwest spirit. Committee members promote the company's unique, caring culture to fellow employees and they can appear anywhere, at any time, to lend a helping hand. Southwest also has a blog called 'Nuts about Southwest' which addresses employees' concerns, relays information about changes in the company, and tries to boost employee moral.

Finally, a growing number of organizations are offering customers a service guarantee, promising that if service delivery fails to meet predefined standards, the customer will be entitled to one or more forms of compensation, such as an easy-to-claim replacement, a refund or a credit. They are finding that effective service guarantees can complement the company's service recovery strategy. One of the reasons for having a service guarantee is to build marketing muscle, and research has shown that providing a service guarantee in advertising materials significantly enhances consumers' intentions to buy. Research has also found that a service guarantee has a positive, long-term effect on both employee motivation and customer intention to return (Hart, 1990), although there are suggestions that organizations need to make better use of the information and knowledge gained from invocations of a service guarantee. From the customer's perspective, the primary function of service guarantees is to lower the perceived risks associated with purchase.

SERVICE RECOVERY

Service delivery failure is likely to occur at some point in time for many organizations specializing in hospitality, tourism or events. Though it is unlikely that businesses can eliminate all service failures, they can learn to respond effectively to failures once they do occur. This response is often referred to as service recovery, defined as the process by which a company attempts to rectify a service delivery failure. One study of hotel customers found that their level of satisfaction and their lasting impression of a hotel are based first and foremost on what happens when something goes wrong (Johnston, 2004). Mostly, customers accept that mistakes happen; the problem begins when there is no strategy in place to rectify the situation easily.

Despite the significance of the tourism sector both economically and as a source of customer complaints, there has been little research that explicitly addresses complaining behaviour and service recovery. Research that does exist is relatively recent and still evolving. In the hospitality industry, Lewis and McCann (2004) focused on service failure and recovery in the UK hotel industry, finding that guests who were satisfied with the hotel's response to their problems were much more likely to return than those who were not satisfied with recovery efforts. Leong, Kim and Ham (2002) studied the impact of critical incidents of service failures and recovery efforts in a hotel, finding that only complete resolution results in repeat patronage, while partial resolution and unresolved service failures served as a deterrent to the guest's return patronage. O'Neill and Mattila (2004) presented findings from a survey of 613 hotel guests indicating that guests' overall satisfaction and intention to revisit were much higher when they believed that service failure was unstable and recovery was stable. Finally, the influence of service recovery on satisfaction and revisit intention was also stressed by the study of Yavas et al. (2003).

In the restaurant sector, Hoffman, Kelley and Rotalsky (1995) examined service failures and recovery strategies commonly occurring in the industry, and Leong and Kim (2002) focused on recovery efforts in fast-food restaurants, finding that reasonable care in providing a service failure resolution that meets the customer's expectation may influence customer loyalty. Lastly, Sundaram, Jurowski and Webster (1997) investigated the impacts of four types of service failure recovery efforts in restaurant service consumption situations that differ in the degree of criticality. They argued that the importance of the situation to the consumer plays a significant role in their responses to service failure recovery efforts.

In a study of American customers, AMEX (2014) found that more than nine in ten consumers talk about their good customer service experiences, at least some of the time (93%), while 46 per cent tell someone about them all of the time. When it comes to poor customer service experiences, nearly all (95%) consumers talk about them, with 60 per cent reporting that they talk about these experiences all of the time. AMEX found that on average, consumers tell eight people about their good experiences, and over twice as many people about their bad experiences. Social media is also becoming a more common channel for consumers seeking a customer service response, with one in five (23%) consumers saying they have utilized social media to get a customer service response, a significant increase from 17 per cent in 2012.

THE SERVICE RECOVERY PARADOX

Some researchers have suggested that customers who are dissatisfied, but experience a high level of excellent service recovery may ultimately be even more satisfied and more likely to repurchase than those who were satisfied in the first place (Hart, Heskett and Sasser, 1990; McCollough, Berry and Yadav, 2000). This idea has become known as the service recovery paradox (see Figure 10.6). There are somewhat mixed opinions on whether a recovery paradox exists, but customer complaints about defective services may represent an opportunity for the company to improve its image and perceived quality since it permits the company to make a positive correction or to resolve the complaint (Albrecht and Zemke, 1985; Grönroos, 1990; Heskett, Sasser and Hart, 1990).

McCollough, Berry and Yadav (2000) tested the service recovery paradox for airline passengers, finding that customer satisfaction was lower after service failure and recovery than in the case of error-free service. Hudson and Moreno-Gil (2006),

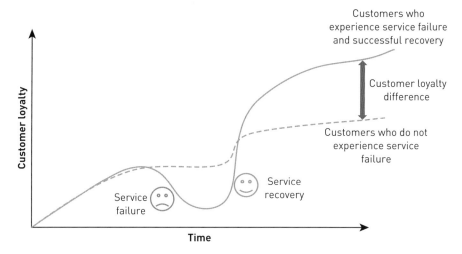

FIGURE 10.6 The service recovery paradox (Source: Adapted from Schindlholzer, 2008)

however, found that hotel customers in Spain who had experienced a recovery encounter, perceived a higher level of service quality for intangible attributes (assurance, trust, reliability, responsiveness and empathy) than noncomplaining customers – supporting, to some extent, the service recovery paradox. The results showed that resolving customer problems related to intangible aspects of the service in a hotel has a strong impact on perceived service quality and thus customer satisfaction. Sousa and Voss (2009) studied service recovery in an e-commerce setting and also found a recovery paradox effect but only for a small proportion of 'delighted' customers: those who perceived an outstanding recovery. They concluded that despite not being a viable strategy in general, delighting customers in the recovery might make sense for profitable customers.

But given the mixed opinions on the extent to which the recovery paradox exists, 'doing it right the first time' is still the best and safest strategy in the long run.

THE SERVICE RECOVERY PROCESS

Every tourism and hospitality organization should have a systematic plan for winning back customers who have been disappointed by some facet of service delivery. One such plan – a five-step procedure – was proposed by Zemke and Schaaf (1989).

1. APOLOGY

The process of service recovery begins with an apology. As Isadore Sharp from the Four Seasons says: 'Whatever the issue, making it right starts with a sincere apology' (Sharp, 2009: 232). Once an organization accepts that failure sometimes occurs, it can instil in its employees the necessity of extending a genuine apology when a customer is disappointed. This simple act can go a long way to framing the customer's perception of his value to the organization and helps pave the path for subsequent steps to regain goodwill (Fisk, Grove and John, 2000). One restaurant study found that recovery strategies that included personal service interaction with customers were more successful than strategies that included monetary compensation (Silber et al., 2009). When contact employees treat customers with respect and courteousness during a service recovery, customers will report significantly higher satisfaction levels (Swanson and Hsu, 2009).

2. URGENT REINSTATEMENT

The next step is to do something to remove the source of customer disappointment. Urgent means the action is taken quickly; reinstatement means making an effort to correct the problem. If an organization is slow to address customer dissatisfaction or fails to present evidence that it is taking some action, the customer is likely to perceive that his or her problems are not important, and may well defect at this point. Customers who complain and have their problems resolved quickly are much more likely to repurchase than those whose complaints are not resolved. In fact, research by TARP (1986) showed that if complaints are resolved quickly, 82 per cent of customers will repurchase. However, if complaints are resolved, but not necessarily quickly, only 52 per cent of customers will return. Urgency is therefore the key, and employees must therefore be empowered to solve problems as they occur.

Sandy Best, former Director of Public Relations for Lake Louise in Canada, helped implement a new 'service with no boundaries' system for employees to deal with service issues. Staff were empowered to solve problems and also compensate for them: 'For example, if a washroom has no toilet paper, the staff solve the issue but if, as the customer, you are still really pissed off, the staff member offers you lunch in return. We train them to do that,' said Best. He found that employees feel good about their work when they are empowered in this way. The extra money spent was well worth the good PR that service recovery engenders. In the era of instant communication through all the far-reaching tentacles of social media, Best deemed it cheaper to solve a problem instantly than to let it escalate into something more serious by leaving it until a guest gets home. Despite initial concerns from 'the money people', Best said that the 'service with no boundaries' system worked well at Lake Louise. It was monitored weekly, he added, as a learning tool for management: 'If the bottom of the totem pole rots out, the management hit the ground hard and fast because they fall from higher up', he explained (Hudson and Hudson, 2015).

3. EMPATHY

Empathy means making the effort to understand why the customer was disappointed with the organization. If service employees can put themselves in the shoes of the customers, they may be able to grasp the disappointment felt by the customer, and successfully display that understanding. An important part of the service recovery process is not economic reimbursement, but empathy and responsiveness of employees (Liden and Skalen, 2003). The payoff of empathy is the customer's realization that the organization is in fact sensitive to the service failure. Tax and Brown (1998) have suggested that customers are looking for three specific types of justice following their complaints: outcome fairness, procedural fairness and interactional fairness. Outcome fairness concerns the results that customers receive from their complaints; procedural fairness refers to the policies, rules and timeliness of the complaint process;

and interactional fairness focuses on the interpersonal treatment received during the complaint process.

4. SYMBOLIC ATONEMENT

The next step in the recovery process is to make amends in some tangible way for the organization's failure, and this may take the form of a room upgrade, a free dessert, or a ticket for a future flight. This step is called symbolic atonement because the gesture is designed not to replace the service, but to communicate to the customer that the organization takes responsibility for the disappointment caused and is willing to pay the price for its failure. At this point, it is important for service organizations to determine customers' thresholds of acceptability. In order to calculate how much compensation a firm should offer after service breakdown, Lovelock and Wirtz (2007) suggest that managers need to consider the positioning of the firm, the severity of the service failure, and who the affected customer is. But the overall rule of thumb for compensation for service failures should be 'well-dosed generosity'. In fact, Timm (2008) believes that companies should go beyond symbolic atonement and always go the extra mile in the eyes of the complaining customer.

Paul Hudson, Operations Director at Luxury Family Hotels, says his company's adage is 'Fix it, plus one'. 'Blow the customer away without costing too much money', he adds. However, Hudson believes that although empowerment is critical, employees have to work within a framework when making decisions on service recovery: 'It is no good throwing money at a problem without working out what the problem was in the first place and how to prevent it in future. It is also important to find out what the customer values in a service, and exactly what we can do to put a problem right. For example, it would be foolish to give a free night's accommodation for a whole family if just one meal was cold in the restaurant. And there is no point giving the customer a free bottle of wine if he/she doesn't drink. A free swimming lesson for the kids might be the perfect remedy, and it costs us very little' (Hudson and Hudson, 2013).

5. FOLLOW-UP

By following up to see if the gesture of symbolic atonement was well received, an organization can gauge how well it placated the customer's dissatisfaction. The follow-up can take many forms depending on the service type and recovery situation. Follow-up gives an organization a chance to evaluate the recovery plan and identify where improvements are necessary. A study of service recovery in the hotel sector found that many hotels did not follow up and were thus missing out on effective way of satisfying guests and informing themselves of the adequacy of their recovery strategies (Lewis and McCann, 2004). The final encounter in a service interaction is critical in determining overall satisfaction, so service providers should ensure that encounters end on a good note.

THE CONSEQUENCES OF AN EFFECTIVE RECOVERY PROCESS

Research has shown that resolving customer problems effectively has a strong impact on customer satisfaction, quality and bottom-line performance (Heskett, Sasser and Hart, 1990; Berry and Parasuraman, 1993; Kelley, Hoffman and Davis, 1993; Tax, Brown and Chandrashenkaran, 1998; Tax and Brown, 1998). An effective recovery will retain customer loyalty regardless of the type of failure. In one study, customer retention exceeded 70 per cent for those customers who perceived effective recovery efforts (Kelley et al., 1993). Retained customers are much more profitable than new ones because they purchase more and they purchase more frequently, while at the same time requiring lower operating costs. British Airways calculates that service recovery efforts return $2 for every dollar invested. In fact, the company finds that 'recovered' customers give the airline more of their business after they have been won back.

An effective recovery process may also lead to positive word of mouth, or at least diminish the negative word of mouth typically associated with poor recovery efforts. One study reported that customers who experienced a service failure told nine or ten individuals about their poor service experience, whereas satisfied customers told only four or five individuals about their satisfactory experience (Collier, 1995). In fact, research by US firm TARP back in 1979 shows that for every 26 unhappy business to business customers, only one will lodge a formal complaint with management. Instead, on average, each unhappy customer will tell ten people, who in turn will tell five others. Therefore, an average of 1300 people will hear about at least one of these unhappy customers' experiences. This 'Customer Complaint Iceberg' is illustrated in Figure 10.7. Furthermore, repeated service failures can aggravate employees. The cost in employee morale is an often overlooked cost of not having an effective service recovery programme.

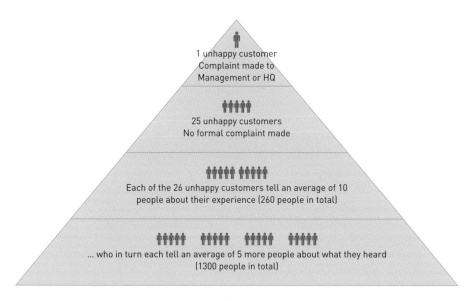

FIGURE 10.7 The Customer Complaint Iceberg (Source: Adapted from TARP, 1979).

The service recovery process can be used to improve the overall quality of service delivery as the service occurs. This is possible if the customer provides feedback during the service experience, which allows the organization to refine its service process. Keeping track of sources of dissatisfaction that create a need for recovery can also help the organization. Careful collection and storage of information regarding the incidents may produce a rich database of information on service quality. In analysing this data, patterns may emerge that specify particularly troublesome aspects of an organization's service delivery system.

CHAPTER SUMMARY

Customer service is the practice of delivering products and services to both internal and external customers via the efforts of employees, and the logic connecting employee satisfaction to customer satisfaction and loyalty (and ultimately profits) is illustrated by the service profit chain. In order to provide top-notch customer service, tourism and hospitality providers need to establish a strong service culture and this requires a strong commitment from management. To avoid broken promises, companies must manage all communications to customers, so that inflated promises do not lead to overly high expectations. Companies also need to recognize the significance of service recovery – responding effectively to failures once they do occur.

REFLECTIVE QUESTIONS

1. Think of a company you are loyal to the extent that you have become an apostle for them. Explain why you are so loyal.

2. Think of a company you know that does not have a strong service culture. Why not? How can they create one?

3. Think of a problem you have experienced recently. After complaining, did the service provider follow the five-step procedure outlined in the text? If not, what steps were missing?

MARKETING IN ACTION: HIGH-PROFILE SPORTING EVENTS IN BRITAIN

High-profile sporting events are becoming increasingly important for Britain's economy, according to an article in the *Daily Telegraph* in May 2015. Sport supports over 450,000 jobs and has become a $29 billion industry there. Top sports events include the Rugby World Cup, Premier League football tournaments, golf championships, lucrative cycling events (such as the Tour de France which kicked off in Yorkshire in 2014) and, of course, the 2012 London Olympics – all of which cast a global spotlight on Britain's sporting and tourism attractions.

In order for these events to have a lasting legacy for tourism growth, customer service is of prime importance. This was exemplified during the preparations for the London Olympics when the People 1st Training Company was given the mandate to bring UK service standards up to scratch. With a traditional reputation for sloppy, rude and slow service in a country where complaining is 'not the done thing', they had their job cut out for them. Research from YouGov in 2010 showed that 73 per cent of the general public in Britain agreed that the country needed to improve customer service ahead of the Olympics, especially with around half a million daily spectators expected from 205 countries. The UK also had to overcome bad publicity generated by the 2011 riots, security worries, and years of economic depression and high costs which had undermined its perceived value for money in the eyes of tourists. Traditionally, service in Britain was considered a second-class occupation, a stop gap or student job and not a career move. This had led to a weak service training culture with reluctant body language, poor eye contact and grudging service delivery proliferating throughout tourism, hospitality, events, and retail.

IMAGE 10.4 Fireworks at the Olympic Stadium in London (Reproduced with permission of Visit Britain)

Planning for the 2012 Summer Olympic Games in London had two main thrusts: (1) infrastructure and (2) people power. Once the redevelopment of venues in various areas of London was set in motion, it was the issue of peopling the Games that was paramount for planners. LOCOG – the London Organizing Committee of the Olympic Games and Paralympic Games – was set up to organize the 17-day event which, if leveraged correctly, could boost England's ailing tourism industry and prompt positive economic impacts for years to come. One of the initiatives set up in advance of the Games was Blue Badge tourist guides, responsible for spreading the word about the Olympics during daily public walking tours around the 2012 site. In 2010 they guided 220 school and college trips and over 1,000 new visitors and tourists per day during the summer. As well as transportation improvements to trains and underground systems, a public waterbus was also planned for the area for 2011 and a flagship bike-hire scheme inaugurated with thousands of bikes available. But the main mandate was to infuse the frontline service providers with a new, top-notch customer service culture.

To train the 70,000-strong cohort of volunteers (dubbed Games Makers by LOCOG), People 1st looked to a Canadian company for help. With customer service training programmes honed during the Vancouver Games, British Columbia's WorldHost™ provided an ideal toolkit for the UK. People 1st adapted the programme for the UK market, supported by leading employers such as McDonald's in sponsorship collaboration. The customized programme included modules on serving customers with disabilities, service across cultures and an ambassador workshop for volunteers assisting overseas visitors.

Through the five-year, renewable licence with WorldHost™, People 1st also intended the training programme to be a lasting legacy of the Games, with 2,000 people living in the vicinity of the main Olympic park gaining hospitality skills transferable

(Continued)

(Continued)

to future careers. In a press release, Brian Wisdom, chief executive of People 1st, said: 'We are also campaigning to train 200,000 frontline staff ahead of the Olympics throughout the wider visitor economy, so that we can effect a cultural change in the perception of the warmth of the UK welcome, which currently lags far behind other countries. It's essential we improve on this if we are to reap the long-term benefits of a successful Games.' Almost a million people worldwide have been trained using WorldHost™ – including 40,000 volunteers and tourism staff who helped make the Vancouver Winter Olympics in 2010 such a success.

The WorldHost™ UK website painted the Games as a chance for the British to impress: 'This presents a unique opportunity for hospitality, tourism, leisure and retail businesses to showcase the best of Britain and increase their sales by providing a warm welcome and impeccable service to visitors to the UK.' WorldHost™ Manager, Yahvel Velazquez said that their training workshops encouraged frontline professionals to go beyond service with a smile: 'It's not just about being nice and friendly... some situations require more tact and very strong listening and communication skills and those are the skills taught and developed by our service professionals.' Intrinsic to WorldHost™'s programme was the message that service providers were a key part in the overall visitor experience. 'They are part of a long chain of interaction that visitors will experience during their stay and if we can collectively deliver good service, individuals will go away with a positive experience,' Velazquez explained. He ascribed the effectiveness of the workshops to the holistic manner in which customer service is viewed: 'We encourage people to believe themselves to be part of a greater mandate, to believe it is something not to be undervalued or underestimated.' This motivation, he said, helped them overcome the often draining and exhausting nature of their daily workload.

A sturdy customer service culture can seriously impact a country's brand strength, affecting goodwill towards the country and boosting its tourism, business and immigration. There are various factors which help create a strong country brand, ranging from tourism, heritage and culture, business, quality of life and value systems. Having a successful Olympics – which is in effect a showcase to the world – can alter or reinforce elements about a nation that people continue to associate it with for years after the event. Positive attributes for the UK's street cred already included music, nightlife, sport, fashion, film, literature, celebrity culture, heritage and, of course, the Royal Family. Recognizing this, VisitBritain came up with an etiquette guide for interactions with visiting foreigners. Called 'Delivering a First Class Welcome', it was based on input from those nationalities featured. It included all the cultural no-no's from mistaking Canadians for Americans to pouring wine incorrectly for Argentinians.

Boris Johnson, London's charismatic mayor at the time, also took on the job of improving London's customer service standards. In the July 2011 issue of *Traveller*, he stressed the importance of a 'warm welcome' for all visitors. He announced the recruitment of 8,000 London Ambassadors from diverse cultural backgrounds, to help out at airports, stations and other key visitor spots. The Queen's Diamond Jubilee in June 2012 was planned as a precursor to the Games, stressing Britain's biggest brand differential – royal pageantry.

Sources: Hudson and Hudson (2013).

CASE STUDY QUESTIONS

1. Why is it important for high-profile events to offer good customer service to attendees?

2. What are the three things that impress you most about the WorldHost programme?

3. Thinks of an event that you have been to recently. Did you experience excellent customer service? Why or why not?

REFERENCES

Albrecht, K. and Zemke, R. (1985) *Service America*. Homewood: Dow Jones-Irwin.

AMEX (2011) 'AMEX Global Service Barometer 2011 Press Release', 1 September. www.thetrainingbank.com (accessed 10 December 2016).

AMEX (2014) *AMEX Global Service Barometer 2014*. http://about.americanexpress.com/news/docs/2014x/2014-global-customer-service-barometer-us.pdf (accessed 10 December 2016).

Berry, L. and Parasuraman, A. (1993) *Marketing de los servicios: La calidad como meta*. Paramón ediciones, S.A. Madrid.

Collier, D. A. (1995) 'Modeling the relationships between process quality errors and overall service process performance', *Journal of Service Industry Management*, 64(4): 4–19.

Dragan, M. (2015) 'The magic formulas: Customer lifetime value and customer acquisition cost', *Sailthru*, 25 September. www.sailthru.com/marketing-blog/written-the-magic-formulas-customer-lifetime-value-and-customer-acquisition-cost (accessed 10 December 2016).

Fisk, R. P., Grove, S. J. and John, J. (2000) *Interactive Services Marketing*. Boston: Houghton Mifflin Company.

Ford, R. C. and Heaton, C. P. (2001) 'Lessons from hospitality that can serve anyone', *Organizational Dynamics*, 30(1): 30–47.

Getz, D. (2007) *Event Studies. Theory, Research and Policy for Planned Events*. Oxford: Butterworth-Heinemann.

Grönroos, C. (1990) *Service Management and Marketing*. Lexington, Mass: Lexington Books.

Hanlon, C. and Stewart, B. (2006) 'Managing personnel in major sport event organizations: What strategies are required?' *Event Management*, 10(1): 77–88.

Hart, C. W. L. (1990) 'The power of unconditional service guarantees', *Harvard Business Review*, 68: 54–62.

Hart, C. W. L., Heskett, J. L. and Sasser, Jr., W. E. (1990) 'The profitable art of service recovery', *Harvard Business Review*, 68(4): 148–56.

Heskett, J., Sasser, W. and Hart, C. (1990) *Service Breakthroughs: Changing the Rules of the Game*. New York: The Free Press.

Heskett, J. L., Sasser, W. E., Jr. and Schlesinger, L. A. (1997) *The Service Profit Chain: How Leading Companies Link Profit and Growth to Loyalty, Satisfaction, and Value.* New York: Free Press.

Hoffman, K. D., Kelley, S. W. and Rotalsky, H. M. (1995) 'Tracking service failures and employee recovery efforts', *Journal of Services Marketing*, 9(2): 49–61.

Hudson, S. and Hudson, L.J. (2013) *Customer Service for Hospitality & Tourism.* Oxford: Goodfellow Publishers Ltd.

Hudson, S. and Hudson, L.J. (2015) *Winter Sport Tourism: Working in Winter Wonderlands.* Oxford: Goodfellow Publishers Ltd.

Hudson, S. and Moreno-Gil, S. (2006) 'The influence of service recovery and loyalty on perceived service quality: A study of hotel customers in Spain', *Journal of Hospitality and Leisure Marketing*, 14(2): 45–66.

Johnston, R. (2004) 'Towards a better understanding of service excellence', *Managing Service Quality*, 14(2/3): 129–33.

Jones, T. O. and Sasser, W. E. (1995) 'Why satisfied customers defect', *Harvard Business Review*, 73 (November–December): 88–99.

Kelley, S. W., Hoffman, K. D. and Davis, M. A. (1993) 'A typology of retail failures and recoveries', *Journal of Retailing*, 69(4): 429–52.

Leong, J. K. and Kim, W. G. (2002) 'Service recovery efforts in fast food restaurants to enhance repeat patronage', *Journal of Travel and Tourism Marketing*, 12(2/3): 65–93.

Leong, J. K., Kim, W. G. and Ham, S. (2002) 'The effects of service recovery on repeat patronage', *Journal of Quality Assurance in Hospitality & Tourism*, 3(1/2): 69–94.

Lewis, B. R. and McCann, P. (2004) 'Service failure and recovery: Evidence from the hotel industry', *International Journal of Contemporary Hospitality Management*, 16(1): 6–17.

Liden, S. B. and Skalen, P. (2003) 'The effect of service guarantees on service recovery', *International Journal of Service Industry Management*, 14(1): 36–58.

Lovelock, C. and Wirtz, J. (2007) *Services Marketing: People, Technology, Strategy*, 6th edn. New Jersey, USA: Prentice Hall International.

Lucas, R. W. (2009) *Customer Service. Skills for Success.* Boston: McGraw Hill.

McCollough, M. A., Berry, L. L. and Yadav, M. S. (2000) 'An empirical investigation of customer satisfaction after service failure and recovery', *Journal of Service Research*, 3(2): 121–37.

MDB (2009) *UK Corporate Hospitality Market Research Report*, February, Market & Business Development, Manchester.

Miller, R. (2011) 'Customer focus in a slow economy', *Customer Service Excellence*, October, 16–17.

Mount, I. (2014) 'A whole town in Colorado pushes to improve its customer service', *New York Times*, 15 October. www.nytimes.com/2014/10/16/business/smallbusiness/a-whole-town-tries-to-improve-its-customer-service-how-could-we-be-a-70.html?_r=0 (accessed 10 December 2016).

Nehring, C. (2015) 'In defence of the notoriously arrogant waiter', *The Wall Street Journal*, 21–2 February: D1 & D8.

O'Neill, J.W. and Mattila, A.S. (2004) 'Towards the development of a lodging service recovery strategy', *Journal of Hospitality & Leisure Marketing*, 11(1): 51–64.

Reichheld, F. F. and Sasser, W. S., Jr. (1990) 'Zero defections: Quality comes to services', *Harvard Business Review,* 68: 105–11.

Sharp, I. (2009) *Four Seasons: The Story of a Business Philosophy.* New York: The Penguin Group.

Silber, I., Israeli, A., Bustin, A. and Zvi, O.B. (2009) 'Recovery strategies for service failures: The case of restaurants', *Journal of Hospitality Marketing and Management,* 18: 730–40.

Snowsports Industries America (2012) 'Revisiting growing the snowsports industry'. http://issuu.com/siasnowsports/docs/growing_the_industry_2011_revisited (accessed 10 December 2016).

Sousa, R. and Voss, C.A. (2009) 'The effects of service failures and recovery on customer loyalty in e-services', *International Journals of Operations & Product Management,* 29(8): 834–64.

Starmer-Smith, C. (2016) 'Our winners all know how to keep the customer satisfied', *Daily Telegraph,* 16 April: 16–20.

STELLA Service (2010) 'The value of great customer service: The economic impact for online retail and other consumer categories'. http://media.stellaservice.com/public/pdf/Value_of_Great_Customer_Service.pdf (accessed 10 December 2016).

Sundaram, D. S., Jurowski, C. and Webster, C. (1997) 'Service failure recovery efforts in restaurant dining: The role of criticality of service consumption', *Hospitality Research Journal,* 20(3): 137–49.

Swanson, S. R. and Hsu, M. K. (2009) 'Critical incidents in tourism: Failure, recovery, customer switching, and word-of-mouth behaviors', *Journal of Travel and Tourism Marketing,* 26: 180–94.

Tax, S. S. and Brown, S. W. (1998) 'Recovering and learning from service failure', *Sloan Management Review,* 40(1): 75–80.

Tax, S. S., Brown, S. W. and Chandrashenkaran, M. (1998) 'Consumer evaluation of service complaint experiences: Implications for relationship marketing', *Journal of Marketing,* 62(2): 60–76.

Technical Assistance Research Program (TARP) (1986) *Consumer Complaint Handling in America: An Update Study.* Washington, DC: White House Office of Consumer Affairs.

Technical Assistance Research Program (TARP) (1979) *Consumer Complaint Handling in America: A Final Report.* Washington, DC: White House Office of Consumer Affairs.

Timm, P. R. (2008) *Customer Service. Career Success through Customer Loyalty.* Upper Saddle River, NJ: Pearson Prentice Hall.

Wen, W. (2016) 'A successful coffee tale from a true believer', *China Daily,* 29 January: 15.

Yavas, U., Karatepe, O. M., Babakus, E. and Avci, T. (2003) 'Customer complaints and organizational responses: A study of hotel guests in Northern Cyprus', *Journal of Hospitality and Leisure Marketing,* 11(1–2): 31–40.

Zeithaml, V. A., Bitner, M. J., Gremler, D., Mahaffey, T. and Hiltz, B. (2007) *Services Marketing: Integrating Customer Focus Across the Firm.* Canadian Edition, New York: McGraw-Hill.

Zemke, R. and Schaaf, D. (1989) *The Service Edge.* New York: Plume.

MARKETING RESEARCH 11

INTRODUCTION

Chapter 11 focuses on marketing research and begins with an introduction to marketing research, its definition and its role in the tourism and hospitality industry. A description of the type of applied research conducted in tourism is followed by an analysis of the various stages in the research process. A section then describes the different methodologies available to researchers and discusses the relative merits of primary versus secondary research. The next part of the chapter looks at sampling, and five common research problems are then highlighted. Case studies focus on marketing research in a chain of luxury family hotels in Portugal, marketing to Millennials, and how the open kitchen concept has spread to hotels.

LESSONS FROM A MARKETING GURU: CHITRA STERN, MARTINHAL, PORTUGAL

How does an engineer turned chartered accountant become the marketing maven for a chain of luxury family hotels and resorts? 'My experience related to tourism really started when both my husband, Roman, and I were involved in a small hotel in West Cork – a 25-room boutique hotel called Liss Ard, set in 160 acres of beautiful West Cork landscape,' says Chitra Stern. 'I developed my knowledge about the tourism industry in West Cork and Ireland through research, case studies and understanding how things worked within the hotel industry.'

IMAGE 11.1 Chitra Stern, Martinhal (Courtesy of Chitra Stern, Martinhal)

Stern – whose family originates from Chennai, India and then Singapore – was educated at University College London where she got her engineering degree, followed by London Business School for her MBA. She also qualified as a chartered accountant with Price Waterhouse in London. 'Entrepreneurship, leadership, marketing and strategy are the cornerstones of what makes me tick in business life,' she says. 'Even during my MBA, I specialized in my second year with course electives like marketing, strategy, branding and entrepreneurship-related electives.'

The enterprising couple now owns the Martinhal chain, dubbed 'Europe's Finest Luxury Family Hotels and Resorts', extending across Portugal's Algarve and in and around the Portuguese capital, Lisbon. The Ireland experience was a 'good kick-start' when it came to developing Martinhal in 2001, says Stern: 'Over the years, we had to develop this knowledge firsthand, through market research, talking to consultants, reading feasibility studies, working with tourism authorities and associations, looking at other hotels in the area and so on. Between 2009 and 2016, I have spent a lot of time developing our marketing strategy, developing the various marketing and sales channels, creating campaigns with our staff and marketing consultants in order to fill our resort.' She acknowledges that the best experience to be gained in business is when you have to do something yourself, when 'the buck stops here'.

Having found 'Europe's California', Stern and her husband developed the first Martinhal resort near the town of Sagres on the Western Algarve coast – and learnt to speak Portuguese. Although initial advice pointed to opening a three-star surf hotel, the couple decided to go for a five-star product to reflect the beautiful and privileged location. 'We also felt that we hadn't moved to Portugal to do something which was not at the upper end of the market. However, differentiation was going to be key,' Stern explains. Having started a family, she saw an opportunity in young professionals with children wanting something more sophisticated than Disneyland:

'Hence, we did further research on several brands like Club Med, Robinson Club, the Swiss ski resorts, as well as brands like Sheraton, Ritz Carlton, etc. to fine-tune what we wanted to do.'

Targeting families at the luxury end of the market, Martinhal provides everything that well-heeled parents might look for during their holiday in terms of childcare, kids' activities, food and facilities in a refined and artfully designed environment. Success in Sagres led to broadening the scope to Quinta da Lago (Martinhal Quinta Family Golf Resort) also in the Algarve region, Cascais near the cities of Lisbon and Estoril (Martinhal Lisbon Cascais Family Resort), and a hotel in the heart of Lisbon. Martinhal Lisbon Chiado Family Suites is the 'world's first city-center elegant family hotel', according to Stern's marketing messages. 'Our pajama club will be central to parents enjoying the sights, sounds, nightlife and great Lisbon restaurants,' she adds. This capital city venture has helped widen their target market beyond Europe.

But it wasn't always plain sailing. Stern says that although market research, in terms of statistics and information available for desk research, was relatively easy to find via tourism associations and foreign investment agencies, the Internet was not as prevalent and far-reaching back in 2001. Also, as the Sagres coastline was an undeveloped area, there was little tourism information on it, especially for 'a start-up with a disruptive idea'. Also, tour operators were the main source of bookings for the Algarve at the time – Expedia and the like had yet to be established there. And the area was originally monopolized by large developers and timeshare operators – such as Four Seasons Fairways, Quinta do Lago, Vale do Lobo, Vilamoura, Oceanico, Parque da Floresta – and large American brands such as Sheraton which commanded consider-able loyalty. 'While the Algarve was well-known – mainly in the British market – Sagres was still relatively unknown and this was the challenge,' Stern says. 'Tour operators were not keen to take on a new product in an unknown area with no critical mass of hotel products, 1.5 hours away from the airport.' This meant the couple had to work very hard and invest a lot of money in marketing both the hotel and the destination itself.

Over the years Stern has refined and fine-tuned her target market in a lengthy process, which has impacted product development, branding and positioning, mar-keting, sales, and delivery of the product including service, guest feedback, product refinement, and price refinement. 'Demographics are changing over half-generations with definitions such as Generation X, Generation Y and Millennials being defined in shorter and shorter times than before,' she says. 'Instant gratification is what people are looking for more and more.' This has led to her delineating exactly the right product and increasingly using word-of-mouth via social media platforms to disperse the message. 'The market research is forever ongoing – you need to keep in touch with the market especially in such dynamic times. You need to keep talking to and listening to your target,' she explains. The digital era is for her both a chal-lenge and an opportunity and she has developed a team of likeminded marketing professionals of various nationalities to keep track of social media traffic and pro-vide feedback. The marketing team also utilizes billboards (with the current tagline 'Eat, Stay, Love'), print ads, social media, FAM trips, and direct mail as well as joint ventures with compatible brands.

Sources: Personal Visit by the authors to Martinhal Sagres, Portugal in May 2016 and interview with Chitra Stern; www.martinhal.com.

MARKETING RESEARCH

The opening case study highlights the critical role that research plays in a business. As Chitra Stern of Martinhal suggests, research should form the basis of an ongoing system for gathering data about a company, its products, and its markets. Often managers, in the course of their everyday duties, gather intelligence informally and subconsciously by observing, listening to discussions, talking to colleagues in the industry, and reading trade journals and papers. Valuable as this process is, it should be supported by more formal procedures carried out in a systematic and scientific manner. The way in which an organization gathers, uses, and disseminates its research in the marketing context is generally referred to as the marketing information system (MIS). The success of an MIS depends on the quality of the information, its accuracy and relevance, and the way it is collected, interpreted, and applied. A key component of the MIS is the marketing research process.

Researchers and managers seldom address the definition of what constitutes marketing research. To complicate the issue further, the terms 'market research' and 'marketing research' are often used interchangeably, sometimes within the same document. Gerhold (1993) asserts that there is no difference between the two terms and that they can both be defined as 'any scientific effort to understand and measure markets or improve marketing performance'. Kinnear et al. (1993) distinguish between the two terms, arguing that the focus of market research is on the analysis of markets, whereas marketing research extends the role and character of research and emphasizes the contact between researchers and the marketing management process. This chapter adopts the term marketing research exclusively, defining it as the systematic and objective search for and analysis of information relevant to the identification and solution of any problem in the field of marketing (Green, Tull and Albaum, 1988).

According to Goeldner and Ritchie (2009), there are six reasons for conducting tourism and hospitality research:

(1) to identify, describe, and solve problems in order to increase the efficiencies of day-to-day tourism operations;

(2) to keep tourism and hospitality firms in touch with trends, changes, predictions, etc. related to their markets;

(3) to reduce the waste produced by tourists and tourist organizations;

(4) to develop new areas of profit by finding new products, services, markets, etc.;

(5) to help promote sales in situations where research findings are of interest to the public; and

(6) to develop goodwill, as the public thinks well of firms that are doing research in order to meet consumers' needs.

Unfortunately, in tourism and hospitality many smaller organizations feel that 'real' marketing research is a costly and time-consuming luxury only available to large companies that have professional research staff, sophisticated computers, and almost unlimited budgets. Other organizations see marketing research as something to be undertaken when a major event is about to occur – the introduction of a new product, the acquisition of a new property, or a change in target markets. Its value at these junctures is recognized, but its ability to contribute to an organization's success on a day-to-day basis is often overlooked.

Another common problem in the tourism industry is that organizations are not making full use of the information that already exists and is easily accessed. Disney was guilty of this when it developed the Paris theme park. When researchers tried to understand why tourists were not visiting during the summer of 1992, they discovered that due to the combination of transatlantic airfare wars and currency movements plus domestic economic recession, it was actually cheaper to go to Disney World in Orlando than an equivalent trip to Paris. Why would tourists flock to the new, smaller park when they could just as easily go to the home of Disney with all its other facilities plus guaranteed sunshine and beautiful beaches – and why did researchers not consider this?

As mentioned in Chapter 3, travel companies have access to mind-boggling data: everything from basic personal information to preferred airline seats, in-flight entertainment preferences, favoured television channels in hotels, meals in restaurants, and credit card usage. They have the means to paint detailed pictures of consumers that will drive marketing initiatives to engage them deeply (Carey, Kang and Zea, 2012). According to McKinsey, we are on the cusp of a new golden age for marketing, with marketing science boosting the precision of real-time operating decisions (Gordon and Perrey, 2015). Leading marketers are using research and analytics to shed light on who buys what, and why; and then, in the consumer decision journey, marketing efforts are likely to yield the greatest return. At major hotel companies, for example, marketing analysts are able to study the performance of a particular property over a weekend and then drill down on individual customer segments to access how to make improvements. If the data show that a profitable segment of weekend travellers are shortening their stays, the company can create special offers (such as late checkouts or upgrades) to encourage repeat business.

APPLIED RESEARCH IN TOURISM AND HOSPITALITY

Most marketing research is classified as applied research, which is undertaken to answer specific questions. It differs from pure research (done by scientists at universities or by government authorities), which is aimed at the discovery of new information. Applied research in tourism and hospitality can be grouped into eight categories: research on consumers; research on products and services; research on pricing; research on place and distribution; research on promotion; research on competition; research on the operating environment; and research on a destination. Table 11.1 lists some of the typical research programmes undertaken within these categories.

Consumer research is the first category in the table, and is of particular interest to those interested in the study of tourism and hospitality marketing. As the table suggests, there may be a number of objectives in carrying out consumer research, and one is to measure customer loyalty. Enterprise Rent-A-Car has found from research that 'completely satisfied' customers were three times more likely to rent with Enterprise than those who were 'somewhat satisfied', so it is important to gauge customer satisfaction on an ongoing basis (Hudson and Hudson, 2013). One common way of measuring customer loyalty is calculating a Net Promoter Score for consumers. Researchers ask one question: 'How likely are you to recommend this product or service to a friend

TABLE 11.1 Applied research in tourism and hospitality

1. Research on consumers	2. Research on products and services
• Identifying existing markets • Identifying potential markets • Identifying lapsed consumers • Testing customer loyalty • Developing detailed consumer profiles • Identifying general trends in demographics and psychographics • Identifying changes in attitudes and behaviour patterns (generally) • Identifying changes in attitudes and behaviour patterns (product specific)	• Measuring attitudes towards existing products or services • Identifying potential new products which may be at the end of their product life cycle • Identifying products that are considered acceptable substitutes/alternatives • Evaluating competitors' products • Evaluating consumer attitudes towards décor, presentation and packaging • Evaluating consumer attitudes about combinations of products and services
3. Research on pricing	4. Research on place and distribution
• Identifying attitudes towards prices • Testing attitudes towards packages and individual pricing • Identifying costs • Identifying costing policies of competitors • Testing alternative pricing strategies • Testing payment processes (credit cards, electronic funds transfer, etc.)	• Identifying attitudes towards location • Identifying attitudes towards buildings/premises • Identifying attitudes on virtual sites • Identifying potential demand for product or services at other locations • Identifying cooperative opportunities for distribution of information or services
5. Research on promotion	6. Research on competition
• Testing and comparing media options • Testing alternative messages • Testing competitors' messages and their effectiveness • Identifying cooperative opportunities • Measuring advertising and promotion effectiveness	• Measuring awareness • Measuring usage • Identifying levels of customer loyalty • Identifying competitors' strengths and weaknesses • Identifying specific competitive advantages (locations, suppliers, etc.) • Identifying cooperative opportunities
7. Research on the operating environment	8. Research on a destination
• Economic trends • Social trends • Environmental issues • Political climate and trends • Impacts of technological developments	• Measuring residents attitudes • Benchmarking • Measuring customer loyalty • Identifying tourism activities • Identifying spending patterns • Branding research

or colleague?' When offered a scale of 0 to 10, the responses will fall in to three categories: promoters (those rating the service a 9 or 10), who are loyal fans; passives (the 7s and 8s); and detractors (those giving scores of 0–6). By taking the percentage of promoters and deducting the percentage of detractors, executives can determine a metric known as Net Promoter Score (NPS).

Another category of applied research is competitor research, sometimes called competitor intelligence. If a company wants to keep track of competition, it requires a clear understanding of who the competition is, as well as knowledge of how the company is doing in comparison to the competitors. Competitor intelligence is available through a variety of sources, including competitors' annual reports, local tourism authorities and state tourism departments, magazine articles, speeches, media releases, brochures, and advertisements. The form of competitor intelligence

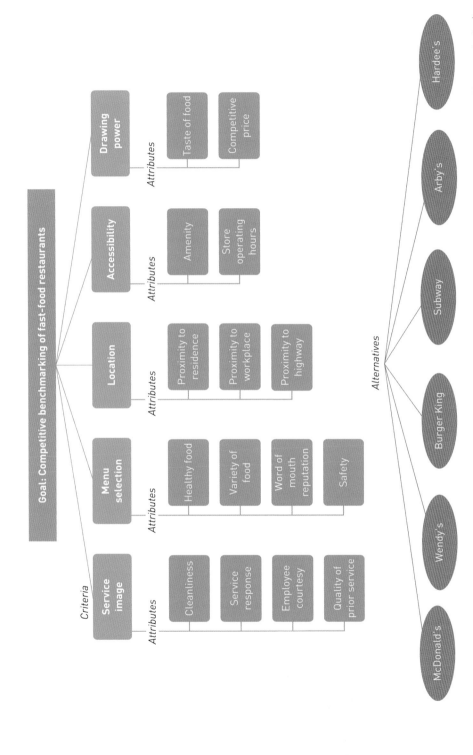

FIGURE 11.1 A hierarchy of benchmarking fast-food restaurants (©Emerald Group Publishing Limited. All rights reserved. Reprinted by permission)

research will vary from business to business. For a tourist attraction or food opera-tion, it could be as simple as counting the number of cars in the parking lot at various times, or actually going into the facility to see how busy it is. For a hotel, it might mean checking room availability at particular times or watching for advertisements of special offers and discounts. For tour operators, it may involve counting the num-ber of competing coaches at major destinations and collecting tour brochures and schedules. Participant observation is also often used to gather competitor intelligence. For example, executives of airlines might travel with competitors, or hotel managers might check in to competitor hotels. These are effective ways of gathering valuable knowledge for research purposes.

More recently, the practice of benchmarking has received attention from tourism mar-keting researchers. Benchmarking is essentially a management technique that allows companies to compare how well they are performing relative to their competitors (Kozak and Rimmington, 1999). Benchmarking initiatives might include collecting guest satisfaction scores. For Sheraton Hotels and Resorts, for example, measur-ing and comparing guest satisfaction is a crucial part of the company's marketing research. Guest satisfaction scores (GSS) are closely monitored by the research group, and results are shared with all hotels and all employees. Restaurants are also using benchmarking to measure service performance against competitors. Min and Min (2011) developed a series of benchmarks for the fast-food sector to help them moni-tor their service-delivery processes, identify relative weaknesses, and take corrective actions for continuous service improvements using an analytic hierarchy process. As shown in Figure 11.1, the top level of the hierarchy represents the ultimate goal of determining the best-practice fast-food restaurant. At the second level of the hierarchy are five distinct service criteria, generally considered important in measuring fast-food restaurant service quality: service image, menu selection, location, accessibility and drawing power. The attributes belonging to one of the five service criteria were con-nected to the bottom level of the hierarchy represented by six fast-food restaurants under evaluation.

APPLIED RESEARCH IN EVENTS TOURISM

Getz and Page (2015) have provided a framework for understanding and creating knowledge about events tourism. At the centre of the model is the core phenomenon (event experiences and meanings), and other key elements in the framework are the antecedents and choices (including motivation research), planning and managing event tourism, patterns and processes (including spatial, temporal, policy-making and knowledge creation), outcomes and the impacted. The authors present a summary of established research themes and key concepts and terms within event tourism, categorized by reference to the main elements in the framework. They also consider future directions by pinpointing emerging or desired lines of research, as well as methodologies, so that these can be viewed as a research agenda.

Certainly, research tends to support the use of local tax dollars to promote events tourism and foster community enrichment (Ahmed and Krohn, 1990; Gooroochurn and Sinclair, 2005). One study found that the use of tax funds for the promotion of the arts, cultural events and other tourism-related events is a successful strategy, enabling tourism growth, while feeding a virtuous cycle that yields still greater tour-ism dollars for the community (Litvin et al., 2006). The study suggested, at least for

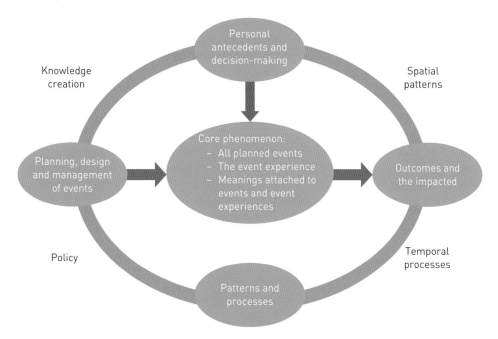

FIGURE 11.2 A framework for studying knowledge on event tourism (Reprinted from *Tourism Management*, 52, Getz and Page, 'Progress and prospects for event tourism research', pages 593–631. ©2016. With permission from Elsevier)

smaller tourism communities, that their long-term interests are best served by allocating tourism taxes towards initiatives that will provide special reasons for visitors to come to their community. Festivals and special events seem to provide the best path for growth, leading to a healthy tourism sector that can directly and indirectly be an economic engine for the community.

Other researchers agree that investment in events and festival can be the most effective use of tax dollars (Crompton and McKay, 1997; Goldblatt and Nelson, 2001). Special events have become one of the fastest growing types of tourist attractions, due to their uniqueness and the celebratory and festive ambience they provide, presenting visitors with 'the opportunity to participate in a collective experience which is distinct from the everyday life' (Getz, 1989). Events give tourists a way to experience diverse cultural forms while providing the host city with a hook to attract tourism revenue (Hall, 1992). From a community's perspective, the literature notes that festival-based tourism can generate significant economic benefits, filling local hotel rooms and restaurants while generally requiring minimal capital investment by taking advantage of existing infrastructure. In addition, from an intangible perspective, successful festivals can serve as a way to increase quality of life for residents, building community pride and cohesiveness (Gursoy, Kim and Uysal, 2004; Liburd and Derkzen, 2009). Successful events create a reason for tourists to visit, serving as catalysts to increase demand for food and beverages, generating increased tax revenue and feeding the virtuous cycle that proponents of these taxes espouse (Litvin, Smith and Blackwell, 2012). Finally, planned events are regarded as a key element in a destination image and brand strategy (Richards and Wilson, 2004).

One area of event studies, receiving increasing attention from researchers and prac-titioners, is the topic of event leveraging. Event leveraging is a subtle but significant strategy for extending the range of tangible and intangible benefits from events. It involves using the power and momentum of event investments and developments to 'kick-start' and/or accelerate the creation of additional tangible and intangible legacies (Faulkner and Tideswell, 1999). In recent years, policy-makers have become increas-ingly interested in using major sporting events as catalysts for generating beneficial economic, social and environmental legacies for host communities (Faulkner et al., 2000). For instance, the staging of mega sporting events has become a strategy for justifying a range of ancillary urban projects related to urban renewal and regenera-tion, place brand adjustment, as well as public and private sector investment in local businesses (Essex and Chalkley, 2004).

STAGES IN THE RESEARCH PROCESS

In undertaking research, there are a number of steps that should be followed, as outlined in Figure 11.3.

FIGURE 11.3 Stages in the research process

1. IDENTIFY AND DEFINE THE PROBLEM

Before beginning the task of gathering information, it is first necessary to identify the problem for which research is required. This step is crucial to ensure that any information collected is relevant. As well as formulating an aim, specific research questions (objectives) should be stipulated at the outset. These objectives will deter-mine the type of information required. A research project recently completed by the authors in South Carolina was instigated by a local chamber of commerce which identified the need to create a new brand for its destination (Bluffton) in order to attract people to live, work and play. Key leaders in the town realized that Bluffton needed to differentiate itself from competitors as well as articulate a unique identity in order to succeed not only as a place to visit but a place in which future investment and development may also take place. To begin with, a committee of business and community leaders was assembled as the Bluffton Branding Task Force to help guide the six-month branding process (Hudson et al., 2016).

2. INVESTIGATE AVAILABLE SOURCES

There is little point embarking upon a research programme involving the collection of primary data if information is already available. Seeking out available information will involve a search of internal data generated and recorded by the organization as well as an examination of available secondary sources of data. Such information should then be assessed to establish the extent to which the research questions can be tackled using this information alone. For the Bluffton project referred to above, the researchers were starting from scratch, but before deciding on the methods to be employed for the branding research, the team conducted an extensive review of branding work of this nature, and after examining best practices they recognized that stakeholder engagement would be crucial in the branding development process.

3. DEVELOP THE RESEARCH PLAN

Specific information should be determined from the research objectives. Research objectives must be translated into specific information needs. Two types of data may be used to meet the manager's information needs: secondary data, consisting of information that already exists somewhere, having been collected for another purpose, and primary data, consisting of information collected for the specific purpose at hand. For the Bluffton project, it was decided that research would include both qualitative and quantitative research in two principal stages, namely: (1) a series of charettes (workshops in which designers work intensively on a problem and present their findings and proposals in a public forum) and in-depth interviews with local decision-makers and key individuals; and (2) surveys of local leaders and business owners, potential business owners, visitors and area residents.

4. COLLECT DATA

Upon development of a research plan, data should be collected using the method(s) selected. The data collection phase of the marketing research process is generally the most expensive and the one most frequently subject to error. Great care should be taken to avoid bias, which, if introduced, could render results meaningless. This is a particular problem associated with the interview and observation methods. In Bluffton, to establish the core values and paint a picture of the future, the research team conducted four charettes attended by an average of 25–30 people. They are often used in the development of place brands. The second part of the qualitative research involved conducting 30 in-depth interviews with key decision-makers and stakeholders in the region. Following this, over 600 surveys were administered to existing and potential businesses, local government officials/people of influence, visitors, and Town of Bluffton residents. Electronic, mailed and intercept surveys explored the perceptions towards the Town of Bluffton as a brand, the Town's image, and test iterations of brand positioning.

5. ANALYSE DATA

At this stage, the collected data must be processed and analysed to pull out important information and findings. The methods used and the type of information collected will determine the analysis needed. Raw data taken from questionnaires, in-depth interviews, checklists, etc. need to be recorded, analysed, and interpreted. Researchers are constantly searching for similarities and differences, for groupings, patterns and items of particular significance. Commonly used statistical packages among tourism researchers are SPSS (Statistical Package for the Social Sciences), MINITAB, and NCSS (Number Cruncher Statistical System). These packages are continually being monitored, reviewed and updated to reflect the process of continuous evolution in computer software. The qualitative data from the Bluffton project were recorded and transcribed for analysis using NVivo software, whereas SPSS was used to analyse the data from the surveys.

6. PRESENT RESEARCH RESULTS

Information needs to be tabulated and interpreted, so that recommendations can be made regarding an appropriate course of action to take. This will almost certainly involve the presentation of a report that summarizes the results of the research. This report enables the management of the organization to make decisions based on the newly acquired information. Initially, the research results from the Bluffton research were presented to the Bluffton Branding Task Force, and led to the development of the 'Heart of the Lowcountry' brand that was rolled out through a variety of media outlets including radio, TV, social media, print and billboards. A report was then developed (see Figure 11.4) and widely disseminated.

FIGURE 11.4 Cover of the Bluffton Brand Assessment and Development Report.

DIGITAL SPOTLIGHT: MARKETING TO MILLENNIALS

A click of a mouse, the scroll of a finger, the press of a button – this is how Millennials have grown up and how they now conduct business, reservations, purchasing, communication and social transactions. Increasingly, marketers have been turning their attention away from Baby Boomers and towards gratifying the instantaneous needs of the Now Generation.

There are currently around 79 million Millennials just in North America – that's three million more than Baby Boomers who are predicted to dwindle to just 58 million by 2030. According to a recent study by Moosylvania, a digital marketing company, Millennials already represent $1.3 trillion in consumer spending worldwide, out of total spending of nearly $11 trillion. Young adults, the study found, need a lot of reassurance but don't like to be marketed to. 'No one truly understands Millennials,' the researchers summarized. 'Not even Millennials.' Risk-averse and socially conscious, Millennials are savvy shoppers, and brands are finding them a tough nut to crack. The most diverse and educated generation to date, they are using their comfort with technology not only to

IMAGE 11.2 Millennials at Gstaad in Switzerland enjoying lunch (Courtesy of Gstaad Saanenland Tourismus - Photographer: Roger Grütter)

locate the best prices, but also influence 'how things are done'. Millennials have been called a lot of names by marketers: narcissistic, lazy, indecisive and self-promoting. They have been labelled the 'boomerang generation' for the many who are unwilling to leave the nest or the 'Peter Pan generation' because they supposedly won't grow up. But businesses are now realizing that this generation – born between 1980 and the early 2000s – should be treated with a little more respect. Given their numbers, they have the ability to reshape the economy, and are changing the way everything is sold, including hospitality.

While the younger component of these children of the Digital Age is still financially dependent on parents, older Millennials are at peak purchasing power and an ideal target market for destinations and resorts. So what are the keys to attracting, satisfying and retaining this demanding demographic?

Here are a few 'Must-Haves for Millennials':

- Free wi-fi throughout hotels, venues, resorts, destinations
- Social and wired areas in lobbies (providing Howard Schultz's 'third place')
- High-tech, smartphone-friendly websites
- Apps to replace traditional maps and brochures
- Real time reporting and responding to their social media comments
- Trustworthy peer reviews
- Speedy automated check in/out and automated bill paying
- Smart technology and plentiful power outlets in hotels, restaurants, airports, etc.
- Cool factors: unique facilities, emotional component, age-appropriate freebies
- Social responsibility programmes at resorts, restaurants, hotels, venues, destinations
- Fresh, organic foods with gluten-free, lactose-free, vegetarian and vegan options
- Health and wellness facilities
- Pod hotels – reducing accommodation costs in order to have a larger budget for more active vacation experiences

A Swiss ski resort which has responded to this high-tech trend is Gstaad, particularly in regard to apps. Visitors can benefit from up to date information from many different

(Continued)

(Continued)

sources including iSKI Swiss, Skiresort.de, Snocountry, Skitude, myswitzerland, Skiline, Schee & Mehr. Gstaad's piste map is interactive and Pistenbericht gives a daily updated snow report, slope report, weather and web cams.

Gstaad is also active on social media. Its Facebook, tagged 'Gstaad – come up, slow down', is updated daily and the resort has a strong presence on Instagram and Twitter. Gstaad incorporated a responsive design into its website – www.gstaad.ch – which is compatible with every gadget, smartphone and computer. It is also able to track users. 'During 2014, 64.02 per cent of the users were desktop-users, 19.15 per cent mobile users and 16.83 per cent tablet-users,' says Antje Buchs, Project Manager Public Relations for Gstaad Saanenland Tourismus. 'Thanks to the responsive design, it is also possible to book hotels and apartments with smartphones.'

Despite their reliance on online communication, Millennials are actually more sociable offline than previous generations – so long as technology is close at hand. With such constant access to images of social activity, they are subject to the FOMO (Fear of Missing Out) phenomenon. Around 58 per cent prefer to travel with friends: that's 20 per cent more than other demographic groups. Free wi-fi around the slopes of Gstaad in social spots such as the Eggli, Rellerli, Saanerslochgrat and Wispile mountain restaurants means that digital devotees can relax in between runs and socialize while still keeping in touch online.

Wow factors for Gstaad include the chance to visit the world's first peak-to-peak suspension bridge, Peak Walk. Spanning 107 m, with spectacular mountain views, the bridge starts at the top of View Point on Glacier 3000 and finishes at Scex Rouge peak. Glacier 3000 also gives Gstaad the longest ski season in the area. While every Alpine resort offers fondue evenings, Gstaad has gone a step further with its fabulous Fondueland. Here guests enjoy fondue while sitting in one of two giant wooden fondue-pots which each seat up to eight people. The specially designated huts are open year round and accessible by foot, bike, sledge or snowshoes. Catering to Millennial music mania, Gstaad's Ride on Music is a three-day festival with a mix of hiphop, street, rock and folk music, with satellite events on the slopes by day and in town by night.

The Superpass satisfies another Millennial Must-Have: value for money. It covers three ski areas with one lift ticket, encompassing 188 lifts and 630 km of skiing. Although Gstaad is by no means a cheap ski resort, it prides itself on making skiing accessible to youth and families. The resort also has several affordable lodging options including Spitzhorn, Hamilton Lodge and a new youth hostel in the holiday region of Gstaad, which was incidentally dubbed by actress, Julie Andrews as 'the last paradise in a crazy world'.

Environmental sustainability is an important issue for Millennials, who have grown up with recycling and the notion of reducing environmental footprints. In this respect, Sustainable Gstaad has various ongoing ecological projects including traditional alpine farming, hydroelectric power stations, a central hotel laundry, and green fuel for piste equipment as well as GPS for PistenBullys.

Sources: Personal interview with Kerstin Sonnekalb for Gstaad Saanenland Tourismus, January 2015; personal interview with Antje Buchs, Project Manager Public Relations for Gstaad Saanenland Tourismus, May 2016; http://expediablog.co.uk/wp-content/uploads/2013/10/Future-of-Travel-Report1.pdf

RESEARCH METHODOLOGY

The increased importance of tourism management decision-making has caused more attention to be focused on the theories and methodologies of the tourism research process. A recurrent theme has emerged in the travel research literature concerning the appropriateness of specific types of tourism research and certain methodological applications. There are several approaches to collecting data, but two key decisions that have to be made are as follows:

(1) **Primary versus secondary data.** In planning a research project, it is sensible to consider whether it is worth going to the expense of collecting new information (primary data, where the researcher is the primary user) or whether existing data (secondary data, where the researcher is the secondary user) will be sufficient. In practice, it may be necessary to collect both types of information. As Chitra Stern said in the opening case study, although statistics and information about the Algarve in Portugal was relatively easy to find via tourism associations and foreign investment agencies, she still needed to collect her own primary data in order to start the new business. The various types of primary and secondary research are explored later in this chapter.

(2) **Qualitative versus quantitative research.** Qualitative research methods and techniques give rise to qualitative (subjective) information, whereas quantitative research is research to which numerical (empirical) estimates can be attached. There has been much debate recently about appropriate methods for leisure research, with some authors arguing for extended use of qualitative research over quantitative research. In tourism research, quantitative and qualitative research approaches seem to coexist without the sort of apparent rivalry seen in leisure studies. It is possible for research to be conducted entirely quantitatively, entirely qualitatively, or using a mixture of both. In fact, it is common for large-scale quantitative research to be planned on the basis of prior exploratory qualitative studies.

The distinction between the two methods is indicated in Table 11.2. Both research methods possess distinct limitations and weaknesses, but both also have redeeming characteristics. The choice between the two must be determined by the situation in which research takes place, not by some misguided search for rigor simply for its own sake.

SECONDARY RESEARCH

Secondary data is data that already exists for an established purpose, and secondary research is also referred to as documents and desk research. It includes information

TABLE 11.2 Qualitative versus quantitative research (Source: Adapted from McDaniel and Gates, 1993)

Comparison dimension	Qualitative research	Quantitative research
Types of questions	Probing	Limited probing
Sample size	Small	Large
Information per respondent	Much	Varies
Administration	Interviewer with special skills required	Fewer special skills required
Types of analysis	Subjective, interpretive	Statistical, summarizing
Hardware	Digital recorders, projection devices, video equipment, pictures	Questionnaires, computers, printouts
Ability to replicate	Low	High
Training of the researcher	Psychology, sociology, social psychology, consumer behaviour marketing, marketing research	Statistics, decision models, decision support systems, computer programming, marketing research
Types of research	Exploratory	Descriptive or causal

collected from internal sources such as occupancy rates, sales figures, attendance figures, types of services sold, etc. In-house surveys can also be valuable sources of data. As well, data can be collected from external sources. Government agencies such as VisitBritain, Tourism Australia or the Canadian Tourism Commission (CTC) compile statistics on visitor arrivals, how much they spend, where they are coming from, etc. As well as generating a considerable amount of statistical data at the macro level, government is also responsible for a number of tourism-related publications. The World Tourism Organization (UNWTO), for example, produces numerous publications to support the tourism sector in advancing knowledge and tourism policies worldwide. The UNWTO is the United Nations agency responsible for the promotion of responsible, sustainable and universally accessible tourism.

The trade press can also provide a regular supply of information. Popular travel trade publications include *Travel Weekly* in the UK, *Tourism* in Canada and *Travel Trade* in the US. Research journals, periodicals, and special reports can be useful sources of information, as can conference papers, speeches and annual reports. A veritable explosion of new journals has been introduced as the outlet for academic publication of research in hospitality and tourism. A recent inventory, while neither exhaustive nor exclusive, yielded a count of over 100 journals, as listed in Table 11.3.

Searching the Internet, while sometimes a time-consuming process, can also reveal other potential sources of information, as can chat groups and online newsletters. It is worth noting, however, that the accuracy of such information is not guaranteed, so checking the reliability of the source is important.

TABLE 11.3 An inventory of tourism and hospitality publications

General Interest	Tourism	Foodservice
The Cornell Hotel & Restaurant Administration Quarterly	Annals of Tourism Research	Journal of Restaurant & Foodservice Marketing
International Journal of Hospitality Management	ACTA Turistica	Journal of Nutrition, Recipe and Menu Development
Journal of Hospitality and Tourism Research	Asia Pacific Journal of Tourism Research	Journal of College and University Foodservice
FIU Hospitality Review	Current Issues in Tourism	Journal of Foodservice Systems
International Journal of Contemporary Hospitality Management	Event Tourism	Journal of Agricultural & Food Information
Journal of Quality Assurance in Hospitality & Tourism	Information Technology & Tourism	Journal of Nutrition for the Elderly
The Journal of Applied Hospitality Management	International Journal of Tourism Research	Journal of the American Dietetic Association
Australian Journal of Hospitality Management	Journal of Convention & Exhibition Management	NACUFS Journal (National Association of College & University Foodservices)
The Consortium Journal: Journal of HBCU	Journal of Ecotourism	School Foodservice Research Review
International Journal of Hospitality and Tourism Administration	Journal of Sports Tourism	Journal of Food Production Management
Praxis – The Journal of Applied Hospitality Management	Journal of Sustainable Tourism	Journal of Food Products Marketing
Anatolia Journal	Journal of Travel Research	Journal of Foodservice Business Research
Scandinavian Journal of Hospitality and Tourism	Journal of Travel & Tourism Research	Journal of Culinary Science
Tourism and Hospitality Research	Journal of Vacation Marketing	Annual Review of Food Science and Technology
Journal of Hospitality & Leisure for the Elderly	Pacific Tourism Review	Trend in Food Science and Technology
Journal of Convention & Exhibition Management	Teoros International	Critical Reviews in Food Science and Nutrition
Journal of Hospitality & Leisure Marketing	Tourism analysis	Food and Nutrition Research
Journal of Tourism and Hospitality Education	TOURISM: An International Interdisciplinary Journal	Journal of the Science of Food and Agriculture
Hotel & Motel Management	The Tourist Review	The Journal of Foodservice Management and Education
International Journal of Hospitality Information Technology	Tourism, Culture & Communication	Journal of the Academy of Nutrition and Dietetics

(Continued)

TABLE 11.3 (Continued)

General Interest	Tourism	Foodservice
Journal of Gambling Studies	Tourism Economics	Journal of Food Products Marketing
Journal of Hospitality Financial Management	Tourism Geographies	Comprehensive Reviews in Food Science and Food Safety
Australian Leisure Management	Tourism Management	
Journal of Service Management	Tourism Recreation Research	
Journal of Hospitality Marketing and Management	Tourism Today	
Applied Geography	Tourismus Journal	
Leisure Studies	Tourist Studies	
Leisure Sciences	Travel & Tourism Analyst	
UNLV Journal of Hospitality, Tourism and Leisure Science	Journal of Teaching in Travel & Tourism	
International Journal of Retail and Distribution Management	Journal of Human Resources in Hospitality & Tourism	
Journal of Leisure Research	Journal of Travel & Tourism Marketing	
Journal of Place Management and Development	Journal of Tourism Studies	
Journal of Policy Research in Tourism, Leisure and Events	Tourism Intelligence Quarterly	
Journal of Hospitality, Leisure, Sports and Tourism Education	Papers de Turisme	
Managing Leisure	Journal of Hospitality and Tourism Management	
The Journal of Applied Hospitality Management	European Journal of Tourism Research	
Advances in Hospitality and Tourism Research	International Journal of Tourism Policy and Research	
Annals of Leisure Research	Journal of Travel and Tourism Marketing	
ASEAN Journal of Tourism and Hospitality Research	Journal of Outdoor Recreation and Tourism	
Event Management	Tourism Management Perspectives	
International Journal of Culture, Tourism and Hospitality Research	Visitor Studies	
International Journal of Hospitality Knowledge Management	Tourism Planning and Development	

General Interest	Tourism	Foodservice
Journal of Hospitality and Tourism Management	Journal of China Tourism Research	
Journal of Leisurability	International Journal of Tourism Sciences	
Journal of Park and Recreation Administration	e-Review of Tourism Research	
Journal of Retail and Leisure Property	Festival Management and Event Tourism	
Journal of the Canadian Association for Leisure Studies	Journal of Convention & Event Tourism	
	Journal of Heritage Tourism	
	Journal of Tourism and Cultural Change	
	Journal of Tourism and Cultural Heritage	
	Journal of Tourism Consumption and Practice	
	Progress in Tourism and Hospitality Research	
	Tourism in Marine Environments	
	Tourismos: an International Multidisciplinary Journal of Tourism	

PRIMARY RESEARCH

QUALITATIVE RESEARCH TECHNIQUES

The term 'qualitative' is used to describe research methods and techniques that use, and give rise to, subjective rather than empirical information. In general, the approach is to collect a great amount of 'rich' information from relatively few people. Potential purposes of qualitative research include developing hypotheses concerning relevant behaviour and attitudes; identifying the full range of issues, views and attitudes that should be pursued in large-scale research; and understanding how a buying decision is made. Qualitative research can be used in unstructured and structured situations.

UNSTRUCTURED SITUATIONS

Participative observation falls into this category, in which a tourism field researcher may adopt one of four different roles. The first is the 'complete participant', where the researcher becomes a genuine participant, and the second is the 'participant as observer', where researchers reveal their intentions. Third, 'observers as participants' also reveal themselves as researchers, and will participate in the normal social process, but make no pretence of being participants. The fourth type, 'the complete observer', simply observes without being involved. The highly successful 'What Happens in Vegas, Stays in Vegas' advertising campaign was developed following extensive qualitative research to understand consumer behaviour that including observational research and 'tag-alongs' (following visitors around from the moment they arrived until the moment they left).

Mystery shopping, the name given to participant observation in the commercial sector, has become a common marketing research technique in tourism and hospitality (Hudson et al., 2001). In the services context, mystery shopping provides information about the service experience as it unfolds, and helps to develop a richer knowledge of the experiential nature of services. According to the Mystery Shopping Providers Association (MSPA), there are some 30,000 mystery shoppers in the US hired by luxury hotel brands to check-in anonymously and judge standards of the properties (O'Shea-Evans, 2012). 'In the late 1980s, Hilton was among the first luxury hotel brands to utilize the service,' says Mike Bare, co-owner and president of Bare International and one of the original founders of the MSPA. Three decades later, it is common practice among hotel brands around the world. Table 11.4 summarizes the various advantages and disadvantages of using this method of participative observation.

TABLE 11.4 Advantages and disadvantages of covert participative observation or mystery shopping

Advantages	Disadvantages
Offers deep insights into feelings and motivations behind service/practice	Raises ethical issues by observing people without their knowledge
Experience is natural and not contrived for the sake of the observer	Based on assumptions that need to be made explicit and addressed
Serves as a management tool for improving standards in customer service by providing actionable recommendations	Information collected may be biased as a result of arbitrary or careless selection of observation periods, or the observer's own prejudices
Ideal for investigating services	In the long term, advantages for improving customer service can wear off if not integrated with other measures of service delivery process
Serves as a management tool for enhancing human resource management	Can be very costly and time-consuming

STRUCTURED SITUATIONS

Qualitative research also permits more structured situations in which the researcher can play a more proactive role, although that role is more facilitative than directive. At the initial stages of tourism research, it may be necessary to follow up a conversation, and, if the research is intended to generate quantitative data, to develop items for scales to be used on a questionnaire. Hence, there is a need to identify clearly the constructs that inform the attitudes towards specific destinations, behaviours, or experiences that are being surveyed. The idea of interviewing groups of people together rather than individually is becoming increasingly popular in marketing research. In a focus group, the interviewer becomes the facilitator of a discussion rather than an interviewer as such, in order to obtain representative views of a wider population. A focus group is usually fairly homogeneous in nature and comprises eight to ten people. It is important that those selected have little experience of working in a focus group, as the researcher wishes to obtain views representative of a wider population, not from expert 'opinion givers' who are used to the dynamics of a focus group.

Focus groups are commonly used in commercial research, especially in the development and monitoring of advertising campaigns. They are beginning to be widely used in the world of tourism, and are often used for obtaining feedback on holiday brochures. Groups are asked to respond to the layout, pictures, text and typeface of brochures, to help companies find those that appeal most to various market niches. Charettes have also been used in tourism research, but are less common than focus groups. As mentioned before, a charette is a workshop in which designers work intensively on a problem and present their findings and proposals in a public forum (Kelbaugh, 1997). They are often used in the development of place brands but have not been used extensively in tourism research. These intense planning sessions are intended to provide practical, stakeholder-driven solutions based on collaborative vision and values from the general public (Mara, 2006).

IMAGE 11.3 Researchers conduct a charette in Bluffton, South Carolina

In-depth interviews tend to be used for three main reasons. Firstly, they are used in situations where the limited number of subjects renders quantitative methods inappropriate. Secondly, they are used when information obtained from each subject is expected to vary considerably, i.e. when the question of 'what percentage of respondents said what' is not relevant. Thirdly, in-depth interviews can be used to explore a topic as a preliminary stage in planning a more formal questionnaire-based survey.

Interviews can be structured, unstructured, or a combination of the two. The unstructured interview differs from a conversation in the sense that both parties are aware of an underlying agenda of question and answer. The structured interview involves a number of skills on the part of the researcher. For example, questionnaire-drafting skills, such as determining the sequence of questions and their precise content, are key. Other required skills are the interpersonal skills involved in conversation and being able to 'lead' the interviewee. Also, the researcher must develop the skills of recording responses accurately; very often interviews are recorded and a word-for-word transcription is prepared.

There are various ways of going about the analysis of interview transcripts, but it is imperative that the researcher returns to the terms of reference and statement of objectives and begins to evaluate the information gathered in relation to the questions posed. Recently, a variety of computer packages have become available to analyse interview transcripts. In the Bluffton research project referred to above, interview transcriptions were analysed using NVivo software, and were organized and subsequently analysed around the main questions or key themes accordingly. This form of analysis is analogous to template analysis, which, in general terms, is a technique that allows for a comparison of perspectives (King, 1998) in this case between respondents and is helpful in organizing large amounts of text (Crabtree and Miller, 1999).

QUANTITATIVE RESEARCH TECHNIQUES

A review of the methods used in collecting tourism and hospitality research data shows that the questionnaire technique or survey method is the most frequently used. The survey method includes factual surveys, opinion surveys, or interpretive surveys, all of which can be conducted by personal interview, telephone, mail or by electronic means. Factual surveys are by far the most beneficial. 'When you are on holiday, what activities do you engage in?' is a question where respondents should be able to give accurate information in response. In an opinion survey, the respondent is asked to express an opinion or make an evaluation or appraisal. In interpretive surveys, the respondent acts as an interpreter as well as a reporter. Subjects are asked why they chose a certain course of action – why they chose a particular package, for example. While respondents can reply accurately to 'what' questions, they often have difficulty replying to 'why' questions. Therefore, while interpretive research may give a researcher a feel for consumer behaviour, the usefulness of the results tends to be limited.

Personal interviews tend to be much more flexible than either mail or telephone surveys because the interviewer can adapt to the situation and the respondent. Typically, one can obtain much more information by personal interview than by other means, as personal interviewers can observe the situation as well as ask questions. A major limitation of the personal interview method, however, is its relatively high cost. An interview takes a considerable amount of time to conduct, and there is always the possibility of personal interviewer bias. Telephone surveys are conducted much more rapidly and at less cost than personal interviews. Speed and low cost are the primary advantages of telephone interviews; however, these interviews tend to be less flexible than personal interviews, and they also have to be brief. Computer-assisted telephone interviewing using random dialling is very popular in North America. Mail surveys involve mailing the questionnaire to carefully selected sample respondents and requesting them to return the completed questionnaires. Advantages are that a large geographical area can be covered, respondents can fill out the survey at their own convenience and personal interview bias is absent. The greatest problems with mail surveys are the lack of a good list and lack of adequate response.

A popular way of conducting research these days is the use of electronic surveys that ask consumers questions and immediately record and tabulate the results. Computer-type electronic equipment might be placed in a hotel lobby, mall or other high-traffic location – for example, Whistler Resort collects data from its skiers using electronic devices placed up and down the main street. Alternatively, respondents may be asked to complete a survey online. Internet-based survey methodology is gaining increasing popularity. Meliá Hotels International engaged marketing consultants Market Metrix to move their infrequent paper questionnaire data collection method online in order to increase sample size and data reliability. Every guest is now invited to participate to better represent the entire guest experience every day. Customer input is available instantly, not only to the head office, but also to the general manager and frontline staff at every property. It is now possible to use customer feedback for instant service recovery as well as long-term service improvement. Meliá's own customer feedback is compared with relevant industry benchmarks in the local markets where they compete in order to ensure that competitive standards are met and guest value remains high.

New technology is impacting other areas of marketing research. Virtual focus groups are becoming more common. Online 'chat' sessions, in which one to dozens of pre-recruited respondents type in responses to a guided online discussion, can be used effectively to bring together participants from virtually anywhere to discuss experiences with a service or provide feedback on products. While virtual focus groups will not always be able to replace in-person interviews, the time- and cost-saving benefits of such groups make them a very useful tool for researchers – especially for gathering website feedback with participants when they are using the Internet. Companies are also using virtual worlds to gather useful consumer feedback. Starwood Hotels and Resorts used Second Life, an online world with a virtual economy, as a three-dimensional test bed for its new chain of hotels called Aloft. The company created an elaborate digital prototype for the new chain not just to promote the venture, but also to give its designers feedback from prospective guests before the first real hotel opened in 2008.

Advances in technology are also allowing companies to tap into human emotions, seeking patterns that can predict emotional reactions and behaviour on a massive scale (Dwoskin and Rusli, 2015). Emotient, for example, a San Diego startup, has developed software that can recognize emotions from a database of micro-expressions that happen in a fraction of a second, and has worked with Honda and Procter & Gamble to gauge people's emotions as they try out products. 'Neuromarketing' is also lighting up the eyes of marketing researchers, promising to target the unconscious desires of consumers, which are supposedly revealed by measuring the brain (Bell, 2015). Neuromarketing is a scientifically sound, genuinely interesting field in cognitive science, where the response to products and consumer decision-making is understood on the level of body and mind. This might involve looking at how familiar brand logos engage the memory systems in the brain, or examining whether the direction of eye gaze of people in ads affects how attention-grabbing they are, or testing whether the brain's electrical activity varies when watching subtly different ads. Like most of cognitive neuroscience, the studies are abstract, ultra-focused and a long way from everyday experience.

Finally, an increasing number of organizations are employing social media listening tools in order to keep a track on customers, improve services or brand relationships, and ultimately improve the bottom line (see Digital Spotlight on M Live in Chapter 3). Virgin Atlantic Airways, for example, monitors social media to gather insights to drive continual incremental improvements in its service. In response to online-community suggestions, it launched a system to arrange taxi sharing on arrival with passengers from the same flight. Brandwatch (2014) suggests that researchers in the travel industry need to monitor the effect that social media has at 'three points of contact'. These are before departure, travel and stay, and back home (see Figure 11.5).

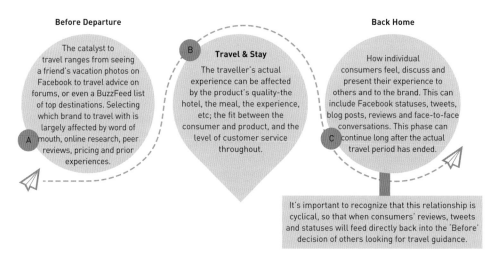

FIGURE 11.5 The cyclical nature of travel decisions (©2017 Brandwatch. All rights reserved. Reprinted by permission)

In their 2014 report on social media listening, Brandwatch gives examples from various sectors of the tourism and hospitality industry on how listening to social media has benefited individual companies. For example, by listening to branded conversation, accommodation providers LateRooms noticed that a number of forums featured lengthy and frequent discussion of their services, quite a revelation for the brand. One particular forum that generated considerable brand discussion was Blonde Poker, a poker news website. LateRooms quickly recognized the value in this conversation and capitalized on the opportunity to capture the business of travelling poker fans. The company managed to foster a healthy marketing relationship with the forum, helping to drive targeted and relevant traffic to LateRoom's website.

Another example of social media listening comes from the travel agency sector. In 2013, Expedia released an advertisement in Canada calling for viewers to 'escape winter' through travelling. The ad was poorly received by some a few weeks later, thanks to an apparently annoying violin noise during the repetitive commercial showings. Negative sentiment soon rippled throughout social media. Referring to the particularly abrasive violin featured, hundreds of watchers took to Twitter to voice their unhappiness. Expedia's creative agency, Grip Limited was listening carefully. Grip replaced the original with three new, specially created TV spots, and a potentially damaging campaign was cleverly adjusted. In the first replacement video, the violin is thrown out of the house, a direct response to the complaints about its unpleasant noise online. After isolating the scores of commenters that had grumbled about the original advert, another more aggressive ad was created and sent by the Expedia Canada Twitter and Facebook accounts directly to the dissenters, complete with a joking apology about the first commercial. The third video takes the viewer directly to Cam Charron's house (who was one of the many that took to Twitter to complain), where he is personally given the opportunity to destroy the violin (Brandwatch, 2014).

SAMPLING

Because of the expenses associated with research, marketing managers often find themselves grappling with the question of how many people must be surveyed in order to obtain accurate responses. It is almost impossible – and not very cost effective – to interview every product user or potential product user. Therefore, a company's decisions are based on the opinions and reactions of a sample of the population. The sample selection process is as follows:

(1) **Define the population.** The first stage in the sampling process is specification of the target population.

(2) **Specify the sample frame.** This is a specification of the listing, directory, or roster from which the sample will be chosen.

(3) **Select the sampling method.** The researcher has to decide whether a probability or nonprobability approach will be applied to draw the sample and exactly how the sample members will be selected. There is a wide range of both probability and nonprobability sampling methods. The key difference between the two is that in probability sampling, a statistical evaluation of sampling error can be undertaken; such an assessment is not possible for samples drawn by nonprobabilistic methods. Therefore the more accurate form of sampling is the probability method, in which each unit of the population has a known, but not necessarily an equal, chance of selection. Techniques subsumed within this method are simple, random, systematic, stratified, cluster, multiphase and area sampling.

(4) **Determine sample size.** The selection of sample size has received considerable attention from critics of tourism research. (Baker, Hozier and Rogers, 1994). suggest that there are two basic approaches for the tourism researcher interested in accountability and efficiency: required size per cell and the traditional statistical model. The required size per cell approach requires approximately 30 responses for each demographic cell of data. For example, two genders, four ethnic groups and four age groups would require a sample size of 960 ($2 \times 4 \times 4 \times 30$). The traditional statistical model is based on a management specification of allowable error (e), the level of confidence in the sampling process (z), and the variance in the population (@). The sampling size is thus expressed as: $n = z@ / e$. One important aspect of the traditional statistical method of sample size determination is that the sample must be randomly selected; every member of the population of interest must have a known chance of being selected. This is a key to eliminating systematic bias. Another important point is that if questionnaire respondents are all basically alike, a small sample size

is required, no matter how large the population. This is often a fundamentally difficult concept for researchers and managers to accept. Sample size is not a function of population size: it is a function of population variance. Large-scale data collection is very costly, and quite often not needed.

(5) **Draw the sample and collect the data.** The final stage in the sampling process is the implementation stage, in which the sample is chosen and surveyed. The sampling procedure adopted will have a direct impact on the validity of the results, so if the survey is to be the principal tool for data collection, careful consideration must be given to the technique employed and the sample size chosen.

COMMON RESEARCH ERRORS

There are many potential pitfalls in conducting research; the most common four errors are discussed here.

1. NOT INCLUDING ENOUGH QUALITATIVE INFORMATION

As mentioned earlier in the chapter, EuroDisney in France got off to a poor start partly due to a lack of in-depth, qualitative research. A key problem was a lack of sufficient understanding of the potential customer. Researchers failed to understand domestic tourists and those travelling from other parts of Europe. For example, the original ban on alcohol at the park had to be lifted due to public demand as no self-respecting French person could contemplate lunch without a glass of wine. Pets also had to be accommodated as the French routinely take dogs and even cats on their road holidays. Other errors were made in the way visitors booked their Disney vacations. Reservations started out as direct bookings made by telephone or by Internet. This alienated British tourists who usually book holidays via travel agencies. Disney also expected European tourists to change their travel habits for their park. Traditionally French tourists travel in August during a one-month vacation period when factories and offices shut down and the British take two weeks some time between the end of July and the first week of September. Disney predicted erroneously that both nationalities would take their children out of school for shorter periods outside of the main vacation periods.

2. AN IMPROPER USE OF SOPHISTICATED STATISTICAL ANALYSIS

It is possible for a multitude of errors to creep into the research process if collection, tabulation, and analysis are not done properly. In today's environment, tabulation is likely to take place on the computer; a number of excellent packages are available for this purpose. However, statistical conclusions must be interpreted in terms of the best action or policy for the organization to follow. This reduction of the interpretation to recommendations is one of the most difficult tasks in the research process. Hotels will often use statistical reports on which to base decision-making. Shaun Durant, General Manager of the Residence Inn by Marriott in Florence, South Carolina, relies heavily on the services of Smith Travel Research (STR). 'Smith Travel Research offers a great tool called the STAR report that is utilized by a number of hotels to analyse industry trends. With this report we can easily compare occupancy percentages and average daily rates across our competitive set,' he says.

3. FAILURE TO HAVE A SAMPLE THAT IS REPRESENTATIVE OF THE POPULATION

A sample is a segment of the population selected to represent the population as a whole. Ideally, the sample should be representative, so that the researcher can make accurate estimates of the thoughts and behaviours of the larger population. The Sheraton Suites Calgary Eau Claire, Canada, mainly targets the business traveller, so it is important to get feedback from this segment when they stay during the business week. Every Wednesday, the hotel holds a weekly cocktail party. Four or five managers are on hand to greet the guests, and it is a unique opportunity for business travellers to meet hotel managers and get to know them. The meetings are an opportunity for managers to build relationships, gain more knowledge about guest preferences, and listen to any concerns, so that they can ultimately improve customer service.

4. PROBLEMS WITH INTERPRETATION

The task of interpretation is not an easy job – rather it requires a great skill and dexterity on the part of the researcher. One should always remember that even if the data are properly collected and analysed, wrong interpretation would lead to inaccurate conclusions. When measuring service quality, for example, there are several options open to researchers, including simply asking for perceptions of performance. However, this measure offers little diagnostic potential and, indeed, may result in inappropriate priorities being established. From a managerial perspective, it would seem important to track trends of the extent to which expectations are met over time as well as trends in performance, and even levels of importance for various services. The use of difference scores (between expectation and performance or importance and performance) gives managers a better understanding of whether increasing expectations or diminishing performance might be responsible for declining service quality and customer satisfaction. An examination of minimum expectations may also be fruitful. Similarly, disregarding importance may mean losing useful insights. Without considering attribute importance, one has no indication of the relative importance that respondents attach to particular aspects of service performance (Hudson, Hudson and Miller, 2004).

CHAPTER SUMMARY

The way in which an organization gathers, uses, and disseminates its research in the marketing context is generally referred to as the Marketing Information System (MIS). A key component of the MIS is the marketing research process: the systematic and objective search for and analysis of information relevant to the identification and solution of any problem in the field of marketing. In undertaking research, these steps should be followed: identify and define the problem; investigate available sources; develop the research plan; collect data; analyse data; and present research results. There are several approaches to collecting data, but two key decisions that have to be made are whether to use primary or secondary data and whether to use qualitative or quantitative research. There are many potential pitfalls in conducting research, the most common four errors being not including enough qualitative information, an improper use of statistical analysis, failure to have a representative sample, and problems with interpretation.

REFLECTIVE QUESTIONS

1. Do some research and find an example of a local tourism or hospitality organiza-
    tion that has recently published research results. How have they used the results
    for decision-making?
2. If you owned a high-class restaurant and wanted to improve the level of service
    offered by your staff, how could observational research help you accomplish
    your goal?
3. Differentiate between qualitative and quantitative research and give specific
    examples of how each could be used by a hotel.

MARKETING IN ACTION: OPEN KITCHEN CONCEPT SPREADS TO HOTELS

While TV chefs have morphed into global celebrities in the era of TV reality shows, a
new restaurant trend in Open Kitchen Dining has emerged. Although the concept is not
totally novel – after all, sushi bars have been doing it for years – it is the polished level of performance, highbrow cuisine and the proliferation of the trend that is more recent. All around the world, restaurants are putting their executive chefs on display, cooking part, or even all, of a meal right in front of diners who often sit at counters, watching every move. Cooking has become a reality show, adding an extra cachet to the restaurant experience. This ascendance of culinary scrutiny has gone hand in hand with a heightened interest in farm fresh ingredients and a general food fetishism, which encompasses new fads in organic, gluten-free, lactose-free, vegan and vegetarian eating.

IMAGE 11.4 Kitchen Table in London's Soho district
(Courtesy of Kitchen Table)

The open kitchen trend seems to have been born in big cities such as New York,
where chefs originally cooked within view of diners largely due to tight space constraints, but it has now spread worldwide, as far as Kenya, South Africa and Kobe,
Japan. Investors are renovating their restaurants to accommodate the model in a bid
to offer their customers a unique experience. A good example is the 19-seat Kitchen
Table, in London's Soho district, a restaurant that encourages full interaction with
the chefs as they prepare the food. Awarded a Michelin star in 2014, Kitchen Table
prepares, cooks and serves a daily changing 10–15 course menu of meticulously

sourced and foraged British ingredients. Head Chef James Knappett, who has previously spent time in the kitchens at The Ledbury, Noma and Per Se, says the idea of the restaurant came from wanting to do something completely different: 'In my previous jobs I was cooking for over 100 people a day in other people's restaurants and I went home not really knowing if anyone enjoyed their meal or what their experience was like. So I wanted to put the guests right in front of us and really find out what they are thinking about food. We can also interact with them, and tell them in detail where the ingredients come from.'

Forward-thinking hotels are also experimenting with the open kitchen concept. Just outside San Diego, California, the Kitchen Counter experience at the Seasons Restaurant is advertised as 'culinary magic'. 'Socializing and dining around the kitchen is the heart of Seasons Restaurant's operating philosophy,' says Demi Ortega, Regional Vice President and General Manager of Four Seasons. 'We wanted to create an environment where guests felt at home and could stay as long as they please. Here you'll know the chef's making the food and know that our team will take care of your personal needs and understand your discerning taste.' The culinary team at Seasons Restaurant prepares a five-course menu before a group of six diners, explaining about the choices of seasonal ingredients, cooking techniques and flavours. Rather than mere nourishment, the experience is touted as a 'thrilling culinary adventure', which can be customized to different tastes and dietary requirements. Appropriate wines are served with each course, adding an educational viticulture element. 'There is no official menu, the Kitchen Counter experience is seasonally driven and allows the chefs to share their personal story of what inspires them,' Ortega explains. 'It showcases the creative soul of the kitchen and give guests a sneak peak of what takes place, from the preparation, to the plating, to the story behind why the chef selected these ingredients, flavour combinations and preparation style.'

With elegant décor and a relaxing ambiance, the Four Seasons Aviara is a rambling complex of top-notch apartments and villas with pools, spa, fitness centre, salon and shop set on a lush, landscaped hillside near Carlsbad, around 45 minutes from downtown San Diego. But the signature culinary experiences at Seasons Restaurant – which also include private chef, chef's table and private dining room options – have put the Aviara's celebrity chefs at the forefront of San Diego's culinary scene. 'This kitchen is reminiscent of dining at your own home, providing comforts of your kitchen and enjoying the relaxed atmosphere of interacting with members of the family,' says Ortega.

According to a study carried out by the Harvard Business School (2014), better food would seem to be served in those restaurants where chefs and customers can see eye to eye. For two weeks, researchers experimented with four different scenarios in a cafeteria converted into an authentic laboratory. The results showed that when cooks could see patrons, food quality got higher ratings. One reason for this, according to the researchers, is that contact – at least a visual one – with the end-users of their work is a strong stimulus for the chefs, who thus realize the importance of their job, feeling more appreciated, satisfied and motivated. This is certainly the case at Four Seasons Aviara: 'Kitchen and chef will be the heart of the personality of

(Continued)

(Continued)

this place,' says Ortega. 'Everything from food on table, to the food to go, will speak about chef's passion and connection to food. Chef will come out and interact with the guests while the manager will be able to help select the right wine for the guests to buy for their dinner.'

Certainly, consumers are on board with the concept. Gathering data from 277 regular restaurant customers, Alonso and O'Neill (2010) explored images of open restaurant kitchens. Overall, respondents' comments demonstrate positive views about the open kitchen concept, including fun, entertainment, cleanliness, trust and being able to see both the chefs and the food being prepared. While clearly an open kitchen concept may not be appropriate, convenient or feasible in all hospitality scenarios, the findings suggest that many consumers do appreciate elements of the concept that can be experienced during the consumption of their meals. What may be even more important is the 'reassuring' aspect of how food is being prepared, including cleanliness, attention to allergies and food intolerances and hygienic measures.

The National Restaurant Association (2016) asked two industry experts how to make an open kitchen worthy of a standing ovation. 'An open kitchen is no longer just a hole in the wall where you can see someone working,' says William Eaton, chairman of the board of Cini-Little International, the world's largest foodservice design consultancy. 'Display kitchens serve as a focal point,' says Rodolfo Farber, co-founder and partner of San Diego-based Jaime Partners, a construction and project management company specializing in the hospitality industry (National Restaurant Association, 2016).

The two experts came up with guidelines to make the open kitchen a harmonious experience for culinary teams as well as diners. Acoustics are integral to this and they recommend careful attention to kitchen clatter and, in particular, dishwashing noise. Ventilation and smells have to be addressed, preferably using an air modulation system: 'You also want to draw the air from the dining room gently into the kitchen,' says Eaton. Aesthetics are equally important: 'Plan sight lines strategically. Build a counter high enough to shield the kitchen work area and the floor, but low enough to give guests a glimpse into the action,' says Eaton. With this heightened transparency, the aesthetic planning of the restaurant should also extend to kitchen equipment, although attention should also be given to functionality, cleanliness and tidiness. Cooking crews literally become cast members in the open kitchen concept and they need special preparation and training for their starring roles.

Sources: Hudson, S. (2016). "Open Kitchen Concept Spreads to Hotels." Hotel Business Review, August. http://hotelexecutive.com/business_review/

CASE STUDY QUESTIONS

1. Account for the popularity of the open kitchen concept
2. Critique the study conducted by the Harvard Business School. Was the methodology sound?
3. What further research could be done to confirm the findings from the Harvard study?

REFERENCES

Ahmed, Z. U. and Krohn, F. B. (1990) 'Marketing dynamics of a hotel tax: The case of Chautauqua County, New York', *Hospitality Review*, 8(2): 15–26.

Alonso, A. D. and O'Neill, M. A. (2010) 'Exploring consumers' images of open restaurant kitchen design', *Journal of Retail and Leisure Property*, 9: 247–59.

Baker, K. J., Hozier, G. C., Jr. and Rogers, R. D. (1994) 'Marketing research theory and methodology and the tourism industry: A nontechnical discussion', *Journal of Travel Research*, 32(3): 3–7.

Bell, V. (2015) 'The marketing industry has started using neuroscience, but the results are more glitter than gold', *Guardian*, 28 June. https://www.theguardian.com/science/2015/jun/28/vaughan-bell-neuroscience-marketing-advertising (accessed 10 December 2016).

Brandwatch (2014) *Brandwatch Report Travel and Hospitality. Social Listening and the Tourism Industry: A Snapshot.* Brighton: Brandwatch.

Bruni, F. (2005) 'Yes, the Kitchen's Open. Too Open', 27 July. www.nytimes.com/2005/07/27/dining/yes-the-kitchens-open-too-open.html?_r=0 (accessed 10 December 2016).

Carey, R., Kang, D. and Zea, M. (2012) 'The trouble with travel distribution', *McKinsey Quarterly*, February.

Crabtree, B. F. and Miller, W. L. (eds) (1999) *Doing Qualitative Research*, 2nd edn. London: Sage.

Crompton, J. L. and McKay, S. L. (1997) 'Motives of visitors attending festival events,' *Annals of Tourism Research*, 24(2): 425–39.

Dwoskin, E. and Rusli, E.M. (2015) 'The technology that unmasks your hidden emotions', *Wall Street Journal*, 29 January: B1.

Essex, S. and Chalkley, B. (2004) 'Mega-sporting events in urban and regional policy: A history of the Winter Olympics', *Planning Perspectives,* 19(2): 201–4.

Faulkner, B., Chalip, L., Brown, G., Jago, L., March, R. and Woodside, A. (2000) 'Monitoring the tourism impacts of the Sydney 2000 Olympics', *Event Management*, 6: 1–16.

Faulkner, B. and Tideswell, C. (1999) 'Leveraging tourism benefits from the Sydney 2000 Olympics', *Pacific Tourism Review*, 3: 227–38.

Fine Dining TV (2014) 'Inside Kitchen Table – the up close and personal dining experience. YouTube video. https://www.youtube.com/watch?v=GYktGY1GEuw (accessed 10 December 2016).

Gerhold, P. (1993) 'Defining marketing (or is it market?) research', *Marketing Research*, 5(Fall): 6–7.

Getz, D. (1989) 'Special events: Defining the product', *Tourism Management*, 10(2): 125–37.

Getz, D. and Page, S.J. (2015) 'Progress and prospects for event tourism research', *Tourism Management*, 52: 593–631.

Goeldner, C. R. and Ritchie, J. R. B. (2009) *Tourism: Principles, Practices, Philosophies*, 11th edn. New York: Wiley.

Goldblatt, J. and Nelson, K. S. (2001) *The International Dictionary of Event Management*. 2nd edn. New York: John Wiley.

Gooroochurn, N. and Sinclair, M. T. (2005) 'Economics of tourism taxation: Evidence from Mauritius', *Annals of Tourism Research*, 32(2): 478–98.

Gordon, J. and Perrey, J. (2015) The dawn of marketing's new golden age', *McKinsey Quarterly*, February.

Green, P., Tull, D. and Albaum, A. (1988) *Research for Marketing Decisions*, 5th edn. Englewood Cliffs, NJ: Prentice-Hall.

Gursoy, D., Kim, K. and Uysal, M. (2004) 'Perceived impacts of festivals and special events by organizers: An extension and validation', *Tourism Management*, 25(2): 171–81.

Hall, C.M. (1992) *Hallmark Tourist Events*. London: Belhaven.

Harvard Business Review (2014) 'Cooks make tastier food when they can see their customers', *Harvard Business Review*, November. https://hbr.org/2014/11/cooks-make-tastier-food-when-they-can-see-their-customers/ar/1 (accessed 10 December 2016).

Hudson, S., Cardenas, D., Meng, F. and Thal, K. (2016) 'Building a place brand from the bottom up: A case study from the US', *Journal of Vacation Marketing*. Online first – doi: 10.1177/1356766716649228.

Hudson, S. and Hudson, L. J. (2013) *Customer Service for Hospitality and Tourism*. Oxford: Goodfellow Publishers Ltd.

Hudson, S., Hudson, P. and Miller, G. A. (2004) 'The measurement of service quality in the UK tour operating sector: A methodological comparison', *Journal of Travel Research*, 42(3): 305–12.

Hudson, S., Snaith, T., Miller, G. A. and Hudson, P. (2001) 'Distribution channels in the travel industry: Using mystery shoppers to understand the influence of travel agency recommendations', *Journal of Travel Research*, 40 (2): 148–54.

Kelbaugh, D. (1997) *Common Place: Toward Neighborhood and Regional Design*. Seattle: University of Washington Press.

King, N. (1998) 'Template analysis'. In G, Symon and C. Cassell (eds), *Qualitative Methods and Analysis in Organizational Research*, pp. 118–34. London: Sage.

Kinnear, T., Taylor, J., Johnson, L. and Armstrong, R. (1993) *Australian Marketing Research*. Sydney, Australia: McGraw-Hill.

Kozak, M. and Rimmington, M. (1999) 'Measuring tourist destination competitiveness: conceptual considerations and empirical findings', *Hospitality Management*, 18: 273–83.

Liburd, J. J. and Derkzen, P. (2009) 'Emic perspectives on quality of life: The case of the Danish Wadden Sea festival', *Tourism and Hospitality Research*, 9(2): 132–46.

Litvin, S. W., Crotts, J. C., Blackwell, C. and Styles, A. K. (2006) 'Expenditures of accommodations tax revenue: A South Carolina study', *Journal of Travel Research*, 45(2): 150–7.

Litvin, S. W., Smith, W. W. and Blackwell, C. (2012) 'Destination marketing, accommodation taxes, and mandated promotional expenditures: May be time to reconsider', *Current Issues in Tourism*, 15(4): 385–90.

Mara, A. (2006) 'Using charettes to perform civic engagement in technical communication classrooms and workplaces', *Technical Communication Quarterly*, 15(2): 215–36.

McDaniel, C. D., Jr. and Gates, R. (1993) *Contemporary Marketing Research*, 2nd edn. Minneapolis–St. Paul, MN: West, 126.

Min, H. and Min, H. (2011) 'Benchmarking the service quality of fast-food restaurant franchises in the USA: A longitudinal study', *Benchmarking: An International Journal*, 18(2): 282–300.

National Restaurant Association (2016) 'Open kitchens take center stage', www. restaurant.org/Manage-My-Restaurant/Operations/Back-of-House/Open-kitchens-take-center-stage (accessed 10 December 2016).

O'Shea-Evans, K. (2012) 'Confessions of a hotel mystery shopper', *Travel + Leisure*, 23 July. http://edition.cnn.com/2012/07/23/travel/confessions-hotel-mystery-shopper/index.html (accessed 10 December 2016).

Richards, G. and Wilson, J. (2004) 'The impact of cultural events on city image: Rotterdam, cultural capital of Europe 2001', *Urban Studies*, 41(10): 1931–1951.

Tuttle, B. (2012) 'Nothing to hide: Why restaurants embrace the open kitchen', *Time*, 20 August. http://business.time.com/2012/08/20/nothing-to-hide-why-restaurants-embrace-the-open-kitchen (accessed 10 December 2016).

TOURISM MARKETING ETHICS   12

INTRODUCTION

Chapter 12 begins with a discussion about the principles of ethical marketing and the growth of research into tourism and hospitality ethics. The second section looks at ethical consumption and how travellers are increasingly demanding openness from companies – more information, responsibility and accountability. The next two next sections of the chapter cover the related topics of sustainable tourism and responsible marketing of tourism, and the final section discusses cause-related marketing in the tourism and hospitality sector. Case studies look at accessible tourism in Scandinavia, sustainable golf in Portugal, and war tourism in Vietnam.

PLEASE
DO NOT
DISTURB

LESSONS FROM A MARKETING GURU: ACCESSIBLE TRAVEL EXPERT, MAGNUS BERGLUND

Millions of people around the world with a disability have the means and desire to travel, yet many choose to stay at home because of the lack of accessible facilities. The potential size of the accessible tourism market is estimated at between 600 and 900 million people worldwide, suggesting that roughly 10 per cent of the population is looking for barrier-free or accessible travel. With an ageing population, this percentage will continue to grow and there is an increasing recognition that this is no longer a niche market. According to a study conducted by Open Doors, a well-recognized training firm in the US, people with a disability take 31.7 million trips per year spending $13.6 billion on travel. Furthermore, people with a disability tend not to travel alone and are often accompanied by carers, family or friends. If their expenditure is factored in, too, this increases the 'clout' of accessible tourism considerably in the overall tourism market.

IMAGE 12.1   Magnus Berglund, Accessibility Director for Scandic (Courtesy of Scandic)

In order to nurture an accessible tourism market, a cultural shift needs to occur along with facility and service advancements in the travel and hospitality industry. Some destinations have recognized this need to change, and have introduced initiatives to position themselves as 'accessible tourism-friendly'. Examples are: the Accessible Tourism for All programme in the UK; the Freedom without Barriers project in San Marino; Hospitality for All in Germany; IMSERSO programmes in Spain; the Accessible San Diego initiative; Peru's Tourism for All programme; the Barrier-Free Thailand project; and Belgium's Accessible Tourism Destination Certification Programme.

Perhaps the most proactive hotel group in terms of providing accessibility is Scandic, the Nordic region's leading hotel chain with 230 hotels across Europe. The policies dedicated to accessibility were initiated by Magnus Berglund, who was originally a cook with Scandic. Due to a muscle disease, Berglund was on sick leave for five years. When he was able to start work again, he contacted his former employer with his ideas on how the hotel chain could increase accessibility and use it to gain competitive advantage. In 2003, Berglund, who walks with the help of a special cane and travels with a rehab dog, was appointed Accessibility Director for Scandic, reporting directly to the Group Executive Committee. 'Guests with special needs are a growing market due to the population getting older,' says Berglund. 'This will continue as disabilities are no longer seen as a hindrance that stops people from travelling. At Scandic we work hard to make all our hotels more accessible. It is not always about investing in the building – many times it is the smallest things that make a difference.'

Scandic has an accessibility standard that was drawn up in 2003 as a platform for all special needs work at Scandic. This standard works as a checklist and template for the hotels and, in particular, when Scandic opens a new hotel or renovates an existing hotel. The standard has grown over the years and today it contains 135 checkpoints to follow. Ninety of these points are mandatory for all hotels and, for new hotels, all of the points must be considered. Scandic's accessibility standards can be found at: www.scandichotels.com/Always-at-Scandic/Special-needs/. 'We have a lot of focus on design and we try to build our accessible rooms so that they are as good as any other room,' says Berglund.

Special features in the hotels include alarm clocks that vibrate or shine a blue light for the hard of hearing, braille hotel fact sheets, accessible rooms, elevator and other controls at two heights, and a can-do attitude towards accommodating disabilities. A lowered reception desk for wheelchair users, a guest computer in the lobby at a comfortable height for a wheelchair and an ordinary chair, and a hearing loop in conference facilities and reception, are other examples of a high level of accessibility. 'On every hotel page our guests can see what kind of service we offer regarding special needs,' says Berglund.

Primarily a customer service provision, this attention to detail also makes sound business sense. 'Since there is a growing market for travellers with special needs we do see that the work we do gives us competitive advantage,' Berglund explains. 'We are probably the first hotel chain in the world that has undertaken so many activities when it comes to accessibility. When we started with this work in 2003 we didn't have any contracts with handicap organizations. Today we have contracts with over 100 different handicap organizations and we think that says a lot about the kind of effect our work has. There are also more and more conferences where organizers are asking about accessibility before they book.' The market is growing from both the conference and the leisure sectors, he says, particularly due to an ageing population, which increasingly expects to travel.

Training, of course, is critical and Berglund educates all the hotels on how to accommodate disabilities. As part of this training, he asks hotel executives to navigate their hotels in wheelchairs, to familiarize them with the challenges facing those with disabilities. Scandic also has an excellent interactive online e-learning course on accessibility that is available for both staff and anyone outside of the chain. Participants can navigate in three different 3D panoramic environments – a reception and lobby, a hotel room, and a hotel restaurant.

Ongoing research into clients' needs is important, too, for Scandic: 'We receive feedback from our customers via email and we have a great cooperation with different organizations, such as handicap organizations,' says Berglund. 'We continuously develop

(Continued)

(Continued)

our work and we have workshops every two years with our technical department and we listen to our guests.' This level of customer interaction and service is reflected in the Scandic marketing department which includes accessibility in various ways: 'We are sponsors to different organizations within accessibility, as an example we are partners with the Paralympics team for Sweden, Norway, Denmark and Finland. We have information in different channels, our website and also sales brochure and much more. We work closely together with the marketing department.'

Research suggests that once disabled travellers have found accommodation that suits their needs, they can be loyal customers returning year on year. Given that approximately 20 per cent of North Americans and Europeans are living with a disability, it is a market that cannot be ignored by the hotel sector.

Sources: Darcy (2010); Grady and Ohlin (2009).

ETHICS IN MARKETING

As the opening case study posits, with an increased awareness and a focused attention on issues such as accessibility, the tourism and hospitality sector is having to adapt. Magnus Berglund would argue that accommodating people with disabilities is just the 'right thing to do', and essentially, marketing ethics refers to what is morally right and wrong, good and bad in marketing, and particularly the moral challenges of marketing practitioners as they engage in marketing practice (Smith and Murphy, 2012). In the last few decades, marketing ethics has moved from being regarded as an oxymoron in some quarters to a position of relative academic legitimacy. Increasingly, more scholarship is devoted to the topic, fuelled by specialty journals like the *Journal of Business Ethics*. Ethical marketing is less of a marketing strategy and more of a philosophy that informs all marketing efforts. It is not a hard and fast list of rules, but a general set of guidelines to assist companies as they evaluate new marketing strategies. Table 12.1 lists some of the common principles of ethical marketing, but ethical questions commonly arise in regard to fairness in pricing, truth in advertising and other marketing communications, and product safety. More recently, media attention has focused on ethical issues in relation to marketing practices online (e.g. privacy in marketing through social networks) and marketing and sustainability (e.g. where marketing is seen to promote increased consumption and a disposable society).

Attention has also turned to the tourism and hospitality industry in regard to ethical practices. In fact, in addition to the oft-cited economic indicators displaying the dominance of the tourism industry, there has been a commensurate and almost equally well-publicized rise and recognition of the potentially negative impacts that the growth of this industry can have (Archer, Cooper and Ruhanen, 2005). Researchers have been critical of the pernicious social and environmental impacts the industry brings with it from reinforcing Western domination over developing countries through the 'host/guest' relationship (Smith and Brent, 2001), to the visual scars on the landscape caused by ski resorts or golf courses (Hudson, 2000). This has led to calls for the industry to exercise greater responsibility and 'professionalism' (Sheldon, 1989) in order to protect the 'golden goose' (Manning and Dougherty, 1995), and mirrors the

TABLE 12.1 Principles of ethical marketing (Based on Marketing-schools.com, 2016 and the Institute for Advertising Ethics).

1. All marketing communications share the common standard of truth
2. Marketing professionals abide by the highest standard of personal ethics
3. Advertising is clearly distinguished from news and entertainment content
4. Marketers should be transparent about who they pay to endorse their products
5. Consumers should be treated fairly based on the nature of the product and the nature of the consumer (e.g. extra care is needed when marketing to children)
6. The privacy of the consumer should never be compromised
7. Marketers should follow federal, state and local advertising laws, and cooperate with industry self-regulatory programmes for the resolution of marketing practices
8. Ethics should be discussed openly and honestly during all marketing decisions

arguments for greater corporate and social responsibility in other industries. In the last few decades, therefore, responsible tourism has emerged as a significant trend in the Western world, as wider consumer market trends towards lifestyle marketing and ethical consumption have spread to tourism (Goodwin and Francis, 2003). As the opening case highlights, tourism organizations are beginning to realize that promoting their ethical stance can be good business as it potentially enhances a company's profits, management effectiveness, public image and employee relations (Fleckenstein and Huebsch, 1999; Hudson and Miller, 2005b).

As a consequence of these changes, research into tourism and hospitality ethics is growing in areas such as tourism advertising ethics (Campelo, Aitken and Gnoth; 2011); ethical marketing of tourism products (Babaitia, Munteanu and Ispas, 2010); accessibility in tourism (see case study above); unethical sales practices (Stoller, 2011); the ethics of last-chance tourism (Dawson et al., 2011); environmental ethics in tourism (Jovičić and Sinosich, 2012); and the ethics of visiting war-torn countries (Hudson, 2007). For managers in the industry, other key ethical issues arise in four main areas: the supply chain, the local community (in the tourism destination), the workplace, and customers (Leadlay, 2011). There may be concerns about forced labour in the supply chain or exploitation of migrant workers in the workplace, for example; or local people may perceive that they have little or no share in the economic benefits of tourism, while bearing a disproportionate burden from environmental degradation.

The case study in Chapter 8 on Brazil touched on the negative consequences of producing controversial advertisements, but provocative advertising can have both positive and negative impacts. Hudson (2008) provides a good example of this in his case study about Thomas Cook's Club 18–30 brand, which sells overseas holidays to young people. Club 18–30 was first launched in the 1960s targeting the affluent youth, but by the mid-80s, was increasingly associated with cutting-edge licentiousness – sex, sex and more sex – and bad publicity was as good as any publicity when its outrageous ads, as well as the much-publicized bad behaviour of both its clients and some of its overseas staff, engendered endless debate and criticism in the media. By the mid-90s, Club 18–30 was thriving thanks to headline-grabbing advertising campaigns featuring such *double entendre* slogans as 'Beaver Espana', 'Summer of 69' and 'Wake up at the crack of Dawn'.

However, by 2003 the high-profile, self-styled sex-on-the beach tour company had been undermined by its own risqué image. What had once been tongue in cheek had now become sullied and non-PC. The Club 18–30 management team decided to reinvigorate the brand and reinvent it through advertising, a review of its core overseas offering and promotions. Women, in particular, were targeted as a key element in rebranding the company in an effort to attract a different type of customer. The gaudy, high-profile logo was replaced by a softer, sleek, monochrome design, banners were removed from destinations, and company literature was upgraded to resemble a lifestyle magazine rather than the traditional brochures which had always featured scantily clad young people on the beach and in night clubs. Bar crawls and beach parties featuring lewd drinking games were stopped and night-based club and bar crawls were supplemented with shopping trips, scuba diving, golf, spas, cultural visits and, in particular, an emphasis on music events and the upmarket club scene.

Campelo, Aitken and Gnoth (2011) have also looked at the ethics of advertising, focusing on the ethics of representing people and places through the visual rhetoric of advertising campaigns. The idea of ethical representation deals with how close particular advertising campaigns come to representing a common reality. Based on an analysis of advertisements in the '100% Pure New Zealand' campaign, they offer some ethical principles to condition the visual rhetoric of the marketing of destinations and place brands. These principles are: (1) represent the place's ethos based on the perceived reality of a place's social capital; (2) frame representations that identify and celebrate traditions, lifestyle, and cultural manifestations of relationships between people and place; (3) avoid deliberate misrepresentations; (4) create a balance in the representation of cultures comprising a mosaic of heritages and ethnicities; and (5) recognize that the ethos of a place is represented not just by its content but also by its form. The authors conclude that the marketing and branding of destinations should identify and enhance the ethos of the place with representations that are authentic and equitable. This means participation of local people in the discussion of destination branding campaigns to authenticate and enlighten the representation of a place's ethos as a fair and ethical representation.

Finally, there are some ethical concerns over the use of product placement as a marketing tool, the main concern centring on the issue of deception. Product placements are not labelled as advertisements and therefore may be viewed as hidden but paid messages (Balasubramanian, 1994). Research has confirmed that consumers are concerned about the 'subliminal' effect of product placement (Tiwsakul, Hackley and Szmigin, 2005). The idea of advertising that affects people below their level of conscious awareness, so that they are not able to exercise conscious control over their acceptance or rejection of the message, creates ethical issues for both marketers and consumers.

For managers in the tourism and hospitality industry, approaches for making ethical decision tend to vary, and Table 12.2 summarizes those approaches. The United Nations World Tourism Organization (UNWTO) has developed a Global Code of Ethics for Tourism (GCET), a comprehensive set of principles designed to guide key-players in tourism development (see http://ethics.unwto.org/en/content/global-code-ethics-tourism). The Code's ten principles amply cover the economic, social, cultural and environmental components of travel and tourism. The World Committee on Tourism Ethics is the impartial body responsible for interpreting, applying and evaluating the provisions of this code. The tasks assigned to the Committee include the promotion and dissemination of the code, as well as the evaluation and monitoring of the implementation of the principles enshrined therein.

TABLE 12.2 Approaches to ethical decision-making

Jaszay's ethics analysis model (2002)	Blanchard and Peale's quick 'ethics check' (1988)	Hall's five-step test for ethics (1992)
What are we trying to accomplish?	Is it legal? Will I be violating either civil law or company policy?	Is the decision legal?
Is what we are trying to accomplish ethical?	Is it balanced? Is it fair to all concerned in the short term as well as the long term? Does it promote win–win relationships?	Is the decision fair?
Where do our loyalties belong?	How will it make me feel about myself? Will it make me proud? Would I feel good if my decision were published in the newspaper?	Does the decision hurt anyone?
Who are the stakeholders that will be affected by our decision?	Would I feel good if my family knew about it?	Have I been honest with those affected?
What are our decision options? (Is there a better alternative?)		Can I live with my decision?
Are there any ethical principles that might be violated by any of the options?		
What are the consequences (positive and negative) to all the stakeholders for each option?		

Some tourism researchers have studied ethical decision-making in tourism. Hudson and Miller (2005a), for example, developed six ethical scenarios (social, environmental and economic) with pertinence to the challenges faced by industry practitioners today. They then applied the Multidimensional Ethics Scale (MES) (Reidenbach and Robin, 1988) to tourism students to see how they responded to these scenarios. The MES captures the extent to which respondents feel that a particular action is unethical according to the ethical theories of justice (the equitable distribution of reward and punishment), relativism (there are no universal standards of moral value only cultural norms) and deontology and utilitarianism. Respondents as a whole were least satisfied with the decisions taken with the environmental scenarios. This supports the contention that students are more exposed to ethical scenarios related to the environment (Hughes, 2005). There is a need, therefore, for the tourism curriculum to integrate more social and economic ethical dilemmas. Similar to many prior studies, the results indicated that female students are more sensitive to ethical issues than males in terms of their ethical intention – particularly for environmental issues.

ETHICAL CONSUMERISM

As mentioned in Chapter 2, wider consumer market trends towards lifestyle marketing and ethical consumption have spread to tourism. Travellers are increasingly demanding openness from companies – more information, responsibility and accountability. International leisure travellers are also increasingly motivated to select a destination for the quality of its environmental health and the diversity and integrity of its natural and cultural resources. The Digital Spotlight in this chapter shows how the popular golf destination of Portugal has implemented environmentally friendly measures aimed at reducing the impact of golf course construction and operation.

Creative hospitality providers are also responding and benefiting from this trend. A hotel owner in Aruba, for example, has won numerous awards for green practices, and maintains an enviable 90 per cent occupancy rate. Ewald Biemans, owner of Bucuti & Tara Beach Resort, is well known on the island for being an environmental preservation pioneer, and his Eagle Beach property is the first resort in the Americas to be certified ISO 14001 – a classification that requires superior environmental management. Biemans maintains that operating green does not necessarily mean sacrificing luxury. 'You have to be creative.' he says. 'You must find ways to increase a guest's sense of VIP treatment while at the same time expand their consciousness about their environmental responsibility. And I have found that the more guests realize that they are contributing to the well-being of the planet and are welcome to get involved in community efforts, the more they enjoy their vacation. It's win–win' (Media, 2013). Even in the hotel's fitness centre, energy-saving light bulbs and motion sensor lights have been installed, plastic cups have been replaced with paper, the towels are old beach towels that have been converted, there are recycling bins for aluminum, green glass and paper, and the hotel's Environmental Policy is posted.

A more environmentally conscious society is often attributed to the influence of the younger generation. Consumer research specialists Nielsen have found that twenty and

IMAGE 12.2 Fitness Center at Bucuti & Tara Beach Resort (©Bucuti & Tara Beach Resort. Reproduced with permission)

thirty year-olds are more willing to pay extra for environmentally friendly products than any other age group (nearly three-quarters said they would, versus just half of Baby Boomers) (Jullien, 2016). They are also civic-minded, compassionate and progressive, preoccupied with issues such as unemployment and inequality (63% donate to charities and 43% volunteer or are a member of a community organization). Related to volunteering, 'voluntourism' or traveller philanthropy is also gathering momentum, whereby these civic-minded travellers or travel businesses are giving time, talent and financial resources to further the well-being of the places that they visit. The phenomenon is expected to grow exponentially, benefiting from trends in giving, travel, and globalization. The trend has spread to the corporate world, an opportunity noticed by Hands-Up Incentives, a company specializing in sustainability-focused incentive trips in over 30 difference destinations. 'There are many opportunities for companies to give back and improve their corporate social responsibility reputations,' said founder Christopher Hill, who notes over the past five years such give-back trips increased 300 per cent. Groups can volunteer for social sustainable travel experiences incorporating wildlife and communities. The company has several case studies on its website at www.handsupincentives.com/case-studies/.

But it is not just the younger generation that is influencing more ethical consumption. Chapter 2 referred to the 'LOHAS' segment, an acronym for Lifestyles of Health and Sustainability, responsible for an estimated $290 billion in goods and services focused on health, the environment, social justice, personal development and sustainable living (Thiyagaraj, 2015). Research shows that one in four adult Americans is part of this group – nearly 41 million people. LOHAS tourists will tend to look for destinations and resorts that are sustainable and 'eco' (i.e. in harmony with the environment, its wildlife and human communities). One consequence of this trend is the development of eco-spas. Eco-spas are usually located in attractive natural landscapes that are designed and built in harmony with the surroundings, using local and sustainable materials. Some eco-spas are even temporary and are dismantled at the end of the tourist season leaving no trace. Networks such as Ecospas (www.ecospas.com) provide guidelines and support for those spas who want to become more environmentally friendly or green. Examples of eco initiatives might include: limiting and recycling water; using local and seasonal produce for cuisine; respecting indigenous and tribal communities and traditions; using cosmetics not tested on animals; and protecting wildlife. One of the challenges with this new trend is the abuse of the 'eco' label, with many spas claiming to be eco-spas but not following adequate guidelines. Eco-spas can technically be located anywhere if they are environmentally friendly, but it is most common to find them in beautiful landscapes such as the rainforests of Central America, the outback of Australia, or the bush in Africa.

Ethical consumption in tourism and hospitality has spread to the restaurant business, with customers seeking foods that adhere to animal welfare, organic and other standards. Restaurant chains like Chipotle are catering to these changing consumer tastes. The company, whose slogan is 'Food with Integrity', creatively promotes its concerns about sustainable agriculture and the humane treatment of animals used for meat. It hopes that preaching the gospel of sustainable agriculture will translate into consumers buying Chipotle fast food (Cohen, 2014). From its beginnings in Denver in 1993, Chipotle has styled itself as a different kind of fast-food restaurant, one that cares about the supply chain. Today, the company has about 2,000 restaurants and a stock market value of more than $12 billion. Chipotle has also created the *Cultivate Festival*, a travelling festival series that 'encourages attendees to think and talk about food and food issues', according to the company. Attendees see musical performances from top national acts, combined with educational opportunities about how food can be raised responsibly and prepared safely. During the events, customers can check out various learning exhibits that cover topics such as genetically modified organisms (GMOs), fresh versus processed food, and factory versus farm foods.

In fact, event attendees in general are looking to event organizers to take a more ethical stance, although Laing and Frost (2010) suggest that more research is needed to explore aspects of behaviour of event-goers, including their motivations, the influence of their interest in green issues on their decision-making processes with respect to attending events, and their expectations as to the green 'content' of events, as well as levels of satisfaction with current offerings. They make the observation that the lack of academic research focused on green events is juxtaposed with increasing interest by organizers of events in highlighting their green credentials and an increasingly sophisticated market that is more knowledgeable about sustainability practices than ever before. They also refer to the growing trend of promoting an ethical message through events (as in the Chipotle-sponsored event referred to above), through avenues such as sponsorship, themed displays or stalls, presentations, and sale of food and beverages that fit with the sustainable theme.

As mentioned in Chapter 2, authenticity is increasingly important to travellers, who want more interaction with local people with more emotional and cultural links to the communities they visit. According to Gilmore and Pine (2007), management of the customer perception of authenticity is a source of competitive advantage. However, it has

IMAGE 12.3 Goats in trees in southwest Morocco (photo courtesy of Stephanie Green).

been suggested that the practice of 'staged authenticity' (MacCannell, 1973) – creating the impression that an experience is authentic, whereas in fact it is not – is unethical and can be a deterrent to tourists (Ruitz, 2008). A good example comes from southwest Morocco, where the authors were travelling in 2016. In that area, it is quite common to find dozens of goats hanging out lazily in the tree-tops, munching absentmindedly like overgrown crows (see Image 12.3 above). The goats are drawn to the fruit of the Argan tree, which ripens in June each year. Naturally, tourists are also drawn to the trees for the photo opportunity. However, our driver informed us that the goats are often 'placed' in the trees, so that buses will stop for photographs – and then pay a small 'fee' to the local farmers (or guide) for the privilege.

ETHICS AND SUSTAINABLE TOURISM

A tourism marketer must have an understanding of the principles of sustainable tourism, a concept that is closely tied to ethics (Hudson and Miller, 2003). Wight (1995) suggests that there is an overlap between special interest tourism like ecotourism, cultural tourism and adventure tourism, and that the motivations to participate in these types of tourism are overlain by an ethical dimension. Wight argues that only when the ethical principle is overlain as the key motivation, can tourism be considered sustainable (see Figure 12.1).

Butler describes sustainable tourism development as 'tourism which is developed and maintained in an area in such a manner and at such a scale that it remains viable over an indefinite period and does not degrade or alter the environment (human and

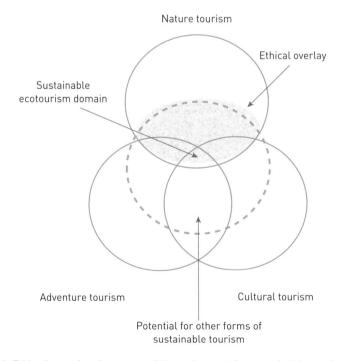

FIGURE 12.1 Ethics in tourism is an essential requirement for sustainable tourism (Wight, 1995, Reprinted with permission of Taylor and Francis Group LLC Books)

physical) in which it exists to such a degree that it prohibits the successful development and well-being of other activities and processes' (Butler, 1993).

Over-popularity as a tourism attraction can often lead to a destination becoming the unsustainable victim of its own success. Machu Picchu, Peru, an Inca site rediscovered in 1911, is a good example. Attracting around 400,000 visitors by the early 2000s, there was little restriction to either access or visitor behaviour within the sacred sites which reportedly generate US$40 million annually for the Peruvian economy. Aguas Calientes, the village at the base of Machu Picchu, mushroomed in size, garbage lined the banks of the nearby Urubamba River, and the Inca Trail had deteriorated due to many years of unrestricted over-use. Overcrowding, erosion and the exploitation of local people as guides and porters were all endemic before January 2001 when the government finally intervened and initiated a system of regulations and permits. Increasing pressure from UNESCO, the World Tourism Organization (WTO) and numerous nongovernment agencies has encouraged a limit on the number of visitors to the ancient Inca ruins. Laws limit numbers on the trail to 500 per day now, and visitors must join guided tours with registered companies to ensure adherence to conservation regulations. To promote continued sustainability in the area, the tourists themselves have to admit some responsibility as well as the government and the tourism industry. Prices are rising to visit the site – general admission is now around US$45 per person and the Inca Trail permit has gone up in the last ten years from US$20 to US$80 in order to pay for trail maintenance, monitoring of regulations and better facilities.

Another good example of a destination being the victim of its own success comes from Mallorca in Spain. The municipality of Calvià on the Spanish island suffered over-development and environmental degradation in the 1970s and 1980s, due to massive tourism investment. Tourism development was based on short-term interests, unlimited building out of tune with local conditions, and an unsustainable exploitation of exceptional natural resources. In order to restore the communities, radical changes had to be implemented, so a local Agenda 21 process led to the closing of many run-down hotels, landscape restoration, establishment of new protected areas and the creation of an environmental charge on the sales of hotel rooms. These changes coincided with public awareness and marketing campaigns to improve the city's image, leading to increased employment opportunities as well as popularity among visitors. Visitor spending also rose as the destination was able to charge higher prices for a higher quality product. An article in the British tabloid, the *Sun*, complained about this, with a headline 'Your hols will Costa packet'. But as one commentator said: 'If fewer *Sun* readers can afford to travel to the island, Mallorca refining its tourism product for the higher end of the market could prove to be of economic merit as well as benefiting the environment, heritage and culture' (Royle, 2009).

Dawson et al. (2011) have discussed the ethics of an emerging travel trend that has been labelled 'last chance tourism' (LCT). In LCT, tourism demand is based on the desire to see vulnerable places and features before they disappear or are essentially and irrevocably changed. The paradox in this new form of travel lies in the fact that the tourists often travel long distances to these places, and are thus disproportionately responsible per capita for increased greenhouse gas emissions and various other stressors that have the potential to alter further the very attractions being visited. Through a praxis/reflective approach, Dawson et al. discuss the various ethical issues associated with marketing and managing LCT, using one of the most evocative symbols of climate change, the polar bears of Churchill, Manitoba, Canada, as a source of empirical evidence and a foundation for exploring ethical considerations. They conclude that since there are currently no existing precedents set for managing LCT, the responsibility for maintaining a sustainable and ethically supported polar bear viewing industry lies in the hands of the operators involved and the regulators governing the sector.

DIGITAL SPOTLIGHT: PORTUGAL'S GOLF RICH ALGARVE AREA STRIVES TO ACHIEVE ENVIRONMENTAL SUSTAINABILITY

Portugal's Algarve region was one of the first destinations to recognize the potential for golf tourism to bolster off-season visitation. With an abundance of beautiful beaches fulfilling tourists' needs in the summer, the area actively encouraged high-end golf course developments in the 1980s throughout its 500 square kilometre domain at a time when only lip service was paid to sustainability and environmental responsibility worldwide. The area was voted Established Golf Destination of the Year by IAGTO (International Association of Golf Tour Operators) in 2006, and the 'Best Golf Destination in the World' at the World Travel Awards in Qatar in 2014.

IMAGE 12.4 Espiche Golf Club (©Espiche Golf SA. All rights reserved. Reproduced with permission)

In October 2015 at the annual IAGTO Awards, the Algarve was vaunted as a great example of the benefits and value of working towards sustainability, according to an article in *The Golf Environment* e-mag. It had also won European Golf Destination of the Year in 2014. The conference in Tenerife saw the announcement of a new environmental award, the Sustainable Golf Destination of the Year Award, which would be presented at the 2016 ceremony in Mallorca. This new award would recognize golf destinations across the world, which are collectively committed to protecting nature, using resources efficiently and providing value to the community. The award aimed to encourage destinations to work together to embed sustainable practices for the benefit of their businesses, their community and the environment.

It was back in 2000 that local government regulation in Portugal kicked in with an Environmental Impact Assessment (EIA) Decree-Law limiting golf development to designated tourism areas. Two years later, the University of Algarve developed an

(Continued)

(Continued)

environmental sustainability blueprint for the region with its Algarve Golf Study. Most courses and developments were built before 2000 and therefore any environmental management plans would involve retrospective damage limitation.

With over a million rounds played per year, golf tourism is now huge for the area's economy. A golf course can generate 150 new beds in a hotel and up to $14 million in revenue, with wealthy golfers spending double the amount of other types of tourists. Over 60 per cent of their spending is outside the actual golf course. The golf industry adds 10,000 jobs to the Algarve region, and has a strategic importance for the Algarve since it operates in a counter-cycle to sun-beach tourism.

But the impact of around 27 million visitors annually, 12,000 registered golfers and 42 golf courses in the Algarve leads to an obvious challenge to long-term sustainability and, therefore, future competitiveness. The major environmental issues for the Algarve are consumption of water for irrigation, consumption of phytopharmaceuticals and fertilizers, energy consumption, waste production, location of courses and implementation of environmental practices by the golf clubs. Around $450 million is generated per year by Algarve's golf tourism, making environmental management affordable particularly for the bigger golf courses and developments.

Golf was identified as one of the ten priority products to be developed in Portugal between 2007 and 2015 as part of the National Strategic Plan for Tourism (PENT). The plan recognizes that the golf sector 'will be strengthened by the adoption of principles of sustainability, respect for the environment, active participation by resident populations, on-going training of human resources, innovation in all business areas, guarantee of quality and safety, compliance with a code of good practices and correct positioning in the purchasing markets'. Conclusions reached by a 2008 Conference included connecting the golf product to landscape heritage factors and to natural resources. 'The golf offer should therefore be tailored to territorial planning instruments, urban and landscape contexts, and environmental management practices, which play a decisive factor in guaranteeing the sustainability of the golf destination', the report stated. Good environmental practices were recommended during the design, construction and operational stages of golf course development for both financial and ethical reasons.

One club which has followed these precepts is Espiche Golf Club (www.espiche-golf.com), located on an Ecological Reserve near Lagos, Western Algarve. And it is using its ecological status as a digital differential in its marketing and advertising. Its website starts with the tagline 'A Visionary Commitment to Sustainability'. Scroll down the home page to read a segment on 'Espiche: eco-friendly, sustainable golf', describing the experience as unique within the Algarve, with its indigenous planting scheme which enriches the local biodiversity. Employing low-herbicide, low-water grass use on greens, fairways and rough, the eco-aware company plans to promote the green side of Espiche even more in the future. 'It's too early to say if it gives us a competitive advantage. But the "E" word is great PR,' General Manager, Luis Rocha says. 'We will definitely see an ROI. We're already paying a lot less in bills – power is expensive in Portugal. So we see savings now and even more in the long-term.' Rocha adds that the sustainably nurtured course is being improved all the time.

It is not only the course design and management that is catching ethical golfing attention, though. The cutting-edge club was awarded third place in *Golf Inc.* magazine's 'Clubhouse of the Year' competition for 2014–15. Although the 18-hole course opened in 2012, it took two more years for the launch of the stunning new eco-friendly clubhouse to follow in 2014. Sensitively integrated into the existing landscape, the ultra-mod clubhouse was built with stone from original farmhouse buildings in the lower walls of the outer structure to maintain the sense of history. It also uses solar energy from panels hidden within the roof design, to ensure a state of the art approach to sustainability. Designed by architect Nadine Berger, it reflects the club's ethos of preservation, conservation and innovation. 'Water is now a worldwide issue,' says owner Peter Thornton. 'We bought the land when things were in a transitional stage as Portugal was getting into the EU. Since then it was designated an ecological preserve. The end result is that we have built something for the future.'

Sources: Visit and interview with Espiche Golf Club (2015); Hudson and Hudson (2014).

CASE STUDY QUESTIONS

1. Would you say that the golf industry in general has a negative impact on the environment?

2. Which particular environmentally friendly initiative from the case impresses you most?

3. What more could the golf sector do to protect the environment?

RESPONSIBLE MARKETING OF TOURISM

If environmental improvement is to provide a competitive opportunity, an organization must consider responsible marketing, which is the balancing of environmental initiatives and environmental communication in order to achieve sustainable competitive advantage (Hudson and Miller, 2005b). Unfortunately, there has been no consistent approach to environmental marketing practices in tourism. Some companies neglect their environmental obligations, perhaps because of a lack of guidelines and examples of best practice, or perhaps because they don't understand the benefits. Others exploit environmental communication for short-term gains or fail to tell visitors about their environmental initiatives. Many studies indicate that environmental considerations are now a significant element of travellers' destination-choosing process, and much of what first-time visitors learn about a destination's environmental qualities that may influence their choice depends on the effectiveness of information and the motivation stimulated by commercial brochures or websites.

Figure 12.2 is a model of responsible marketing that managers in the tourism industry can use to improve their environmental marketing practices. The model is based on previous literature in marketing and in strategic and environmental management, and it adopts the view that an organization or destination can be plotted on a two-by-two matrix to identify its position regarding responsible marketing. The vertical axis represents environmental action and the horizontal axis represents communication of these activities. Organizations can take up one of four theoretical positions within the model. They can be classified as *inactive* when they tend not to see the benefits of allocating any resources towards environmental activities and when they have a low level of commitment to both environmental improvement and communication of environmental activities. Those that see the benefits of environmental action (perhaps for regulatory purposes) but fail to communicate these efforts are *reactive*. Organizations that exploit consumer interests in environmentally friendly products without considering resource characteristics, environmental ethics, or a long-term perspective are seen as *exploitive*. The position in the model most likely to remain sustainable (and competitive) is that in which both environmental action and environmental communication of this action are high, and these organizations are labelled as *proactive*. In the proactive position, products and services are developed sensitively, with regard to their long-term future, and consumers are aware (both before purchase and during the visit) of the concern for the resources involved.

It is important to recognize that an organization's position in the model may only be temporary, as it may be in transit between one place in the model and the next. Further, there is likely to be a variety of contingency factors that will affect the position on the model. Previous research suggests that these influences include the level of environmental pressures from stakeholders, managerial interpretations of environmental issues, the level of environmental regulations, and the size and the financial position of the company.

The Walt Disney Company is a good example of an organization that takes up a proactive position on this model, having been selected as a member of the Dow Jones Sustainability Indexes. The Disney Conservation Fund, for example, founded in 1995, is a key pillar in Disney's efforts to protect the planet and help kids develop

ENVIRONMENTALLY RESPONSIBLE ACTION	ENVIRONMENTAL COMMUNICATION	
	LOW	HIGH
LOW	**INACTIVE** No support or involvement from top management Environmental management not necessary No environmental reporting No employee environmental training or involvement	**EXPLOITIVE** Some involvement of top management Environmental issues dealt with only when necessary External reporting but no internal reporting Little employee training or involvement
HIGH	**REACTIVE** Some involvement of top management Environmental management is a worthwhile function Internal reporting but no external reporting Some employee environmental training or involvement	**PROACTIVE** Top management involved in environmental issues Environmental management is a priority item Regular internal and external reporting including an environmental plan or report Employee environmental training or involvement encouraged

FIGURE 12.2 A model for responsible marketing

lifelong conservation values. The fund supports the study of wildlife; the protection of habitats; the development of community conservation and education programmes in critical ecosystems; and experiences that connect children to nature across the globe. But being proactive with regard to responsible tourism doesn't have to be limited to large companies. As mentioned in Chapter 9, the Stellenbosch tour company, Bites and Sites, is a member of Unashamedly Ethical, and includes a detailed 'Responsible Tourism' segment on its website with commitments to social, economic and environmental responsibility.

Other proactive pioneers of sustainable travel are seeking to move beyond the environment, and tackle social issues such as global poverty through tourism (sometimes referred to as 'pro-poor tourism' (Ashley, Boyd and Goodwin, 2000)). Bruce Poon Tip, founder and owner of travel operator G Adventures, for example, recently announced a partnership with National Geographic – one of the world's largest organizations dedicated to exploration, education, and conservation – and a commitment to develop 50 additional social enterprises at G Adventures destinations around the world. 'We believe that if done right, travel can be the greatest form of wealth distribution the world has ever seen,' he said (Birnbaum, 2015). The largest small-group adventure company in the world, G Adventures has carved its award-winning global reputation on sustainable travel – intimate, authentic experiences that fully immerse travellers in local culture. As mentioned in Chapter 4, many of its trips offer a unique opportunity to help the underserved communities that travellers visit, often through its Planeterra Foundation, an organization founded in 2003 with a focus on social enterprise support and development. Today, 25 social enterprise projects are incorporated in the supply chain of G Adventure itineraries with the goal of helping communities become more sustainable, and Poon Tip plans to triple that number by 2020.

Another company attempting to tackle the root causes of poverty is the Taj Group, the largest hotel, leisure and hospitality company in Southeast Asia. Taj runs many hospitality training programmes within the company's 36 rural vocational schools, where underprivileged youth and marginalized groups such as India's dalits, or untouchable caste, get training. Taj worked with the government to create the schools, which are run in partnership with NGOs. 'India is grappling with multiple issues,' says Vasant Ayyapan, director of corporate sustainability for the Taj Group. 'It's a bottomless pit. If you just give out money or food, that won't help people in the long run. That's why we decided to tackle the root causes of poverty, helping people earn a sustainable livelihood' (Buchmeyer, 2013). Taj's poverty-relief work extends to purchases made for the hotels. Holiday Village in Goa, for example, buys shell garland welcome gifts from underprivileged artisans. Also, the bags for newspapers and slippers are made by the Women's India Trust, which employs 100 poor women.

One hotel in Amsterdam is training scores of long-term unemployed people, preparing them for jobs in the hospitality sector. 'We don't look at a person's background. We look for their talents,' said a spokesperson for the non-for-profit Good Hotel (Farrow, 2016). The company is looking for expansion opportunities, and in 2016 opened a boutique property in Antigua, Guatemala, where it provides training for young people, offering an alternative to drugs and gangs. 'Our aim is to invest in people,' said the spokesperson. 'And get the best out of them.'

Finally, events can also take a proactive approach to responsibility. Many event organizers are recognizing that large events do not have to have a huge climate impact and, in fact, can play a positive role by becoming low-carbon or even carbon neutral. Through the establishment of greenhouse gas reduction and offsetting initiatives, event organizers can take responsibility for their emissions, use their larger purchasing power and profile to lead in climate change action, and support the transition to more sustainable energy use. Benefits include the opportunity to demonstrate publicly a commitment to sustainability and to inspire participants and spectators to choose low-carbon options in their own lives, as well as saving money through measures such as reducing energy consumption. An example is the transportation used in the Vancouver Winter Olympic Games that was intended to influence green behaviour. The public transportation system included the latest low and no emission technologies, and the Olympic fleet used hybrid, electric and propane vehicles. Event organizers can also incorporate other greening initiatives at their event to complement their climate-friendly practices: water conservation or promoting positive social and economic development, for example.

As Figure 12.2 suggests, promoting such initiatives is important. Los Cabos Green Fest in Mexico, for instance, touts itself as the 'first sustainable festival'. The annual festival combines international music and entertainment acts, sports – like yoga master classes, paddle boarding, soccer, eco trails runs and more – with environmental awareness workshops and events. Workshops are on topics such as permaculture, health and nutrition, green business, protected areas and natural wonders. Local and US-based companies are also on hand to introduce and offer sustainable products and services. Waste from the event is recycled and repurposed to reduce its carbon footprint, and a portion of the proceeds benefits local nonprofit organizations.

The alignment of an event with a key social issue is another way that event organizers can act in a responsible manner. In Australia, for example, the importance of reconciliation between Aboriginals and white Australians is a significant social issue. The organizers of the 2000 Summer Olympics therefore utilized the profile of gold medal-winning Aboriginal athlete Cathy Freeman to initiate national discourse about the reconciliation issue in Australia (Chalip, 2006). Likewise, Vancouver's sustainability efforts during the 2010 Winter Olympics included participation of Aboriginal communities. But social issues can also work against event organizers. Qatar's harsh treatment of foreign contract and domestic workers, seen by many as slave labour in the richest per capita state on earth, has placed the 2022 World Cup competition in doubt (*Independent*, 2014).

Events can also generate large amounts of money for charities. For example, nearly all of the 100-plus golf tournaments on the American PGA, Web.com Tour and Champions Tours are structured as nonprofit organizations designed to donate 100 per cent of net proceeds to local charities. Collectively, The PGA TOUR and its tournaments raised more than $160 million for charity in 2015. The all-time total donated to charity is $2.3 billion since the first-ever charitable contribution of $10,000 was made by the 1938 Palm Beach Invitational. 'This incredible record is due to the selfless work and tireless efforts of all the tournaments, sponsors, players and, especially, our volunteers,' said PGA TOUR Commissioner Tim Finchem. 'Passing this milestone ensures that many lives will continue to be positively impacted in the communities where we play' (PGA TOUR, 2016).

Finally, a number of researchers have argued that sporting events can have positive impacts on community citizenship. The hosting of sporting events is often a key element that enables communities devastated by economic downturns to regain and enhance their financial foothold in regional, national and global economies. However, criticisms are often raised that local community residents are often left out of the process, especially with one-off events. Misener and Mason (2006) suggest that community involvement in the hosting of sporting events – by organizing, watching or participating in an event – can positively impact community citizenship. They argue that so-called 'flexible citizenship' allows those who are seemingly unattached or disconnected from places to develop a sense of place and identity. Proponents of flexible citizenship consider members of a community as more actively involved in the development and shaping of their own civic identity, rather than static recipients of ascribed citizenship status.

CAUSE-RELATED MARKETING

Cause-related marketing (CRM), said to be corporate philanthropy organized to increase the bottom line (Barnes and Fitzgibbons, 1991), is a rapidly expanding trend in marketing communications, and is growing at a time when the public is increasingly cynical about big business. It is basically a marketing programme that strives to achieve two objectives – improve corporate performance and help worthy causes – by linking fundraising for the benefit of a cause to the purchase of the firm's products and/or services. Companies use CRM to contribute to the well-being of society and to associate themselves with a respected cause that will reflect positively on their corporate image. Companies, and their brands, can benefit from strategic alignments with causes or with not-for-profit organizations. It is hoped the emotional attributes associated with cause-linked brands differentiate them from their rivals (sometimes referred to as 'cause branding'). Lindblad Expeditions is a good example of a travel company engaging in CRM activities. With ten ships visiting some of the world's most sensitive destinations, the company (via donations from passengers) supports crucial research on sharks in the Galapagos and a project tagging killer whales in the Antarctic, among other conservation efforts (Buchmeyer, 2013).

CRM efforts can be categorized into autonomously branded, co-branded, house branded, and industry branded approaches (Hudson, 2008), the distinctive features of each being summarized in Table 12.3. Autonomously branded philanthropic collaborations are characterized by an arm's length relationship between the corporate sponsor's brand and the brand of the charity/cause that it supports. These are the quickest and easiest kind of relationships to arrange and are the dominant form of philanthropic activity. Mt. Bachelor in Oregon, for example, has Charity Ski Weeks whereby lift ticket vouchers are provided to several Charity Week partners that can be redeemed for $25 full day lift tickets. This offers a great deal for local skiers and riders while generating cash contributions with 100 per cent of the proceeds donated directly to the issuing nonprofit organization.

In co-branded collaborations, the company and the charity form a new brand co-sponsored and marketed by both organizations. An example of this type of branding approach is Avon's sponsorship of the *Race for the Cure* in partnership with the Breast Cancer Coalition. Collaborations of this type are more strategic than autonomously branded programmes because the company can differentiate itself by becoming the sole sponsor of an event or cause, and because co-ownership implies increased commitment and effort. In the ski industry, Stowe Mountain Resort Ski

Table 12.3 Branding approaches to CRM (Source: Adapted from Hudson, 2008)

Features	Autonomously branded	Co-branded	House branded	Industry branded
Charity reputation	Established/ independent of company	Tied to company and charity	Company dependent	Established/ independent of industry
Company's involvement in charity administration	None	Partial to jointly administered	Company controlled	None
Company control over charity use of funds raised by CRM programme	Limited	Some influence	Complete	Limited
Strategic opportunity	Leverage external brand	Leverage brand congruence	Support existing company/product brand	Leverage industry brand
CRM promotional objective	Demonstrate firm-charity congruence where not obvious	Demonstrate firm-charity brand congruence	Promote firm's commitment	Promote industry's commitment

and Snowboard School partners with Friends of Stowe Adaptive Sports, to put on an annual event called the Adaptive Ski Bash. Friends of Stowe is a nonprofit organization that supports access to sports and recreational opportunities for people living with permanent disabilities.

With the house branded approach, the firm takes ownership of a cause and develops an entirely new organization to deliver benefits associated with the cause (Hoeffler and Keller, 2002). Similar to private label products, house branded charities are by definition differentiated from other charities, and in the increasingly crowded marketplace for philanthropic programme partners, the firm has unfettered access to its own charity. Vail Resorts has its own house branded charity, setting up Vail Resort Echo in 2008 to bring a more focused approach to local charitable giving. Local leaders representing each division of the company are part of Giving Councils in each of the communities in which Vail Resorts operates. Together, these Councils work to identify key local organizations that are implementing successful programmes that will change the lives of children and protect the resources that make the resort towns unique. The Giving Councils award cash grants and in-kind donations once a year through a grant application process. Chipotle, referred to above, also takes a house branded approach. In 2011, the company established the Chipotle Cultivate Foundation to extend its commitment to creating a more sustainable food future. The foundation is dedicated to providing resources and promoting good stewardship for farmers; promoting better livestock husbandry; encouraging regenerative agriculture practices; and fostering food literacy, cooking education, and nutritious eating. Since its inception, the foundation has contributed more than $3 million to likeminded organizations committed to cultivating a better world through food.

Finally, industry branded initiatives are those that involve contributions to a cause from the industry as a whole, rather than separate corporations. As with house branded CRM initiatives, few examples exist in tourism, but the Travel Foundation in the UK fits this typology. The Travel Foundation was established in 2003 as a partnership between government, NGOs and the travel industry to acknowledge that tour operators have a responsibility to help protect the places that tourists visit and ensure that the benefits of tourism reach the local communities. The Travel Foundation supports tourism stakeholders – including tour operators from the relevant source markets, destination authorities, local tourism businesses and local communities – to develop and deliver a programme of activities that optimizes the overall benefits of tourism. The Travel Foundation also aims to change industry policy and practice, to help the tourism industry become a more sustainable one. The Travel Foundation's approach is depicted in Figure 12.3. Since 2003, the Foundation has worked in 25 countries, on over 35 projects that have generated more than £1 million in local incomes.

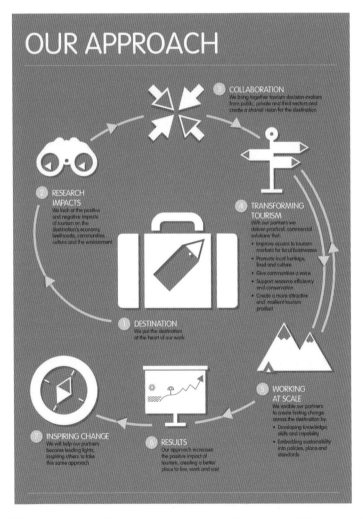

FIGURE 12.3 The Travel Foundation's approach to sustainable tourism (©The Travel Foundation. Used with kind permission)

CHAPTER SUMMARY

Marketing ethics refers to what is morally right and wrong, good and bad in marketing, and particularly the moral challenges of marketing practitioners as they engage in marketing practice. Research into tourism and hospitality ethics is growing in areas such as tourism advertising ethics, accessibility, unethical sales practices and environmental ethics. Travellers are increasingly demanding openness from companies – more information, responsibility and accountability. International leisure travellers are also increasingly motivated to select a destination for the quality of its environmental health and the diversity and integrity of its natural and cultural resources. A tourism marketer must therefore have an understanding of the principles of sustainable tourism, a concept that is closely tied to ethics.

REFLECTIVE QUESTIONS

1. The text suggests that research into tourism and hospitality ethics is growing. Why is this? Is the tourism industry behind or ahead of other sectors in responding to ethical issues?

2. Find an example of an advertisement that could be considered unethical. What are the problems with the ad?

3. The text suggests that travellers are increasingly motivated to select a destination for the quality of its environmental health. Find an example (outside of those in the book) of a tourism/hospitality provider that is responding and benefiting from this trend. Where would you position the company on Figure 2.2?

MARKETING IN ACTION: THE ETHICS OF PORTRAYING WAR AS A TOURISM ATTRACTION IN VIETNAM

War tourism has been around for hundreds of years. Admiral Lord Nelson's battleship, *The Victory*, for example, has long been a successful tourist attraction drawing millions of visitors to Portsmouth, England. Heroes from the American Civil War have likewise been venerated in the US with statues, artifacts, memorials and reenactments of their battles, attracting tourists in their thousands. The eerie reminders of World War II atrocities at Belsen and Auschwitz are still major tourism destinations as well as the city of Hiroshima in Japan and Pearl Harbor in Hawaii. However, it is only more recently that tourism marketers in Vietnam have identified the cultural value of their war-ravaged country in terms of an attraction to encourage more overseas visitors.

Having suffered more than 30 years of war (first with France, then with the US, and finally civil war), Vietnam has been engaged in renovation and rebuilding since its 1987 economic reform policy, *doi moi*. The reform promoted open-door policies and a free market economy. Through the establishment of the Vietnam National Administration of Tourism (VNAT), war tourism has been actively encouraged and targeted as part of a government and private sector marketing plan. VNAT is focusing on increasing state

IMAGE 12.5 Dien Bien Phu Victory Museum (©Vietnam National Administration of Tourism. Source: Tourism Information Technology Center-TITC. Used with permission)

management of tourism, strategic planning and forecasting, human resource training, and the easing of formalities within the industry. The intention is to attract overseas investment and develop tourism as a dominant foreign exchange earner for Vietnam.

War in Vietnam in the twentieth century led to the deaths of more than three million inhabitants along with 75,000 French and 59,000 US soldiers. The environmental, social, political and economic repercussions of this devastation still persist. VNAT predicts that two million Vietnamese immigrants will revisit their native country as tourists from the 80 different countries where they now live. Former American soldiers also seek the closure of revisiting the scenes of their nightmares in order to 'remember the fallen', to come to terms with the past and also to participate in a more positive future for Vietnam. Already there are several nonprofit organizations and tour companies in the US providing tailor-made trips to these former scenes of battle. 'We're promoting all the war history, but American tourism is really our aim,' said Luong Minh Sam, Director of the Tourism Department of Danang. 'Six million Americans were directly involved in the Vietnam War, and 20 million more were indirectly involved. That's a big market for us.'

The challenge of providing authentic and sensitive war memoirs can raise ethical issues. For example, how to package it all, encourage visitors and provide for their comforts, without it all becoming a de-sensitized fun family day out. Added to this are the many fundamental problems for tourism development in Vietnam. There is poor infrastructure with low standard roads and inadequate transport links between the north and south of the country. The system of business laws and policies can be inadequate and confusing, undermining investment confidence. Safety can be another tourist concern as petty crime is prolific in the cities and exacerbated at night by poor or nonexistent street lighting in some areas. Skilled workers and qualified management personnel are often lacking.

However, Vietnam is geographically ripe for mass tourism. Three-quarters of the mainly agricultural country is tropical forest and wild mountains and 3200 km of coastline is home to 125 mostly unspoilt beaches. The climate is mainly hot, humid and dry although there are tropical monsoons from May to October. There is a huge variety of historic sites, French colonial architecture, diverse traditions, top cuisine and couture, and thriving northern tribal hill culture. Vietnam's wartime heritage enables anything relating to the conflict with the US and its allies to be an important component of tourism marketing.

In Ho Chi Minh City (formerly Saigon), huge crowds visit the War Remnants Museum to view a grisly montage of photos of torture and shocking war crimes. Included is a

(Continued)

(Continued)

mock prison with tiger-cage cells, emaciated models and evidence of beheadings and dismembering. As ghoulish as it now seems, some of the most blood-curdling exhibits have been removed or toned down. Likewise the name of the place has also been changed; it used to be the Museum of American War Crimes. War buffs will find even better pickings at Ho Chi Minh's Military Museum, which sports a fine array of American and Vietnamese military hardware, including tanks, shells, bombs and the wreckage of downed aircraft. For those interested in digging deeper into Vietnam's long history of conflict, the Ho Chi Minh City Museum (formerly the Revolutionary Museum) offers over a dozen rooms of resistance memorabilia dating back to the first campaigns against the French in the 1800s. Besides old weapons, medals, uniforms, homemade bombs and booby traps, there are fine archival pictures. Here, and at all the war museums, it's easy to shop for souvenirs that include dogtags, military hats and clothing, knives, medals and lighters – mostly fake.

Another major war tourism attraction in Vietnam is the Cu Chi Tunnels, 40 miles from Ho Chi Minh City. Cu Chi was made famous during the Vietnam war for its extensive network of underground tunnels spanning almost 200 kilometres. The tunnels were first used by the Viet Minh to hide from the French in the 1940s, then later became hideouts, living quarters and sniper bases for the Viet Cong, who at one point had even tunnelled under the Mekong Delta headquarters of the US Army's 25th Division. Guerillas and villagers often lived underground for months, surviving on tapioca, and breathing with the help of an elaborate ventilation system which also served to direct cooking smoke away from the inhabited areas. From these hiding places, the Viet Cong were able to make sneak attacks on their enemies, often within the US garrison. The American soldiers made every effort to destroy them, trying manpower, firepower, bombs, dogs and even gas, but ultimately failed.

Today short sections of the tunnel cobweb are open to the public and, on request, tourists can explore even further into the narrow, dark, dusty and bat-filled tunnels. These tunnels have been enlarged for the Western frame, but some, just 30 inches in diameter, were originally only accessible to the diminutive Vietnamese 'tunnel rats'. The subterranean lifestyle in the dirty, hot and claustrophobic confines can be relived by tourists now as they fumble their way through, bent double or on hands and knees for a few hundred metres. The area is encircled by bomb craters, testament to the 500,000 tons of bombs dropped in the area. Such bombarding often collapsed the upper tunnels, killing all inhabitants and unexploded ordnance continued to maim local people for many years after the wars. The Cu Chi tunnels are a vivid testament to the ingenuity and perseverance that eventually helped the Vietnamese win the war.

Diverse tourist facilities now support the tunnel tours, with lectures, propaganda videos from the 1960s, shooting ranges, gift shops featuring rice wine with cobras and scorpions inside the bottles as well as necklaces of silver bullets, and refreshments all established in an education/entertainment format. Visitors are shown vicious mantraps made of sharpened bamboo spikes concealed by foliage-covered trapdoors. There are gun-totting mannequins dressed in guerilla warfare jungle gear both above ground in the forest and below in the tunnel rooms. Such commodification of war relics, sites and memorabilia could be seen by some as trivialization of suffering and death, parodying a harrowing chapter of history. Conversely, it could be applauded for its educational message to younger people who would otherwise know nothing of Vietnam's beleaguered past as well as providing a grim reminder of past mistakes for future generations to learn from. Whichever viewpoint prevails, this pragmatic exploitation of Vietnam's past is also helping to create a prosperous commercial base to counteract poverty in some of the country's rural and urban areas that were hardest hit by the wars.

Source: Personal visits by the authors to Vietnam in 2006 and 2016.

CASE STUDY QUESTIONS

1. In your view, is promoting war tourism in Vietnam an ethical practice?
2. Give other examples from around the world of war tourism.
3. What more could Vietnamese marketers do to sensitively promote their war attractions?

REFERENCES

Archer, B., Cooper, C. and Ruhanen, L. (2005) 'The positive and negative impacts of tourism'. In W. F. Theobald (ed.), *Global Tourism*, pp. 79–102. New York: Butterworth-Heinemann/Elsevier.

Ashley, C., Boyd, C. and Goodwin, H. (2000) 'Pro-poor tourism: Putting poverty at the heart of the tourism agenda', *Natural Resource Objectives*, 51: 1–6.

Babaitia, C., Munteanu, V. and Ispas, A. (2010) 'The effects of ethical marketing in tourism'. In V. Mladenov and Z. Bojkovoc (eds), *Latest Trends on Cultural Heritage and Tourism, 3rd WSEAS International Conference on Cultural Heritage and Tourism, Corfu, Greece*, pp. 99–102.

Balasubramanian, S. K. (1994) 'Beyond advertising and publicity: Hybrid messages and public policy issues', *Journal of Advertising*, 23(4), 29–47.

Barnes, N. G. and Fitzgibbons, D. (1991) 'Is cause related marketing in your future?' *Business Forum*, 16(4): 20.

Birnbaum, E. (2015) 'Sharing the wealth: G Adventures ups its game in sustainable tourism', *Financial Post*, 23 October. www.financialpost.com/m/wp/news/blog.html?b=business.financialpost.com/small-business/sharing-the-wealth-g-adventures-ups-its-game-in-sustainable-tourism&pubdate=2015-10-25 (accessed 10 December 2016).

Blanchard, K. and Peale, N. V. (1988) *The Power of Ethical Management*. New York: William Morrow.

Buchmeyer, J.P. (2013) 'Can luxury like this change lives?' *Condé Nast Traveler*, September: 87–90.

Butler, R. (1993) 'Tourism – an evolutionary perspective'. In R. W. Butler, J. G. Nelson, G. Wall (eds), *Tourism and Sustainable Development: Monitoring, Planning, Managing*, Chapter 2, p. 29. Department of Geography Publication 37, University of Waterloo, Waterloo.

Campelo, A., Aitken, R. and Gnoth, J. (2011) 'Visual rhetoric and ethics in marketing of destinations', *Journal of Travel Research,* 50(1): 3–14.

Chalip, L. (2006) 'Towards social leverage of sport events', *Journal of Sport Tourism,* 11(2): 109–27.

Cohen, N. (2014) 'Chipotle blurs lines with a satirical series about industrial farming', *New York Times,* 27 January: B3.

Darcy, S. (2010) 'Inherent complexity: Disability, accessible tourism and accommodation information preferences', *Tourism Management,* 31(6): 816–26.

Dawson, J., Johnston, M. J., Stewart, E. J., Lemieux, C. J., Lemelin, R. H., Maher, P. T. and Grimwood, B. S. R. (2011) 'Ethical considerations of last chance tourism', *Journal of Ecotourism,* 10(3): 250–65.

Farrow, B. (2016) 'Turnaround service', *Hemispheres,* July: 18.

Fleckenstein, M. P. and Huebsch, P. (1999) 'Ethics in tourism – reality or hallucination', *Journal of Business Ethics,* 19(1): 137–43.

Gilmore, J. H. and Pine, J. (2007) *Authenticity.* Boston, MA: Harvard Business School Publishing.

Goodwin, H., and Francis, J. (2003) 'Ethical and responsible tourism: Consumer trends in the UK', *Journal of Vacation Marketing,* 9(3): 271–82.

Grady, J. and Ohlin, J. B. (2009) 'Equal access to hospitality services for guests with mobility impairments under the Americans with Disabilities Act: Implications for the hospitality industry', *International Journal of Hospitality Management,* 28: 161–9.

Hall, S. J. (1992) *Ethics in Hospitality Management.* East Lansing, Michigan: Educational Institute of the American Hotel and Motel Association.

Hoeffler, S. and Keller, K. L. (2002) 'Building brand equity through corporate societal marketing', *Journal of Public Policy & Marketing,* 21(1): 84.

Hudson, S. (2000) *Snow Business: A Study of the International Ski Industry.* London: The Continuum International Publishing Group.

Hudson, S. (2007) 'To go or not to go? Ethical perspectives on tourism in an outpost of tyranny', *Journal of Business Ethics,* 76(4): 385–96.

Hudson, S. (2008) *Tourism and Hospitality Marketing: A Global Perspective.* London: Sage.

Hudson, S. and Hudson, L. J. (2014) *Golf Tourism,* 2nd edn. Oxford: Goodfellow Publishers Ltd.

Hudson, S. and Hudson, L. J. (2015) *Winter Sport Tourism: Working in Winter Wonderlands.* Oxford: Goodfellow Publishers Ltd.

Hudson, S. and Miller, G. (2003) 'Ethical considerations in sustainable tourism'. In L. Taylor and A. Ryall (eds), *Proceedings of the Sustainable Mountain Communities Conference, Banff, Canada,* pp. 192–9.

Hudson, S. and Miller, G. (2005a) 'Ethical orientation and awareness of tourism students', *Journal of Business Ethics,* 62(4): 383–96.

Hudson, S. and Miller, G. (2005b) 'The responsible marketing of tourism: The case of Canadian Mountain Holidays', *Tourism Management,* 26(2): 133–42.

Hughes, M. (2005) 'An analysis of the sustainable tourism literature', *CAUTHE Conference, Alice Springs, Australia*, 1–5 February.

Independent (2014) 'The power of football', *The Independent*, 10 June: 2.

Jaszay, C. (2002) 'Teaching ethics in hospitality programs', *Journal of Hospitality and Tourism Education*, 14(3): 57–63.

Jovičić, D. and Sinosich, R. (2012) 'Ethical bases of sustainable tourism', *Conference Proceedings from Tourism andHospitality Management 2012*, pp. 308–15.

Jullien, J. (2016) 'Shiny happy people', *ES Magazine*, 22 April: 25–7.

Laing, J. and Frost, W. (2010) 'How green was my festival: Exploring challenges and opportunities associated with staging green events', *International Journal of Hospitality Management*, 29: 261–7.

Leadlay, F. (2011) 'Integrating ethics into tourism: Beyond codes of conduct', *Guardian*, 25 August. www.theguardian.com/sustainable-business/blog/integrating-ethics-into-tourism (accessed 10 December 2016).

MacCannell, D. (1973) 'Staged authenticity: Arrangements of social space in tourist settings', *American Journal of Sociology*, 79(3): 589–603.

Manning, E. W. and Dougherty, T. (1995) 'Sustainable tourism: Preserving the golden goose', *Cornell Hotel and Restaurant Administration Quarterly,* April: 29–42.

Marketing-schools.com (2016) 'Ethical marketing'. www.marketing-schools.org/types-of-marketing/ethical-marketing.html (accessed 10 December 2016).

Media, C. (2013) 'Owner of Bucuti & Tara Beach Resorts invited as keynote speaker at the 14th Annual Sustainable Tourism Conference', *Visit Aruba News*. http://news.visitaruba.com/news/owner-of-bucuti-tara-beach-resorts-invited-as-keynote-speaker-at-the-14th-annual-sustainable-tourism-conference (accessed 10 December 2016).

Misener, L. and Mason, D. S. (2006) 'Developing local citizenship through sporting events: Balancing community involvement and tourism development', *Current Issues in Tourism*, 9(4/5): 384–98.

PGA TOUR (2016) 'PGA TOUR and its tournaments set record for charitable giving', *PGATOUR.com*, 16 March. http://together.pgatour.com/stories/2016/03/pga-tour-charity-total.html (accessed 10 December 2016).

Reidenbach, R. E. and Robin, D. P. (1988) 'Some initial steps towards improving the measurement of ethical evaluations of marketing activities', *Journal of Business Ethics*, 7: 871–9.

Royle, S. A. (2009) 'Tourism changes on a Mediterranean island: Experiences from Mallorca', *Island Studies Journal*, 4(2): 225–40.

Ruitz, R. (2008) 'How authentic is your vacation?' *Forbes*, 18 June. www.forbes.com/2008/06/18/travel-destinations-authentic-forbeslife-cx_rr_0618travel.html (accessed 10 December 2016).

Sheldon, P. (1989) 'Professionalism in tourism and hospitality', *Annals of Tourism Research*, 16: 492–503.

Smith, V. L. and Brent, M. (2001) *Hosts and Guests Revisited: Tourism Issues of the 21 Century*. New York: Cognizant.

Smith, N. C. and Murphy, P. E. (2012) *Marketing Ethics*. London: Sage.

Stoller, G. (2011) 'Some hotels don't live up to online hype, disappointed guests say', *USA Today*, 5 May. www.hospitalitynet.org/news/4051257.html (accessed 12 December 2016).

Thiyagaraj, V. (2015) 'Lohas: The rise of ethical consumerism', *International Journal of Scientific Research*, 4(7): 702–3.

Tiwsakul, R., Hackley, C. and Szmigin, I. (2005) 'Explicit, non-integrated product placement in British television programmes', *International Journal of Advertising*, 24(1), 95–111.

Wight, P. (1995) 'Sustainable ecotourism: Balancing economic, environmental and social goals within an ethical framework', *Tourism Recreation Research*, 20(1): 5–13.

INDEX